# TensorFlow 2.0 Computer Vision Cookbook

Implement machine learning solutions to overcome various computer vision challenges

**Jesús Martínez**

BIRMINGHAM—MUMBAI

# TensorFlow 2.0 Computer Vision Cookbook

**Group Product Manager**: Kunal Parikh

**Publishing Product Manager**: Sunith Shetty

**Senior Editor**: David Sugarman

**Content Development Editor**: Nathanya Dias

**Technical Editor**: Arjun Varma

**Copy Editor**: Safis Editing

**Project Coordinator**: Aishwarya Mohan

**Proofreader**: Safis Editing

**Indexer**: Manju Arasan

**Production Designer**: Joshua Misquitta

First published: February 2021

Production reference: 1210121

Published by Packt Publishing Ltd.

Livery Place

35 Livery Street

Birmingham

B3 2PB, UK.

ISBN 978-1-83882-913-1

www.packt.com

`Packt.com`

Subscribe to our online digital library for full access to over 7,000 books and videos, as well as industry leading tools to help you plan your personal development and advance your career. For more information, please visit our website.

## Why subscribe?

- Spend less time learning and more time coding with practical eBooks and Videos from over 4,000 industry professionals

- Improve your learning with Skill Plans built especially for you

- Get a free eBook or video every month

- Fully searchable for easy access to vital information

- Copy and paste, print, and bookmark content

Did you know that Packt offers eBook versions of every book published, with PDF and ePub files available? You can upgrade to the eBook version at `packt.com` and as a print book customer, you are entitled to a discount on the eBook copy. Get in touch with us at `customercare@packtpub.com` for more details.

At `www.packt.com`, you can also read a collection of free technical articles, sign up for a range of free newsletters, and receive exclusive discounts and offers on Packt books and eBooks.

# Contributors

## About the author

**Jesús Martínez** is the founder of the computer vision e-learning site DataSmarts. He is a computer vision expert and has worked on a wide range of projects in the field, such as a piece of people-counting software fed with images coming from an RGB camera and a depth sensor, using OpenCV and TensorFlow. He developed a self-driving car in a simulation, using a convolutional neural network created with TensorFlow, that worked solely with visual inputs. Also, he implemented a pipeline that uses several advanced computer vision techniques to track lane lines on the road, as well as providing extra information such as curvature degree.

*This book is dedicated to my parents, Armando and Maris, who have always pushed me toward excellence.*

## About the reviewers

**Vincent Kok** is a maker and a software platform application engineer in the transportation industry. He graduated from University of Science, Malaysia, with an MSc in embedded system engineering. Vincent actively involves himself with the developer community, as well as attending Maker Faire events held around the world, such as in Shenzhen in 2014 and in Singapore and Tokyo in 2015. Designing electronics hardware kits and giving soldering/Arduino classes for beginners are some of his favorite ways to spend his free time. Currently, his focus is on computer vision technology, software test automation, deep learning, and constantly keeping himself up to date with the latest technology.

Rajeev Ratan is a data scientist with an MSc in artificial intelligence from the University of Edinburgh and a BSc in electrical and computer engineering from the University of the West Indies. He has worked in several London tech start-ups as a data scientist, mostly in computer vision. He was a member of Entrepreneur First, a London-based start-up incubator, where he co-founded an Edtech start-up. Later on, he worked in AI tech start-ups involved in the real estate and gambling sectors. Before venturing into data science, Rajeev worked as a radio frequency engineer for 8 years. His research interests lie in deep learning and computer vision. He has created several online courses that are hosted on Udemy, Packt, and Manning Publications.

## Packt is searching for authors like you

If you're interested in becoming an author for Packt, please visit `authors.packtpub.com` and apply today. We have worked with thousands of developers and tech professionals, just like you, to help them share their insight with the global tech community. You can make a general application, apply for a specific hot topic that we are recruiting an author for, or submit your own idea.

# Table of Contents

**Preface**

## 1

## Getting Started with TensorFlow 2.x for Computer Vision

| | | | |
|---|---|---|---|
| Technical requirements | 2 | See also | 16 |
| Working with the basic building blocks of the Keras API | 3 | Saving and loading a model | 16 |
| | | How to do it... | 16 |
| Getting ready | 3 | How it works... | 20 |
| How to do it... | 3 | There's more... | 20 |
| How it works... | 6 | | |
| See also | 7 | Visualizing a model's architecture | 20 |
| | | Getting ready | 20 |
| Loading images using the Keras API | 7 | How to do it... | 20 |
| | | How it works... | 25 |
| Getting ready | 7 | | |
| How to do it... | 8 | Creating a basic image classifier | 25 |
| How it works... | 11 | Getting ready | 25 |
| See also | 12 | How to do it... | 25 |
| | | How it works... | 32 |
| Loading images using the tf.data.Dataset API | 12 | See also | 32 |
| How to do it... | 12 | | |
| How it works... | 15 | | |

## 2

## Performing Image Classification

| | | | |
|---|---|---|---|
| Technical requirements | 34 | Getting ready | 34 |
| Creating a binary classifier to detect smiles | 34 | How to do it... | 35 |
| | | How it works... | 39 |

See also                                    39

**Creating a multi-class classifier
to play rock paper scissors**        39
Getting ready                               40
How to do it...                             40
How it works...                             44

**Creating a multi-label classifier
to label watches**                   45
Getting ready                               45
How to do it...                             46
How it works...                             51
See also                                    52

**Implementing ResNet from
scratch**                            52
Getting ready                               52
How to do it...                             53
How it works...                             59
See also                                    60

**Classifying images with a pre-
trained network using the
Keras API**                          60
Getting ready                               60
How to do it...                             61

How it works...                             63
See also                                    64

**Classifying images with a
pre-trained network using
TensorFlow Hub**                     64
Getting ready                               64
How to do it...                             65
How it works...                             67
See also                                    67

**Using data augmentation to
improve performance with the
Keras API**                          68
Getting ready                               68
How to do it...                             69
How it works...                             75
See also                                    75

**Using data augmentation to
improve performance with the
tf.data and tf.image APIs**          75
Getting ready                               75
How to do it...                             76
How it works...                             83
See also                                    83

# 3

# Harnessing the Power of Pre-Trained Networks with Transfer Learning

**Technical requirements**           86
**Implementing a feature
extractor using a pre-trained
network**                            87
Getting ready                               87
How to do it...                             88
How it works...                             93
See also                                    94

**Training a simple classifier on
extracted features**                 94
Getting ready                               95
How to do it...                             95
How it works...                             97
See also                                    97

**Spot-checking extractors and
classifiers**                        97

Getting ready                                98
How to do it...                              99
How it works...                              104

### Using incremental learning to train a classifier                     104
Getting ready                                105
How to do it...                              105
How it works...                              109

### Fine-tuning a network using the Keras API                            109

Getting ready                                110
How to do it...                              110
How it works...                              114
See also                                     115

### Fine-tuning a network using TFHub                                     115
Getting ready                                115
How to do it...                              116
How it works...                              119
See also                                     119

# 4
# Enhancing and Styling Images with DeepDream, Neural Style Transfer, and Image Super-Resolution

Technical requirements                       122
Implementing DeepDream                       122
Getting ready                                123
How to do it...                              123
How it works...                              127
See also                                     128

### Generating your own dreamy images                                     128
Getting ready                                128
How to do it...                              129
How it works...                              133

### Implementing Neural Style Transfer                                    134
Getting ready                                134
How to do it...                              134
How it works...                              140
See also                                     141

### Applying style transfer to custom images                             141
Getting ready                                141

How to do it...                              142
How it works...                              146
See also                                     146

### Applying style transfer with TFHub                                    147
Getting ready                                147
How to do it...                              147
How it works...                              151
See also                                     151

### Improving image resolution with deep learning                        151
Getting ready                                152
How to do it...                              152
How it works...                              159
See also                                     159

# 5

## Reducing Noise with Autoencoders

| | | | |
|---|---|---|---|
| Technical requirements | 162 | Spotting outliers using autoencoders | 182 |
| Creating a simple fully connected autoencoder | 162 | Getting ready | 182 |
| Getting ready | 162 | How to do it... | 182 |
| How to do it... | 163 | How it works... | 187 |
| How it works... | 167 | Creating an inverse image search index with deep learning | 188 |
| See also | 168 | Getting ready | 188 |
| Creating a convolutional autoencoder | 168 | How to do it... | 188 |
| Getting ready | 168 | How it works... | 193 |
| How to do it... | 168 | See also | 194 |
| How it works... | 174 | Implementing a variational autoencoder | 194 |
| See also | 175 | Getting ready | 194 |
| Denoising images with autoencoders | 175 | How to do it... | 194 |
| Getting ready | 175 | How it works... | 201 |
| How to do it... | 175 | See also | 201 |
| How it works... | 181 | | |

# 6

## Generative Models and Adversarial Attacks

| | | | |
|---|---|---|---|
| Technical requirements | 204 | How it works... | 221 |
| Implementing a deep convolutional GAN | 204 | See also | 222 |
| Getting ready | 205 | Translating images with Pix2Pix | 222 |
| How to do it... | 205 | Getting ready | 222 |
| How it works... | 212 | How to do it... | 223 |
| See also | 213 | How it works... | 235 |
| Using a DCGAN for semi-supervised learning | 213 | See also | 236 |
| Getting ready | 213 | Translating unpaired images with CycleGAN | 236 |
| How to do it... | 213 | Getting ready | 236 |

How to do it...                        237
How it works...                        251
See also                               251

Implementing an adversarial
attack using the Fast Gradient

Signed Method                          252
Getting ready                          252
How to do it                           252
How it works...                        256
See also                               256

# 7

# Captioning Images with CNNs and RNNs

Technical requirements                 258
Implementing a reusable image
caption feature extractor              258
Getting ready                          259
How to do it...                        259
How it works...                        267
See also                               268

Implementing an image
captioning network                     268
Getting ready                          268
How to do it...                        269
How it works...                        276

See also                               277

Generating captions for your
own photos                             277
Getting ready                          278
How to do it...                        278
How it works...                        283

Implementing an image
captioning network on COCO
with attention                         283
Getting ready                          284
How to do it...                        284

# 8

# Fine-Grained Understanding of Images through Segmentation

Technical requirements                 304
Creating a fully convolutional
network for image
segmentation                           304
Getting ready                          304
How to do it...                        305
How it works...                        318
See also                               319

Implementing a U-Net from
scratch                                319

Getting ready                          319
How to do it...                        320
How it works...                        331
See also                               331

Implementing a U-Net with
transfer learning                      332
Getting ready                          332
How to do it...                        333
How it works...                        343
See also                               344

Segmenting images using Mask-RCNN and TensorFlow Hub  344
Getting ready  344

How to do it...  345
How it works...  349
See also  350

# 9
# Localizing Elements in Images with Object Detection

Technical requirements  352
Creating an object detector with image pyramids and sliding windows  352
Getting ready  353
How to do it...  353
How it works...  361
See also  361

Detecting objects with YOLOv3  361
Getting ready  362
How it works...  378
See also  378

Training your own object detector with TensorFlow's Object Detection API  379
Getting ready  379
How to do it...  380
How it works...  390
See also  391

Detecting objects using TFHub  392
Getting ready  392
How to do it...  392
How it works...  396
See also  396

# 10
# Applying the Power of Deep Learning to Videos

Technical requirements  398
Detecting emotions in real time  398
Getting ready  398
How to do it...  399
How it works...  412
See also  412

Recognizing actions with TensorFlow Hub  412
Getting ready  413
How to do it...  413
How it works...  418
See also  419

Generating the middle frames

of a video with TensorFlow Hub  419
Getting ready  420
How to do it...  420
How it works...  424
See also  425

Performing text-to-video retrieval with TensorFlow Hub  425
Getting ready  425
How to do it...  426
How it works...  432
See also  432

# 11
# Streamlining Network Implementation with AutoML

Technical requirements                     434
Creating a simple image
classifier
with AutoKeras                             435
How to do it...                            435
How it works...                            436
See also                                   436

Creating a simple image
regressor with AutoKeras                   437
Getting ready                              437
How to do it...                            437
How it works...                            440
See also                                   441

Exporting and importing a
model in AutoKeras                         441

How to do it...                            441
How it works...                            444
See also                                   445

Controlling architecture
generation with AutoKeras'
AutoModel                                  445
How to do it...                            445
How it works...                            449
See also                                   449

Predicting age and gender with
AutoKeras                                  449
Getting ready                              450
How to do it...                            452
How it works...                            459
See also                                   460

# 12
# Boosting Performance

Technical requirements                     462
Using convolutional neural
network ensembles to improve
accuracy                                   462
Getting ready                              462
How to do it...                            463
How it works...                            469
See also                                   470

Using test time augmentation
to improve accuracy                        470
Getting ready                              470
How to do it...                            471
How it works...                            476

Using rank-N accuracy to
evaluate performance                       477
Getting ready                              477
How to do it...                            478
How it works...                            483
See also                                   483

Using label smoothing to
increase performance                       483
Getting ready                              484
How to do it...                            484
How it works...                            489

Checkpointing model                        490
How to do it...                            490

**Customizing the training process using tf.GradientTape**   **497**

How to do it...   497
How it works...   501

Getting ready   502
How to do it...   502
How it works...   507
See also   507

## Other Books You May Enjoy

## Index

# Preface

The release of TensorFlow 2.x in 2019 was one of the biggest and most anticipated events in the deep learning and artificial intelligence arena, because it brought with it long-overdue improvements to this popular and relevant framework, mainly focused on simplicity and ease of use.

The adoption of Keras as the official TensorFlow high-level API, the ability to switch back and forth between eager and graph-based execution (thanks to `tf.function`), and the ability to create complex data pipelines with `tf.data` are just a few of the great additions that TensorFlow 2.x brings to the table.

In this book, you will discover a vast amount of recipes that will teach you how to take advantage of these advancements in the context of deep learning applied to computer vision. We will cover a wide gamut of applications, ranging from image classification to more challenging ones, such as object detection, image segmentation, and **Automated Machine Learning (AutoML)**.

By the end of this book, you'll be prepared and confident enough to tackle any computer vision problem that comes your way with the invaluable help of TensorFlow 2.x!

## Who this book is for

This book is for computer vision developers, computer vision engineers, and deep learning practitioners looking for go-to solutions to various problems faced in computer vision. You will discover how to employ modern machine learning techniques and deep learning architectures to perform a plethora of computer vision tasks. Basic knowledge of Python programming and computer vision is required.

# What this book covers

*Chapter 1, Getting Started with TensorFlow 2.x for Computer Vision*, serves as an overview of basic deep learning concepts, as well as being a first look at some important TensorFlow 2.x features, such as the Keras and `tf.data.Dataset` APIs. It also teaches you about common and necessary tasks such as saving and loading a model and visualizing a network architecture. It ends with the implementation of a simple image classifier.

*Chapter 2, Performing Image Classification*, goes in-depth about the most common application of deep neural networks to computer vision: image classification. It explores the common varieties of classification, such as binary and multiclass classification, and then transitions to examples of multilabel classification and out-of-the-box solutions using transfer learning and TensorFlow Hub.

*Chapter 3, Harnessing the Power of Pre-Trained Networks with Transfer Learning*, focuses on transfer learning, a powerful technique to reuse networks pre-trained on massive datasets to increase development productivity and the performance of deep learning-powered computer vision applications. This chapter starts by seeing you use pre-trained networks as feature extractors. Then, you will learn how to combine deep learning with traditional machine learning algorithms through a procedure called incremental learning. Finally, the chapter closes with two examples of fine-tuning: the first using the Keras API and the second relying on TensorFlow Hub.

*Chapter 4, Enhancing and Styling Images with DeepDream, Neural Style Transfer, and Image Super-Resolution*, focuses on fun and less conventional applications of deep neural networks in computer vision, namely DeepDream, neural style transfer, and image super-resolution.

*Chapter 5, Reducing Noise with Autoencoders*, goes over autoencoders, a composite architecture used in domains such as image restoration, inverse image search indexes, and image denoising. It starts by introducing the dense and convolutional variants of autoencoders and then explains several applications, such as inverse image search engines and outlier detection.

*Chapter 6, Generative Models and Adversarial Attacks*, introduces you to many examples and applications of **Generative Adversarial Networks** (**GANs**). The chapter ends with an example of how to perform an adversarial attack on convolutional neural networks.

*Chapter 7, Captioning Images with CNNs and RNNs*, focuses on how to combine both convolutional and recurrent neural networks to generate textual descriptions of images.

*Chapter 8, Fine-Grained Understanding of Images through Segmentation*, focuses on image segmentation, a fine-grained version of image classification, at the pixel level. It covers seminal segmentation architectures, such as U-Net and Mask-RCNN.

*Chapter 9, Localizing Elements in Images with Object Detection*, covers the complex and yet common task of object detection. It goes over both traditional approaches based on image pyramids and sliding windows and more modern solutions, such as YOLO. It includes a thorough explanation of how to leverage the TensorFlow Object Detection API to train state-of-the-art models on custom datasets.

*Chapter 10, Applying the Power of Deep Learning to Videos*, expands the application of deep neural networks to videos. Here, you will find examples of how to detect emotions, recognize actions, and generate frames in a video.

*Chapter 11, Streamlining Network Implementation with AutoML*, explores the exciting subfield of AutoML using Autokeras, an experimental library built on top of TensorFlow 2.x, which uses **Neural Architecture Search** (**NAS**) to arrive at the best model possible for a given problem. The chapter starts by exploring the basic features of Autokeras and closes by using AutoML to create an age and gender prediction tool.

*Chapter 12, Boosting Performance*, explains in detail many different techniques that can be used to boost the performance of a network, from simple but powerful methods, such as using ensembles, to more advanced ones, such as using GradientTape to tailor the training process to the specific needs of a project.

# To get the most out of this book

You will need a version of TensorFlow 2 installed. All the recipes in this book have been implemented and tested using TensorFlow 2.3 on macOS X and Ubuntu 20.04, but they should work with future stable versions as well. Please note that Windows is not supported.

Although not strictly necessary, access to a GPU-enabled machine, either on-premises or in the cloud, is highly encouraged, as it reduces the runtime of the examples dramatically.

| Software/hardware covered in the book | OS requirements |
|---|---|
| Python 3.6+ | macOS X or Linux (Debian-based) |
| TensorFlow 2.3+ | macOS X or Linux (Debian-based) |

**If you are using the digital version of this book, we advise you to type the code yourself or access the code via the GitHub repository (link available in the next section). Doing so will help you avoid any potential errors related to the copying and pasting of code.**

Because this is a hands-on book, focused on practical examples to solve varied situations, I encourage you to expand your knowledge on any topics that you find interesting in any particular recipe. In the *See also* section of each recipe, you will find links, references, and suggestions for recommended reads or extension points that will cement your understanding of the techniques explained in that example.

## Download the example code files

You can download the example code files for this book from GitHub at `https://github.com/PacktPublishing/Tensorflow-2.0-Computer-Vision-Cookbook`. In case there's an update to the code, it will be updated on the existing GitHub repository.

We also have other code bundles from our rich catalog of books and videos available at `https://github.com/PacktPublishing/`. Check them out!

# Code in Action

Code in Action videos for this book can be viewed at `https://bit.ly/2NmdZ5G`.

# Download the color images

We also provide a PDF file that has color images of the screenshots/diagrams used in this book. You can download it here: `https://static.packt-cdn.com/downloads/9781838829131_ColorImages.pdf`.

# Conventions used

There are a number of text conventions used throughout this book.

`Code in text`: Indicates code words in text, database table names, folder names, filenames, file extensions, pathnames, dummy URLs, user input, and Twitter handles. Here is an example: "Using `image_generator`, we'll pick and display a random batch of 10 images directly from the directory they are stored in."

A block of code is set as follows:

```
iterator = (image_generator
            .flow_from_directory(directory=data_directory,
                                 batch_size=10))
for batch, _ in iterator:
plt.figure(figsize=(5, 5))
for index, image in enumerate(batch, start=1):
ax = plt.subplot(5, 5, index)
plt.imshow(image)
plt.axis('off')
plt.show()
break
```

When we wish to draw your attention to a particular part of a code block, the relevant lines or items are set in bold:

```
[default]
exten => s,1,Dial(Zap/1|30)
exten => s,2,Voicemail(u100)
exten => s,102,Voicemail(b100)
exten => i,1,Voicemail(s0)
```

Any command-line input or output is written as follows:

```
$ pip install tensorflow-hub Pillow
$ pip install tensorflow-datasets tqdm
```

**Bold**: Indicates a new term, an important word, or words that you see onscreen. For example, words in menus or dialog boxes appear in the text like this. Here is an example: "Select **System info** from the **Administration** panel."

> **Tips or important notes**
> We'll use the modified version of the Stanford Cars dataset we just worked on in future recipes in this chapter.

# Sections

In this book, you will find several headings that appear frequently (*Getting ready, How to do it..., How it works..., There's more...,* and *See also*).

To give clear instructions on how to complete a recipe, use these sections as follows:

## Getting ready

This section tells you what to expect in the recipe and describes how to set up any software or any preliminary settings required for the recipe.

## How to do it...

This section contains the steps required to follow the recipe.

## How it works...

This section usually consists of a detailed explanation of what happened in the previous section.

## There's more...

This section consists of additional information about the recipe in order to make you more knowledgeable about the recipe.

## See also

This section provides helpful links to other useful information for the recipe.

# Get in touch

Feedback from our readers is always welcome.

**General feedback**: If you have questions about any aspect of this book, mention the book title in the subject of your message and email us at customercare@packtpub.com.

**Errata**: Although we have taken every care to ensure the accuracy of our content, mistakes do happen. If you have found a mistake in this book, we would be grateful if you would report this to us. Please visit www.packtpub.com/support/errata, selecting your book, clicking on the Errata Submission Form link, and entering the details.

**Piracy**: If you come across any illegal copies of our works in any form on the Internet, we would be grateful if you would provide us with the location address or website name. Please contact us at copyright@packt.com with a link to the material.

**If you are interested in becoming an author**: If there is a topic that you have expertise in and you are interested in either writing or contributing to a book, please visit authors.packtpub.com.

# Reviews

Please leave a review. Once you have read and used this book, why not leave a review on the site that you purchased it from? Potential readers can then see and use your unbiased opinion to make purchase decisions, we at Packt can understand what you think about our products, and our authors can see your feedback on their book. Thank you!

For more information about Packt, please visit packt.com.

# 1

# Getting Started with TensorFlow 2.x for Computer Vision

One of the greatest features of TensorFlow 2.x is that it finally incorporates Keras as its high-level API. Why is this so important? While it's true that Keras and TensorFlow have had very good compatibility for a while, they have remained separate libraries with different development cycles, which causes frequent compatibility issues. Now that the relationship between these two immensely popular tools is official, they'll grow in the same direction, following a single roadmap and making the interoperability between them completely seamless. In the end, Keras is TensorFlow and TensorFlow is Keras.

Perhaps the biggest advantage of this merger is that by using Keras' high-level features, we are not sacrificing performance by any means. Simply put, Keras code is production-ready!

Unless the requirements of a particular project demand otherwise, in the vast majority of the recipes in this book, we'll rely on TensorFlow's Keras API.

The reason behind this decision is twofold:

- Keras is easier to understand and work with.
- It's the encouraged way to develop using TensorFlow 2.x.

In this chapter, we will cover the following recipes:

- Working with the basic building blocks of the Keras API
- Loading images using the Keras API
- Loading images using the tf.data.Dataset API
- Saving and loading a model
- Visualizing a model's architecture
- Creating a basic image classifier

Let's get started!

## Technical requirements

For this chapter, you will need a working installation of TensorFlow 2.x. If you can access a GPU, either physical or via a cloud provider, your experience will be much more enjoyable. In each recipe, in the *Getting ready* section, you will find the specific preliminary steps and dependencies to complete it. Finally, all the code shown in this chapter is available in this book's GitHub repository at `https://github.com/ PacktPublishing/Tensorflow-2.0-Computer-Vision-Cookbook/tree/ master/ch1`.

Check out the following link to see the Code in Action video:

`https://bit.ly/39wkpGN`.

# Working with the basic building blocks of the Keras API

Keras is the official high-level API for TensorFlow 2.x and its use is highly encouraged for both experimental and production-ready code. Therefore, in this first recipe, we'll review the basic building blocks of Keras by creating a very simple fully connected neural network.

Are you ready? Let's begin!

## Getting ready

At the most basic level, a working installation of TensorFlow 2.x is all you need.

## How to do it...

In the following sections, we'll go over the sequence of steps required to complete this recipe. Let's get started:

1. Import the required libraries from the Keras API:

```
from sklearn.model_selection import train_test_split
from sklearn.preprocessing import LabelBinarizer
from tensorflow.keras import Input
from tensorflow.keras.datasets import mnist
from tensorflow.keras.layers import Dense
from tensorflow.keras.models import Model
from tensorflow.keras.models import Sequential
```

2. Create a model using the Sequential API by passing a list of layers to the Sequential constructor. The numbers in each layer correspond to the number of neurons or units it contains:

```
layers = [Dense(256, input_shape=(28 * 28 * 1,),
                activation='sigmoid'),
          Dense(128, activation='sigmoid'),
          Dense(10, activation='softmax')]
sequential_model_list = Sequential(layers)
```

3.  Create a model using the add() method to add one layer at a time. The numbers in each layer correspond to the number of neurons or units it contains:

```
sequential_model = Sequential()
sequential_model.add(Dense(256,
                     input_shape=(28 * 28 * 1,),
                     activation='sigmoid'))
sequential_model.add(Dense(128, activation='sigmoid'))
sequential_model.add(Dense(10, activation='softmax'))
```

4.  Create a model using the Functional API. The numbers in each layer correspond to the number of neurons or units it contains:

```
input_layer = Input(shape=(28 * 28 * 1,))
dense_1 = Dense(256, activation='sigmoid')(input_layer)
dense_2 = Dense(128, activation='sigmoid')(dense_1)
predictions = Dense(10, activation='softmax')(dense_2)
functional_model = Model(inputs=input_layer,
                         outputs=predictions)
```

5.  Create a model using an object-oriented approach by sub-classing tensorflow. keras.models.Model. The numbers in each layer correspond to the number of neurons or units it contains:

```
class ClassModel(Model):
    def __init__(self):
        super(ClassModel, self).__init__()
        self.dense_1 = Dense(256, activation='sigmoid')
        self.dense_2 = Dense(256, activation='sigmoid')
        self.predictions = Dense(10,activation='softmax')

    def call(self, inputs, **kwargs):
        x = self.dense_1(inputs)
        x = self.dense_2(x)
    return self.predictions(x)
class_model = ClassModel()
```

6. Prepare the data so that we can train all the models we defined previously. We must reshape the images into vector format because that's the format that's expected by a fully connected network:

```
(X_train, y_train), (X_test, y_test) = mnist.load_data()

X_train = X_train.reshape((X_train.shape[0], 28 * 28 *
                          1))
X_test = X_test.reshape((X_test.shape[0], 28 * 28 *
                        1))

X_train = X_train.astype('float32') / 255.0
X_test = X_test.astype('float32') / 255.0
```

7. One-hot encode the labels to break any undesired ordering bias:

```
label_binarizer = LabelBinarizer()
y_train = label_binarizer.fit_transform(y_train)
y_test = label_binarizer.fit_transform(y_test)
```

8. Take 20% of the data for validation:

```
X_train, X_valid, y_train, y_valid = train_test_split(X_
train, y_train, train_size=0.8)
```

9. Compile, train the models for 50 epochs, and evaluate them on the test set:

```
models = {
    'sequential_model': sequential_model,
    'sequential_model_list': sequential_model_list,
    'functional_model': functional_model,
    'class_model': class_model
}

for name, model in models.items():
    print(f'Compiling model: {name}')
    model.compile(loss='categorical_crossentropy',
                  optimizer='adam',
                  metrics=['accuracy'])
```

```
print(f'Training model: {name}')
model.fit(X_train, y_train,
          validation_data=(X_valid, y_valid),
          epochs=50,
          batch_size=256,
          verbose=0)

_, accuracy = model.evaluate(X_test, y_test,
                             verbose=0)
print(f'Testing model: {name}. \nAccuracy:
    {accuracy}')
print('---')
```

After 50 epochs, all three models should have obtained around 98% accuracy on the test set.

## How it works...

In the previous section, we went over the basic building blocks we'll need to build most deep learning-powered computer vision projects using TensorFlow 2.x.

First, we imported the Keras API, the high-level interface for the second version of TensorFlow. We learned that all Keras-related functionality is located inside the tensorflow package.

Next, we found that TensorFlow 2.x offers great flexibility when it comes to defining models. In particular, we have two main APIs we can use to build models:

- **Symbolic**: Also known as the declarative API, it allows us to define a model as a **Directed Acyclic Graph (DAG)**, where each layer constitutes a node and the interactions or connections between layers are the edges. The pros of this API are that you can examine the model by plotting it or printing its architecture; compatibility checks are run by the framework, diminishing the probability of runtime errors; and if the model compiles, it runs. On the other hand, the main con is that it's not suited for non-DAG architectures (networks with loops), such as Tree-LSTMs.

- **Imperative**: Also known as the **model sub-classing API**, this API is a more Pythonic, developer-friendly way of specifying a model. It also allows for more flexibility in the forward pass than its symbolic counterpart. The pros of this API are that developing models becomes no different than any other object-oriented task, which speeds up the process of trying out new ideas; specifying a control flow is easy using Python's built-in constructs; and it's suited for non-DAG architectures, such as Tree-RNNs. In terms of its cons, reusability is lost because the architecture is hidden within the class; almost no inter-layer compatibility checks are run, thus moving most of the debugging responsibility from the framework to the developer; and there's loss of transparency because information about the interconnectedness between layers is not available.

We defined the same architecture using both the Sequential and Functional APIs, which correspond to the symbolic or declarative way of implementing networks, and also a third time using an imperative approach.

To make it clear that, in the end, the three networks are the same, no matter which approach we took, we trained and evaluated them on the famous `MNIST` dataset, obtaining a decent 98% accuracy on the test set.

## See also

If you're interested in learning more about Tree-LSTMs, you can read the paper where they were first introduced here: `https://nlp.stanford.edu/pubs/tai-socher-manning-acl2015.pdf`.

# Loading images using the Keras API

In this recipe, we will learn how to load images using the Keras API, a very important task considering that, in computer vision, we'll always work with visual data. In particular, we'll learn how to open, explore, and visualize a single image, as well as a batch of them. Additionally, we will learn how to programmatically download a dataset.

## Getting ready

Keras relies on the `Pillow` library to manipulate images. You can install it easily using `pip`:

```
$> pip install Pillow
```

Let's get started!

## How to do it...

Now, let's begin this recipe:

1.  Import the necessary packages:

```
import glob
import os
import tarfile
import matplotlib.pyplot as plt
from tensorflow.keras.preprocessing.image import
ImageDataGenerator
from tensorflow.keras.preprocessing.image
import load_img, img_to_array
from tensorflow.keras.utils import get_file
```

2.  Define the URL and destination of the CINIC-10 dataset, an alternative to the famous CIFAR-10 dataset:

```
DATASET_URL = 'https://datashare.is.ed.ac.uk/bitstream/
handle/10283/3192/CINIC-10.tar.gz?sequence=4&isAllowed=y'
DATA_NAME = 'cinic10'
FILE_EXTENSION = 'tar.gz'
FILE_NAME = '.'.join([DATA_NAME, FILE_EXTENSION])
```

3.  Download and decompress the data. By default, it will be stored in ~/.keras/ datasets/<FILE_NAME>:

```
downloaded_file_location = get_file(origin=DATASET_URL,
fname=FILE_NAME, extract=False)


# Build the path to the data directory based on the
location of the downloaded file.
data_directory, _ = downloaded_file_location.rsplit(os.
path.sep, maxsplit=1)
data_directory = os.path.sep.join([data_directory,
                                 DATA_NAME])


# Only extract the data if it hasn't been extracted
already
if not os.path.exists(data_directory):
```

```
    tar = tarfile.open(downloaded_file_location)
    tar.extractall(data_directory)
```

4. Load all image paths and print the number of images found:

```
data_pattern = os.path.sep.join([data_directory,
                                 '*/*/*.png'])
image_paths = list(glob.glob(data_pattern))
print(f'There are {len(image_paths):,} images in the
    dataset')
```

The output should be as follows:

```
There are 270,000 images in the dataset
```

5. Load a single image from the dataset and print its metadata:

```
sample_image = load_img(image_paths[0])
print(f'Image type: {type(sample_image)}')
print(f'Image format: {sample_image.format}')
print(f'Image mode: {sample_image.mode}')
print(f'Image size: {sample_image.size}')
```

The output should be as follows:

```
Image type: <class 'PIL.PngImagePlugin.PngImageFile'>
Image format: PNG
Image mode: RGB
Image size: (32, 32)
```

6. Convert an image into a NumPy array:

```
sample_image_array = img_to_array(sample_image)
print(f'Image type: {type(sample_image_array)}')
print(f'Image array shape: {sample_image_array.shape}')
```

Here's the output:

```
Image type: <class 'numpy.ndarray'>
Image array shape: (32, 32, 3)
```

7.  Display an image using `matplotlib`:

```
plt.imshow(sample_image_array / 255.0)
```

This gives us the following image:

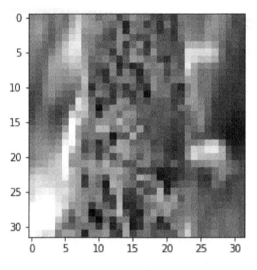

Figure 1.1 – Sample image

8.  Load a batch of images using `ImageDataGenerator`. As in the previous step, each image will be rescaled to the range [0, 1]:

```
image_generator = ImageDataGenerator(horizontal_
flip=True, rescale=1.0 / 255.0)
```

9.  Using `image_generator`, we'll pick and display a random batch of 10 images directly from the directory they are stored in:

```
iterator = (image_generator
        .flow_from_directory(directory=data_directory,
                             batch_size=10))
for batch, _ in iterator:
    plt.figure(figsize=(5, 5))
    for index, image in enumerate(batch, start=1):
        ax = plt.subplot(5, 5, index)
        plt.imshow(image)
        plt.axis('off')
```

```
        plt.show()
        break
```

The displayed batch is shown here:

Figure 1.2 – Batch of images

Let's see how it all works.

## How it works...

First, we downloaded a visual dataset with the help of the get_file() function, which, by default, stores the file with a name of our choosing inside the ~/.keras/datasets directory. If the file already exists in this location, get_files() is intelligent enough to not download it again.

Next, we decompressed the CINIC-10 dataset using untar. Although these steps are not required to load images (we can manually download and decompress a dataset), it's often a good idea to automate as many steps as we can.

We then loaded a single image into memory with load_img(), a function that uses Pillow underneath. Because the result of this invocation is in a format a neural network won't understand, we transformed it into a NumPy array with img_to_array().

Finally, to load batches of images instead of each one individually, we used
`ImageDataGenerator`, which had been configured to also normalize each image.
`ImageDataGenerator` is capable of much more, and we'll often use it whenever we
want to implement data augmentation, but for this recipe, we only used it to load groups
of 10 images at a time directly from disk, thanks to the `flow_from_directory()`
method. As a final remark, this last method returns batches of images and labels, but we
ignored the latter as we're only interested in the former.

## See also

To learn more about processing images with Keras, please consult the official
documentation here: `https://www.tensorflow.org/api_docs/python/tf/`
`keras/preprocessing/image`. For more information on the `CINIC-10` dataset,
visit this link: `https://datashare.is.ed.ac.uk/handle/10283/3192`.

# Loading images using the tf.data.Dataset API

In this recipe, we will learn how to load images using the `tf.data.Dataset` API,
one of the most important innovations that TensorFlow 2.x brings. Its functional style
interface, as well as its high level of optimization, makes it a better alternative than the
traditional Keras API for large projects, where efficiency and performance is a must.

In particular, we'll learn how to open, explore, and visualize a single image, as well as a
batch of them. Additionally, we will learn how to programmatically download a dataset.

## How to do it...

Let's begin this recipe:

1.  First, we need to import all the packages we'll need for this recipe:

```
import os
import tarfile
import matplotlib.pyplot as plt
import numpy as np
import tensorflow as tf
from tensorflow.keras.utils import get_file
```

2.  Define the URL and destination of the CINIC-10 dataset, an alternative to the famous CIFAR-10 dataset:

```
DATASET_URL = 'https://datashare.is.ed.ac.uk/bitstream/
handle/10283/3192/CINIC-10.tar.gz?sequence=4&isAllowed=y'
DATA_NAME = 'cinic10'
FILE_EXTENSION = 'tar.gz'
FILE_NAME = '.'.join([DATA_NAME, FILE_EXTENSION])
```

3.  Download and decompress the data. By default, it will be stored in ~/keras/dataset/<FILE_NAME>:

```
downloaded_file_location = get_file(origin=DATASET_URL,
fname=FILE_NAME, extract=False)


# Build the path to the data directory based on the
location of the downloaded file.
data_directory, _ = downloaded_file_location.rsplit(os.
path.sep, maxsplit=1)
data_directory = os.path.sep.join([data_directory,
                                   DATA_NAME])


# Only extract the data if it hasn't been extracted
already
if not os.path.exists(data_directory):
    tar = tarfile.open(downloaded_file_location)
    tar.extractall(data_directory)
```

4.  Create a dataset of image paths using a glob-like pattern:

```
data_pattern = os.path.sep.join([data_directory, '*/*/*.
png'])
image_dataset = tf.data.Dataset.list_files(data_pattern)
```

5.  Take a single path from the dataset and use it to read the corresponding image:

```
for file_path in image_dataset.take(1):
    sample_path = file_path.numpy()
sample_image = tf.io.read_file(sample_path)
```

6.  Even though the image is now in memory, we must convert it into a format a neural network can work with. For this, we must decode it from its PNG format into a NumPy array, as follows:

```
sample_image = tf.image.decode_png(sample_image,
                                    channels=3)
sample_image = sample_image.numpy()
```

7.  Display the image using matplotlib:

```
plt.imshow(sample_image / 255.0)
```

Here's the result:

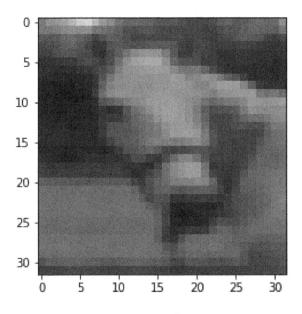

Figure 1.3 – Sample image

8.  Take the first 10 elements of image_dataset, decode and normalize them, and then display them using matplotlib:

```
plt.figure(figsize=(5, 5))
for index, image_path in enumerate(image_dataset.
take(10), start=1):
    image = tf.io.read_file(image_path)
    image = tf.image.decode_png(image, channels=3)
    image = tf.image.convert_image_dtype(image,
```

```
                                                        np.float32)

    ax = plt.subplot(5, 5, index)
    plt.imshow(image)
    plt.axis('off')

plt.show()
plt.close()
```

Here's the output:

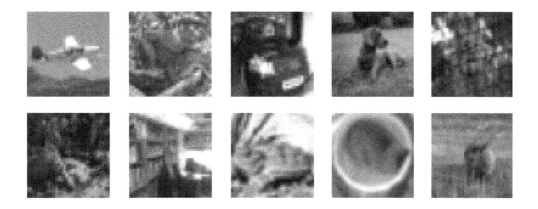

Figure 1.4 – Batch of images

Let's explain this in more detail.

## How it works...

First, we downloaded the CINIC-10 dataset using the get_file() helper function, which saves the fetched file with a name we give it inside the ~/.keras/datasets directory by default. If the file was downloaded before, get_files() won't download it again.

Because CINIC-10 is compressed, we used untar to extract its contents. This is certainly not required to execute these steps each time we want to load images, given that we can manually download and decompress a dataset, but it's a good practice to automate as many steps as possible.

To load the images into memory, we created a dataset of their file paths, which enabled us to follow almost the same process to display single or multiple images. We did this using the path to load the image into memory. Then, we decoded it from its source format (PNG, in this recipe), converted it into a `NumPy` array, and then pre-processed it as needed.

Finally, we took the first 10 images in the dataset and displayed them with `matplotlib`.

## See also

If you want to learn more about the `tf.data.Dataset` API, please refer to the official documentation here: `https://www.tensorflow.org/api_docs/python/tf/data/Dataset`. For more information regarding the CINIC-10 dataset, go to this link: `https://datashare.is.ed.ac.uk/handle/10283/3192`.

# Saving and loading a model

Training a neural network is hard work and time-consuming. That's why retraining a model every time is impractical. The good news is that we can save a network to disk and load it whenever we need it, whether to improve its performance with more training or to use it to make predictions on fresh data. In this recipe, we'll learn about different ways to persist a model.

Let's get started!

## How to do it...

In this recipe, we'll train a **CNN** on `mnist` just to illustrate our point. Let's get started:

1.  Import everything we will need:

```
import json
import numpy as np
from sklearn.model_selection import train_test_split
from sklearn.preprocessing import LabelBinarizer
from tensorflow.keras import Model
from tensorflow.keras.datasets import mnist
from tensorflow.keras.layers import BatchNormalization
from tensorflow.keras.layers import Conv2D
from tensorflow.keras.layers import Dense
from tensorflow.keras.layers import Dropout
```

```
from tensorflow.keras.layers import Flatten
from tensorflow.keras.layers import Input
from tensorflow.keras.layers import MaxPooling2D
from tensorflow.keras.layers import ReLU
from tensorflow.keras.layers import Softmax
from tensorflow.keras.models import load_model
from tensorflow.keras.models import model_from_json
```

2. Define a function that will download and prepare the data by normalizing the train and test sets and one-hot encoding the labels:

```
def load_data():
  (X_train, y_train), (X_test, y_test) = mnist.load_data()

    # Normalize data.
    X_train = X_train.astype('float32') / 255.0
    X_test = X_test.astype('float32') / 255.0

    # Reshape grayscale to include channel dimension.
    X_train = np.expand_dims(X_train, axis=3)
    X_test = np.expand_dims(X_test, axis=3)

    # Process labels.
    label_binarizer = LabelBinarizer()
    y_train = label_binarizer.fit_transform(y_train)
    y_test = label_binarizer.fit_transform(y_test)

    return X_train, y_train, X_test, y_test
```

3. Define a function for building a network. The architecture comprises a single convolutional layer and two fully connected layers:

```
def build_network():
    input_layer = Input(shape=(28, 28, 1))
    convolution_1 = Conv2D(kernel_size=(2, 2),
                           padding='same',
                           strides=(2, 2),
                           filters=32)(input_layer)
```

```
activation_1 = ReLU()(convolution_1)
batch_normalization_1 = BatchNormalization()
                              (activation_1)
pooling_1 = MaxPooling2D(pool_size=(2, 2),
                              strides=(1, 1),
    padding='same')(batch_normalization_1)
dropout = Dropout(rate=0.5)(pooling_1)


flatten = Flatten()(dropout)
dense_1 = Dense(units=128)(flatten)
activation_2 = ReLU()(dense_1)
dense_2 = Dense(units=10)(activation_2)
output = Softmax()(dense_2)


network = Model(inputs=input_layer, outputs=output)


return network
```

4.  Implement a function that will evaluate a network using the test set:

```
def evaluate(model, X_test, y_test):
    _, accuracy = model.evaluate(X_test, y_test,
                              verbose=0)
    print(f'Accuracy: {accuracy}')
```

5.  Prepare the data, create a validation split, and instantiate the neural network:

```
X_train, y_train, X_test, y_test = load_data()
X_train, X_valid, y_train, y_valid = train_test_split(X_
train, y_train, train_size=0.8)
model = build_network()
```

6.  Compile and train the model for 50 epochs, with a batch size of `1024`. Feel free to tune these values according to the capacity of your machine:

```
model.compile(loss='categorical_crossentropy',
              optimizer='adam',
              metrics=['accuracy'])
model.fit(X_train, y_train,
          validation_data=(X_valid, y_valid),
          epochs=50,
          batch_size=1024,
          verbose=0)
```

7.  Save the model, along with its weights, in HDF5 format using the `save()` method. Then, load the persisted model using `load_model()` and evaluate the network's performance on the test set:

```
# Saving model and weights as HDF5.
model.save('model_and_weights.hdf5')


# Loading model and weights as HDF5.
loaded_model = load_model('model_and_weights.hdf5')


# Predicting using loaded model.
evaluate(loaded_model, X_test, y_test)
```

The output is as follows:

```
Accuracy: 0.9836000204086304
```

Here, we can see that our loaded model obtains 98.36% accuracy on the test set. Let's take a look at this in more detail.

## How it works...

We just learned how to persist a model to disk and back into memory using TensorFlow's 2.0 Keras API, which consists of saving both the model and its weights in a single **HDF5** file using the save() method. Although there are other ways to achieve the same goal, this is the preferred and most commonly used method because we can simply restore a network to its saved state using the load_model() function, and then resume training or use it for inference.

## There's more...

You can also store the model separately from the weights – the former in **JSON** format and the latter in HDF5 – using to_json() and save_weights(), respectively. The advantage of this approach is that we can copy a network with the same architecture from scratch using the model_from_json() function. The downside, though, is that we need more function calls, and this effort is rarely worth it.

# Visualizing a model's architecture

Due to their complexity, one of the most effective ways to debug a neural network is by visualizing its architecture. In this recipe, we'll learn about two different ways we can display a model's architecture:

- Using a text summary
- Using a visual diagram

## Getting ready

We'll need both Pillow and pydot to generate a visual representation of a network's architecture. We can install both libraries using pip, as follows:

```
$> pip install Pillow pydot
```

## How to do it...

Visualizing a model's architecture is pretty easy, as we'll learn in the following steps:

1.  Import all the required libraries:

    ```
    from PIL import Image
    from tensorflow.keras import Model
    from tensorflow.keras.layers import BatchNormalization
    ```

```
from tensorflow.keras.layers import Conv2D
from tensorflow.keras.layers import Dense
from tensorflow.keras.layers import Dropout
from tensorflow.keras.layers import Flatten
from tensorflow.keras.layers import Input
from tensorflow.keras.layers import LeakyReLU
from tensorflow.keras.layers import MaxPooling2D
from tensorflow.keras.layers import Softmax
from tensorflow.keras.utils import plot_model
```

2. Implement a model using all the layers we imported in the previous step. Notice that we are naming each layer for ease of reference later on. First, let's define the input:

```
input_layer = Input(shape=(64, 64, 3),
                    name='input_layer')
```

Here's the first convolution block:

```
convolution_1 = Conv2D(kernel_size=(2, 2),
                       padding='same',
                       strides=(2, 2),
                       filters=32,
                       name='convolution_1')(input_layer)
activation_1 = LeakyReLU(name='activation_1')
(convolution_1)
batch_normalization_1 = BatchNormalization(name='batch_
normalization_1')(activation_1)
pooling_1 = MaxPooling2D(pool_size=(2, 2),
                         strides=(1, 1),
                         padding='same',
                         name='pooling_1')(batch_
normalization_1)
```

Here's the second convolution block:

```
convolution_2 = Conv2D(kernel_size=(2, 2),
                       padding='same',
                       strides=(2, 2),
                       filters=64,
                       name='convolution_2')(pooling_1)
```

```
activation_2 = LeakyReLU(name='activation_2')
(convolution_2)
batch_normalization_2 = BatchNormalization(name='batch_
normalization_2')(activation_2)
pooling_2 = MaxPooling2D(pool_size=(2, 2),
                                strides=(1, 1),
                                padding='same',
                                name='pooling_2')
                                (batch_normalization_2)
dropout = Dropout(rate=0.5, name='dropout')(pooling_2)
```

Finally, we'll define the dense layers and the model itself:

```
flatten = Flatten(name='flatten')(dropout)
dense_1 = Dense(units=256, name='dense_1')(flatten)
activation_3 = LeakyReLU(name='activation_3')(dense_1)
dense_2 = Dense(units=128, name='dense_2')(activation_3)
activation_4 = LeakyReLU(name='activation_4')(dense_2)
dense_3 = Dense(units=3, name='dense_3')(activation_4)
output = Softmax(name='output')(dense_3)


model = Model(inputs=input_layer, outputs=output,
                name='my_model')
```

3.  Summarize the model by printing a text representation of its architecture, as follows:

```
print(model.summary())
```

Here's the summary. The numbers in the **Output Shape** column describe the dimensions of the volume produced by that layer, while the number in the **Param #** column states the number of parameters in that layer:

```
Model: "my_model"
_____
Layer (type)                 Output Shape            Param #
=================================================================
input_layer (InputLayer)     [(None, 64, 64, 3)]     0
_____
convolution_1 (Conv2D)       (None, 32, 32, 32)      416
_____
activation_1 (LeakyReLU)     (None, 32, 32, 32)      0
_____
batch_normalization_1 (Batch (None, 32, 32, 32)      128
_____
pooling_1 (MaxPooling2D)     (None, 32, 32, 32)      0
_____
convolution_2 (Conv2D)       (None, 16, 16, 64)      8256
_____
activation_2 (LeakyReLU)     (None, 16, 16, 64)      0
_____
batch_normalization_2 (Batch (None, 16, 16, 64)      256
_____
pooling_2 (MaxPooling2D)     (None, 16, 16, 64)      0
_____
dropout (Dropout)            (None, 16, 16, 64)      0
_____
flatten (Flatten)            (None, 16384)           0
_____
dense_1 (Dense)              (None, 256)             4194560
_____
activation_3 (LeakyReLU)     (None, 256)             0
_____
dense_2 (Dense)              (None, 128)             32896
_____
activation_4 (LeakyReLU)     (None, 128)             0
_____
dense_3 (Dense)              (None, 3)               387
_____
output (Softmax)             (None, 3)               0
=================================================================
Total params: 4,236,899
Trainable params: 4,236,707
Non-trainable params: 192
_____
```

Figure 1.5 – Text representation of the network

The last few lines summarize the number of trainable and non-trainable parameters. The more parameters a model has, the harder and slower it is to train.

4. Plot a diagram of the network's architecture:

```
plot_model(model,
           show_shapes=True,
           show_layer_names=True,
           to_file='my_model.jpg')
model_diagram = Image.open('my_model.jpg')
```

This produces the following output:

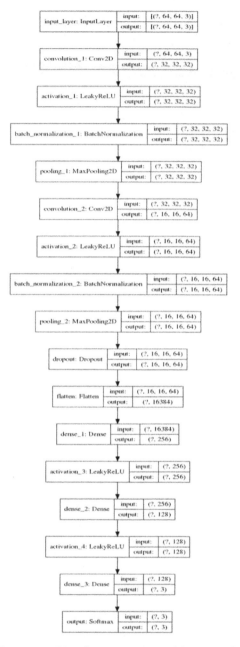

Figure 1.6 – Visual representation of the network

Now, let's learn how this all works.

# How it works...

Visualizing a model is as simple as calling `plot_model()` on the variable that holds it. For it to work, however, we must ensure we have the required dependencies installed; for instance, `pydot`. Nevertheless, if we want a more detailed summary of the number of parameters in our network layer-wise, we must invoke the `summarize()` method.

Finally, naming each layer is a good convention to follow. This makes the architecture more readable and easier to reuse in the feature because we can simply retrieve a layer by its name. One remarkable application of this feature is **neural style transfer**.

# Creating a basic image classifier

We'll close this chapter by implementing an image classifier on `Fashion-MNIST`, a popular alternative to `mnist`. This will help us consolidate the knowledge we've acquired from the previous recipes. If, at any point, you need more details on a particular step, please refer to the previous recipes.

## Getting ready

I encourage you to complete the five previous recipes before tackling this one since our goal is to come full circle with the lessons we've learned throughout this chapter. Also, make sure you have `Pillow` and `pydot` on your system. You can install them using pip:

```
$> pip install Pillow pydot
```

Finally, we'll use the `tensorflow_docs` package to plot the loss and accuracy curves of the model. You can install this library with the following command:

```
$> pip install git+https://github.com/tensorflow/docs
```

## How to do it...

Follow these steps to complete this recipe:

1.  Import the necessary packages:

    ```
    import matplotlib.pyplot as plt
    import numpy as np
    import tensorflow as tf
    import tensorflow_docs as tfdocs
    import tensorflow_docs.plots
    ```

```
from sklearn.model_selection import train_test_split
from sklearn.preprocessing import LabelBinarizer
from tensorflow.keras import Model
from tensorflow.keras.datasets import fashion_mnist as fm
from tensorflow.keras.layers import BatchNormalization
from tensorflow.keras.layers import Conv2D
from tensorflow.keras.layers import Dense
from tensorflow.keras.layers import Dropout
from tensorflow.keras.layers import ELU
from tensorflow.keras.layers import Flatten
from tensorflow.keras.layers import Input
from tensorflow.keras.layers import MaxPooling2D
from tensorflow.keras.layers import Softmax
from tensorflow.keras.models import load_model
from tensorflow.keras.utils import plot_model
```

2.  Define a function that will load and prepare the dataset. It will normalize the data, one-hot encode the labels, take a portion of the training set for validation, and wrap the three data subsets into three separate `tf.data.Dataset` instances to increase performance using `from_tensor_slices()`:

```
def load_dataset():
    (X_train, y_train), (X_test, y_test) = fm.load_data()

    X_train = X_train.astype('float32') / 255.0
    X_test = X_test.astype('float32') / 255.0

    # Reshape grayscale to include channel dimension.
    X_train = np.expand_dims(X_train, axis=3)
    X_test = np.expand_dims(X_test, axis=3)

    label_binarizer = LabelBinarizer()
    y_train = label_binarizer.fit_transform(y_train)
    y_test = label_binarizer.fit_transform(y_test)

    (X_train, X_val,
     y_train, y_val) = train_test_split(X_train, y_train,
```

```
                              train_size=0.8)
    train_ds = (tf.data.Dataset
                   .from_tensor_slices((X_train,
                                        y_train)))
    val_ds = (tf.data.Dataset
                 .from_tensor_slices((X_val, y_val)))
    test_ds = (tf.data.Dataset
                  .from_tensor_slices((X_test, y_test)))
```

3. Implement a function that will build a network similar to **LeNet** with the addition of `BatchNormalization`, which we'll use to make the network faster and most stable, and `Dropout` layers, which will help us combat overfitting, a situation where the network loses generalization power due to high variance:

```python
def build_network():
    input_layer = Input(shape=(28, 28, 1))
    x = Conv2D(filters=20,
               kernel_size=(5, 5),
               padding='same',
               strides=(1, 1))(input_layer)
    x = ELU()(x)
    x = BatchNormalization()(x)
    x = MaxPooling2D(pool_size=(2, 2),
                     strides=(2, 2))(x)
    x = Dropout(0.5)(x)

    x = Conv2D(filters=50,
               kernel_size=(5, 5),
               padding='same',
               strides=(1, 1))(x)
    x = ELU()(x)
    x = BatchNormalization()(x)
    x = MaxPooling2D(pool_size=(2, 2),
                     strides=(2, 2))(x)
    x = Dropout(0.5)(x)
```

```
x = Flatten()(x)
x = Dense(units=500)(x)
x = ELU()(x)
x = Dropout(0.5)(x)

x = Dense(10)(x)
output = Softmax()(x)

model = Model(inputs=input_layer, outputs=output)
return model
```

4.  Define a function that takes a model's training history, along with a metric of interest, to create a plot corresponding to the training and validation of the curves of such a metric:

```
def plot_model_history(model_history, metric, ylim=None):
    plt.style.use('seaborn-darkgrid')
    plotter = tfdocs.plots.HistoryPlotter()
    plotter.plot({'Model': model_history}, metric=metric)

    plt.title(f'{metric.upper()}')
    if ylim is None:
        plt.ylim([0, 1])
    else:
        plt.ylim(ylim)

    plt.savefig(f'{metric}.png')
    plt.close()
```

5. Consume the training and validation datasets in batches of 256 images at a time. The `prefetch()` method spawns a background thread that populates a buffer of size `1024` with image batches:

```
BATCH_SIZE = 256
BUFFER_SIZE = 1024

train_dataset, val_dataset, test_dataset = load_dataset()

train_dataset = (train_dataset
                .shuffle(buffer_size=BUFFER_SIZE)
                .batch(BATCH_SIZE)
                .prefetch(buffer_size=BUFFER_SIZE))
val_dataset = (val_dataset
                .batch(BATCH_SIZE)
                .prefetch(buffer_size=BUFFER_SIZE))
test_dataset = test_dataset.batch(BATCH_SIZE)
```

6. Build and train the network:

```
EPOCHS = 100

model = build_network()
model.compile(loss='categorical_crossentropy',
optimizer='adam', metrics=['accuracy'])

model_history = model.fit(train_dataset, validation_
data=validation_dataset, epochs=EPOCHS, verbose=0)
```

7. Plot the training and validation loss and accuracy:

```
plot_model_history(model_history, 'loss', [0., 2.0])
plot_model_history(model_history, 'accuracy')
```

The first graph corresponds to the loss curve both on the training and validation sets:

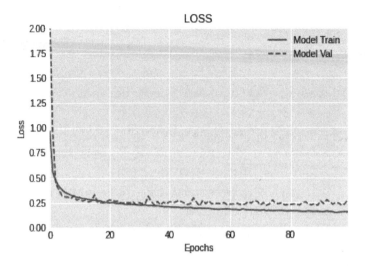

Figure 1.7 – Loss plot

The second plot shows the accuracy curve for the training and validation sets:

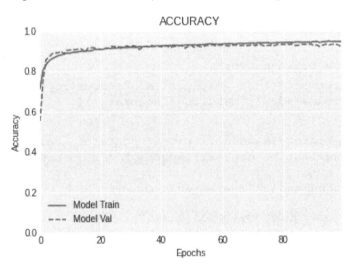

Figure 1.8 – Accuracy plot

8.  Visualize the model's architecture:

```
plot_model(model, show_shapes=True, show_layer_
names=True, to_file='model.png')
```

The following is a diagram of our model:

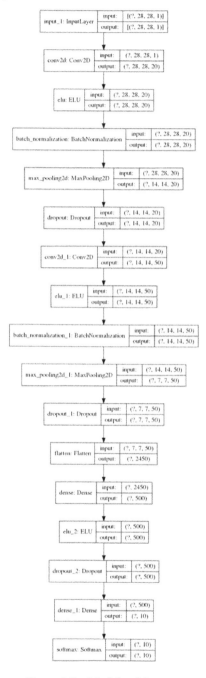

Figure 1.9 – Model architecture

9.  Save the model:

```
model.save('model.hdf5')
```

10. Load and evaluate the model:

```
loaded_model = load_model('model.hdf5')
results = loaded_model.evaluate(test_dataset, verbose=0)
print(f'Loss: {results[0]}, Accuracy: {results[1]}')
```

The output is as follows:

```
Loss: 0.2943768735975027, Accuracy: 0.9132000207901001
```

That completes the final recipe of this chapter. Let's review how it all works.

## How it works...

In this recipe, we used all the lessons learned in this chapter. We started by downloading Fashion-MNIST and used the tf.data.Dataset API to load its images so that we could feed them to our network, which we implemented using the declarative Functional high-level Keras API. After fitting our model to the data, we examined its performance by reviewing the loss and accuracy curves on the training and validation sets with the help of matplotlib and tensorflow_docs. To gain a better understanding of the network, we visualized its architecture with plot_model() and then saved it to disk, along with its weights, in the convenient HDF5 format. Finally, we loaded the model with load_model() to evaluate it on new, unseen data – that is, the test set – obtaining a respectable 91.3% accuracy rating.

## See also

For a deeper explanation of Fashion-MNIST, visit this site: https://github.com/zalandoresearch/fashion-mnist. The GitHub repository for the TensorFlow docs is available here: https://github.com/tensorflow/docs.

# 2
# Performing Image Classification

Computer vision is a vast field that takes inspiration from many places. Of course, this means that its applications are wide and varied. However, the biggest breakthroughs over the past decade, especially in the context of deep learning applied to visual tasks, have occurred in a particular domain known as **image classification**.

As the name suggests, image classification consists of the process of discerning what's in an image based on its visual content. Is there a dog or a cat in this image? What number is in this picture? Is the person in this photo smiling or not?

Because image classification is such an important and pervasive task in deep learning applied to computer vision, the recipes in this chapter will focus on the ins and outs of classifying images using TensorFlow 2.x.

We'll cover the following recipes:

- Creating a binary classifier to detect smiles
- Creating a multi-class classifier to play Rock Paper Scissors
- Creating a multi-label classifier to label watches
- Implementing ResNet from scratch

- Classifying images with a pre-trained network using the Keras API
- Classifying images with a pre-trained network using TensorFlow Hub
- Using data augmentation to improve performance with the Keras API
- Using data augmentation to improve performance with the tf.data and tf.image APIs

# Technical requirements

Besides a working installation of TensorFlow 2.x, it's highly recommended to have access to a GPU, given that some of the recipes are very resource-intensive, making the use of a CPU an inviable option. In each recipe, you'll find the steps and dependencies needed to complete it in the *Getting ready* section. Finally, the code shown in this chapter is available in full here: `https://github.com/PacktPublishing/Tensorflow-2.0-Computer-Vision-Cookbook/tree/master/ch2`.

Check out the following link to see the Code in Action video:

`https://bit.ly/3bOjqnU`

# Creating a binary classifier to detect smiles

In its most basic form, image classification consists of discerning between two classes, or signaling the presence or absence of some trait. In this recipe, we'll implement a binary classifier that tells us whether a person in a photo is smiling.

Let's begin, shall we?

## Getting ready

You'll need to install `Pillow`, which is very easy with `pip`:

```
$> pip install Pillow
```

We'll use the `SMILEs` dataset, located here: `https://github.com/hromi/SMILEsmileD`. Clone or download a zipped version of the repository to a location of your preference. In this recipe, we assume the data is inside the `~/.keras/datasets` directory, under the name `SMILEsmileD-master`:

Figure 2.1 – Positive (left) and negative (right) examples

Let's get started!

## How to do it...

Follow these steps to train a smile classifier from scratch on the SMILEs dataset:

1.  Import all necessary packages:

```
import os
import pathlib
import glob
import numpy as np
from sklearn.model_selection import train_test_split
from tensorflow.keras import Model
from tensorflow.keras.layers import *
from tensorflow.keras.preprocessing.image import *
```
← load.img()
img_to_array()

2.  Define a function to load the images and labels from a list of file paths:

```
def load_images_and_labels(image_paths):
    images = []
    labels = []

    for image_path in image_paths:
        image = load_img(image_path, target_size=(32,32),
                         color_mode='grayscale')
        image = img_to_array(image)
```

```
        label = image_path.split(os.path.sep)[-2]
        label = 'positive' in label
        label = float(label)

        images.append(image)
        labels.append(label)

    return np.array(images), np.array(labels)
```

Notice that we are loading the images in grayscale, and we're encoding the labels by checking whether the word *positive* is in the file path of the image.

3.  Define a function to build the neural network. This model's structure is based on **LeNet** (you can find a link to LeNet's paper in the *See also* section):

```
def build_network():
    input_layer = Input(shape=(32, 32, 1))
    x = Conv2D(filters=20,
               kernel_size=(5, 5),
               padding='same',
               strides=(1, 1))(input_layer)
    x = ELU()(x)
    x = BatchNormalization()(x)
    x = MaxPooling2D(pool_size=(2, 2),
                     strides=(2, 2))(x)
    x = Dropout(0.4)(x)

    x = Conv2D(filters=50,
               kernel_size=(5, 5),
               padding='same',
               strides=(1, 1))(x)
    x = ELU()(x)
    x = BatchNormalization()(x)
    x = MaxPooling2D(pool_size=(2, 2),
                     strides=(2, 2))(x)
    x = Dropout(0.4)(x)
```

```
x = Flatten()(x)
x = Dense(units=500)(x)
x = ELU()(x)
x = Dropout(0.4)(x)

output = Dense(1, activation='sigmoid')(x)

model = Model(inputs=input_layer, outputs=output)
return model
```

Because this is a binary classification problem, a single Sigmoid-activated neuron is enough in the output layer.

4. Load the image paths into a list:

```
files_pattern = (pathlib.Path.home() / '.keras' /
                 'datasets' /
                 'SMILEsmileD-master' / 'SMILEs' / '*'
                 / '*' /
                 '*.jpg')
files_pattern = str(files_pattern)
dataset_paths = [*glob.glob(files_pattern)]
```

5. Use the `load_images_and_labels()` function defined previously to load the dataset into memory:

```
X, y = load_images_and_labels(dataset_paths)
```

6. Normalize the images and compute the number of positive, negative, and total examples in the dataset:

```
X /= 255.0
total = len(y)
total_positive = np.sum(y)
total_negative = total - total_positive
```

7. Create train, test, and validation subsets of the data:

```
(X_train, X_test,
 y_train, y_test) = train_test_split(X, y,
                                     test_size=0.2,
```

```
                                          stratify=y,
                                          random_state=999)
(X_train, X_val,
 y_train, y_val) = train_test_split(X_train, y_train,
                                    test_size=0.2,
                                    stratify=y_train,
                                    random_state=999)
```

8. Instantiate the model and compile it:

```
model = build_network()
model.compile(loss='binary_crossentropy',
              optimizer='rmsprop',
              metrics=['accuracy'])
```

9. Train the model. Because the dataset is unbalanced, we are assigning weights to each class proportional to the number of positive and negative images in the dataset:

```
BATCH_SIZE = 32
EPOCHS = 20
model.fit(X_train, y_train,
          validation_data=(X_val, y_val),
          epochs=EPOCHS,
          batch_size=BATCH_SIZE,
          class_weight={
              1.0: total / total_positive,
              0.0: total / total_negative
          })
```

10. Evaluate the model on the test set:

```
test_loss, test_accuracy = model.evaluate(X_test,
                                          y_test)
```

After 20 epochs, the network should get around 90% accuracy on the test set. In the following section, we'll explain the previous steps.

# How it works...

We just trained a network to determine whether a person is smiling or not in a picture. Our first big task was to take the images in the dataset and load them into a format suitable for our neural network. Specifically, the `load_image_and_labels()` function is in charge of loading an image in grayscale, resizing it to 32x32x1, and then converting it into a `numpy` array. To extract the label, we looked at the containing folder of each image: if it contained the word positive, we encoded the label as 1; otherwise, we encoded it as 0 (a trick we used here was casting a Boolean as a float, like this: `float(label)`).

Next, we built the neural network, which is inspired by the LeNet architecture. The biggest takeaway here is that because this is a binary classification problem, we can use a single Sigmoid-activated neuron to discern between the two classes.

We then took 20% of the images to comprise our test set, and from the remaining 80% we took an additional 20% to create our validation set. With these three subsets in place, we proceeded to train the network over 20 epochs, using `binary_crossentropy` as our loss function and `rmsprop` as the optimizer.

To account for the imbalance in the dataset (out of the 13,165 images, only 3,690 contain smiling people, while the remaining 9,475 do not), we passed a `class_weight` dictionary where we assigned a weight conversely proportional to the number of instances of each class in the dataset, effectively forcing the model to pay more attention to the 1.0 class, which corresponds to *smile*.

Finally, we achieved around 90.5% accuracy on the test set.

# See also

For more information on the SMILEs dataset, you can visit the official GitHub repository here: `https://github.com/hromi/SMILEsmileD`. You can read the LeNet paper here (it's pretty long, though): `http://yann.lecun.com/exdb/publis/pdf/lecun-98.pdf`.

# Creating a multi-class classifier to play rock paper scissors

More often than not, we are interested in categorizing an image into more than two classes. As we'll see in this recipe, implementing a neural network to differentiate between many categories is fairly straightforward, and what better way to demonstrate this than by training a model that can play the widely known Rock Paper Scissors game?

Are you ready? Let's dive in!

## Getting ready

We'll use the `Rock-Paper-Scissors Images` dataset, which is hosted on Kaggle at the following location: `https://www.kaggle.com/drgfreeman/rockpaperscissors`. To download it, you'll need a Kaggle account, so sign in or sign up accordingly. Then, unzip the dataset in a location of your preference. In this recipe, we assume the unzipped folder is inside the `~/.keras/datasets` directory, under the name `rockpaperscissors`.

Here are some sample images:

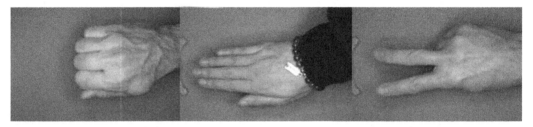

Figure 2.2 – Example images of rock (left), paper (center), and scissors (right)

Let's begin implementing.

## How to do it...

The following steps explain how to train a multi-class **Convolutional Neural Network** (**CNN**) to distinguish between the three classes of the Rock Paper Scissors game:

1.  Import the required packages:

```
import os
import pathlib
import glob
import numpy as np
import tensorflow as tf
from sklearn.model_selection import train_test_split
from tensorflow.keras import Model
from tensorflow.keras.layers import *
from tensorflow.keras.losses import
CategoricalCrossentropy
```

2. Define a list with the three classes, and also an alias to `tf.data.experimental.AUTOTUNE`, which we'll use later:

```
CLASSES = ['rock', 'paper', 'scissors']
AUTOTUNE = tf.data.experimental.AUTOTUNE
```

The values in `CLASSES` match the names of the directories that contain the images for each class.

3. Define a function to load an image and its label, given its file path:

```
def load_image_and_label(image_path, target_size=(32,
32)):
    image = tf.io.read_file(image_path)
    image = tf.image.decode_jpeg(image, channels=3)
    image = tf.image.rgb_to_grayscale(image)
    image = tf.image.convert_image_dtype(image,
                                         np.float32)
    image = tf.image.resize(image, target_size)

    label = tf.strings.split(image_path,os.path.sep)[-2]
    label = (label == CLASSES)  # One-hot encode.
    label = tf.dtypes.cast(label, tf.float32)

    return image, label
```

Notice that we are one-hot encoding by comparing the name of the folder that contains the image (extracted from `image_path`) with the `CLASSES` list.

4. Define a function to build the network architecture. In this case, it's a very simple and shallow one, which is enough for the problem we are solving:

```
def build_network():
    input_layer = Input(shape=(32, 32, 1))
    x = Conv2D(filters=32,
               kernel_size=(3, 3),
               padding='same',
               strides=(1, 1))(input_layer)
    x = ReLU()(x)
    x = Dropout(rate=0.5)(x)
```

```
x = Flatten()(x)
x = Dense(units=3)(x)
output = Softmax()(x)


return Model(inputs=input_layer, outputs=output)
```

5.  Define a function to, given a path to a dataset, return a `tf.data.Dataset` instance of images and labels, in batches and optionally shuffled:

```
def prepare_dataset(dataset_path,
                    buffer_size,
                    batch_size,
                    shuffle=True):
    dataset = (tf.data.Dataset
                .from_tensor_slices(dataset_path)
                .map(load_image_and_label,
                    num_parallel_calls=AUTOTUNE))

    if shuffle:
        dataset.shuffle(buffer_size=buffer_size)

    dataset = (dataset
                .batch(batch_size=batch_size)
                .prefetch(buffer_size=buffer_size))

    return dataset
```

6.  Load the image paths into a list:

```
file_patten = (pathlib.Path.home() / '.keras' /
                'datasets' /
                'rockpaperscissors' / 'rps-cv-images' /
                '*' /
                '*.png')
file_pattern = str(file_patten)
dataset_paths = [*glob.glob(file_pattern)]
```

7.  Create train, test, and validation subsets of image paths:

```
train_paths, test_paths = train_test_split(dataset_paths,
                                            test_size=0.2,
                                            random_state=999)
train_paths, val_paths = train_test_split(train_paths,
                                           test_size=0.2,
                                           random_state=999)
```

8.  Prepare the training, test, and validation datasets:

```
BATCH_SIZE = 1024
BUFFER_SIZE = 1024
train_dataset = prepare_dataset(train_paths,
                         buffer_size=BUFFER_SIZE,
                         batch_size=BATCH_SIZE)
validation_dataset = prepare_dataset(val_paths,
                         buffer_size=BUFFER_SIZE,
                         batch_size=BATCH_SIZE,
                         shuffle=False)
test_dataset = prepare_dataset(test_paths,
                         buffer_size=BUFFER_SIZE,
                         batch_size=BATCH_SIZE,
                         shuffle=False)
```

9.  Instantiate and compile the model:

```
model = build_network()
model.compile(loss=CategoricalCrossentropy
             (from_logits=True),
             optimizer='adam',
             metrics=['accuracy'])
```

10. Fit the model for 250 epochs:

```
EPOCHS = 250
model.fit(train_dataset,
          validation_data=validation_dataset,
          epochs=EPOCHS)
```

11. Evaluate the model on the test set:

```
test_loss, test_accuracy = model.evaluate(test_dataset)
```

After 250 epochs, our network achieves around 93.5% accuracy on the test set. Let's understand what we just did.

## How it works...

We started by defining the CLASSES list, which allowed us to quickly one-hot encode the labels of each image, based on the name of the directory where they were contained, as we observed in the body of the load_image_and_label() function. In this same function, we read an image from disk, decoded it from its JPEG format, converted it to grayscale (color information is not necessary in this problem), and then resized it to more manageable dimensions of 32x32x1.

build_network() creates a very simple and shallow CNN, comprising a single convolutional layer, activated with ReLU(), followed by an output, a fully connected layer of three neurons, corresponding to the number of categories in the dataset. Because this is a multi-class classification task, we use Softmax() to activate the outputs.

prepare_dataset() leverages the load_image_and_label() function defined previously to convert file paths into batches of image tensors and one-hot encoded labels.

Using the three functions explained here, we prepared three subsets of data, with the purpose of training, validating, and testing the neural network. We trained the model for 250 epochs, using the adam optimizer and CategoricalCrossentropy(from_logits=True) as our loss function (from_logits=True produces a bit more numerical stability).

Finally, we got around 93.5% accuracy on the test set. Based on these results, you could use this network as a component of a Rock Paper Scissors game to recognize the hand gestures of a player and react accordingly.

## See also

For more information on the `Rock-Paper-Scissors Images` dataset, refer to the official Kaggle page where it's hosted: `https://www.kaggle.com/drgfreeman/rockpaperscissors`.

# Creating a multi-label classifier to label watches

A neural network is not limited to modeling the distribution of a single variable. In fact, it can easily handle instances where each image has multiple labels associated with it. In this recipe, we'll implement a CNN to classify the gender and style/usage of watches.

Let's get started.

## Getting ready

First, we must install `Pillow`:

```
$> pip install Pillow
```

Next, we'll use the `Fashion Product Images (Small)` dataset hosted in Kaggle, which, after signing in, you can download here: `https://www.kaggle.com/paramaggarwal/fashion-product-images-small`. In this recipe, we assume the data is inside the `~/.keras/datasets` directory, under the name `fashion-product-images-small`. We'll only use a subset of the data, focused on watches, which we'll construct programmatically in the *How to do it...* section.

Here are some sample images:

Figure 2.3 – Example images

Let's begin the recipe.

## How to do it...

Let's review the steps to complete the recipe:

1.  Import the necessary packages:

```
import os
import pathlib
from csv import DictReader
import glob
import numpy as np
from sklearn.model_selection import train_test_split
from sklearn.preprocessing import MultiLabelBinarizer
from tensorflow.keras.layers import *
from tensorflow.keras.models import Model
from tensorflow.keras.preprocessing.image import *
```

2.  Define a function to build the network architecture. First, implement the convolutional blocks:

```
def build_network(width, height, depth, classes):
    input_layer = Input(shape=(width, height, depth))
    x = Conv2D(filters=32,
               kernel_size=(3, 3),
               padding='same')(input_layer)
```

```
x = ReLU()(x)
x = BatchNormalization(axis=-1)(x)
x = Conv2D(filters=32,
           kernel_size=(3, 3),
           padding='same')(x)
x = ReLU()(x)
x = BatchNormalization(axis=-1)(x)
x = MaxPooling2D(pool_size=(2, 2))(x)
x = Dropout(rate=0.25)(x)

x = Conv2D(filters=64,
           kernel_size=(3, 3),
           padding='same')(x)
x = ReLU()(x)
x = BatchNormalization(axis=-1)(x)
x = Conv2D(filters=64,
           kernel_size=(3, 3),
           padding='same')(x)
x = ReLU()(x)
x = BatchNormalization(axis=-1)(x)
x = MaxPooling2D(pool_size=(2, 2))(x)
x = Dropout(rate=0.25)(x)
```

Next, add the fully convolutional layers:

```
x = Flatten()(x)
x = Dense(units=512)(x)
x = ReLU()(x)
x = BatchNormalization(axis=-1)(x)
x = Dropout(rate=0.5)(x)

x = Dense(units=classes)(x)
output = Activation('sigmoid')(x)

return Model(input_layer, output)
```

3.  Define a function to load all images and labels (gender and usage), given a list of image paths and a dictionary of metadata associated with each of them:

```
def load_images_and_labels(image_paths, styles,
                           target_size):
    images = []
    labels = []
    for image_path in image_paths:
        image = load_img(image_path,
                         target_size=target_size)
        image = img_to_array(image)
        image_id = image_path.split(os.path.sep)[-
                                     1][:-4]

        image_style = styles[image_id]
        label = (image_style['gender'],
                 image_style['usage'])

        images.append(image)
        labels.append(label)

    return np.array(images), np.array(labels)
```

4.  Set the random seed to guarantee reproducibility:

```
SEED = 999
np.random.seed(SEED)
```

5.  Define the paths to the images and the `styles.csv` metadata file:

```
base_path = (pathlib.Path.home() / '.keras' /
             'datasets' /
             'fashion-product-images-small')
styles_path = str(base_path / 'styles.csv')
images_path_pattern = str(base_path / 'images/*.jpg')
image_paths = glob.glob(images_path_pattern)
```

6. Keep only the `Watches` images for `Casual`, `Smart Casual`, and `Formal` usage, suited to `Men` and `Women`:

```
with open(styles_path, 'r') as f:
    dict_reader = DictReader(f)
    STYLES = [*dict_reader]

    article_type = 'Watches'
    genders = {'Men', 'Women'}
    usages = {'Casual', 'Smart Casual', 'Formal'}
    STYLES = {style['id']: style
              for style in STYLES
              if (style['articleType'] == article_type
                                        and
                  style['gender'] in genders and
                  style['usage'] in usages)}

image_paths = [*filter(lambda p:
                   p.split(os.path.sep)[-1][:-4]
                                    in STYLES.keys(),
                   image_paths)]
```

7. Load the images and labels, resizing the images into a 64x64x3 shape:

```
X, y = load_images_and_labels(image_paths, STYLES,
                              (64, 64))
```

8. Normalize the images and multi-hot encode the labels:

```
X = X.astype('float') / 255.0
mlb = MultiLabelBinarizer()
y = mlb.fit_transform(y)
```

9. Create the train, validation, and test splits:

```
(X_train, X_test,
 y_train, y_test) = train_test_split(X, y,
                                     stratify=y,
                                     test_size=0.2,
```

```
                                     random_state=SEED)
(X_train, X_valid,
 y_train, y_valid) = train_test_split(X_train, y_train,
                                      stratify=y_train,
                                      test_size=0.2,
                                      random_state=SEED)
```

10. Build and compile the network:

```
model = build_network(width=64,
                      height=64,
                      depth=3,
                      classes=len(mlb.classes_))
model.compile(loss='binary_crossentropy',
              optimizer='rmsprop',
              metrics=['accuracy'])
```

11. Train the model for 20 epochs, in batches of 64 images at a time:

```
BATCH_SIZE = 64
EPOCHS = 20
model.fit(X_train, y_train,
          validation_data=(X_valid, y_valid),
          batch_size=BATCH_SIZE,
          epochs=EPOCHS)
```

12. Evaluate the model on the test set:

```
result = model.evaluate(X_test, y_test,
                        batch_size=BATCH_SIZE)
print(f'Test accuracy: {result[1]}')
```

This block prints as follows:

```
Test accuracy: 0.90233546
```

13. Use the model to make predictions on a test image, displaying the probability of each label:

```
test_image = np.expand_dims(X_test[0], axis=0)
probabilities = model.predict(test_image)[0]
for label, p in zip(mlb.classes_, probabilities):
    print(f'{label}: {p * 100:.2f}%')
```

That prints this:

```
Casual: 100.00%
Formal: 0.00%
Men: 1.08%
Smart Casual: 0.01%
Women: 99.16%
```

14. Compare the ground truth labels with the network's prediction:

```
ground_truth_labels = np.expand_dims(y_test[0],
                                     axis=0)
ground_truth_labels = mlb.inverse_transform(ground_truth_labels)
print(f'Ground truth labels: {ground_truth_labels}')
```

The output is as follows:

```
Ground truth labels: [('Casual', 'Women')]
```

Let's see how it all works in the next section.

## How it works...

We implemented a smaller version of a **VGG** network, which is capable of performing multi-label, multi-class classification, by modeling independent distributions for the gender and usage metadata associated with each watch. In other words, we modeled two binary classification problems at the same time: one for gender, and one for usage. This is the reason we activated the outputs of the network with Sigmoid, instead of Softmax, and also why the loss function used is binary_crossentropy and not categorical_crossentropy.

We trained the aforementioned network over 20 epochs, on batches of 64 images at a time, obtaining a respectable 90% accuracy on the test set. Finally, we made a prediction on an unseen image from the test set and verified that the labels produced with great certainty by the network (100% certainty for Casual, and 99.16% for Women) correspond to the ground truth categories Casual and Women.

## See also

For more information on the Fashion Product Images (Small) dataset, refer to the official Kaggle page where it is hosted: https://www.kaggle.com/ paramaggarwal/fashion-product-images-small. I recommend you read the paper where the seminal **VGG** architecture was introduced: https://arxiv.org/ abs/1409.1556.

# Implementing ResNet from scratch

**Residual Network**, or **ResNet** for short, constitutes one of the most groundbreaking advancements in deep learning. This architecture relies on a component called the residual module, which allows us to ensemble networks with depths that were unthinkable a couple of years ago. There are variants of **ResNet** that have more than 100 layers, without any loss of performance!

In this recipe, we'll implement **ResNet** from scratch and train it on the challenging drop-in replacement to CIFAR-10, CINIC-10.

## Getting ready

We won't explain **ResNet** in depth, so it is a good idea to familiarize yourself with the architecture if you are interested in the details. You can read the original paper here: https://arxiv.org/abs/1512.03385.

# How to do it...

Follow these steps to implement **ResNet** from the ground up:

1.  Import all necessary modules:

```
import os
import numpy as np
import tarfile
import tensorflow as tf
from tensorflow.keras.callbacks import ModelCheckpoint
from tensorflow.keras.layers import *
from tensorflow.keras.models import *
from tensorflow.keras.regularizers import l2
from tensorflow.keras.utils import get_file
```

2.  Define an alias to the `tf.data.experimental.AUTOTUNE` option, which we'll use later:

```
AUTOTUNE = tf.data.experimental.AUTOTUNE
```

3.  Define a function to create a residual module in the **ResNet** architecture. Let's start by specifying the function signature and implementing the first block:

```
def residual_module(data,
                    filters,
                    stride,
                    reduce=False,
                    reg=0.0001,
                    bn_eps=2e-5,
                    bn_momentum=0.9):
    bn_1 = BatchNormalization(axis=-1,
                              epsilon=bn_eps,
                              momentum=bn_momentum)(data)
    act_1 = ReLU()(bn_1)
    conv_1 = Conv2D(filters=int(filters / 4.),
                    kernel_size=(1, 1),
                    use_bias=False,
                    kernel_regularizer=l2(reg))(act_1)
```

Let's now implement the second and third blocks:

```
    bn_2 = BatchNormalization(axis=-1,
                              epsilon=bn_eps,
                              momentum=bn_momentum)(conv_1)
    act_2 = ReLU()(bn_2)
    conv_2 = Conv2D(filters=int(filters / 4.),
                    kernel_size=(3, 3),
                    strides=stride,
                    padding='same',
                    use_bias=False,
                    kernel_regularizer=l2(reg))(act_2)
    bn_3 = BatchNormalization(axis=-1,
                              epsilon=bn_eps,
                              momentum=bn_momentum)
(conv_2)
    act_3 = ReLU()(bn_3)
    conv_3 = Conv2D(filters=filters,
                    kernel_size=(1, 1),
                    use_bias=False,
                    kernel_regularizer=l2(reg))(act_3)
```

If reduce=True, we apply a 1x1 convolution:

```
    if reduce:
        shortcut = Conv2D(filters=filters,
                          kernel_size=(1, 1),
                          strides=stride,
                          use_bias=False,
                          kernel_regularizer=l2(reg))(act_1)
```

Finally, we combine the shortcut and the third block into a single layer and return that as our output:

```
    x = Add()([conv_3, shortcut])
    return x
```

4.  Define a function to build a custom **ResNet** network:

```python
def build_resnet(input_shape,
                 classes,
                 stages,
                 filters,
                 reg=1e-3,
                 bn_eps=2e-5,
                 bn_momentum=0.9):
    inputs = Input(shape=input_shape)
    x = BatchNormalization(axis=-1,
                           epsilon=bn_eps,

                           momentum=bn_momentum)(inputs)

    x = Conv2D(filters[0], (3, 3),
               use_bias=False,
               padding='same',
               kernel_regularizer=l2(reg))(x)

    for i in range(len(stages)):
        stride = (1, 1) if i == 0 else (2, 2)
        x = residual_module(data=x,
                            filters=filters[i + 1],
                            stride=stride,
                            reduce=True,
                            bn_eps=bn_eps,
                            bn_momentum=bn_momentum)
        for j in range(stages[i] - 1):
            x = residual_module(data=x,
                               filters=filters[i +
                                                  1],
                               stride=(1, 1),
                               bn_eps=bn_eps,

                               bn_momentum=bn_momentum)
```

```
x = BatchNormalization(axis=-1,
                       epsilon=bn_eps,
                       momentum=bn_momentum)(x)
x = ReLU()(x)
x = AveragePooling2D((8, 8))(x)

x = Flatten()(x)
x = Dense(classes, kernel_regularizer=l2(reg))(x)
x = Softmax()(x)

return Model(inputs, x, name='resnet')
```

5. Define a function to load an image and its one-hot encoded labels, based on its file path:

```
def load_image_and_label(image_path, target_size=(32,
32)):
    image = tf.io.read_file(image_path)
    image = tf.image.decode_png(image, channels=3)
    image = tf.image.convert_image_dtype(image,
                                         np.float32)
    image -= CINIC_MEAN_RGB  # Mean normalize
    image = tf.image.resize(image, target_size)

    label = tf.strings.split(image_path, os.path.sep)[-2]
    label = (label == CINIC_10_CLASSES)  # One-hot
encode.
    label = tf.dtypes.cast(label, tf.float32)

    return image, label
```

6. Define a function to create a `tf.data.Dataset` instance of images and labels from a glob-like pattern that refers to the folder where the images are:

```
def prepare_dataset(data_pattern, shuffle=False):
    dataset = (tf.data.Dataset
               .list_files(data_pattern)
               .map(load_image_and_label,
                  num_parallel_calls=AUTOTUNE)
```

```
                    .batch(BATCH_SIZE))

    if shuffle:
        dataset = dataset.shuffle(BUFFER_SIZE)

    return dataset.prefetch(BATCH_SIZE)
```

7. Define the mean RGB values of the `CINIC-10` dataset, which is used in the `load_image_and_label()` function to mean normalize the images (this information is available on the official `CINIC-10` site):

```
CINIC_MEAN_RGB = np.array([0.47889522, 0.47227842,
0.43047404])
```

8. Define the classes of the `CINIC-10` dataset:

```
CINIC_10_CLASSES = ['airplane', 'automobile', 'bird',
'cat',
                     'deer', 'dog', 'frog', 'horse',
'ship',
                     'truck']
```

9. Download and extract the `CINIC-10` dataset to the `~/.keras/datasets` directory:

```
DATASET_URL = ('https://datashare.is.ed.ac.uk/bitstream/
handle/'
                '10283/3192/CINIC-10.tar.gz?'
                'sequence=4&isAllowed=y')
DATA_NAME = 'cinic10'
FILE_EXTENSION = 'tar.gz'
FILE_NAME = '.'.join([DATA_NAME, FILE_EXTENSION])

downloaded_file_location = get_file(origin=DATASET_URL,
                                    fname=FILE_NAME,
                                    extract=False)

data_directory, _ = (downloaded_file_location
                    .rsplit(os.path.sep, maxsplit=1))
data_directory = os.path.sep.join([data_directory,
```

```
                                         DATA_NAME])
tar = tarfile.open(downloaded_file_location)


if not os.path.exists(data_directory):
    tar.extractall(data_directory)
```

10. Define the glob-like patterns to the train, test, and validation subsets:

```
train_pattern = os.path.sep.join(
    [data_directory, 'train/*/*.png'])
test_pattern = os.path.sep.join(
    [data_directory, 'test/*/*.png'])
valid_pattern = os.path.sep.join(
    [data_directory, 'valid/*/*.png'])
```

11. Prepare the datasets:

```
BATCH_SIZE = 128
BUFFER_SIZE = 1024
train_dataset = prepare_dataset(train_pattern,
                                shuffle=True)
test_dataset = prepare_dataset(test_pattern)
valid_dataset = prepare_dataset(valid_pattern)
```

12. Build, compile, and train a **ResNet** model. Because this is a time-consuming process, we'll save a version of the model after each epoch, using the `ModelCheckpoint()` callback:

```
model = build_resnet(input_shape=(32, 32, 3),
                     classes=10,
                     stages=(9, 9, 9),
                     filters=(64, 64, 128, 256),
                     reg=5e-3)
model.compile(loss='categorical_crossentropy',
              optimizer='rmsprop',
              metrics=['accuracy'])


model_checkpoint_callback = ModelCheckpoint(
    filepath='./model.{epoch:02d}-{val_accuracy:.2f}.
```

```
hdf5',
    save_weights_only=False,
    monitor='val_accuracy')


EPOCHS = 100
model.fit(train_dataset,
          validation_data=valid_dataset,
          epochs=EPOCHS,
          callbacks=[model_checkpoint_callback])
```

13. Load the best model (in this case, `model.38-0.72.hdf5`) and evaluate it on the test set:

```
model = load_model('model.38-0.72.hdf5')
result = model.evaluate(test_dataset)
print(f'Test accuracy: {result[1]}')
```

This prints the following:

```
Test accuracy: 0.71956664
```

Let's learn how it all works in the next section.

## How it works...

The key to **ResNet** is the residual module, which we implemented in *Step 3*. A residual module is a micro-architecture that can be reused many times to create a macro-architecture, thus achieving great depths. The `residual_module()` function receives the input data (`data`), the number of filters (`filters`), the stride (`stride`) of the convolutional blocks, a `reduce` flag to indicate whether we want to reduce the spatial size of the shortcut branch by applying a 1x1 convolution (a technique used to reduce the dimensionality of the output volumes of the filters), and parameters to adjust the amount of regularization (`reg`) and batch normalization applied to the different layers (`bn_eps` and `bn_momentum`).

A residual module comprises two branches: the first one is the skip connection, also known as the shortcut branch, which is basically the same as the input. The second or main branch is composed of three convolution blocks: a 1x1 with a quarter of the filters, a 3x3 one, also with a quarter of the filters, and finally another 1x1, which uses all the filters. The shortcut and main branches are concatenated in the end using the `Add()` layer.

`build_network()` allows us to specify the number of stages to use, and also the number of filters per stage. We start by applying a 3x3 convolution to the input (after being batch normalized). Then we proceed to create the stages. A stage is a series of residual modules connected to each other. The length of the `stages` list controls the number of stages to create, and each element in this list controls the number of layers in that particular stage. The `filters` parameter contains the number of filters to use in each residual block within a stage. Finally, we built a fully connected network, Softmax-activated, on top of the stages with as many units as there are classes in the dataset (in this case, 10).

Because **ResNet** is a very deep, heavy, and slow-to-train architecture, we checkpointed the model after each epoch. In this recipe, we obtained the best model in epoch 38, which produced 72% accuracy on the test set, a respectable performance considering that `CINIC-10` is not an easy dataset and that we did not apply any data augmentation or transfer learning.

## See also

For more information on the `CINIC-10` dataset, visit this link: `https://datashare.is.ed.ac.uk/handle/10283/3192`.

# Classifying images with a pre-trained network using the Keras API

We do not always need to train a classifier from scratch, especially when the images we want to categorize resemble ones that another network trained on. In these instances, we can simply reuse the model, saving ourselves lots of time. In this recipe, we'll use a pre-trained network on ImageNet to classify a custom image.

Let's begin!

## Getting ready

We will need `Pillow`. We can install it as follows:

```
$> pip install Pillow
```

You're free to use your own images in the recipe. Alternatively, you can download the one at this link: `https://github.com/PacktPublishing/Tensorflow-2.0-Computer-Vision-Cookbook/tree/master/ch2/recipe5/dog.jpg`.

Here's the image we'll pass to the classifier:

Figure 2.4 – Image passed to the pre-trained classifier

## How to do it...

As we'll see in this section, re-using a pre-trained classifier is very easy!

1. Import the required packages. These include the pre-trained network used for classification, as well as some helper functions to pre process the images:

```
import matplotlib.pyplot as plt
import numpy as np
from tensorflow.keras.applications import imagenet_utils
from tensorflow.keras.applications.inception_v3 import *
from tensorflow.keras.preprocessing.image import *
```

2. Instantiate an `InceptionV3` network pre-trained on ImageNet:

```
model = InceptionV3(weights='imagenet')
```

3. Load the image to classify. `InceptionV3` takes a 299x299x3 image, so we must resize it accordingly:

```
image = load_img('dog.jpg', target_size=(299, 299))
```

4.  Convert the image to a `numpy` array, and wrap it into a singleton batch:

```
image = img_to_array(image)
image = np.expand_dims(image, axis=0)
```

5.  Pre process the image the same way `InceptionV3` does:

```
image = preprocess_input(image)
```

6.  Use the model to make predictions on the image, and then decode the predictions to a matrix:

```
predictions = model.predict(image)
prediction_matrix = (imagenet_utils
                    .decode_predictions(predictions))
```

7.  Examine the top 5 predictions along with their probability:

```
for i in range(5):
    _, label, probability = prediction_matrix[0][i]
    print(f'{i + 1}. {label}: {probability * 100:.3f}%')
```

This produces the following output:

```
1. pug: 85.538%
2. French_bulldog: 0.585%
3. Brabancon_griffon: 0.543%
4. Boston_bull: 0.218%
5. bull_mastiff: 0.125%
```

8.  Plot the original image with its most probable label:

```
_, label, _ = prediction_matrix[0][0]
plt.figure()
plt.title(f'Label: {label}.')
original = load_img('dog.jpg')
original = img_to_array(original)
plt.imshow(original / 255.0)
plt.show()
```

This block generates the following image:

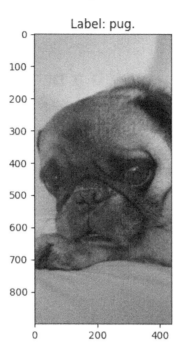

Figure 2.5 – Correctly classified image

Let's see how it all works in the next section.

## How it works...

As evidenced here, in order to classify images effortlessly, using a pre-trained network on ImageNet, we just need to instantiate the proper model with the right weights, like this: `InceptionV3(weights='imagenet')`. This will download the architecture and the weights if it is the first time we are using them; otherwise, a version of these files will be cached in our system.

Then, we loaded the image we wanted to classify, resized it to dimensions compatible with `InceptionV3` (299x299x3), converted it into a singleton batch with `np.expand_dims(image, axis=0)`, and pre processed it the same way `InceptionV3` did when it was trained, with `preprocess_input(image)`.

Next, we got the predictions from the model, which we need to transform to a prediction matrix with the help of `imagenet_utils.decode_predictions(predictions)`. This matrix contains the label and probabilities in the 0th row, which we inspected to get the five most probable classes.

## See also

You can read more about Keras pre-trained models here: `https://www.tensorflow.org/api_docs/python/tf/keras/applications`.

# Classifying images with a pre-trained network using TensorFlow Hub

**TensorFlow Hub** (**TFHub**) is a repository of hundreds of machine learning models contributed to by the big and rich community that surrounds TensorFlow. Here we can find models for a myriad of different tasks, not only for computer vision but for applications in many different domains, such as **Natural Language Processing** (**NLP**) and reinforcement learning.

In this recipe, we'll use a model trained on ImageNet, hosted on TFHub, to make predictions on a custom image. Let's begin!

## Getting ready

We'll need the `tensorflow-hub` and `Pillow` packages, which can be easily installed using `pip`, as follows:

```
$> pip install tensorflow-hub Pillow
```

If you want to use the same image we use in this recipe, you can download it here: `https://github.com/PacktPublishing/Tensorflow-2.0-Computer-Vision-Cookbook/tree/master/ch2/recipe6/beetle.jpg`.

Here's the image we'll classify:

Figure 2.6 – Image to be classified

Let's head to the next section.

# How to do it...

Let's proceed with the recipe steps:

1. Import the necessary packages:

```
import matplotlib.pyplot as plt
import numpy as np
import tensorflow_hub as hub
from tensorflow.keras import Sequential
from tensorflow.keras.preprocessing.image import *
from tensorflow.keras.utils import get_file
```

2. Define the URL of the pre-trained `ResNetV2152` classifier in **TFHub**:

```
classifier_url = ('https://tfhub.dev/google/imagenet/'
                  'resnet_v2_152/classification/4')
```

3. Download and instantiate the classifier hosted on TFHub:

```
model = Sequential([
    hub.KerasLayer(classifier_url, input_shape=(224,
                                                224, 3))])
```

4. Load the image we'll classify, convert it to a numpy array, normalize it, and wrap it into a singleton batch:

```
image = load_img('beetle.jpg', target_size=(224, 224))
image = img_to_array(image)
image = image / 255.0
image = np.expand_dims(image, axis=0)
```

5. Use the pre-trained model to classify the image:

```
predictions = model.predict(image)
```

6. Extract the index of the most probable prediction:

```
predicted_index = np.argmax(predictions[0], axis=-1)
```

7.  Download the ImageNet labels into a file named `ImageNetLabels.txt`:

```
file_name = 'ImageNetLabels.txt'
file_url = ('https://storage.googleapis.com/'
            'download.tensorflow.org/data/ImageNetLabels.txt')
            labels_path = get_file(file_name, file_url)
```

8.  Read the labels into a numpy array:

```
with open(labels_path) as f:
    imagenet_labels = np.array(f.read().splitlines())
```

9.  Extract the name of the class corresponding to the index of the most probable prediction:

```
predicted_class = imagenet_labels[predicted_index]
```

10. Plot the original image with its most probable label:

```
plt.figure()
plt.title(f'Label: {predicted_class}.')
original = load_img('beetle.jpg')
original = img_to_array(original)
plt.imshow(original / 255.0)
plt.show()
```

This produces the following:

Figure 2.7 – Correctly classified image

Let's see how it all works.

## How it works...

After importing the relevant packages, we proceeded to define the URL of the model we wanted to use to classify our input image. To download and convert such a network into a Keras model, we used the convenient `hub.KerasLayer` class in *Step 3*. Then, in *Step 4*, we loaded the image we wanted to classify into memory, making sure its dimensions match the ones the network expects: 224x224x3.

*Steps 5* and *6* perform the classification and extract the most probable category, respectively. However, to make this prediction human-readable, we downloaded a plain text file with all ImageNet labels in *Step 7*, which we then parsed using `numpy`, allowing us to use the index of the most probable category to obtain the corresponding label, finally displayed in *Step 10* along with the input image.

## See also

You can learn more about the pre-trained model we used here: `https://tfhub.dev/google/imagenet/resnet_v2_152/classification/4`.

# Using data augmentation to improve performance with the Keras API

More often than not, we can benefit from providing more data to our model. But data is expensive and scarce. Is there a way to circumvent this limitation? Yes, there is! We can synthesize new training examples by performing little modifications on the ones we already have, such as random rotations, random cropping, and horizontal flipping, among others. In this recipe, we'll learn how to use data augmentation with the Keras API to improve performance.

Let's begin.

## Getting ready

We must install `Pillow` and `tensorflow_docs`:

```
$> pip install Pillow git+https://github.com/tensorflow/docs
```

In this recipe, we'll use the `Caltech 101` dataset, which is available here: `http://www.vision.caltech.edu/Image_Datasets/Caltech101/`. Download and decompress `101_ObjectCategories.tar.gz` to your preferred location. From now on, we assume the data is inside the `~/.keras/datasets` directory, under the name `101_ObjectCategories`.

Here are sample images from `Caltech 101`:

Figure 2.8 – Caltech 101 sample images

Let's implement!

# How to do it...

The steps listed here are necessary to complete the recipe. Let's get started!

1. Import the required modules:

```
import os
import pathlib
import matplotlib.pyplot as plt
import numpy as np
import tensorflow_docs as tfdocs
import tensorflow_docs.plots
from glob import glob
from sklearn.model_selection import train_test_split
from sklearn.preprocessing import LabelBinarizer
from tensorflow.keras.layers import *
from tensorflow.keras.models import Model
from tensorflow.keras.preprocessing.image import *
```

2. Define a function to load all images in the dataset, along with their labels, based on their file paths:

```
def load_images_and_labels(image_paths, target_size=(64,
64)):
    images = []
    labels = []

    for image_path in image_paths:
        image = load_img(image_path,
                             target_size=target_size)
        image = img_to_array(image)

        label = image_path.split(os.path.sep)[-2]

        images.append(image)
        labels.append(label)

    return np.array(images), np.array(labels)
```

3.  Define a function to build a smaller version of **VGG**:

```
def build_network(width, height, depth, classes):
    input_layer = Input(shape=(width, height, depth))

    x = Conv2D(filters=32,
               kernel_size=(3, 3),
               padding='same')(input_layer)
    x = ReLU()(x)
    x = BatchNormalization(axis=-1)(x)
    x = Conv2D(filters=32,
               kernel_size=(3, 3),
               padding='same')(x)
    x = ReLU()(x)
    x = BatchNormalization(axis=-1)(x)
    x = MaxPooling2D(pool_size=(2, 2))(x)
    x = Dropout(rate=0.25)(x)

    x = Conv2D(filters=64,
               kernel_size=(3, 3),
               padding='same')(x)
    x = ReLU()(x)
    x = BatchNormalization(axis=-1)(x)
    x = Conv2D(filters=64,
               kernel_size=(3, 3),
               padding='same')(x)
    x = ReLU()(x)
    x = BatchNormalization(axis=-1)(x)
    x = MaxPooling2D(pool_size=(2, 2))(x)
    x = Dropout(rate=0.25)(x)

    x = Flatten()(x)
    x = Dense(units=512)(x)
    x = ReLU()(x)
    x = BatchNormalization(axis=-1)(x)
    x = Dropout(rate=0.25)(x)
```

```
    x = Dense(units=classes)(x)
    output = Softmax()(x)

    return Model(input_layer, output)
```

4.  Define a function to plot and save a model's training curve:

```
def plot_model_history(model_history, metric,
                       plot_name):
    plt.style.use('seaborn-darkgrid')
    plotter = tfdocs.plots.HistoryPlotter()
    plotter.plot({'Model': model_history},
                 metric=metric)
    plt.title(f'{metric.upper()}')
    plt.ylim([0, 1])
    plt.savefig(f'{plot_name}.png')
    plt.close()
```

5.  Set the random seed:

```
SEED = 999
np.random.seed(SEED)
```

6.  Load the paths to all images in the dataset, excepting the ones of the BACKGROUND_ Google class:

```
base_path = (pathlib.Path.home() / '.keras' /
             'datasets' /
             '101_ObjectCategories')
images_pattern = str(base_path / '*' / '*.jpg')
image_paths = [*glob(images_pattern)]
image_paths = [p for p in image_paths if
               p.split(os.path.sep)[-2] !=
               'BACKGROUND_Google']
```

7.  Compute the set of classes in the dataset:

```
classes = {p.split(os.path.sep)[-2] for p in
           image_paths}
```

8.  Load the dataset into memory, normalizing the images and one-hot encoding the labels:

```
X, y = load_images_and_labels(image_paths)
X = X.astype('float') / 255.0
y = LabelBinarizer().fit_transform(y)
```

9.  Create the training and testing subsets:

```
(X_train, X_test,
 y_train, y_test) = train_test_split(X, y,
                                       test_size=0.2,
                                       random_state=SEED)
```

10. Build, compile, train, and evaluate a neural network without data augmentation:

```
EPOCHS = 40
BATCH_SIZE = 64
model = build_network(64, 64, 3, len(classes))
model.compile(loss='categorical_crossentropy',
              optimizer='rmsprop',
              metrics=['accuracy'])

history = model.fit(X_train, y_train,
                    validation_data=(X_test, y_test),
                    epochs=EPOCHS,
                    batch_size=BATCH_SIZE)
result = model.evaluate(X_test, y_test)
print(f'Test accuracy: {result[1]}')
plot_model_history(history, 'accuracy', 'normal')
```

The accuracy on the test set is as follows:

```
Test accuracy: 0.61347926
```

And here's the accuracy curve:

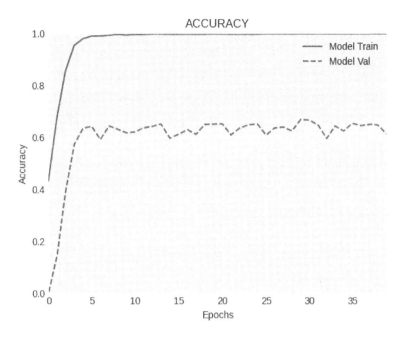

Figure 2.9 – Training and validation accuracy for a network without data augmentation

11. Build, compile, train, and evaluate the same network, this time with data augmentation:

```
model = build_network(64, 64, 3, len(classes))
model.compile(loss='categorical_crossentropy',
              optimizer='rmsprop',
              metrics=['accuracy'])

augmenter = ImageDataGenerator(horizontal_flip=True,
                               rotation_range=30,
                               width_shift_range=0.1,
                               height_shift_range=0.1,
                               shear_range=0.2,
                               zoom_range=0.2,
                               fill_mode='nearest')
train_generator = augmenter.flow(X_train, y_train,
                                 BATCH_SIZE)
hist = model.fit(train_generator,
                 steps_per_epoch=len(X_train) //
```

```
                          BATCH_SIZE,
                          validation_data=(X_test, y_test),
                          epochs=EPOCHS)

result = model.evaluate(X_test, y_test)
print(f'Test accuracy: {result[1]}')
plot_model_history(hist, 'accuracy', 'augmented')
```

The accuracy on the test set when we use data augmentation is as follows:

```
Test accuracy: 0.65207374
```

And the accuracy curve looks like this:

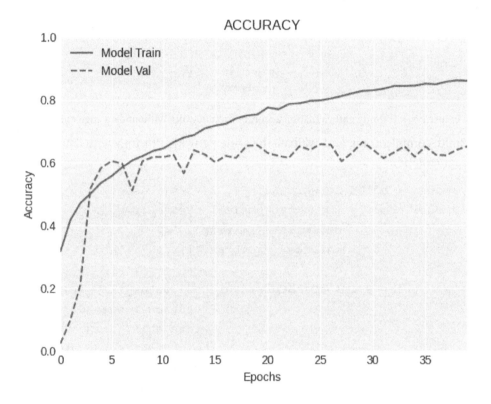

Figure 2.10 – Training and validation accuracy for a network with data augmentation

Comparing *Steps 10* and *11*, we observe a noticeable gain in performance by using data augmentation. Let's understand better what we did in the next section.

# How it works...

In this recipe, we implemented a scaled-down version of **VGG** on the challenging `Caltech 101` dataset. First, we trained a network only on the original data, and then using data augmentation. The first network (see *Step 10*) obtained an accuracy level on the test set of 61.3% and clearly shows signs of overfitting, because the gap that separates the training and validation accuracy curves is very wide. On the other hand, by applying a series of random perturbations, through `ImageDataGenerator()`, such as horizontal flips, rotations, width, and height shifting, among others (see *Step 11*), we increased the accuracy on the test set to 65.2%. Also, the gap between the training and validation accuracy curves is much smaller this time, which suggests a regularization effect resulting from the application of data augmentation.

# See also

You can learn more about `Caltech 101` here: `http://www.vision.caltech.edu/Image_Datasets/Caltech101/`.

# Using data augmentation to improve performance with the tf.data and tf.image APIs

Data augmentation is a powerful technique we can apply to artificially increment the size of our dataset, by creating slightly modified copies of the images at our disposal. In this recipe, we'll leverage the `tf.data` and `tf.image` APIs to increase the performance of a CNN trained on the challenging `Caltech 101` dataset.

# Getting ready

We must install `tensorflow_docs`:

```
$> pip install git+https://github.com/tensorflow/docs
```

In this recipe, we'll use the `Caltech 101` dataset, which is available here: `http://www.vision.caltech.edu/Image_Datasets/Caltech101/`. Download and decompress `101_ObjectCategories.tar.gz` to your preferred location. From now on, we assume the data is inside the `~/.keras/datasets` directory, in a folder named `101_ObjectCategories`.

Here are some sample images from `Caltech 101`:

Figure 2.11 – Caltech 101 sample images

Let's go to the next section.

## How to do it...

Let's go over the steps required to complete this recipe.

1.  Import the necessary dependencies:

```
import os
import pathlib
import matplotlib.pyplot as plt
import numpy as np
import tensorflow as tf
import tensorflow_docs as tfdocs
import tensorflow_docs.plots
from glob import glob
from sklearn.model_selection import train_test_split
from tensorflow.keras.layers import *
from tensorflow.keras.models import Model
```

2.  Create an alias for the `tf.data.experimental.AUTOTUNE` flag, which we'll use later on:

```
AUTOTUNE = tf.data.experimental.AUTOTUNE
```

3. Define a function to create a smaller version of **VGG**. Start by creating the input layer and the first block of two convolutions with 32 filters each:

```
def build_network(width, height, depth, classes):
    input_layer = Input(shape=(width, height, depth))

    x = Conv2D(filters=32,
               kernel_size=(3, 3),
               padding='same')(input_layer)
    x = ReLU()(x)
    x = BatchNormalization(axis=-1)(x)
    x = Conv2D(filters=32,
               kernel_size=(3, 3),
               padding='same')(x)
    x = ReLU()(x)
    x = BatchNormalization(axis=-1)(x)
    x = MaxPooling2D(pool_size=(2, 2))(x)
    x = Dropout(rate=0.25)(x)
```

4. Continue with the second block of two convolutions, this time each with 64 kernels:

```
    x = Conv2D(filters=64,
               kernel_size=(3, 3),
               padding='same')(x)
    x = ReLU()(x)
    x = BatchNormalization(axis=-1)(x)
    x = Conv2D(filters=64,
               kernel_size=(3, 3),
               padding='same')(x)
    x = ReLU()(x)
    x = BatchNormalization(axis=-1)(x)
    x = MaxPooling2D(pool_size=(2, 2))(x)
    x = Dropout(rate=0.25)(x)
```

5.  Define the last part of the architecture, which consists of a series of fully connected layers:

```
x = Flatten()(x)
x = Dense(units=512)(x)
x = ReLU()(x)
x = BatchNormalization(axis=-1)(x)
x = Dropout(rate=0.5)(x)

x = Dense(units=classes)(x)
output = Softmax()(x)

return Model(input_layer, output)
```

6.  Define a function to plot and save the training curves of a model, given its training history:

```
def plot_model_history(model_history, metric,
                       plot_name):
    plt.style.use('seaborn-darkgrid')
    plotter = tfdocs.plots.HistoryPlotter()
    plotter.plot({'Model': model_history},
                 metric=metric)

    plt.title(f'{metric.upper()}')
    plt.ylim([0, 1])

    plt.savefig(f'{plot_name}.png')
    plt.close()
```

7.  Define a function to load an image and one-hot encode its label, based on the image's file path:

```
def load_image_and_label(image_path, target_size=(64,
                                                   64)):
    image = tf.io.read_file(image_path)
    image = tf.image.decode_jpeg(image, channels=3)
    image = tf.image.convert_image_dtype(image,
                                         np.float32)
```

```
    image = tf.image.resize(image, target_size)

    label = tf.strings.split(image_path, os.path.sep)[-2]
    label = (label == CLASSES)  # One-hot encode.
    label = tf.dtypes.cast(label, tf.float32)

    return image, label
```

8. Define a function to augment an image by performing random transformations on it:

```
def augment(image, label):
    image = tf.image.resize_with_crop_or_pad(image,
                                             74, 74)
    image = tf.image.random_crop(image, size=(64, 64, 3))
    image = tf.image.random_flip_left_right(image)
    image = tf.image.random_brightness(image, 0.2)

    return image, label
```

9. Define a function to prepare a `tf.data.Dataset` of images, based on a glob-like pattern that refers to the folder where they live:

```
def prepare_dataset(data_pattern):
    return (tf.data.Dataset
            .from_tensor_slices(data_pattern)
            .map(load_image_and_label,
                 num_parallel_calls=AUTOTUNE))
```

10. Set the random seed:

```
SEED = 999
np.random.seed(SEED)
```

11. Load the paths to all images in the dataset, excepting the ones of the BACKGROUND_ Google class:

```
base_path = (pathlib.Path.home() / '.keras' /
             'datasets' /
             '101_ObjectCategories')
```

```
images_pattern = str(base_path / '*' / '*.jpg')
image_paths = [*glob(images_pattern)]
image_paths = [p for p in image_paths if
               p.split(os.path.sep)[-2] !=
               'BACKGROUND_Google']
```

12. Compute the unique categories in the dataset:

```
CLASSES = np.unique([p.split(os.path.sep)[-2]
                     for p in image_paths])
```

13. Split the image paths into training and testing subsets:

```
train_paths, test_paths = train_test_split(image_paths,
                                           test_size=0.2,
                                           random_state=SEED)
```

14. Prepare the training and testing datasets, without augmentation:

```
BATCH_SIZE = 64
BUFFER_SIZE = 1024
train_dataset = (prepare_dataset(train_paths)
                 .batch(BATCH_SIZE)
                 .shuffle(buffer_size=BUFFER_SIZE)
                 .prefetch(buffer_size=BUFFER_SIZE))
test_dataset = (prepare_dataset(test_paths)
                .batch(BATCH_SIZE)
                .prefetch(buffer_size=BUFFER_SIZE))
```

15. Instantiate, compile, train and evaluate the network:

```
EPOCHS = 40
model = build_network(64, 64, 3, len(CLASSES))
model.compile(loss='categorical_crossentropy',
              optimizer='rmsprop',
              metrics=['accuracy'])
history = model.fit(train_dataset,
                    validation_data=test_dataset,
                    epochs=EPOCHS)
result = model.evaluate(test_dataset)
```

```
print(f'Test accuracy: {result[1]}')
plot_model_history(history, 'accuracy', 'normal')
```

The accuracy on the test set is:

```
Test accuracy: 0.6532258
```

And here's the accuracy curve:

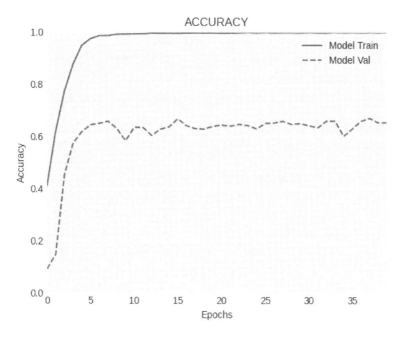

Figure 2.12 – Training and validation accuracy for a network without data augmentation

16. Prepare the training and testing sets, this time applying data augmentation to the training set:

```
train_dataset = (prepare_dataset(train_paths)
                    .map(augment,
                        num_parallel_calls=AUTOTUNE)
                    .batch(BATCH_SIZE)
                    .shuffle(buffer_size=BUFFER_SIZE)
                    .prefetch(buffer_size=BUFFER_SIZE))
test_dataset = (prepare_dataset(test_paths)
                    .batch(BATCH_SIZE)
                    .prefetch(buffer_size=BUFFER_SIZE))
```

17. Instantiate, compile, train, and evaluate the network on the augmented data:

```
model = build_network(64, 64, 3, len(CLASSES))
model.compile(loss='categorical_crossentropy',
              optimizer='rmsprop',
              metrics=['accuracy'])
history = model.fit(train_dataset,
                    validation_data=test_dataset,
                    epochs=EPOCHS)
result = model.evaluate(test_dataset)
print(f'Test accuracy: {result[1]}')
plot_model_history(history, 'accuracy', 'augmented')
```

The accuracy on the test set when we use data augmentation is as follows:

```
Test accuracy: 0.74711984
```

And the accuracy curve looks like this:

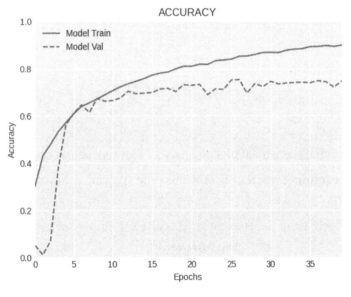

Figure 2.13 – Training and validation accuracy for a network with data augmentation

Let's understand what we just did in the next section.

# How it works...

We just implemented a trimmed down version of the famous **VGG** architecture, trained on the `Caltech 101` dataset. To better understand the advantages of data augmentation, we fitted a first version on the original data, without any modification, obtaining an accuracy level of 65.32% on the test set. This first model displays signs of overfitting, because the gap that separates the training and validation accuracy curves widens early in the training process.

Next, we trained the same network on an augmented dataset (see *Step 15*), using the `augment()` function defined earlier. This greatly improved the model's performance, reaching a respectable accuracy of 74.19% on the test set. Also, the gap between the training and validation accuracy curves is noticeably smaller, which suggests a regularization effect coming out from the application of data augmentation.

# See also

You can learn more about `Caltech 101` here: `http://www.vision.caltech.edu/Image_Datasets/Caltech101/`.

# 3
# Harnessing the Power of Pre-Trained Networks with Transfer Learning

Despite the undeniable power deep neural networks bring to computer vision, they are very complex to tune, train, and make performant. This difficulty comes from three main sources:

- Deep neural networks start to pay off when we have sufficient data, but more often than not, this is not the case. Furthermore, data is expensive and, sometimes, impossible to expand.

- Deep neural networks contain a wide range of parameters that need tuning and can affect the overall performance of the model.

- Deep learning is very resource-intensive in terms of time, hardware, and effort.

Do not be dismayed! With **transfer learning**, we can save ourselves loads of time and effort by leveraging the rich amount of knowledge present in seminal architectures that have been pre-trained on gargantuan datasets, such as ImageNet. And the best part? Besides being such a powerful and useful tool, transfer learning is also easy to apply. We'll learn how to do this in this chapter.

In this chapter, we are going to cover the following recipes:

- Implementing a feature extractor using a pre-trained network

- Training a simple classifier on extracted features

- Spot-checking extractors and classifiers

- Using incremental learning to train a classifier

- Fine-tuning a network using the Keras API

- Fine-tuning a network using TFHub

Let's get started!

# Technical requirements

It's highly encouraged that you have access to a GPU since transfer learning tends to be quite computationally heavy. In the *Getting ready* section of each recipe, you'll receive specific instructions – if they're needed – on how to install the dependencies for that recipe. You can find all the code for this chapter here: `https://github.com/PacktPublishing/Tensorflow-2.0-Computer-Vision-Cookbook/tree/master/ch3`.

Check out the following link to see the Code in Action video:

`https://bit.ly/39wR6DT`.

# Implementing a feature extractor using a pre-trained network

One of the easiest ways to seize the power of transfer learning is to use pre-trained models as feature extractors. This way, we can combine both deep learning and machine learning, something that we normally cannot do, because traditional machine learning algorithms don't work with raw images. In this recipe, we'll implement a reusable `FeatureExtractor` class to produce a dataset of vectors from a set of input images, and then save it in the blazingly fast HDF5 format.

Are you ready? Let's get started!

## Getting ready

You'll need to install `Pillow` and `tqdm` (which we'll use to display a nice progress bar). Fortunately, this is very easy with `pip`:

```
$> pip install Pillow tqdm
```

We'll be using the `Stanford Cars` dataset, which you can download here: `http://imagenet.stanford.edu/internal/car196/car_ims.tgz`. Decompress the data to a location of your preference. In this recipe, we assume the data is inside the `~/.keras/datasets` directory, under the name `car_ims`.

Here are some sample images from the dataset:

Figure 3.1 – Sample images

We'll store the extracted features in HDF5 format, a binary, hierarchical protocol designed to store very large numerical datasets on disk, while keeping ease of access and computation on a row-wise level. You can read more about HDF5 here: `https://portal.hdfgroup.org/display/HDF5/HDF5`.

## How to do it...

Follow these steps to complete this recipe:

1. Import all the necessary packages:

```
import glob
import os
import pathlib
import h5py
import numpy as np
import sklearn.utils as skutils
from sklearn.preprocessing import LabelEncoder
from tensorflow.keras.applications import imagenet_utils
from tensorflow.keras.applications.vgg16 import VGG16
from tensorflow.keras.preprocessing.image import *
from tqdm import tqdm
```

2. Define the `FeatureExtractor` class and its constructor:

```
class FeatureExtractor(object):
    def __init__(self,
                 model,
                 input_size,
                 label_encoder,
                 num_instances,
                 feature_size,
                 output_path,
                 features_key='features',
                 buffer_size=1000):
```

3. We need to make sure the output path can be written:

```
if os.path.exists(output_path):
    error_msg = (f'{output_path} already
                    exists. '
                 f'Please delete it and try
                    again.')
    raise FileExistsError(error_msg)
```

4.  Now, let's store the input parameter as object members:

```
self.model = model
self.input_size = input_size
self.le = label_encoder
self.feature_size = feature_size
self.buffer_size = buffer_size
self.buffer = {'features': [], 'labels': []}
self.current_index = 0
```

5.  `self.buffer` will contain a buffer of both instances and labels, while `self. current_index` will point to the next free location within the datasets in the inner HDF5 database. We'll create this now:

```
self.db = h5py.File(output_path, 'w')
self.features = self.db.create_dataset(features_
 key,
                               (num_instances,
                               feature_size),
                               dtype='float')

self.labels = self.db.create_dataset('labels',
                           (num_instances,),
                           dtype='int')
```

6.  Define a method that will extract features and labels from a list of image paths and store them in the HDF5 database:

```
def extract_features(self,
                     image_paths,
                     labels,
                     batch_size=64,
                     shuffle=True):
    if shuffle:
        image_paths, labels =
        skutils.shuffle(image_paths,
                    labels)

    encoded_labels = self.le.fit_transform(labels)
```

```
            self._store_class_labels(self.le.classes_)
```

7.  After shuffling the image paths and their labels, as well as encoding and storing the latter, we'll iterate over batches of images, passing them through the pre-trained network. Once we've done this, we'll save the resulting features into the HDF5 database (the helper methods we've used here will be defined shortly):

```
for i in tqdm(range(0, len(image_paths),
                    batch_size)):
    batch_paths = image_paths[i: i +
                            batch_size]
    batch_labels = encoded_labels[i:i +
                            batch_size]
    batch_images = []

    for image_path in batch_paths:
        image = load_img(image_path,

                    target_size=self.input_size)
        image = img_to_array(image)
        image = np.expand_dims(image, axis=0)
        image =
        imagenet_utils.preprocess_input(image)

        batch_images.append(image)

    batch_images = np.vstack(batch_images)
    feats = self.model.predict(batch_images,
                        batch_size=batch_size)

    new_shape = (feats.shape[0],
                    self.feature_size)
    feats = feats.reshape(new_shape)
    self._add(feats, batch_labels)

    self._close()
```

8. Define a private method that will add features and labels to the corresponding datasets:

```python
def _add(self, rows, labels):
    self.buffer['features'].extend(rows)
    self.buffer['labels'].extend(labels)

    if len(self.buffer['features']) >=
                        self.buffer_size:
        self._flush()
```

9. Define a private method that will flush the buffers to disk:

```python
def _flush(self):
    next_index = (self.current_index +
                    len(self.buffer['features']))
    buffer_slice = slice(self.current_index,
                    next_index)
    self.features[buffer_slice] =
                    self.buffer['features']
    self.labels[buffer_slice] = self.buffer['labels']
    self.current_index = next_index
    self.buffer = {'features': [], 'labels': []}
```

10. Define a private method that will store the class labels in the HDF5 database:

```python
def _store_class_labels(self, class_labels):
    data_type = h5py.special_dtype(vlen=str)
    shape = (len(class_labels),)
    label_ds = self.db.create_dataset('label_names',
                    shape,
                    dtype=data_type)
    label_ds[:] = class_labels
```

11. Define a private method that will close the HDF5 dataset:

```
def _close(self):
    if len(self.buffer['features']) > 0:
        self._flush()

    self.db.close()
```

12. Load the paths to the images in the dataset:

```
files_pattern = (pathlib.Path.home() / '.keras' /
                 'datasets' /'car_ims' / '*.jpg')
files_pattern = str(files_pattern)
input_paths = [*glob.glob(files_pattern)]
```

13. Create the output directory. We'll create a dataset of rotated car images so that a potential classifier can learn how to correctly revert the photos back to their original orientation, by correctly predicting the rotation angle:

```
output_path = (pathlib.Path.home() / '.keras' /
               'datasets' /
               'car_ims_rotated')
if not os.path.exists(str(output_path)):
    os.mkdir(str(output_path))
```

14. Create a copy of the dataset with random rotations performed on the images:

```
labels = []
output_paths = []
for index in tqdm(range(len(input_paths))):
    image_path = input_paths[index]
    image = load_img(image_path)
    rotation_angle = np.random.choice([0, 90, 180, 270])

    rotated_image = image.rotate(rotation_angle)
    rotated_image_path = str(output_path /
                             f'{index}.jpg')
    rotated_image.save(rotated_image_path, 'JPEG')

    output_paths.append(rotated_image_path)
```

```
        labels.append(rotation_angle)

        image.close()
        rotated_image.close()
```

15. Instantiate `FeatureExtractor` while using a pre-trained `VGG16` network to extract features from the images in the dataset:

```
features_path = str(output_path / 'features.hdf5')
model = VGG16(weights='imagenet', include_top=False)
fe = FeatureExtractor(model=model,
                      input_size=(224, 224, 3),
                      label_encoder=LabelEncoder(),
                      num_instances=len(input_paths),
                      feature_size=512 * 7 * 7,
                      output_path=features_path)
```

16. Extract the features and labels:

```
fe.extract_features(image_paths=output_paths,
                    labels=labels)
```

After several minutes, there should be a file named `features.hdf5` in `~/.keras/datasets/car_ims_rotated`.

## How it works...

In this recipe, we implemented a reusable component in order to use pre-trained networks on ImageNet, such as **VGG16** and **ResNet**, as feature extractors. This is a great way to harness the knowledge encoded in these models, since it allows us to utilize the resulting high-quality vectors to train traditional machine learning models such as `Logistic Regression` and `Support Vector Machines`.

Because image datasets tend to be too big to fit in memory, we resorted to the high-performance, user-friendly HDF5 format, which is perfect for storing large numeric data on disk, while also keeping the ease of access that's typical of NumPy. This means we can interact with HDF5 datasets *as if they were* regular NumPy arrays, making them compatible with the whole SciPy ecosystem.

The result of FeatureExtractor is a hierarchical HDF5 file (think of it as a folder in a filesystem) containing three datasets: features, which contains the feature vectors, labels, which stores the encoded labels, and label_names, which holds the human-readable labels prior to encoding.

Finally, we used FeatureExtractor to create a binary representation of a dataset of car images rotated 0°, 90°, 180°, or 270°.

> **Tip**
>
> We'll use the modified version of the Stanford Cars dataset we just worked on in future recipes in this chapter.

## See also

For more information on the Stanford Cars dataset, you can visit the official page here: https://ai.stanford.edu/~jkrause/cars/car_dataset.html. To learn more about HDF5, head to the official HDF Group website: https://www.hdfgroup.org/.

# Training a simple classifier on extracted features

Machine learning algorithms are not properly equipped to work with tensors, which forbid them from learning directly from images. However, by using pre-trained networks as feature extractors, we close this gap, enabling us to access the power of widely popular, battle-tested algorithms such as **Logistic Regression**, **Decision Trees,** and **Support Vector Machines**.

In this recipe, we'll use the features we generated in the previous recipe (in HDF5 format) to train an image orientation detector to correct the degrees of rotation of a picture, to restore its original state.

# Getting ready

As we mentioned in the introduction to this reipce, we'll use the `features.hdf5` dataset we generated in the previous recipe, which contains encoded information about rotated images from the `Stanford Cars` dataset. We assume the dataset is in the following location: `~/.keras/datasets/car_ims_rotated/features.hdf5`.

Here are some rotated samples:

Figure 3.2 – Example of a car rotated 180º (left), and another rotated 90º (right)

Let's begin!

# How to do it...

Follow these steps to complete this recipe:

1. Import the required packages:

```
import pathlib
import h5py
from sklearn.linear_model import LogisticRegressionCV
from sklearn.metrics import classification_report
```

2. Load the dataset in HDF5 format:

```
dataset_path = str(pathlib.Path.home()/'.
keras'/'datasets'/'car_ims_rotated'/'features.hdf5')
db = h5py.File(dataset_path, 'r')
```

3.  Because the dataset is too big, we'll only work with 50% of the data. The following block splits both the features and labels in half:

```
SUBSET_INDEX = int(db['labels'].shape[0] * 0.5)
features = db['features'][:SUBSET_INDEX]
labels = db['labels'][:SUBSET_INDEX]
```

4.  Take the first 80% of the data to train the model, and the remaining 20% to evaluate it later on:

```
TRAIN_PROPORTION = 0.8
SPLIT_INDEX = int(len(labels) * TRAIN_PROPORTION)
X_train, y_train = (features[:SPLIT_INDEX],
                    labels[:SPLIT_INDEX])
X_test, y_test = (features[SPLIT_INDEX:],
                  labels[SPLIT_INDEX:])
```

5.  Train a cross-validated **Logistic Regression** model on the training set. `LogisticRegressionCV` will find the best C parameter using cross-validation:

```
model = LogisticRegressionCV(n_jobs=-1)
model.fit(X_train, y_train)
```

Notice that `n_jobs=-1` means we'll use all available cores to find the best model in parallel. You can adjust this value based on the capacity of your hardware.

6.  Evaluate the model on the test set. We'll compute a classification report to get a fine-grained view of the model's performance:

```
predictions = model.predict(X_test)
report = classification_report(y_test, predictions,
                    target_names=db['label_names'])
print(report)
```

This prints the following report:

|     | precision | recall | f1-score | support |
| --- | --- | --- | --- | --- |
| 0   | 1.00 | 1.00 | 1.00 | 404 |
| 90  | 0.98 | 0.99 | 0.99 | 373 |
| 180 | 0.99 | 1.00 | 1.00 | 409 |
| 270 | 1.00 | 0.98 | 0.99 | 433 |

| | | | | |
|---|---|---|---|---|
| accuracy | | | 0.99 | 1619 |
| macro avg | 0.99 | 0.99 | 0.99 | 1619 |
| weighted avg | 0.99 | 0.99 | 0.99 | 1619 |

The model does a good job of discriminating between the four classes, achieving an overall accuracy of 99% on the test set!

7.  Finally, close the HDF5 file to free up any resources:

```
db.close()
```

We'll understand how this all works in the next section.

## How it works...

We just trained a very simple **Logistic Regression** model to detect the degree of rotation in an image. To achieve this, we leveraged the rich and expressive features we extracted using a pre-trained **VGG16** network on ImageNet (for a deeper explanation, refer to the first recipe of this chapter).

Because this data is too big, and **scikit-learn**'s machine learning algorithms work with the full data in one go (more specifically, most of them cannot work in batches), we only used 50% of the features and labels, due to memory constraints.

After a couple of minutes, we obtained an incredible performance of 99% on the test set. Moreover, by analyzing the classification report, we can see that the model is very confident in its predictions, achieving an F1 score of at least 0.99 in all four cases.

## See also

For more information on how to extract features from pre-trained networks, refer to the *Implementing a feature extractor using a pre-trained network* recipe in this chapter.

# Spot-checking extractors and classifiers

Often, when we are tackling a new project, we are victims of the Paradox of Choice: we don't know where or how to start due to the presence of so many options to choose from. Which feature extractor is the best? What's the most performant model we can train? How should we pre-process our data?

In this recipe, we will implement a framework that will automatically spot-check feature extractors and classifiers. The goal is not to get the best possible model right away, but to narrow down our options so that we can focus on the most promising ones at a later stage.

## Getting ready

First, we must install `Pillow` and `tqdm`:

```
$> pip install Pillow tqdm
```

We'll use a dataset called `17 Category Flower Dataset`, available here: `http://www.robots.ox.ac.uk/~vgg/data/flowers/17`. However, a curated version, organized into subfolders per class, can be downloaded here: `https://github.com/PacktPublishing/Tensorflow-2.0-Computer-Vision-Cookbook/tree/master/ch3/recipe3/flowers17.zip`. Unzip it in a location of your preference. In this recipe, we assume the data is inside the `~/.keras/datasets` directory, under the name `flowers17`.

Finally, we'll reuse the `FeatureExtractor()` class we defined in the *Implementing a feature extractor using a pre-trained network* recipe, at the start of this chapter. Refer to it if you want to learn more about it.

The following are some example images from the dataset for this recipe, `17 Category Flower Dataset`:

Figure 3.3 – Example images

With the preparation out of the way, let's get to it!

# How to do it...

The following steps will allow us to spot-check several combinations of feature extractors and machine learning algorithms. Follow these steps to complete this recipe:

1. Import the necessary packages:

```
import json
import os
import pathlib
from glob import glob
import h5py
from sklearn.ensemble import *
from sklearn.linear_model import *
from sklearn.metrics import accuracy_score
from sklearn.neighbors import KNeighborsClassifier
from sklearn.preprocessing import LabelEncoder
from sklearn.svm import LinearSVC
from sklearn.tree import *
from tensorflow.keras.applications import *
from tqdm import tqdm
from ch3.recipe1.feature_extractor import
FeatureExtractor
```

2. Define the input size of all the feature extractors:

```
INPUT_SIZE = (224, 224, 3)
```

3. Define a function that will obtain a list of tuples of pre-trained networks, along with the dimensionality of the vectors they output:

```
def get_pretrained_networks():
    return [
        (VGG16(input_shape=INPUT_SIZE,
               weights='imagenet',
               include_top=False),
         7 * 7 * 512),
        (VGG19(input_shape=INPUT_SIZE,
               weights='imagenet',
               include_top=False),
```

```
                7 * 7 * 512),
            (Xception(input_shape=INPUT_SIZE,
                    weights='imagenet',
                    include_top=False),
            7 * 7 * 2048),
            (ResNet152V2(input_shape=INPUT_SIZE,
                    weights='imagenet',
                    include_top=False),
            7 * 7 * 2048),
            (InceptionResNetV2(input_shape=INPUT_SIZE,
                        weights='imagenet',
                        include_top=False),
            5 * 5 * 1536)
        ]
```

4.  Define a function that returns a `dict` of machine learning models to spot-check:

```
    def get_classifiers():
        models = {}
        models['LogisticRegression'] =
                                    LogisticRegression()
        models['SGDClf'] = SGDClassifier()
        models['PAClf'] = PassiveAggressiveClassifier()
        models['DecisionTreeClf'] =
                            DecisionTreeClassifier()
        models['ExtraTreeClf'] = ExtraTreeClassifier()

        n_trees = 100
        models[f'AdaBoostClf-{n_trees}'] = \
            AdaBoostClassifier(n_estimators=n_trees)
        models[f'BaggingClf-{n_trees}'] = \
            BaggingClassifier(n_estimators=n_trees)
        models[f'RandomForestClf-{n_trees}'] = \
            RandomForestClassifier(n_estimators=n_trees)
        models[f'ExtraTreesClf-{n_trees}'] = \
            ExtraTreesClassifier(n_estimators=n_trees)
        models[f'GradientBoostingClf-{n_trees}'] = \
```

```
            GradientBoostingClassifier(n_estimators=n_trees)

    number_of_neighbors = range(3, 25)
    for n in number_of_neighbors:
        models[f'KNeighborsClf-{n}'] = \
            KNeighborsClassifier(n_neighbors=n)

    reg = [1e-3, 1e-2, 1, 10]
    for r in reg:
        models[f'LinearSVC-{r}'] = LinearSVC(C=r)
        models[f'RidgeClf-{r}'] =
            RidgeClassifier(alpha=r)

    print(f'Defined {len(models)} models.')
    return models
```

5.  Define the path to the dataset, as well as a list of all image paths:

```
dataset_path = (pathlib.Path.home() / '.keras' /
                'datasets' 'flowers17')
files_pattern = (dataset_path / 'images' / '*' / '*.jpg')
images_path = [*glob(str(files_pattern))]
```

6.  Load the labels into memory:

```
labels = []
for index in tqdm(range(len(images_path))):
    image_path = images_path[index]
    label = image_path.split(os.path.sep)[-2]
    labels.append(label)
```

7.  Define some variables in order to keep track of the spot-checking process. `final_report` will contain the accuracy of each classifier, trained on the features produced by different pre-trained networks. `best_model`, `best_accuracy`, and `best_features` will contain the name of the best model, its accuracy, and the name of the pre-trained network that produced the features, respectively:

```
final_report = {}
best_model = None
best_accuracy = -1
best_features = None
```

8.  Iterate over each pre-trained network, using it to extract features from the images in the dataset:

```
for model, feature_size in get_pretrained_networks():
    output_path = dataset_path / f'{model.name}_features.hdf5'
    output_path = str(output_path)
    fe = FeatureExtractor(model=model,
                          input_size=INPUT_SIZE,
                          label_encoder=LabelEncoder(),
                          num_instances=len(images_path),
                          feature_size=feature_size,
                          output_path=output_path)
    fe.extract_features(image_paths=images_path,
                        labels=labels)
```

9.  Take 80% of the data to train, and 20% to test:

```
    db = h5py.File(output_path, 'r')

    TRAIN_PROPORTION = 0.8
    SPLIT_INDEX = int(len(labels) * TRAIN_PROPORTION)
    X_train, y_train = (db['features'][:SPLIT_INDEX],
                        db['labels'][:SPLIT_INDEX])
    X_test, y_test = (db['features'][SPLIT_INDEX:],
                      db['labels'][SPLIT_INDEX:])

    classifiers_report = {
```

```
            'extractor': model.name
    }
    print(f'Spot-checking with features from
        {model.name}')
```

10. Using the extracted features in the current iteration, go over all the machine learning models, training them on the training set and evaluating them on the test set:

```
for clf_name, clf in get_classifiers().items():
    try:
        clf.fit(X_train, y_train)
    except Exception as e:
        print(f'\t{clf_name}: {e}')
        continue

    predictions = clf.predict(X_test)
    accuracy = accuracy_score(y_test, predictions)
    print(f'\t{clf_name}: {accuracy}')
    classifiers_report[clf_name] = accuracy
```

11. Check if we have a new best model. If that's the case, update the proper variables:

```
if accuracy > best_accuracy:
    best_accuracy = accuracy
    best_model = clf_name
    best_features = model.name
```

12. Store the results of this iteration in `final_report` and free the resources of the HDF5 file:

```
final_report[output_path] = classifiers_report
db.close()
```

13. Update `final_report` with the information of the best model. Finally, write it to disk:

```
final_report['best_model'] = best_model
final_report['best_accuracy'] = best_accuracy
final_report['best_features'] = best_features
```

```
with open('final_report.json', 'w') as f:
    json.dump(final_report, f)
```

Examining the `final_report.json` file, we can see that the best model is a `PAClf` (`PassiveAggressiveClassifier`), which achieved an accuracy of 0.934 (93.4%) on the test set and was trained on the features we extracted from a **VGG19** network. You can check the full output here: `https://github.com/PacktPublishing/Tensorflow-2.0-Computer-Vision-Cookbook/tree/master/ch3/recipe3/final_report.json`. Let's head over to the next section to study the project we completed in this recipe in more detail.

## How it works...

In this recipe, we developed a framework that automatically enabled us to spot-check 40 different machine learning algorithms by using the features produced by five different pre-trained networks, resulting in 200 experiments. Leveraging the results of this approach, we found that the best model combination for this particular problem was a `PassiveAggressiveClassifier` trained on vectors produced by a **VGG19** network.

Notice that we did not focus on achieving maximal performance, but rather on making an educated decision, based on hard evidence, on where to spend our time and resources if we were to optimize a classifier on this dataset. Now, we know that fine-tuning a **Passive Aggressive Classifier** will, most likely, pay off. How long would it have taken us to arrive at this conclusion? Hours or maybe days.

The power of letting the computer do the heavy lifting is that we don't have to guess and, at the same time, are free to spend our time on other tasks. It's great, isn't it?

# Using incremental learning to train a classifier

One of the problems of traditional machine learning libraries, such as **scikit-learn**, is that they seldom offer the possibility to train models on high volumes of data, which, coincidentally, is the best type of data for deep neural networks. What good is having large amounts of data if we can't use it?

Fortunately, there is a way to circumvent this limitation, and it's called **incremental learning**. In this recipe, we'll use a powerful library, `creme`, to train a classifier on a dataset too big to fit in memory.

# Getting ready

In this recipe, we'll leverage `creme`, an experimental library specifically designed to train machine learning models on huge datasets that are too big to fit in memory. To install `creme`, execute the following command:

```
$> pip install creme==0.5.1
```

We'll use the `features.hdf5` dataset we generated in the *Implementing a feature extractor using a pre-trained network* recipe in this chapter, which contains encoded information about rotated images from the `Stanford Cars` dataset. We assume the dataset is in the following location: `~/.keras/datasets/car_ims_rotated/features.hdf5`.

The following are some sample images from this dataset:

Figure 3.4 – Example of a car rotated 90° (left), and another rotated 0° (right)

Let's begin!

# How to do it...

The following steps will guide us through how to incrementally train a classifier on big data:

1. Import all the necessary packages:

```
import pathlib
import h5py
from creme import stream
from creme.linear_model import LogisticRegression
```

```
from creme.metrics import Accuracy
from creme.multiclass import OneVsRestClassifier
from creme.preprocessing import StandardScaler
```

2. Define a function that will save a dataset as a CSV file:

```
def write_dataset(output_path, feats, labels,
                batch_size):
    feature_size = feats.shape[1]
    csv_columns = ['class'] + [f'feature_{i}'
                            for i in range(feature_
size)]
```

3. We'll have one column for the class of each feature, and as many columns of elements in each feature vector. Next, let's write the contents of the CSV file in batches, starting with the header:

```
dataset_size = labels.shape[0]
with open(output_path, 'w') as f:
    f.write(f'{",".join(csv_columns)}\n')
```

4. Extract the batch in this iteration:

```
for batch_number, index in \
            enumerate(range(0, dataset_size,
                    batch_size)):
        print(f'Processing batch {batch_number +
                            1} of '
            f'{int(dataset_size /
            float(batch_size))}')

        batch_feats = feats[index: index +
                        batch_size]
        batch_labels = labels[index: index +
                        batch_size]
```

5. Now, write all the rows in the batch:

```
for label, vector in \
            zip(batch_labels, batch_feats):
```

```
                  vector = ','.join([str(v) for v in
                                      vector])
                  f.write(f'{label},{vector}\n')
```

6.  Load the dataset in HDF5 format:

```
dataset_path = str(pathlib.Path.home()/'.
keras'/'datasets'/'car_ims_rotated'/'features.hdf5')
db = h5py.File(dataset_path, 'r')
```

7.  Define the split index to separate the data into training (80%) and test (20%)
    chunks:

```
TRAIN_PROPORTION = 0.8
SPLIT_INDEX = int(db['labels'].shape[0] *
                  TRAIN_PROPORTION)
```

8.  Write the training and test subsets to disk as CSV files:

```
BATCH_SIZE = 256
write_dataset('train.csv',
              db['features'][:SPLIT_INDEX],
              db['labels'][:SPLIT_INDEX],
              BATCH_SIZE)
write_dataset('test.csv',
              db['features'][SPLIT_INDEX:],
              db['labels'][SPLIT_INDEX:],
              BATCH_SIZE)
```

9.  `creme` requires us to specify the type of each column in the CSV file as a `dict`.
    instance The following block specifies that `class` should be encoded as `int`, while
    the remaining columns, corresponding to the features, should be of the `float` type:

```
FEATURE_SIZE = db['features'].shape[1]
types = {f'feature_{i}': float for i in range(FEATURE_
SIZE)}
types['class'] = int
```

10. In the following code, we are defining a `creme` pipeline, where each input will be standardized prior to being passed to the classifier. Because this is a multi-class problem, we need to wrap `LogisticRegression` with `OneVsRestClassifier`:

```
model = StandardScaler()
model |= OneVsRestClassifier(LogisticRegression())
```

11. Define `Accuracy` as the target metric and create an iterator over the `train.csv` dataset:

```
metric = Accuracy()
dataset = stream.iter_csv('train.csv',
                          target_name='class',
                          converters=types)
```

12. Train the classifier, one example at a time. Print the running accuracy every 100 examples:

```
print('Training started...')
for i, (X, y) in enumerate(dataset):
    predictions = model.predict_one(X)
    model = model.fit_one(X, y)
    metric = metric.update(y, predictions)

    if i % 100 == 0:
        print(f'Update {i} - {metric}')

print(f'Final - {metric}')
```

13. Create an iterator over the `test.csv` file:

```
metric = Accuracy()
test_dataset = stream.iter_csv('test.csv',
                               target_name='class',
                               converters=types)
```

14. Evaluate the model on the test set once more, one sample at a time:

```
print('Testing model...')
for i, (X, y) in enumerate(test_dataset):
    predictions = model.predict_one(X)
    metric = metric.update(y, predictions)


    if i % 1000 == 0:
        print(f'(TEST) Update {i} - {metric}')


print(f'(TEST) Final - {metric}')
```

After several minutes, we should have a model with around 99% accuracy on the test set. We'll look at this in more detail in the next section.

## How it works...

Often, even though we have massive amounts of data at our disposal, we are unable to use it all due to hardware or software limitations (in the *Training a simple classifier on extracted features* recipe, we had to use only 50%, because we couldn't keep it all in memory). However, with incremental learning (also known as online learning), we can train traditional machine learning models in batches, similar to what we can do with neural networks.

In this recipe, in order to seize the totality of the feature vector from our `Stanford Cars` dataset, we had to write both the training and test sets into CSV files. Next, we trained `LogisticRegression` and wrapped it inside `OneVsRestClassifier`, which learned to detect the degrees of rotation in the feature vectors of the images. Finally, we achieved a very satisfying 99% accuracy on the test set.

## Fine-tuning a network using the Keras API

Perhaps one of the greatest advantages of transfer learning is its ability to seize the tailwind produced by the knowledge encoded in pre-trained networks. By simply swapping the shallower layers in one of these networks, we can obtain remarkable performance on new, unrelated datasets, even if our data is small. Why? Because the information in the bottom layers is virtually universal: It encodes basic forms and shapes that apply to almost any computer vision problem.

In this recipe, we'll fine-tune a pre-trained **VGG16** network on a tiny dataset, achieving an otherwise unlikely high accuracy score.

## Getting ready

We will need `Pillow` for this recipe. We can install it as follows:

```
$> pip install Pillow
```

We'll be using a dataset known as `17 Category Flower Dataset`, which is available here: `http://www.robots.ox.ac.uk/~vgg/data/flowers/17`. A version of it that's been organized into subfolders per class can be found here: `https://github. com/PacktPublishing/Tensorflow-2.0-Computer-Vision-Cookbook/ tree/master/ch3/recipe3/flowers17.zip`. Download and decompress it in a location of your choosing. From now on, we'll assume the data is in `~/.keras/ datasets/flowers17`.

The following are some sample images from this dataset:

Figure 3.5 – Example images

Let's begin!

## How to do it...

Fine-tuning is easy! Follow these steps to complete this recipe:

1.  Import the necessary dependencies:

```
import os
import pathlib
from glob import glob
import numpy as np
```

```
from sklearn.model_selection import train_test_split
from sklearn.preprocessing import LabelBinarizer
from tensorflow.keras import Model
from tensorflow.keras.applications import VGG16
from tensorflow.keras.layers import *
from tensorflow.keras.optimizers import *
from tensorflow.keras.preprocessing.image import *
```

2.  Set the random seed:

```
SEED = 999
```

3.  Define a function that will build a new network from a pre-trained model, where the top fully connected layers will be brand new and adapted to the problem at hand:

```
def build_network(base_model, classes):
    x = Flatten()(base_model.output)
    x = Dense(units=256)(x)
    x = ReLU()(x)
    x = BatchNormalization(axis=-1)(x)
    x = Dropout(rate=0.5)(x)

    x = Dense(units=classes)(x)
    output = Softmax()(x)

    return output
```

4.  Define a function that will load the images and labels in the dataset as NumPy arrays:

```
def load_images_and_labels(image_paths,
                           target_size=(256, 256)):
    images = []
    labels = []

    for image_path in image_paths:
        image = load_img(image_path,
                         target_size=target_size)
```

```
    image = img_to_array(image)

    label = image_path.split(os.path.sep)[-2]

    images.append(image)
    labels.append(label)

return np.array(images), np.array(labels)
```

5. Load the image paths and extract the set of classes from them:

```
dataset_path = (pathlib.Path.home() / '.keras' /
                'datasets' /'flowers17')
files_pattern = (dataset_path / 'images' / '*' / '*.jpg')
image_paths = [*glob(str(files_pattern))]
CLASSES = {p.split(os.path.sep)[-2] for p in
            image_paths}
```

6. Load the images and normalize them, one-hot encode the labels with
   `LabelBinarizer()`, and split the data into subsets for training (80%) and testing
   (20%):

```
X, y = load_images_and_labels(image_paths)
X = X.astype('float') / 255.0
y = LabelBinarizer().fit_transform(y)

(X_train, X_test,
 y_train, y_test) = train_test_split(X, y,
                                      test_size=0.2,

                                      random_state=SEED)
```

7. Instantiate a pre-trained `VGG16`, without the top layers. Specify an input shape of 256x256x3:

```
base_model = VGG16(weights='imagenet',
                   include_top=False,
                   input_tensor=Input(shape=(256, 256,
                                        3)))
```

Freeze all the layers in the base model. We are doing this because we don't want to re-train them, but use their existing knowledge:

```
for layer in base_model.layers:
    layer.trainable = False
```

8. Build the full network with a new set of layers on top using `build_network()` (defined in *Step 3*):

```
model = build_network(base_model, len(CLASSES))
model = Model(base_model.input, model)
```

9. Define the batch size and a set of augmentations to be applied through `ImageDataGenerator()`:

```
BATCH_SIZE = 64
augmenter = ImageDataGenerator(rotation_range=30,
                               horizontal_flip=True,
                               width_shift_range=0.1,
                               height_shift_range=0.1,
                               shear_range=0.2,
                               zoom_range=0.2,
                               fill_mode='nearest')
train_generator = augmenter.flow(X_train, y_train,
                                 BATCH_SIZE)
```

10. Warm up the network. This means we'll only train the new layers (the rest are frozen) for 20 epochs, using **RMSProp** with a learning rate of 0.001. Finally, we'll evaluate the network on the test set:

```
WARMING_EPOCHS = 20
model.compile(loss='categorical_crossentropy',
              optimizer=RMSprop(lr=1e-3),
```

```
            metrics=['accuracy'])
model.fit(train_generator,
            steps_per_epoch=len(X_train) // BATCH_SIZE,
            validation_data=(X_test, y_test),
            epochs=WARMING_EPOCHS)
result = model.evaluate(X_test, y_test)
print(f'Test accuracy: {result[1]}')
```

11. Now that the network has been warmed up, we'll fine-tune the final layers of the base model, specifically from the 16th onward (remember, zero-indexing), along with the fully connected layers, for 50 epochs, using **SGD** with a learning rate of 0.001:

```
for layer in base_model.layers[15:]:
    layer.trainable = True


EPOCHS = 50
model.compile(loss='categorical_crossentropy',
            optimizer=SGD(lr=1e-3),
            metrics=['accuracy'])
model.fit(train_generator,
            steps_per_epoch=len(X_train) // BATCH_SIZE,
            validation_data=(X_test, y_test),
            epochs=EPOCHS)
result = model.evaluate(X_test, y_test)
print(f'Test accuracy: {result[1]}')
```

After warming up, the network achieved 81.6% accuracy on the test set. Then, when we fine-tuned it, after 50 epochs, the accuracy rose to 94.5% on the test set. We'll see how this all works in the next section.

## How it works...

We successfully harnessed the knowledge of a pre-trained **VGG16** on the massive ImageNet database. By replacing the top layers, which are fully connected and are in charge of the actual classification (the rest act as feature extractors), with our own set of deep layers suited to our problem, we managed to obtain a more than decent 94.5% accuracy on the test set.

This result is a demonstration of the power of transfer learning, especially considering we only have 81 images per class in the dataset (81x17=1,377 in total), an insufficient amount for training a good performing deep learning model from scratch.

> **Tip**
>
> Although not always required, when fine-tuning networks, it is a good idea to first *warm up* the *head* (the fully connected layers at the top) to give them time to get accustomed to the features coming from the pre-trained networks.

## See also

You can read more about Keras pre-trained models here: `https://www.tensorflow.org/api_docs/python/tf/keras/applications`.

# Fine-tuning a network using TFHub

One of the easiest ways to fine-tune a network is to rely on the wealth of pre-trained models that live in **TensorFlow Hub** (**TFHub**). In this recipe, we'll fine-tune a **ResNetV1152** feature extractor to classify flowers from a very small dataset.

## Getting ready

We will need `tensorflow-hub` and `Pillow` for this recipe. Both can be installed easily, like this:

```
$> pip install tensorflow-hub Pillow
```

We'll use a dataset known as `17 Category Flower Dataset`, which can be accessed at `http://www.robots.ox.ac.uk/~vgg/data/flowers/17`. I encourage you to get a re-organized copy of the data here: `https://github.com/PacktPublishing/Tensorflow-2.0-Computer-Vision-Cookbook/tree/master/ch3/recipe3/flowers17.zip`. Download and decompress it in a location of your choosing. From now on, we'll assume the data is in `~/.keras/datasets/flowers17`.

The following are some sample images from this dataset:

Figure 3.6 – Example images

Let's get started!

## How to do it...

Follow these steps to successfully complete this recipe:

1.  Import the required packages:

```
import os
import pathlib
from glob import glob
import numpy as np
from sklearn.model_selection import train_test_split
from sklearn.preprocessing import LabelBinarizer
from tensorflow.keras import Sequential
from tensorflow.keras.layers import *
from tensorflow.keras.optimizers import RMSprop
from tensorflow.keras.preprocessing.image import *
from tensorflow_hub import KerasLayer
```

2.  Set the random seed:

```
SEED = 999
```

3.  Define a function that will build a new network from a pre-trained model, where the top fully connected layer will be brand new and adapted to the number of categories in our data:

```
def build_network(base_model, classes):
    return Sequential([
```

```
        base_model,
        Dense(classes),
        Softmax()
    ])
```

4. Define a function that will load the images and labels in the dataset as NumPy
arrays:

```
def load_images_and_labels(image_paths,
                           target_size=(256, 256)):
    images = []
    labels = []

    for image_path in image_paths:
        image = load_img(image_path,
                         target_size=target_size)
        image = img_to_array(image)

        label = image_path.split(os.path.sep)[-2]

        images.append(image)
        labels.append(label)

    return np.array(images), np.array(labels)
```

5. Load the image paths and extract the set of classes from them:

```
dataset_path = (pathlib.Path.home() / '.keras' /
               'datasets' /'flowers17')
files_pattern = (dataset_path / 'images' / '*' / '*.jpg')
image_paths = [*glob(str(files_pattern))]
CLASSES = {p.split(os.path.sep)[-2] for p in image_paths}
```

6.  Load the images and normalize them, one-hot encode the labels with
    `LabelBinarizer()`, and split the data into subsets for training (80%) and testing
    (20%):

```
X, y = load_images_and_labels(image_paths)
X = X.astype('float') / 255.0
y = LabelBinarizer().fit_transform(y)


(X_train, X_test,
 y_train, y_test) = train_test_split(X, y,
                                     test_size=0.2,
                                     random_state=SEED)
```

7.  Instantiate a pre-trained **ResNetV152**, which we'll use as a feature extractor. We are
    passing the model's **TFHub** URL to the `KerasLayer()` class, indicating an input
    shape of 256x256x3:

```
model_url = ('https://tfhub.dev/google/imagenet/'
             'resnet_v1_152/feature_vector/4')
base_model = KerasLayer(model_url, input_shape=(256,
                                                256, 3))
```

    Make the base model untrainable:

```
base_model.trainable = False
```

8.  Build the full network while using the base model as a starting point:

```
model = build_network(base_model, len(CLASSES))
```

9.  Define the batch size and a set of augmentations to be applied through
    `ImageDataGenerator()`:

```
BATCH_SIZE = 32
augmenter = ImageDataGenerator(rotation_range=30,
                               horizontal_flip=True,
                               width_shift_range=0.1,
                               height_shift_range=0.1,
                               shear_range=0.2,
                               zoom_range=0.2,
                               fill_mode='nearest')
```

```
train_generator = augmenter.flow(X_train, y_train,
                                 BATCH_SIZE)
```

10. Train the full model for 20 epochs and evaluate its performance on the test set:

```
EPOCHS = 20
model.compile(loss='categorical_crossentropy',
              optimizer=RMSprop(lr=1e-3),
              metrics=['accuracy'])
model.fit(train_generator,
          steps_per_epoch=len(X_train) // BATCH_SIZE,
          validation_data=(X_test, y_test),
          epochs=EPOCHS)
result = model.evaluate(X_test, y_test)
print(f'Test accuracy: {result[1]}')
```

In a matter of minutes, we obtained a model with an accuracy of around 95.22% on the test set. Awesome, don't you think? Now, let's dive deeper.

## How it works...

We leveraged the knowledge encoded in the pre-trained **ResNetV1152** we used as a starting point, a gargantuan network that we could hardly train on our own, let alone on a such a small dataset as 17 Category Flower Dataset.

With just a quick top layer swap, we managed to obtain an impressive 95.22% accuracy on the test set, which is not a small feat, all constraints considered.

Unlike the *Fine-tuning a network using the Keras API* recipe, we didn't warm up the model's head this time. Again, this is not a hard rule, but yet another tool in our toolbox that we should try on a per-project basis.

## See also

You can read more about the pre-trained model we used in this recipe here: https://tfhub.dev/google/imagenet/resnet_v1_152/feature_vector/4.

# 4

# Enhancing and Styling Images with DeepDream, Neural Style Transfer, and Image Super-Resolution

Although deep neural networks excel in traditional computer vision tasks for purely practical applications, they have a fun side too! As we'll discover in this chapter, we can unlock the artistic side of deep learning with the help of a little bit of cleverness and math, of course!

We'll start this chapter by covering **DeepDream**, an algorithm used to make neural networks produce dream-like images. Next, we'll seize the power of transfer learning to apply the style of famous paintings to our own images (this is known as **Neural Style Transfer**). Finally, we'll close with **Image Super-Resolution**, a deep learning approach that's used to improve the quality of an image.

In this chapter, we will cover the following recipes:

- Implementing DeepDream
- Generating your own dreamy images
- Implementing Neural Style Transfer
- Applying style transfer to custom images
- Applying style transfer with TFHub
- Improving image resolution with deep learning

Let's get started!

# Technical requirements

The usual advice whenever we are working with deep learning applies here: if possible, access a GPU since it greatly improves efficiency and lowers the computing time. In each recipe, you'll find specific preparation instructions in the *Getting ready* section, if needed. You can find all the code for this chapter here: `https://github.com/PacktPublishing/Tensorflow-2.0-Computer-Vision-Cookbook/tree/master/ch4`.

Check out the following link to see the Code in Action video:

`https://bit.ly/3bDns2A`.

# Implementing DeepDream

**DeepDream** is the result of an experiment that aimed to visualize the internal patterns that are learned by a neural network. In order to achieve this goal, we can pass an image through the network, compute its gradient with respect to the activations of a specific layer, and then modify the image to increase the magnitude of such activations to, in turn, magnify the patterns. The result? Psychedelic, surreal photos!

Although this recipe is a bit complex due to the nature of **DeepDream**, we will take it one step at a time, so don't worry.

Let's get started.

# Getting ready

We don't need to install anything extra for this recipe. However, we won't dive deep into the details of **DeepDream**, but if you're interested in the topic, you can read the original blog post by Google here: `https://ai.googleblog.com/2015/06/inceptionism-going-deeper-into-neural.html`.

# How to do it...

Follow these steps and you'll have your own deep dreamer in no time:

1. Import all the necessary packages:

```
import numpy as np
import tensorflow as tf
from tensorflow.keras import Model
from tensorflow.keras.applications.inception_v3 import *
```

2. Define the `DeepDreamer` class and its constructor:

```
class DeepDreamer(object):
    def __init__(self,
                 octave_scale=1.30,
                 octave_power_factors=None,
                 layers=None):
```

3. The constructor parameters specify the scale by which we'll increase the size of an image (`octave_scale`), as well as the factor that will applied to the scale (`octave_power_factors`). `layers` contains the target layers that will be used to generate the dreams. Next, let's store the parameters as object members:

```
        self.octave_scale = octave_scale

        if octave_power_factors is None:
            self.octave_power_factors = [*range(-2, 3)]
        else:
            self.octave_power_factors = \
                octave_power_factors
```

```
if layers is None:
    self.layers = ['mixed3', 'mixed5']
else:
    self.layers = layers
```

4. If some of the inputs are None, we use defaults. If not, we use the inputs. Finally, create the dreamer model by extracting our layers from a pre-trained InceptionV3 network:

```
self.base_model = InceptionV3(weights='imagenet',
                              include_top=False)
outputs = [self.base_model.get_layer(name).output
           for name in self.layers]
self.dreamer_model = Model(self.base_model.input,
                           outputs)
```

5. Define a private method that will compute the loss:

```
def _calculate_loss(self, image):
    image_batch = tf.expand_dims(image, axis=0)
    activations = self.dreamer_model(image_batch)

    if len(activations) == 1:
        activations = [activations]

    losses = []
    for activation in activations:
        loss = tf.math.reduce_mean(activation)
        losses.append(loss)

    total_loss = tf.reduce_sum(losses)
    return total_loss
```

6.  Define a private method that will perform gradient ascent (remember, we want to magnify the patterns of the image). To increase performance, we can wrap this function in `tf.function`:

```python
@tf.function
def _gradient_ascent(self, image, steps, step_size):
    loss = tf.constant(0.0)

    for _ in range(steps):
        with tf.GradientTape() as tape:
            tape.watch(image)
            loss = self._calculate_loss(image)

        gradients = tape.gradient(loss, image)
        gradients /= tf.math.reduce_std(gradients)
                                        + 1e-8

        image = image + gradients * step_size
        image = tf.clip_by_value(image, -1, 1)

    return loss, image
```

7.  Define a private method that will convert the image tensor generated by the dreamer back into a NumPy array:

```python
def _deprocess(self, image):
    image = 255 * (image + 1.0) / 2.0
    image = tf.cast(image, tf.uint8)
    image = np.array(image)

    return image
```

8. Define a private method that will generate a dreamy image by performing _gradient_ascent() for a specific number of steps:

```python
def _dream(self, image, steps, step_size):
    image = preprocess_input(image)
    image = tf.convert_to_tensor(image)
    step_size = tf.convert_to_tensor(step_size)
    step_size = tf.constant(step_size)
    steps_remaining = steps

    current_step = 0
    while steps_remaining > 0:
        if steps_remaining > 100:
            run_steps = tf.constant(100)
        else:
            run_steps = \
                tf.constant(steps_remaining)

        steps_remaining -= run_steps
        current_step += run_steps

        loss, image = self._gradient_ascent(image,
                                            run_steps,
                                            step_size)

    result = self._deprocess(image)
    return result
```

9. Define a public method that will generate dreamy images. The main difference between this and _dream() (defined in *Step 6* and used internally here) is that we'll use different image sizes (called **octaves**), as determined by the original image shape multiplied by a factor, which is the product of powering self.octave_scale to each power in self.octave_power_factors:

```python
def dream(self, image, steps=100, step_size=0.01):
    image = tf.constant(np.array(image))
    base_shape = tf.shape(image)[:-1]
    base_shape = tf.cast(base_shape, tf.float32)
```

```
        for factor in self.octave_power_factors:
            new_shape = tf.cast(
                base_shape * (self.octave_scale **
                                    factor),
                                tf.int32)
            image = tf.image.resize(image,
                                new_shape).numpy()
            image = self._dream(image, steps=steps,
                                step_size=step_size)

        base_shape = tf.cast(base_shape, tf.int32)
        image = tf.image.resize(image, base_shape)
        image = tf.image.convert_image_dtype(image /
                                        255.0,
                                dtype=tf.uint8)
        image = np.array(image)

    return np.array(image)
```

The DeepDreamer() class can be reused to produce dream-like versions of any image we supply to it. We'll see how this works in the next section.

## How it works...

We just implemented a utility class to easily apply **DeepDream**. The algorithm works by calculating the gradient with respect to the activations of a set of layers, then using such gradients to enhance the patterns seen by the network.

In our DeepDreamer() class, the previously described process is implemented in the _gradient_ascent() method (defined in *Step 4*), where we calculated the gradients and added them to the original image over a series of steps. The result was an activation map where, in each subsequent step, the **excitement** of certain neurons in the target layers was magnified.

Generating a dream consists of applying gradient ascent many times, which we basically did in the _dream() method (*Step 6*).

One of the problems of applying gradient ascent at the same scale is that the result looks noisy, with low resolution. Also, the patterns seem to happen at the same granularity level, which produces a uniformity in the result that decreases the dream-like effect we want. To resolve all these issues, the main method, `dream()`, applies gradient ascent at different scales (called **octaves**), where the dreamy output of one octave is the input of the next iteration, at a higher scale.

## See also

To see the dream-like results of passing different combinations of parameters to `DeepDreamer()`, please see the next recipe, *Generating your own dreamy images*.

# Generating your own dreamy images

Deep learning has an entertaining side. **DeepDream** is one application that aims to understand the inner workings of deep neural networks by exciting certain activations on selected layers. However, beyond the investigative intent of the experiment, it also produces psychedelic, dream-like fun images.

In this recipe, we'll experiment with several configurations of **DeepDream** on a test image and see how they affect the results.

## Getting ready

We'll use the `DeepDreamer()` implementation from the first recipe of this chapter (*Implementing DeepDream*). Although I encourage you to try this out with your own images, if you want to follow this recipe as closely as possible, you can download the sample image here: `https://github.com/PacktPublishing/Tensorflow-2.0-Computer-Vision-Cookbook/tree/master/ch4/recipe2/road.jpg`.

Let's take a look at the sample image:

Figure 4.1 – Sample image

Let's begin.

## How to do it...

Follow these steps to cook up your own dreamy photos:

1.  Let's start by importing the required packages. Notice that we are importing `DeepDreamer()` from the previous recipe, *Implementing DeepDream*:

    ```
    import matplotlib.pyplot as plt
    from tensorflow.keras.preprocessing.image import *
    from ch4.recipe1.deepdream import DeepDreamer
    ```

2.  Define the `load_image()` function that will load images from disk into memory as NumPy arrays:

    ```
    def load_image(image_path):
        image = load_img(image_path)
        image = img_to_array(image)

        return image
    ```

3. Define a function that will display an image (represented as a `NumPy` array) using `matplotlib`:

```
def show_image(image):
    plt.imshow(image)
    plt.show()
```

4. Load the original image and display it:

```
original_image = load_image('road.jpg')
show_image(original_image / 255.0)
```

Here, we can see the displayed original image:

Figure 4.2 – Original image that we'll modify shortly

As we can see, it is just a road that cuts through a forest.

5. Generate a dreamy version of the image using the default parameters and display the result:

```
dreamy_image = DeepDreamer().dream(original_image)
show_image(dreamy_image)
```

Here's the result:

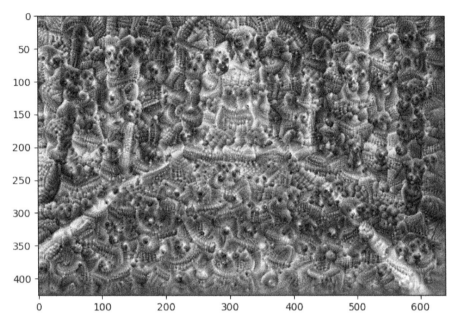

Figure 4.3 – Result of using DeepDream with the default parameters

The result preserves the overall theme of the original photo but adds lots of distortion on top of it in the form of circles, curves, and other basic patterns. Cool – and a bit creepy!

6.  Use three layers. Layers near the top (for instance, `'mixed7'`) encode higher-level patterns:

```
dreamy_image = (DeepDreamer(layers=['mixed2',
                                    'mixed5',
                                    'mixed7'])
                .dream(original_image))
show_image(dreamy_image)
```

Here's the result of using three layers:

Figure 4.4 – Result of using DeepDream with more, higher-level layers

The addition of more layers softened the produced dream. We can see that the patterns are smoother than before, which is likely due to the fact that the 'mixed7' layer encodes more abstract information because it is farther down the architecture. Let's remember that the first layers in a network learn basic patterns, such as lines and shapes, while the layers closer to the output combine these basic patterns to learn more complex, abstract information.

7.  Finally, let's use more **octaves**. The result we expect is an image with less noise and more heterogeneous patterns:

```
dreamy_image = (DeepDreamer(octave_power_factors=[-3, -1,
                                                   0, 3])
                .dream(original_image))
show_image(dreamy_image)
```

Here's the resulting image after using more octaves:

Figure 4.5 – Result of using DeepDream with more octaves

This generated dream contains a satisfying mixture of both high- and low-level patterns, as well as a better color distribution than the one produced in *Step 4*.

Let's go to the next section to understand what we've just done.

## How it works...

In this recipe, we leveraged the hard work we did in the *Implementing DeepDream* recipe in order to produce several dreamy versions of our input image of a road in a forest. By combining different parameters, we discovered that the results could vary widely. Using higher layers, which encode more abstract information, we obtained pictures with less noise and more nuanced patterns.

If we choose to use more octaves, this translates into more images, at different scales, being processed by the network. This approach generates less saturated images, while keeping the more raw, basic patterns typical of the first few layers in a convolutional neural network.

In the end, with just an image and a little creativity, we can obtain pretty interesting results!

An even more entertaining application of deep learning is Neural Style Transfer, which we will cover in the next recipe.

# Implementing Neural Style Transfer

Creativity and artistic expression are not traits that we tend to associate with deep neural networks and AI in general. However, did you know that with the right tweaks, we can turn pre-trained networks into impressive artists, capable of applying the distinctive style of famous painters such as Monet, Picasso, and Van Gogh to our mundane pictures?

This is exactly what Neural Style Transfer does. By the end of this recipe, we'll have the artistic prowess of any painter at our disposal!

## Getting ready

We don't need to install any libraries or bring in extra resources to implement Neural Style Transfer. However, because this is a hands-on recipe, we won't detail the inner workings of our solution extensively. If you're interested in the ins and outs of Neural Style Transfer, I recommend that you read the original paper here: `https://arxiv.org/abs/1508.06576`.

I hope you're ready because we are about to begin!

## How to do it...

Follow these steps to implement your own, reusable, neural style transferrer:

1. Import the necessary packages (notice that we're using a pre-trained **VGG19** network in our implementation):

```
import numpy as np
import tensorflow as tf
from tensorflow.keras import Model
from tensorflow.keras.applications.vgg19 import *
```

2. Define the `StyleTransferrer()` class and its constructor:

```
class StyleTransferrer(object):
    def __init__(self,
                 content_layers=None,
                 style_layers=None):
```

3.  The only relevant parameters are two optional lists of layers for the content and style generation, respectively. If they are None, we'll use defaults internally (as we'll see shortly). Next, load the pre-trained VGG19 and freeze it:

```
self.model = VGG19(weights='imagenet',
                   include_top=False)
self.model.trainable = False
```

4.  Set the weight (importance) of the style and content losses (we'll use these parameters later). Also, store the content and style layers (or use the defaults if necessary):

```
self.style_weight = 1e-2
self.content_weight = 1e4

if content_layers is None:
    self.content_layers = ['block5_conv2']
else:
    self.content_layers = content_layers

if style_layers is None:
    self.style_layers = ['block1_conv1',
                         'block2_conv1',
                         'block3_conv1',
                         'block4_conv1',
                         'block5_conv1']
else:
    self.style_layers = style_layers
```

5.  Define and store the style transferrer model, which takes the **VGG19** input layer as input and outputs all the content and style layers (please take into account that we can use any model, but the best results are usually achieved using either VGG19 or InceptionV3):

```
outputs = [self.model.get_layer(name).output
           for name in
           (self.style_layers +
           self.content_layers)]
```

```
self.style_model = Model([self.model.input],
                              outputs)
```

6. Define a private method that will calculate the **Gram Matrix**, which is used to calculate the style of an image. This is represented by a matrix that contains the means and correlations across different feature maps in the input tensor (for instance, the weights in a particular layer), known as a **Gram Matrix**. For more information on the **Gram Matrix**, please refer to the *See also* section of this recipe:

```
def _gram_matrix(self, input_tensor):
    result = tf.linalg.einsum('bijc,bijd->bcd',
                                  input_tensor,
                                  input_tensor)
    input_shape = tf.shape(input_tensor)
    num_locations = np.prod(input_shape[1:3])
    num_locations = tf.cast(num_locations,tf.float32)
    result = result / num_locations


    return result
```

7. Next, define a private method that will calculate the outputs (content and style). What this private method does is pass the inputs to the model and then compute the **Gram Matrix** of all the style layers, as well as the identity of the content layers, returning dicts that map each layer name to the processed values:

```
def _calc_outputs(self, inputs):
    inputs = inputs * 255
    preprocessed_input = preprocess_input(inputs)
    outputs = self.style_model(preprocessed_input)
    style_outputs = outputs[:len(self.style_layers)]
    content_outputs =
                outputs[len(self.style_layers):]

    style_outputs =
    [self._gram_matrix(style_output)
                        for style_output in
                        style_outputs]
```

```
content_dict = {content_name: value
                    for (content_name, value)
                    in zip(self.content_layers,
                        content_outputs)}

style_dict = {style_name: value
                for (style_name, value)
                in zip(self.style_layers,
                    style_outputs)}

return {'content': content_dict,
        'style': style_dict}
```

8. Define a static helper private method that will clip values between 0 and 1:

```
@staticmethod
def _clip_0_1(image):
    return tf.clip_by_value(image,
                        clip_value_min=0.0,
                        clip_value_max=1.0)
```

9. Define a static helper private method that will compute the loss between a pair of outputs and targets:

```
@staticmethod
def _compute_loss(outputs, targets):
    return tf.add_n([
        tf.reduce_mean((outputs[key] -
                    targets[key]) ** 2)
        for key in outputs.keys()
    ])
```

10. Define a private method that will compute the total loss, which is the result of computing the style and content loss individually, by multiplying them by their respective weight distributed across the corresponding layer and then adding them up:

```
def _calc_total_loss(self,
                     outputs,
                     style_targets,
                     content_targets):
    style_outputs = outputs['style']
    content_outputs = outputs['content']

    n_style_layers = len(self.style_layers)
    s_loss = self._compute_loss(style_outputs,
                                style_targets)
    s_loss *= self.style_weight / n_style_layers

    n_content_layers = len(self.content_layers)
    c_loss = self._compute_loss(content_outputs,
                                content_targets)
    c_loss *= self.content_weight / n_content_layers

    return s_loss + c_loss
```

11. Next, define a private method that will train the model. During a set number of epochs, and for a given number of steps per epoch, we'll calculate the outputs (style and content), compute the total loss, and obtain and apply the gradient to the generated image while using Adam as an optimizer:

```
@tf.function()
def _train(self,
           image,
           s_targets,
           c_targets,
           epochs,
           steps_per_epoch):
    optimizer =
        tf.optimizers.Adam(learning_rate=2e-2,
```

```
                                    beta_1=0.99,
                                    epsilon=0.1)


        for _ in range(epochs):
            for _ in range(steps_per_epoch):
                with tf.GradientTape() as tape:
                    outputs =
                        self._calc_outputs(image)
                    loss =
                        self._calc_total_loss(outputs,
                                              s_targets,
                                              c_targets)

                gradient = tape.gradient(loss, image)
                optimizer.apply_gradients([(gradient,
                                            image)])
                image.assign(self._clip_0_1(image))

        return image
```

12. Define a static helper private method that will convert a tensor into a NumPy image:

```
        @staticmethod
        def _tensor_to_image(tensor):
            tensor = tensor * 255
            tensor = np.array(tensor, dtype=np.uint8)

            if np.ndim(tensor) > 3:
                tensor = tensor[0]

            return tensor
```

13. Finally, define a public `transfer()` method that will take a style image and a content image and generate a new image. This should preserve the content as much as possible while still applying the style of the style image:

```
def transfer(self, s_image, c_image, epochs=10,
             steps_per_epoch=100):
    s_targets = self._calc_outputs(s_image)['style']
    c_targets =
        self._calc_outputs(c_image)['content']

    image = tf.Variable(c_image)

    image = self._train(image,
                        s_targets,
                        c_targets,
                        epochs,
                        steps_per_epoch)

    return self._tensor_to_image(image)
```

That was a lot of work! We'll go a bit deeper in the next section.

## How it works...

In this recipe, we learned that Neural Style Transfer works by optimizing two losses instead of one. On one hand, we want to preserve the content as much as possible, but on the other hand, we want to make this content look like it was produced using the style of the style image.

Quantifying content is achieved by using the content layers, as we would normally do in image classification. How do we quantify style, though? Here's where the **Gram Matrix** plays a crucial role, since it computes the correlations across the feature maps (more precisely, the outputs) of the style layers.

How do we inform the network that the content is more important than the style? By using weights when computing the combined loss. By default, the content weight is *10,000*, while the style weight is just *0.01*. This tells the network that most of its effort should be on reproducing the content, but also optimizing it a bit for style.

In the end, we obtained an image that preserves the coherence of the original one, but with the visual appeal of the style reference image, which is the result of optimizing the output so that it matches the statistics of both input images.

## See also

If you want to learn more the math behind the **Gram Matrix**, go to `https://encyclopediaofmath.org/wiki/Gram_matrix`. To see `StyleTransferrer()` in action, see the next recipe, *Applying style transfer to custom images*.

# Applying style transfer to custom images

Have you ever wondered how a picture of your puppy Fluffy would look if your favorite artist painted it? What if a photo of your car was the product of merging it with the magic of your most beloved painting? Well, you don't have to wonder anymore! With Neural Style Transfer, we can make our favorite images look like wonderful pieces of art effortlessly!

In this recipe, we'll use the `StyleTransferrer()` class we implemented in the *Implementing Neural Style Transfer* recipe to stylize our own images.

## Getting ready

In this recipe, we'll be using the `StyleTransferrer()` implementation from the previous recipe. In order to maximize the fun you'll get out of this recipe, you can find the sample image, along with many different paintings (which you can use as the style reference), here:

`https://github.com/PacktPublishing/Tensorflow-2.0-Computer-Vision-Cookbook/tree/master/ch4/recipe4.`

The following is the sample image we'll be using:

Figure 4.6 – Sample content image

Let's get started!

## How to do it...

The following steps will teach you how to transfer the style of famous paintings to your own images:

1. Import the necessary packages:

   ```
   import matplotlib.pyplot as plt
   import tensorflow as tf
   from chapter4.recipe3.styletransfer import
   StyleTransferrer
   ```

   Notice we're importing `StyleTransferrer()`, which we implemented in the *Implementing Neural Style Transfer* recipe.

2. Tell TensorFlow that we want to run in eager mode because otherwise, it will try to run the `tf.function` decorator functions in `StyleTransferrer()` in graph mode, which will prevent it from working properly:

   ```
   tf.config.experimental_run_functions_eagerly(True)
   ```

3.  Define a function that will load an image as a TensorFlow tensor. Notice that we're rescaling it to a sensible size. We are doing this because Neural Style Transfer is a resource-intensive process, so working on large images can take a long time:

```
def load_image(image_path):
    dimension = 512
    image = tf.io.read_file(image_path)
    image = tf.image.decode_jpeg(image, channels=3)
    image = tf.image.convert_image_dtype(image,
                                         tf.float32)

    shape = tf.cast(tf.shape(image)[:-1], tf.float32)
    longest_dimension = max(shape)
    scale = dimension / longest_dimension

    new_shape = tf.cast(shape * scale, tf.int32)
    image = tf.image.resize(image, new_shape)

    return image[tf.newaxis, :]
```

4.  Define a function that will display an image using `matplotlib`:

```
def show_image(image):
    if len(image.shape) > 3:
        image = tf.squeeze(image, axis=0)

    plt.imshow(image)
    plt.show()
```

5.  Load the content image and display it:

```
content = load_image('bmw.jpg')
show_image(content)
```

Here's the content image:

Figure 4.7 – Content image of a car

We'll apply the style of a painting to this image.

6. Load and display the style image:

```
style = load_image(art.jpg')
show_image(style)
```

Here's the style image:

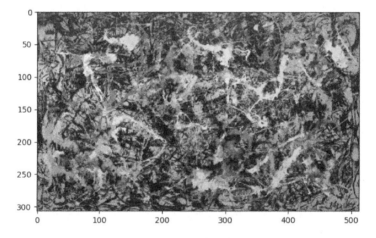

Figure 4.8 – Style image

Can you imagine how our car would look if the artist of this painting painted it?

7.  Use `StyleTransferrer()` to apply the style of the painting to our image of a BMW. Then, display the result:

```
stylized_image = StyleTransferrer().transfer(style,
                                             content)
show_image(stylized_image)
```

Here's the result:

Figure 4.9 – Result of applying the style of the painting to the content image

Impressive, isn't it?

8.  Repeat this process, this time for 100 epochs:

```
stylized_image = StyleTransferrer().transfer(style,
                                             content,
                                             epochs=100)
show_image(stylized_image)
```

Here's the result:

Figure 4.10 – Result of applying the style of the painting to the content image for 100 epochs

This time, the result is sharper. However, we had to wait a while for the process to complete. There's a clear trade-off between time and quality.

Let's move on to the next section.

## How it works...

In this recipe, we leveraged the hard work we did in the *Implementing Neural Style Transfer* recipe. We took an image of a car and applied the style of a cool and captivating piece of art to it. The result, as we saw, is fascinating.

However, we must be aware of how taxing this process is since it takes a long time to complete on a CPU – even on a GPU. Therefore, there's a trade-off to be accounted for between the number of epochs or iterations used to refine the result and the overall quality of the output.

## See also

I encourage you to try this recipe with your own pictures and styles. As a starting point, you can use the images in the following repository to hit the ground running: https://github.com/PacktPublishing/Tensorflow-2.0-Computer-Vision-Cookbook/tree/master/ch4/recipe4. There, you'll find famous artworks from Warhol, Matisse, and Monet, among others.

# Applying style transfer with TFHub

Implementing Neural Style Transfer from scratch is a demanding task. Fortunately, we can use out-of-the-box solutions that live in **TensorFlow Hub** (**TFHub**).

In this recipe, we'll style our own images in just a few lines of code by harnessing the utility and convenience that TFHub provides.

## Getting ready

We must install `tensorflow-hub`. We can do this with just a simple `pip` command:

```
$> pip install tensorflow-hub
```

If you want to access different sample content and style images, please visit this link: `https://github.com/PacktPublishing/Tensorflow-2.0-Computer-Vision-Cookbook/tree/master/ch4/recipe5`.

Let's take a look at the sample image:

Figure 4.11 – Content image

Let's get started!

## How to do it...

Neural Style Transfer with TFHub is a breeze! Follow these steps to complete this recipe:

1.  Import the necessary dependencies:

    ```
    import matplotlib.pyplot as plt
    import numpy as np
    ```

```
import tensorflow as tf
from tensorflow_hub import load
```

2.  Define a function that will load an image as a TensorFlow tensor. We need to rescale the image in order to save time and resources, given that Neural Style Transfer is a taxing process, so working on large images can take a long time:

```
def load_image(image_path):
    dimension = 512
    image = tf.io.read_file(image_path)
    image = tf.image.decode_jpeg(image, channels=3)
    image = tf.image.convert_image_dtype(image,
                                         tf.float32)

    shape = tf.cast(tf.shape(image)[:-1], tf.float32)
    longest_dimension = max(shape)
    scale = dimension / longest_dimension

    new_shape = tf.cast(shape * scale, tf.int32)
    image = tf.image.resize(image, new_shape)

    return image[tf.newaxis, :]
```

3.  Define a function that will convert a tensor into an image:

```
def tensor_to_image(tensor):
    tensor = tensor * 255
    tensor = np.array(tensor, dtype=np.uint8)

    if np.ndim(tensor) > 3:
        tensor = tensor[0]

    return tensor
```

4.  Define a function that will display an image using `matplotlib`:

```
def show_image(image):
    if len(image.shape) > 3:
        image = tf.squeeze(image, axis=0)
```

```
        plt.imshow(image)
        plt.show()
```

5.  Define the path to the style transfer implementation in TFHub and load the model:

```
    module_url = ('https://tfhub.dev/google/magenta/'
                  'arbitrary-image-stylization-v1-256/2')
    hub_module = load(module_url)
```

6.  Load the content image. Then, display it:

```
    image = load_image('bmw.jpg')
    show_image(image)
```

Here it is:

Figure 4.12 – Content image of a car

We'll apply style transfer to this photo in the next step.

7.  Load and display the style image:

```
    style_image = load_image('art4.jpg')
    show_image(style_image)
```

Here, you can see the style image:

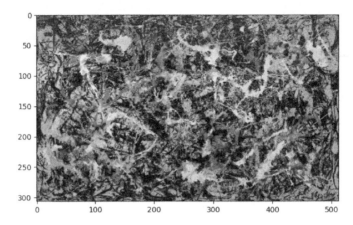

Figure 4.13 – This is our style image of choice

We'll pass this and the content image to the TFHub module we recently created and wait for the result.

8. Apply Neural Style Transfer using the model we downloaded from TFHub and display the result:

```
results = hub_module(tf.constant(image),
                        tf.constant(style_image))
stylized_image = tensor_to_image(results[0])
show_image(stylized_image)
```

Here's the result of applying Neural Style Transfer with TFHub:

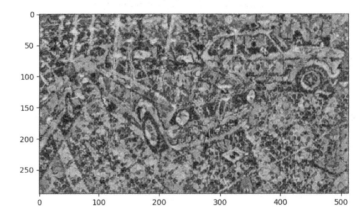

Figure 4.14 – Result of applying style transfer using TFHub

*Voilà!* The result looks pretty good, don't you think? We'll dive a bit deeper in the next section.

## How it works...

In this recipe, we learned that using TFHub to stylize images is substantially easier than implementing the algorithm from scratch. However, it gives us less control since it acts as a black box.

Either way, the result is quite satisfactory because it preserves the coherence and meaning of the original scene, while adding the artistic traits of the style image on top.

The most important part is downloading the correct module from TFHub, and then loading it using the `load()` function.

For the pre-packaged module to work, we must pass both the content and style images as `tf.constant` constants.

Finally, because we received a tensor, in order to properly display the result on-screen, we used our custom function, `tensor_to_image()`, to turn it into a `NumPy` array that can easily be plotted using `matplotlib`.

## See also

You can read more about the TFHub module we used here at `https://tfhub.dev/google/magenta/arbitrary-image-stylization-v1-256/2`.

Also, why don't you play around with your own images and other styles? You can use the assets here as a starting point: `https://github.com/PacktPublishing/Tensorflow-2.0-Computer-Vision-Cookbook/tree/master/ch4/recipe5`.

# Improving image resolution with deep learning

**Convolutional Neural Networks (CNNs)** can also be used to improve the resolution of low-quality images. Historically, we can achieve this by using interpolation techniques, example-based approaches, or low- to high-resolution mappings that must be learned.

As we'll see in this recipe, we can obtain better results faster by using an end-to-end deep learning-based approach.

Sound interesting? Let's get to it!

# Getting ready

We will need `Pillow` in this recipe, which you can install with the following command:

```
$> pip install Pillow
```

In this recipe, we are using the `Dog and Cat Detection` dataset, which is hosted on Kaggle: `https://www.kaggle.com/andrewmvd/dog-and-cat-detection`. In order to download it, you'll need to sign in on the website or sign up. Once you're logged in, save it in a place of your preference as `dogscats.zip`. Finally, decompress it in a folder named `dogscats`. From now on, we'll assume the data is in `~/.keras/datasets/dogscats`.

The following is a sample from the two classes in the dataset:

Figure 4.15 – Example images

Let's get started!

# How to do it...

Follow these steps to implement a fully convolutional network in order to perform image super-resolution:

1.  Import all the necessary modules:

    ```
    import pathlib
    from glob import glob
    import matplotlib.pyplot as plt
    import numpy as np
    from PIL import Image
    ```

```
from tensorflow.keras import Model
from tensorflow.keras.layers import *
from tensorflow.keras.optimizers import Adam
from tensorflow.keras.preprocessing.image import *
```

2.  Define a function that will build the network architecture. Notice that this is a fully convolutional network, which means only convolutional layers (besides the activations) comprise it, including the output:

```
def build_srcnn(height, width, depth):
    input = Input(shape=(height, width, depth))

    x = Conv2D(filters=64, kernel_size=(9, 9),
                kernel_initializer='he_normal')(input)
    x = ReLU()(x)
    x = Conv2D(filters=32, kernel_size=(1, 1),
                kernel_initializer='he_normal')(x)
    x = ReLU()(x)
    output = Conv2D(filters=depth, kernel_size=(5, 5),
                    kernel_initializer='he_normal')(x)

    return Model(input, output)
```

3.  Define a function that will resize an image based on a scale factor. Take into consideration that it receives an image represented as a NumPy array:

```
def resize_image(image_array, factor):
    original_image = Image.fromarray(image_array)
    new_size = np.array(original_image.size) * factor
    new_size = new_size.astype(np.int32)
    new_size = tuple(new_size)

    resized = original_image.resize(new_size)
    resized = img_to_array(resized)
    resized = resized.astype(np.uint8)

    return resized
```

4.  Define a function that will tightly crop an image. We are doing this because we want the image to fit nicely when we apply a sliding window to extract patches later. SCALE is the factor we want the network to learn how to enlarge images by:

```
def tight_crop_image(image):
    height, width = image.shape[:2]
    width -= int(width % SCALE)
    height -= int(height % SCALE)
    return image[:height, :width]
```

5.  Define a function that will purposely reduce the resolution of an image by downsizing it and then upsizing it:

```
def downsize_upsize_image(image):
    scaled = resize_image(image, 1.0 / SCALE)
    scaled = resize_image(scaled, SCALE / 1.0)
    return scaled
```

6.  Define a function that will crop patches from input images. INPUT_DIM is the height and width of the images we will feed into the network:

```
def crop_input(image, x, y):
    y_slice = slice(y, y + INPUT_DIM)
    x_slice = slice(x, x + INPUT_DIM)

    return image[y_slice, x_slice]
```

7.  Define a function that will crop patches of output images. LABEL_SIZE is the height and width of the images outputted by the network. On the other hand, PAD is the number of pixels that will be used as padding to ensure we are cropping the region of interest properly:

```
def crop_output(image, x, y):
    y_slice = slice(y + PAD, y + PAD + LABEL_SIZE)
    x_slice = slice(x + PAD, x + PAD + LABEL_SIZE)

    return image[y_slice, x_slice]
```

8. Set the random seed:

```
SEED = 999
np.random.seed(SEED)
```

9. Load the paths to all the images in the dataset:

```
file_patten = (pathlib.Path.home() / '.keras' /
               'datasets' /
               'dogscats' / 'images' / '*.png')
file_pattern = str(file_patten)
dataset_paths = [*glob(file_pattern)]
```

10. Because the dataset is huge and we don't need all the images in it to achieve our goal, let's randomly pick 1,500 of them:

```
SUBSET_SIZE = 1500
dataset_paths = np.random.choice(dataset_paths,
                                 SUBSET_SIZE)
```

11. Define the parameters that will be used to create our dataset of low-resolution patches as input and high-resolution patches (the labels) as output. All of these parameters were defined in previous steps, except for STRIDE, which is the number of pixels we'll slide both in the horizontal and vertical axes to extract patches:

```
SCALE = 2.0
INPUT_DIM = 33
LABEL_SIZE = 21
PAD = int((INPUT_DIM - LABEL_SIZE) / 2.0)
STRIDE = 14
```

12. Build the dataset. The inputs will be low-resolution patches that have been extracted from the images after being downsized and upsized. The labels will be patches from the unaltered image:

```
data = []
labels = []
for image_path in dataset_paths:
    image = load_img(image_path)
    image = img_to_array(image)
    image = image.astype(np.uint8)
```

```
    image = tight_crop_image(image)
    scaled = downsize_upsize_image(image)

    height, width = image.shape[:2]

    for y in range(0, height - INPUT_DIM + 1, STRIDE):
        for x in range(0, width - INPUT_DIM + 1, STRIDE):
            crop = crop_input(scaled, x, y)
            target = crop_output(image, x, y)

            data.append(crop)
            labels.append(target)

data = np.array(data)
labels = np.array(labels)
```

13. Instantiate the network, which we'll train for 12 epochs while using `Adam()` as our optimizer with learning rate decay. The loss function is `'mse'`. Why? Because our goal is not to achieve great accuracy, but to learn a set of filters that correctly map patches from low to high resolution:

```
EPOCHS = 12
optimizer = Adam(lr=1e-3, decay=1e-3 / EPOCHS)
model = build_srcnn(INPUT_DIM, INPUT_DIM, 3)
model.compile(loss='mse', optimizer=optimizer)
```

14. Train the network:

```
BATCH_SIZE = 64
model.fit(data, labels, batch_size=BATCH_SIZE,
          epochs=EPOCHS)
```

15. Now, to evaluate our solution, we'll load a test image, convert it into a `NumPy` array, and reduce its resolution:

```
image = load_img('dogs.jpg')
image = img_to_array(image)
image = image.astype(np.uint8)
```

```
image = tight_crop_image(image)
scaled = downsize_upsize_image(image)
```

16. Display the low-resolution image:

```
plt.title('Low resolution image (Downsize + Upsize)')
plt.imshow(scaled)
plt.show()
```

Let's see the result:

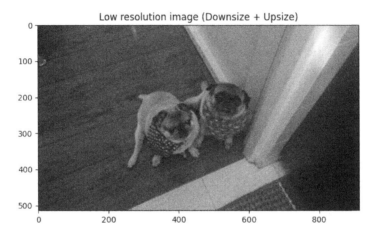

Figure 4.16 – Low-resolution test image

Now, we want to create a sharper version of this photo.

17. Create a canvas with the same dimensions of the input image. This is where we'll store the high-resolution patches generated by the network:

```
output = np.zeros(scaled.shape)
height, width = output.shape[:2]
```

18. Extract low-resolution patches, pass them through the network to obtain their high-resolution counterparts, and place them in their proper location in the output canvas:

```
for y in range(0, height - INPUT_DIM + 1, LABEL_SIZE):
    for x in range(0, width - INPUT_DIM + 1, LABEL_SIZE):
        crop = crop_input(scaled, x, y)
```

```
image_batch = np.expand_dims(crop, axis=0)
prediction = model.predict(image_batch)
new_shape = (LABEL_SIZE, LABEL_SIZE, 3)
prediction = prediction.reshape(new_shape)


output_y_slice = slice(y + PAD, y + PAD +
                       LABEL_SIZE)
output_x_slice = slice(x + PAD, x + PAD +
                       LABEL_SIZE)
output[output_y_slice, output_x_slice] =
                       prediction
```

19. Finally, display the high-resolution result:

```
plt.title('Super resolution result (SRCNN output)')
plt.imshow(output / 255)
plt.show()
```

Here's the super-resolution output:

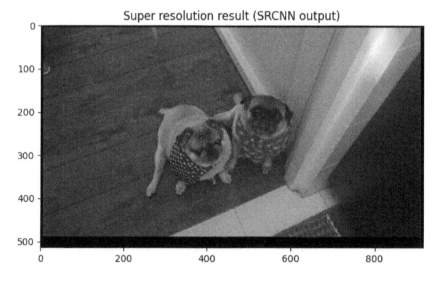

Figure 4.17 – High-resolution test image

Compared to the low-resolution image, this photo does a better job of detailing the dogs and the overall scene, don't you think?

> **Tip**
>
> I recommend that you open both the low- and high-resolution images in a PDF or photo viewer. This will help you closely examine the differences between them and convince yourself that the network did its job well. It can be hard to judge the distinction in the print version of this book.

## How it works...

In this recipe, we created a model capable of improving the resolution of a blurry or low resolution image. The biggest takeaway of this implementation is that it is powered by a **fully convolutional neural network**, meaning that it comprises only convolutional layers and their activations.

This is a regression problem, where each pixel in the output is a feature we want to learn.

However, our goal is not to optimize for accuracy, but to train the model so the feature maps encode the necessary information to produce high-resolution patches from low-resolution ones.

Now, we must ask ourselves: why patches? We don't want to *learn* what's in the image. Instead, again, we want our network to figure out how to go from low to high resolution. Patches are good enough for this purpose as they enclose localized patterns that are easier to grasp.

You might have noticed that we didn't train for many epochs (only 12). This is by design because it's been shown that training for too long can actually hurt the network's performance.

Finally, it must be noted that because this network was trained on images of dogs and cats, its expertise lies in upscaling photos of these animals. Nonetheless, by switching the dataset, we can easily create a super-resolution network that specializes in other kind of data.

## See also

Our implementation is based on the great work of Dong et al., whose paper on the subject can be read here: https://arxiv.org/abs/1501.00092.

# 5
# Reducing Noise with Autoencoders

Among the most interesting families of deep neural networks is the autoencoder family. As their name suggests, their sole purpose is to digest their input, and then reconstruct it back into its original shape. In other words, an autoencoder learns to copy its input to its output. Why? Because the side effect of this process is what we are after: not to produce a tag or classification, but to learn an efficient, high-quality representation of the images that have been passed to the autoencoder. The name of such a representation is **encoding**.

How do they achieve this? By training two networks in tandem: an **encoder**, which takes images and produces the encoding, and a **decoder**, which takes the encoding and tries to reconstruct the input from its information.

In this chapter, we will cover the basics, starting with a simple fully connected implementation of an autoencoder. Later, we'll create a more common and versatile convolutional autoencoder. We will also learn how to apply autoencoders in more practical contexts, such as denoising images, detecting outliers in a dataset, and creating an inverse image search index. Sound interesting?

In this chapter, we will cover the following recipes:

- Creating a simple fully connected autoencoder
- Creating a convolutional autoencoder
- Denoising images with autoencoders
- Spotting outliers using autoencoders
- Creating an inverse image search index with deep learning
- Implementing a variational autoencoder

Let's get started!

# Technical requirements

Although using a GPU is always a good idea, some of these recipes (especially *Creating a simple fully connected autoencoder*) work well with a mid-tier CPU, such as an Intel i5 or i7. If any particular recipe depends on external resources or requires preparatory steps, you'll find specific preparation instructions in the *Getting ready* section. You can promptly access all the code for this chapter here: `https://github.com/PacktPublishing/Tensorflow-2.0-Computer-Vision-Cookbook/tree/master/ch5`.

Check out the following link to see the Code in Action video:

`https://bit.ly/3qrHYaF`.

# Creating a simple fully connected autoencoder

**Autoencoders** are unusual in their design, as well as in terms of their functionality. That's why it's a great idea to master the basics of implementing, perhaps, the simplest version of an autoencoder: a fully connected one.

In this recipe, we'll implement a fully connected autoencoder to reconstruct the images in `Fashion-MNIST`, a standard dataset that requires minimal preprocessing, allowing us to focus on the autoencoder itself.

Are you ready? Let's get started!

# Getting ready

Fortunately, `Fashion-MNIST` comes bundled with TensorFlow, so we don't need to download it on our own.

We'll use `OpenCV`, a famous computer vision library, to create a mosaic so that we can compare the original images with the ones reconstructed by the autoencoder. You can install `OpenCV` effortlessly with `pip`:

```
$> pip install opencv-contrib-python
```

Now that all the preparations have been handled, let's take a look at the recipe!

## How to do it...

Follow these steps, to implement a simple yet capable autoencoder:

1. Import the necessary packages to implement the fully connected autoencoder:

```
import cv2
import numpy as np
from tensorflow.keras import Model
from tensorflow.keras.datasets import fashion_mnist
from tensorflow.keras.layers import *
```

2. Define a function that will build the autoencoder's architecture. By default, the encoding or latent vector dimension is *128*, but *16*, *32*, and *64* are good values too:

```
def build_autoencoder(input_shape=784, encoding_dim=128):
    input_layer = Input(shape=(input_shape,))
    encoded = Dense(units=512)(input_layer)
    encoded = ReLU()(encoded)
    encoded = Dense(units=256)(encoded)
    encoded = ReLU()(encoded)

    encoded = Dense(encoding_dim)(encoded)
    encoding = ReLU()(encoded)

    decoded = Dense(units=256)(encoding)
    decoded = ReLU()(decoded)
    decoded = Dense(units=512)(decoded)
    decoded = ReLU()(decoded)
    decoded = Dense(units=input_shape)(decoded)
```

```
decoded = Activation('sigmoid')(decoded)


return Model(input_layer, decoded)
```

3. Define a function that will plot a sample of general images against their original counterparts, in order to visually assess the autoencoder's performance:

```
def plot_original_vs_generated(original, generated):
    num_images = 15
    sample = np.random.randint(0, len(original),
                               num_images)
```

4. The previous block selects 15 random indices, which we'll use to pick the same sample images from the `original` and `generated` batches. Next, let's define an inner function so that we can stack a sample of 15 images in a 3x5 grid:

```
def stack(data):
    images = data[sample]
    return np.vstack([np.hstack(images[:5]),
                      np.hstack(images[5:10]),
                      np.hstack(images[10:15])])
```

5. Now, define another inner function so that we can add text on top of an image. This will be useful for distinguishing the generated images from the originals, as we'll see shortly:

```
def add_text(image, text, position):
    pt1 = position
    pt2 = (pt1[0] + 10 + (len(text) * 22),
           pt1[1] - 45)
    cv2.rectangle(image,
                  pt1,
                  pt2,
                  (255, 255, 255),
                  -1)
    cv2.putText(image, text,
                position,
                fontFace=cv2.FONT_HERSHEY_SIMPLEX,
                fontScale=1.3,
```

```
                    color=(0, 0, 0),
                    thickness=4)
```

6. Wrap up this function by selecting the same images from the original and generated groups. Then, stack both groups together to form a mosaic, resize it so that it's 860x860 in size, label the original and generated tiles in the mosaic using add_text(), and display the result:

```
original = stack(original)
generated = stack(generated)

mosaic = np.vstack([original,
                    generated])
mosaic = cv2.resize(mosaic, (860, 860),
                    interpolation=cv2.INTER_AREA)
mosaic = cv2.cvtColor(mosaic, cv2.COLOR_GRAY2BGR)

add_text(mosaic, 'Original', (50, 100))
add_text(mosaic, 'Generated', (50, 520))

cv2.imshow('Mosaic', mosaic)
cv2.waitKey(0)
```

7. Download (or load, if cached) Fashion-MNIST. Because this is not a classification problem, we are only keeping the images, not the labels:

```
(X_train, _), (X_test, _) = fashion_mnist.load_data()
```

8. Normalize the images:

```
X_train = X_train.astype('float32') / 255.0
X_test = X_test.astype('float32') / 255.0
```

9. Reshape the images into vectors:

```
X_train = X_train.reshape((X_train.shape[0], -1))
X_test = X_test.reshape((X_test.shape[0], -1))
```

10. Build the autoencoder and compile it. We'll use `'adam'` as the optimizer and mean squared Error (`'mse'`) as the loss function. Why? We're not interested in getting the classification right but reconstructing the input as closely as possible, which translates into minimizing the overall error:

```
autoencoder = build_autoencoder()
autoencoder.compile(optimizer='adam', loss='mse')
```

11. Fit the autoencoder over 300 epochs, a figure high enough to allow the network to learn a good representation of the input. To speed up the training process a bit, we'll pass batches of `1024` vectors at a time (feel free to change the batch size based on your hardware capabilities). Notice how the input features are also the labels or targets:

```
EPOCHS = 300
BATCH_SIZE = 1024
autoencoder.fit(X_train, X_train,
                epochs=EPOCHS,
                batch_size=BATCH_SIZE,
                shuffle=True,
                validation_data=(X_test, X_test))
```

12. Make predictions on the test set (basically, generate copies of the test vectors):

```
predictions = autoencoder.predict(X_test)
```

13. Reshape the predictions and test vectors back to grayscale images of dimensions 28x28x1:

```
original_shape = (X_test.shape[0], 28, 28)
predictions = predictions.reshape(original_shape)
X_test = X_test.reshape(original_shape)
```

14. Generate a comparative plot of the original images against the ones produced by the autoencoder:

```
plot_original_vs_generated(X_test, predictions)
```

Here's the result:

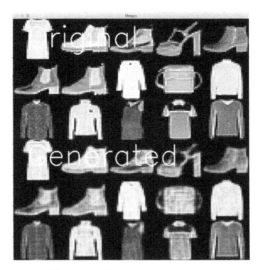

Figure 5.1 – Mosaic of the original images (top three rows) compared with the
generated ones (bottom three rows)

Judging by the results, our autoencoder did a pretty decent job. In all cases, the shape
of the clothing items is well-preserved. However, it isn't as accurate at reconstructing
the inner details, as shown by the T-shirt in the sixth row, fourth column, where the
horizontal stripe in the original is missing in the produced copy.

## How it works...

In this recipe, we learned that autoencoders work by combining two networks into one:
the encoder and the decoder. In the `build_autoencoder()` function, we implemented
a fully connected autoencoding architecture, where the encoder portion takes a
784-element vector and outputs an encoding of 128 numbers. Then, the decoder picks
up this encoding and expands it through several stacked dense (fully connected) layers,
where the last one creates a 784-element vector (the same dimensions that the input
contains).

The training process thus consists of minimizing the distance or error between the input
the encoder receives and the output the decoder produces. The only way to achieve this is
to learn encodings that minimize the information loss when compressing the inputs.

Although the loss function (in this case, `MSE`) is a good measure to see if the autoencoder
is progressing in its learning, with these particular networks, visual verification is
just as relevant, if not more. That's why we implemented the `plot_original_vs_`
`generated()` function: to check that the copies look like their original counterparts.

Why don't you try changing the encoding size? How does it affect the quality of the copies?

## See also

If you're wondering why `Fashion-MNIST` exists at all, take a look at the official repository here: `https://github.com/zalandoresearch/fashion-mnist`.

# Creating a convolutional autoencoder

As with regular neural networks, when it comes to images, using convolutions is usually the way to go. In the case of autoencoders, this is no different. In this recipe, we'll implement a convolutional autoencoder to reproduce images from `Fashion-MNIST`.

The distinguishing factor is that in the decoder, we'll use reverse or transposed convolutions, which upscale volumes instead of downscaling them. This is what happens in traditional convolutional layers.

This is an interesting recipe. Are you ready to begin?

## Getting ready

Because there are convenience functions in TensorFlow for downloading `Fashion-MNIST`, we don't need to do any manual preparations on the data side. However, we must install `OpenCV` so that we can visualize the outputs of the autoencoder. This can be done with the following command:

```
$> pip install opencv-contrib-python
```

Without further ado, let's get started.

## How to do it...

Follow these steps to implement a fully functional convolutional autoencoder:

1.  Let's import the necessary dependencies:

    ```
    import cv2
    import numpy as np
    from tensorflow.keras import Model
    from tensorflow.keras.datasets import fashion_mnist
    from tensorflow.keras.layers import *
    ```

2.  Define the `build_autoencoder()` function, which internally builds the autoencoder architecture and returns the encoder, the decoder, and the autoencoder itself. Start defining the input and the first set of 32 convolutional filters:

```
def build_autoencoder(input_shape=(28, 28, 1),
                      encoding_size=32,
                      alpha=0.2):
    inputs = Input(shape=input_shape)
    encoder = Conv2D(filters=32,
                     kernel_size=(3, 3),
                     strides=2,
                     padding='same')(inputs)
    encoder = LeakyReLU(alpha=alpha)(encoder)
    encoder = BatchNormalization()(encoder)
```

Define the second set of convolutions (64 this time):

```
    encoder = Conv2D(filters=64,
                     kernel_size=(3, 3),
                     strides=2,
                     padding='same')(encoder)
    encoder = LeakyReLU(alpha=alpha)(encoder)
    encoder = BatchNormalization()(encoder)
```

Define the output layers of the encoder:

```
    encoder_output_shape = encoder.shape
    encoder = Flatten()(encoder)
    encoder_output = Dense(units=encoding_size)(encoder)

    encoder_model = Model(inputs, encoder_output)
```

3.  In *Step 2*, we defined the encoder model, which is a regular convolutional neural network. The next block defines the decoder model, starting with the input and 64 transposed convolution filters:

```
    decoder_input = Input(shape=(encoding_size,))
    target_shape = tuple(encoder_output_shape[1:])
    decoder = Dense(np.prod(target_shape))(decoder_input)
    decoder = Reshape(target_shape)(decoder)
    decoder = Conv2DTranspose(filters=64,
```

```
                             kernel_size=(3, 3),
                             strides=2,
                             padding='same')(decoder)
decoder = LeakyReLU(alpha=alpha)(decoder)
decoder = BatchNormalization()(decoder)
```

Define the second set of transposed convolutions (32 this time):

```
decoder = Conv2DTranspose(filters=32,
                             kernel_size=(3, 3),
                             strides=2,
                             padding='same')(decoder)
decoder = LeakyReLU(alpha=alpha)(decoder)
decoder = BatchNormalization()(decoder)
```

Define the output layer of the decoder:

```
decoder = Conv2DTranspose(filters=1,
                             kernel_size=(3, 3),
                             padding='same')(decoder)
outputs = Activation('sigmoid')(decoder)

decoder_model = Model(decoder_input, outputs)
```

4.  The decoder uses `Conv2DTranspose` layers, which expand their inputs to generate larger output volumes. Notice that the further we go into the decoder, the fewer filters the `Conv2DTranspose` layers use. Finally, define the autoencoder:

```
encoder_model_output = encoder_model(inputs)
decoder_model_output =
    decoder_model(encoder_model_output)
autoencoder_model = Model(inputs,
    decoder_model_output)

return encoder_model, decoder_model, autoencoder_model
```

The autoencoder is the end-to-end architecture. This starts with the input layer, which goes into the encoder, and ends with an output layer, which is the result of passing the encoder's output through the decoder.

5. Define a function that will plot a sample of general images against their original counterparts. This will help us visually assess the autoencoder's performance. (This is the same function we defined in the previous recipe. For a more complete explanation, refer to the *Creating a simple fully connected autoencoder* recipe of this chapter.) Take a look at the following code:

```
def plot_original_vs_generated(original, generated):
    num_images = 15
    sample = np.random.randint(0, len(original),
                               num_images)
```

6. Define an inner helper function in order to stack a sample of images in a 3x5 grid:

```
def stack(data):
    images = data[sample]
    return np.vstack([np.hstack(images[:5]),
                      np.hstack(images[5:10]),
                      np.hstack(images[10:15])])
```

7. Next, define a function that will put text on an image in a given position:

```
def add_text(image, text, position):
    pt1 = position
    pt2 = (pt1[0] + 10 + (len(text) * 22),
           pt1[1] - 45)
    cv2.rectangle(image,
                  pt1,
                  pt2,
                  (255, 255, 255),
                  -1)
    cv2.putText(image, text,
                position,
                fontFace=cv2.FONT_HERSHEY_SIMPLEX,
                fontScale=1.3,
                color=(0, 0, 0),
                thickness=4)
```

8.  Finally, create a mosaic containing both the original and generated images:

```
original = stack(original)
generated = stack(generated)

mosaic = np.vstack([original,
                    generated])
mosaic = cv2.resize(mosaic, (860, 860),
                    interpolation=cv2.INTER_AREA)
mosaic = cv2.cvtColor(mosaic, cv2.COLOR_GRAY2BGR)

add_text(mosaic, 'Original', (50, 100))
add_text(mosaic, 'Generated', (50, 520))

cv2.imshow('Mosaic', mosaic)
cv2.waitKey(0)
```

9.  Download (or load, if cached) `Fashion-MNIST`. We are only interested in the images; therefore, we can drop the labels:

```
(X_train, _), (X_test, _) = fashion_mnist.load_data()
```

10. Normalize the images and add a channel dimension to them:

```
X_train = X_train.astype('float32') / 255.0
X_test = X_test.astype('float32') / 255.0

X_train = np.expand_dims(X_train, axis=-1)
X_test = np.expand_dims(X_test, axis=-1)
```

11. Here, we are only interested in the autoencoder, so we'll ignore the other two return values of the `build_autoencoder()` function. However, in different circumstances, we could want to keep them. We'll train the model using `'adam'` and use `'mse'` as the loss function since we want to reduce the error, not optimize for classification accuracy:

```
_, _, autoencoder = build_autoencoder(encoding_size=256)
autoencoder.compile(optimizer='adam', loss='mse')
```

12. Train the autoencoder over 300 epochs, in batches of 512 images at a time. Notice how the input images are also the labels:

```
EPOCHS = 300
BATCH_SIZE = 512
autoencoder.fit(X_train, X_train,
                epochs=EPOCHS,
                batch_size=BATCH_SIZE,
                shuffle=True,
                validation_data=(X_test, X_test),
                verbose=1)
```

13. Make copies of the test set:

```
predictions = autoencoder.predict(X_test)
```

14. Reshape both the predictions and the test images back to 28x28 (no channel dimension):

```
original_shape = (X_test.shape[0], 28, 28)
predictions = predictions.reshape(original_shape)
X_test = X_test.reshape(original_shape)
predictions = (predictions * 255.0).astype('uint8')
X_test = (X_test * 255.0).astype('uint8')
```

15. Generate a comparative mosaic of the original images and the copies outputted by the autoencoder:

```
plot_original_vs_generated(X_test, predictions)
```

Let's take a look at the result:

Figure 5.2 – Mosaic of the original images (top three rows), compared with those produced by the convolutional autoencoder (bottom three rows)

As we can see, the autoencoder has learned a good encoding, which allowed it to reconstruct the input images with minimal detail loss. Let's head over to the next section to understand how it works!

## How it works...

In this recipe, we learned that a convolutional autoencoder is one of the most common yet powerful members of this family of neural networks. The encoder portion of the architecture is a regular convolutional neural network that relies on convolutions and dense layers to downsize the output and produce a vector representation. The decoder is the interesting part because it has to deal with the converse problem: to reconstruct the input based on the synthesized feature vector, also known as an encoding.

How does it do this? By using a transposed convolution (`Conv2DTranspose`). Unlike traditional `Conv2D` layers, these produce shallower volumes (fewer filters), but they are wider and taller. The result is an output layer with only one filter, and 28x28 dimensions, which is the same shape as the input. Fascinating, isn't it?

The training process consists of minimizing the error between the output (the generated copies) and the input (the original images). Therefore, MSE is a fitting loss function because it provides us with this very information.

Finally, we assessed the performance of the autoencoder by visually inspecting a sample of test images, along with their synthetic counterparts.

> **Tip**
> In an autoencoder, the size of the encoding is crucial to guarantee the decoder has enough information to reconstruct the input.

## See also

Here's a great explanation of transposed convolutions: `https://towardsdatascience.com/transposed-convolution-demystified-84ca81b4baba`.

# Denoising images with autoencoders

Using images to reconstruct their input is great, but are there more useful ways to apply autoencoders? Of course there are! One of them is image denoising. As the name suggests, this is the act of restoring damaged images by replacing the corrupted pixels and regions with sensible values.

In this recipe, we'll purposely damage the images in `Fashion-MNIST`, and then train an autoencoder to denoise them.

## Getting ready

`Fashion-MNIST` can easily be accessed using the convenience functions TensorFlow provides, so we don't need to manually download the dataset. On the other hand, because we'll be creating some visualizations using `OpenCV`, we must install it, as follows:

```
$> pip install opencv-contrib-python
```

Let's get started!

## How to do it...

Follow these steps to implement a convolutional autoencoder capable of restoring damaged images:

1. Import the required packages:

```
import cv2
import numpy as np
from tensorflow.keras import Model
```

```
from tensorflow.keras.datasets import fashion_mnist
from tensorflow.keras.layers import *
```

2.  Define the `build_autoencoder()` function, which creates the corresponding neural architecture. Notice that this is the same architecture we implemented in the previous recipe; therefore, we won't go into too much detail here. For an in-depth explanation, please refer to the *Creating a convolutional autoencoder* recipe:

```
def build_autoencoder(input_shape=(28, 28, 1),
                      encoding_size=128,
                      alpha=0.2):
    inputs = Input(shape=input_shape)
    encoder = Conv2D(filters=32,
                     kernel_size=(3, 3),
                     strides=2,
                     padding='same')(inputs)
    encoder = LeakyReLU(alpha=alpha)(encoder)
    encoder = BatchNormalization()(encoder)
    encoder = Conv2D(filters=64,
                     kernel_size=(3, 3),
                     strides=2,
                     padding='same')(encoder)
    encoder = LeakyReLU(alpha=alpha)(encoder)
    encoder = BatchNormalization()(encoder)

    encoder_output_shape = encoder.shape
    encoder = Flatten()(encoder)
    encoder_output =
        Dense(units=encoding_size)(encoder)

    encoder_model = Model(inputs, encoder_output)
```

3.  Now that we've created the encoder model, let's create the decoder:

```
    decoder_input = Input(shape=(encoding_size,))
    target_shape = tuple(encoder_output_shape[1:])
    decoder =
        Dense(np.prod(target_shape))(decoder_input)
```

```
        decoder = Reshape(target_shape)(decoder)

        decoder = Conv2DTranspose(filters=64,
                                  kernel_size=(3, 3),
                                  strides=2,
                                  padding='same')(decoder)
        decoder = LeakyReLU(alpha=alpha)(decoder)
        decoder = BatchNormalization()(decoder)

        decoder = Conv2DTranspose(filters=32,
                                  kernel_size=(3, 3),
                                  strides=2,
                                  padding='same')(decoder)
        decoder = LeakyReLU(alpha=alpha)(decoder)
        decoder = BatchNormalization()(decoder)

        decoder = Conv2DTranspose(filters=1,
                                  kernel_size=(3, 3),
                                  padding='same')(decoder)
        outputs = Activation('sigmoid')(decoder)

        decoder_model = Model(decoder_input, outputs)
```

4. Finally, define the autoencoder itself and return the three models:

```
        encoder_model_output = encoder_model(inputs)
        decoder_model_output =
        decoder_model(encoder_model_output)
        autoencoder_model = Model(inputs,
                                  decoder_model_output)

        return encoder_model, decoder_model, autoencoder_
    model
```

5.  Define the `plot_original_vs_generated()` function, which creates a comparative mosaic of the original and generated images. We'll use this function later to show the noisy images and their restored counterparts. Similar to `build_autoencoder()`, this function works in the same way we defined it in the *Creating a simple fully connected autoencoder* recipe, so if you want a detailed explanation, please review that recipe:

```python
def plot_original_vs_generated(original, generated):
    num_images = 15
    sample = np.random.randint(0, len(original),
                               num_images)
```

6.  Define an inner helper function that will stack a sample of images in a 3x5 grid:

```python
def stack(data):
    images = data[sample]
    return np.vstack([np.hstack(images[:5]),
                      np.hstack(images[5:10]),
                      np.hstack(images[10:15])])
```

7.  Define a function that will put custom text on top of an image, in a certain location:

```python
def add_text(image, text, position):
    pt1 = position
    pt2 = (pt1[0] + 10 + (len(text) * 22),
           pt1[1] - 45)
    cv2.rectangle(image,
                  pt1,
                  pt2,
                  (255, 255, 255),
                  -1)
    cv2.putText(image, text,
                position,
                fontFace=cv2.FONT_HERSHEY_SIMPLEX,
                fontScale=1.3,
                color=(0, 0, 0),
                thickness=4)
```

8. Create the mosaic with both the original and the generated images, label each sub-grid, and display the result:

```
original = stack(original)
generated = stack(generated)

mosaic = np.vstack([original,
                    generated])
mosaic = cv2.resize(mosaic, (860, 860),
                    interpolation=cv2.INTER_AREA)
mosaic = cv2.cvtColor(mosaic, cv2.COLOR_GRAY2BGR)

add_text(mosaic, 'Original', (50, 100))
add_text(mosaic, 'Generated', (50, 520))

cv2.imshow('Mosaic', mosaic)
cv2.waitKey(0)
```

9. Load `Fashion-MNIST` using TensorFlow's handy function. We will only keep the images since the labels are unnecessary:

```
(X_train, _), (X_test, _) = fashion_mnist.load_data()
```

10. Normalize the images and add a single color channel to them using `np.expand_dims()`:

```
X_train = X_train.astype('float32') / 255.0
X_test = X_test.astype('float32') / 255.0

X_train = np.expand_dims(X_train, axis=-1)
X_test = np.expand_dims(X_test, axis=-1)
```

11. Generate two tensors with the same dimensions as `X_train` and `X_test`, respectively. These will correspond to random **Gaussian** noise that has a mean and standard deviation equal to `0.5`:

```
train_noise = np.random.normal(loc=0.5, scale=0.5,
                               size=X_train.shape)
test_noise = np.random.normal(loc=0.5, scale=0.5,
                              size=X_test.shape)
```

12. Purposely damage both X_train and X_test by adding train_noise and test_noise, respectively. Make sure that the values remain between 0 and 1 using np.clip():

```
X_train_noisy = np.clip(X_train + train_noise, 0, 1)
X_test_noisy = np.clip(X_test + test_noise, 0, 1)
```

13. Create the autoencoder and compile it. We'll use 'adam' as our optimizer and 'mse' as our loss function, given that we're interested in reducing the error instead of improving accuracy:

```
_, _, autoencoder = build_autoencoder(encoding_size=128)
autoencoder.compile(optimizer='adam', loss='mse')
```

14. Fit the model for 300 epochs, on batches of 1024 noisy images at a time. Notice that the features are the noisy images, while the labels or targets are the original ones, prior to being damaged:

```
EPOCHS = 300
BATCH_SIZE = 1024
autoencoder.fit(X_train_noisy, X_train,
                epochs=EPOCHS,
                batch_size=BATCH_SIZE,
                shuffle=True,
                validation_data=(X_test_noisy,X_test))
```

15. Make predictions with the trained model. Reshape both the noisy and generated images back to 28x28, and scale them up to the [0, 255] range:

```
predictions = autoencoder.predict(X_test)

original_shape = (X_test_noisy.shape[0], 28, 28)
predictions = predictions.reshape(original_shape)
X_test_noisy = X_test_noisy.reshape(original_shape)

predictions = (predictions * 255.0).astype('uint8')
X_test_noisy = (X_test_noisy * 255.0).astype('uint8')
```

16. Finally, display the mosaic of noisy versus restored images:

```
plot_original_vs_generated(X_test_noisy, predictions)
```

Here's the result:

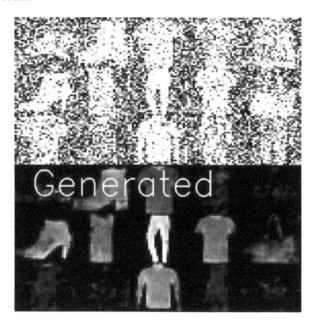

Figure 5.3 – Mosaic of noisy images (top) versus the ones restored by the network (bottom)

Look how damaged the images at the top are! The good news is that, in most instances, the autoencoder did a good job of restoring them. However, it couldn't denoise the images closer to the edges of the mosaic properly, which is a sign that more experimentation can be done to improve their performance (to be fair, these bad examples are hard to discern, even for humans).

## How it works...

The novelty in this recipe is the practical use of the convolutional autoencoder. Both the network and other building blocks have been covered in depth in the last two recipes, so let's focus on the denoising problem itself.

To recreate a real-life scenario of damaged images, we added a heavy amount of Gaussian noise to both the training and test sets in the Fashion-MNIST dataset. This kind of noise is known as salt and pepper because the damaged image looks as though it had these seasonings spilled all over it.

To teach our autoencoder how the images once looked, we used the noisy ones as the features and the originals as the target or labels. This way, after 300 epochs, the network learned an encoding capable of, on many occasions, mapping salt and peppered instances to satisfyingly restored versions of them.

Nonetheless, the model is not perfect, as we saw in the mosaic, where the network was unable to restore the images at the edges of the grid. This is a demonstration of how difficult repairing a damaged image can be.

# Spotting outliers using autoencoders

Another great application of autoencoders is outlier detection. The idea behind this use case is that the autoencoder will learn an encoding with a very small error for the most common classes in a dataset, while its ability to reproduce scarcely represented categories (outliers) will be much more error-prone.

With this premise in mind, in this recipe, we'll rely on a convolutional autoencoder to detect outliers in a subsample of `Fashion-MNIST`.

Let's begin!

## Getting ready

To install `OpenCV`, use the following `pip` command:

```
$> pip install opencv-contrib-python
```

We'll rely on TensorFlow's built-in convenience functions to load the `Fashion-MNIST` dataset.

## How to do it...

Follow these steps to complete this recipe:

1.  Import the required packages:

```
import cv2
import numpy as np
from sklearn.model_selection import train_test_split
from tensorflow.keras import Model
from tensorflow.keras.datasets import fashion_mnist as
fmnist
from tensorflow.keras.layers import *
```

2.  Set a random seed to guarantee reproducibility:

```
SEED = 84
np.random.seed(SEED)
```

3.  Define a function that will build the autoencoder architecture. This function follows the same structure we studied in the *Creating a convolutional autoencoder* recipe, so if you want a deeper explanation, please go back to that recipe. Let's start by creating the encoder model:

```
def build_autoencoder(input_shape=(28, 28, 1),
                      encoding_size=96,
                      alpha=0.2):
    inputs = Input(shape=input_shape)
    encoder = Conv2D(filters=32,
                     kernel_size=(3, 3),
                     strides=2,
                     padding='same')(inputs)
    encoder = LeakyReLU(alpha=alpha)(encoder)
    encoder = BatchNormalization()(encoder)
    encoder = Conv2D(filters=64,
                     kernel_size=(3, 3),
                     strides=2,
                     padding='same')(encoder)
    encoder = LeakyReLU(alpha=alpha)(encoder)
    encoder = BatchNormalization()(encoder)

    encoder_output_shape = encoder.shape
    encoder = Flatten()(encoder)
    encoder_output = Dense(encoding_size)(encoder)

    encoder_model = Model(inputs, encoder_output)
```

4.  Next, build the decoder:

```
    decoder_input = Input(shape=(encoding_size,))
    target_shape = tuple(encoder_output_shape[1:])
    decoder = Dense(np.prod(target_shape))(decoder_input)
    decoder = Reshape(target_shape)(decoder)
```

```
decoder = Conv2DTranspose(filters=64,
                          kernel_size=(3, 3),
                          strides=2,
                          padding='same')(decoder)
decoder = LeakyReLU(alpha=alpha)(decoder)
decoder = BatchNormalization()(decoder)

decoder = Conv2DTranspose(filters=32,
                          kernel_size=(3, 3),
                          strides=2,
                          padding='same')(decoder)
decoder = LeakyReLU(alpha=alpha)(decoder)
decoder = BatchNormalization()(decoder)

decoder = Conv2DTranspose(filters=1,
                          kernel_size=(3, 3),
                          padding='same')(decoder)
outputs = Activation('sigmoid')(decoder)

decoder_model = Model(decoder_input, outputs)
```

5.  Lastly, build the autoencoder and return the three models:

```
encoder_model_output = encoder_model(inputs)
decoder_model_output =
decoder_model(encoder_model_output)
autoencoder_model = Model(inputs,
                          decoder_model_output)

return encoder_model, decoder_model, autoencoder_
model
```

6. Next, define a function that will contrive a dataset of two classes, where one of them represents an anomaly or outlier. Start by selecting the instances corresponding to the two classes of interest, and then shuffle them to break any possible ordering bias:

```
def create_anomalous_dataset(features,
                             labels,
                             regular_label,
                             anomaly_label,
                             corruption_proportion=0.01):
    regular_data_idx = np.where(labels ==
                                regular_label)[0]
    anomalous_data_idx = np.where(labels ==
                                  anomaly_label)[0]

    np.random.shuffle(regular_data_idx)
    np.random.shuffle(anomalous_data_idx)
```

7. Next, from the anomalous category, select a number of instances proportional to `corruption_proportion`. Finally, create the final dataset by merging the regular instances with the outliers:

```
    num_anomalies = int(len(regular_data_idx) *
                        corruption_proportion)
    anomalous_data_idx =
            anomalous_data_idx[:num_anomalies]

    data = np.vstack([features[regular_data_idx],
                      features[anomalous_data_idx]])
    np.random.shuffle(data)

    return data
```

8. Load `Fashion-MNIST`. Merge both the train and test sets into a single dataset:

```
(X_train, y_train), (X_test, y_test) = fmnist.load_data()
X = np.vstack([X_train, X_test])
y = np.hstack([y_train, y_test])
```

9.  Define the regular and anomalous labels, and then create the anomalous dataset:

```
REGULAR_LABEL = 5  # Sandal
ANOMALY_LABEL = 0  # T-shirt/top


data = create_anomalous_dataset(X, y,
                                REGULAR_LABEL,
                                ANOMALY_LABEL)
```

10. Add a channel dimension to the dataset, normalize it, and divide it into 80% for training and 20% for testing:

```
data = np.expand_dims(data, axis=-1)
data = data.astype('float32') / 255.0
X_train, X_test = train_test_split(data,
                                   train_size=0.8,
                                   random_state=SEED)
```

11. Build the autoencoder and compile it. We'll use 'adam' as the optimizer and 'mse' as the loss function since this gives us a good measure of the model's error:

```
_, _, autoencoder = build_autoencoder(encoding_size=256)
autoencoder.compile(optimizer='adam', loss='mse')
```

12. Train the autoencoder for 300 epochs, on batches of 1024 images at a time:

```
EPOCHS = 300
BATCH_SIZE = 1024
autoencoder.fit(X_train, X_train,
                epochs=EPOCHS,
                batch_size=BATCH_SIZE,
                validation_data=(X_test, X_test))
```

13. Make predictions on the data to find the outliers. We'll compute the mean squared error between the original image and the one produced by the autoencoder:

```
decoded = autoencoder.predict(data)
mses = []
for original, generated in zip(data, decoded):
    mse = np.mean((original - generated) ** 2)
    mses.append(mse)
```

14. Select the indices of the images with errors greater than the 99.9% quantile. These will be our outliers:

```
threshold = np.quantile(mses, 0.999)
outlier_idx = np.where(np.array(mses) >= threshold)[0]
print(f'Number of outliers: {len(outlier_idx)}')
```

15. Save a comparative image of the original and generated images for each outlier:

```
decoded = (decoded * 255.0).astype('uint8')
data = (data * 255.0).astype('uint8')

for i in outlier_idx:
    image = np.hstack([data[i].reshape(28, 28),
                       decoded[i].reshape(28, 28)])
    cv2.imwrite(f'{i}.jpg', image)
```

Here's an example of an outlier:

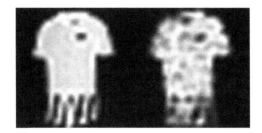

Figure 5.4 – Left: Original outlier. Right: Reconstructed image.

As we can see, we can harness the knowledge stored in the encoding learned by the autoencoder to easily detect anomalous or uncommon images in a dataset. We'll look at this in more detail in the next section.

## How it works...

The idea behind this recipe is very simple: outliers, by definition, are rare occurrences of an event or class within a dataset. Therefore, when we train an autoencoder on a dataset that contains outliers, it won't have sufficient time nor examples to learn a proper representation of them.

By leveraging the low confidence (in other words, the high error) the network will display when reconstructing anomalous images (in this example, T-shirts), we can select the worst copies in order to spot outliers.

However, for this technique to work, the autoencoder must be great at reconstructing the regular classes (for instance, sandals); otherwise, the false positive rate will be too high.

# Creating an inverse image search index with deep learning

Because the whole point of an autoencoder is to learn an encoding or a low-dimensional representation of a set of images, they make for great feature extractors. Furthermore, we can use them as the perfect building blocks of image search indices, as we'll discover in this recipe.

## Getting ready

Let's install `OpenCV` with `pip`. We'll use it to visualize the outputs of our autoencoder, in order to visually assess the effectiveness of the image search index:

```
$> pip install opencv-python
```

We'll start implementing the recipe in the next section.

## How to do it...

Follow these steps to create your own image search index:

1. Import the necessary libraries:

```
import cv2
import numpy as np
from tensorflow.keras import Model
from tensorflow.keras.datasets import fashion_mnist
from tensorflow.keras.layers import *
```

2. Define `build_autoencoder()`, which instantiates the autoencoder. First, let's assemble the encoder part:

```
def build_autoencoder(input_shape=(28, 28, 1),
                      encoding_size=32,
                      alpha=0.2):
    inputs = Input(shape=input_shape)
    encoder = Conv2D(filters=32,
                     kernel_size=(3, 3),
```

```
                        strides=2,
                        padding='same')(inputs)
        encoder = LeakyReLU(alpha=alpha)(encoder)
        encoder = BatchNormalization()(encoder)
        encoder = Conv2D(filters=64,
                        kernel_size=(3, 3),
                        strides=2,
                        padding='same')(encoder)
        encoder = LeakyReLU(alpha=alpha)(encoder)
        encoder = BatchNormalization()(encoder)

        encoder_output_shape = encoder.shape
        encoder = Flatten()(encoder)
        encoder_output = Dense(units=encoding_size,
                            name='encoder_output')
    (encoder)
```

3. The next step is to define the decoder portion:

```
        target_shape = tuple(encoder_output_shape[1:])
        decoder = Dense(np.prod(target_shape))(encoder _
    output)
        decoder = Reshape(target_shape)(decoder)

        decoder = Conv2DTranspose(filters=64,
                                kernel_size=(3, 3),
                                strides=2,
                                padding='same')(decoder)
        decoder = LeakyReLU(alpha=alpha)(decoder)
        decoder = BatchNormalization()(decoder)

        decoder = Conv2DTranspose(filters=32,
                                kernel_size=(3, 3),
                                strides=2,
                                padding='same')(decoder)
        decoder = LeakyReLU(alpha=alpha)(decoder)
        decoder = BatchNormalization()(decoder)
```

```
decoder = Conv2DTranspose(filters=1,
                          kernel_size=(3, 3),
                          padding='same')(decoder)
outputs = Activation(activation='sigmoid',

                     name='decoder_output')(decoder)
```

4.  Finally, build the autoencoder and return it:

```
autoencoder_model = Model(inputs, outputs)
return autoencoder_model
```

5.  Define a function that will compute the Euclidean distance between two vectors:

```
def euclidean_dist(x, y):
    return np.linalg.norm(x - y)
```

6.  Define the search() function, which uses the search index (a dictionary of feature vectors paired with their corresponding images) to retrieve the most similar results to a query vector:

```
def search(query_vector, search_index,
           max_results=16):
    vectors = search_index['features']
    results = []

    for i in range(len(vectors)):
        distance = euclidean_dist(query_vector,
                                  vectors[i])
        results.append((distance,
                        search_index['images'][i]))

    results = sorted(results,
                     key=lambda p: p[0])[:max_results]
    return results
```

7. Load the `Fashion-MNIST` dataset. Keep only the images:

```
(X_train, _), (X_test, _) = fashion_mnist.load_data()
```

8. Normalize the images and add a color channel dimension:

```
X_train = X_train.astype('float32') / 255.0
X_test = X_test.astype('float32') / 255.0
X_train = np.expand_dims(X_train, axis=-1)
X_test = np.expand_dims(X_test, axis=-1)
```

9. Build the autoencoder and compile it. We'll use `'adam'` as the optimizer and `'mse'` as the loss function since this gives us a good measure of the model's error:

```
autoencoder = build_autoencoder()
autoencoder.compile(optimizer='adam', loss='mse')
```

10. Train the autoencoder for 10 epochs, on batches of `512` images at a time:

```
EPOCHS = 50
BATCH_SIZE = 512
autoencoder.fit(X_train, X_train,
                epochs=EPOCHS,
                batch_size=BATCH_SIZE,
                shuffle=True,
                validation_data=(X_test, X_test))
```

11. Create a new model, which we'll use as a feature extractor. It'll receive the same inputs as the autoencoder and will output the encoding learned by the autoencoder. In essence, we are using the encoder part of the autoencoder to turn images into vectors:

```
fe_input = autoencoder.input
fe_output = autoencoder.get_layer('encoder_output').output
feature_extractor = Model(inputs=fe_input,
                          outputs=fe_output)
```

12. Create the search index, comprised of the feature vectors of `X_train`, along with the original images (which must be reshaped back to 28x28 and rescaled to the range [0, 255]):

```
train_vectors = feature_extractor.predict(X_train)

X_train = (X_train * 255.0).astype('uint8')
X_train = X_train.reshape((X_train.shape[0], 28, 28))
search_index = {
    'features': train_vectors,
    'images': X_train
}
```

13. Compute the feature vectors of `X_test`, which we will use as our sample of query images. Also, reshape `X_test` to 28x28 and rescale its values to the range [0, 255]:

```
test_vectors = feature_extractor.predict(X_test)

X_test = (X_test * 255.0).astype('uint8')
X_test = X_test.reshape((X_test.shape[0], 28, 28))
```

14. Select 16 random test images (with their corresponding feature vectors) to use as queries:

```
sample_indices = np.random.randint(0, X_test.shape[0],16)
sample_images = X_test[sample_indices]
sample_queries = test_vectors[sample_indices]
```

15. Perform a search for each of the images in the test sample and save a side-to-side visual comparison of the test query, along with the results fetched from the index (which, remember, is comprised of the train data):

```
for i, (vector, image) in \
        enumerate(zip(sample_queries, sample_images)):
    results = search(vector, search_index)
    results = [r[1] for r in results]
    query_image = cv2.resize(image, (28 * 4, 28 * 4),
                             interpolation=cv2.INTER_AREA)

    results_mosaic =
```

```
np.vstack([np.hstack(results[0:4]),
           np.hstack(results[4:8]),
           np.hstack(results[8:12]),
           np.hstack(results[12:16])])
result_image = np.hstack([query_image,
                          results_mosaic])
cv2.imwrite(f'{i}.jpg', result_image)
```

Here's an example of a search result:

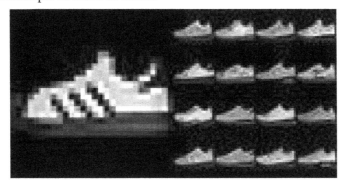

Figure 5.5 – Left: Query image of a shoe. Right: The best 16 search results, all of which contain shoes too

As the preceding image demonstrates, our image search index is a success! We'll see how it works in the next section.

## How it works...

In this recipe, we learned how to leverage the distinguishing trait of an autoencoder, which is to learn an encoding that greatly compresses the information in the input images, resulting in minimal loss of information. Then, we used the encoder part of a convolutional autoencoder to extract the features of fashion item photos and construct an image search index.

By doing this, using this index as a search engine is as easy as computing the Euclidean distance between a query vector (corresponding to a query image) and all the images in the index, selecting only those that are closest to the query.

The most important aspect in our solution is to train an autoencoder that is good enough to produce high-quality vectors, since they make or break the search engine.

## See also

The implementation is based on the great work of Dong *et al.*, whose paper can be read here: `https://github.com/PacktPublishing/Tensorflow-2.0-Computer-Vision-Cookbook/tree/master/ch5/recipe5`.

# Implementing a variational autoencoder

Some of the most modern and complex use cases of autoencoders are **Variational Autoencoders (VAEs)**. They differ from the rest of the autoencoders in that, instead of learning an arbitrary function, they learn a probability distribution of the input images. We can then sample this distribution to produce new, unseen data points.

A **VAE** is, in fact, a generative model, and in this recipe, we'll implement one.

## Getting ready

We don't need any special preparation for this recipe, so let's get started right away!

## How to do it...

Follow these steps to learn how to implement and train a **VAE**:

1.  Import the necessary packages:

```python
import matplotlib.pyplot as plt
import numpy as np
import tensorflow as tf
from tensorflow.keras import Model
from tensorflow.keras import backend as K
from tensorflow.keras.datasets import fashion_mnist
from tensorflow.keras.layers import *
from tensorflow.keras.losses import mse
from tensorflow.keras.optimizers import Adam
```

2. Because we'll be using the `tf.function` annotation soon, we must tell TensorFlow to run functions eagerly:

```
tf.config.experimental_run_functions_eagerly(True)
```

3. Define a class that will encapsulate our implementation of the **variational autoencoder**. The constructor receives the dimensions of the input vector, the dimensions of the intermediate encoding, and the dimensions of the latent space (the probability distribution):

```
class VAE(object):
    def __init__(self,
                 original_dimension=784,
                 encoding_dimension=512,
                 latent_dimension=2):
        self.original_dimension = original_dimension
        self.encoding_dimension = encoding_dimension
        self.latent_dimension = latent_dimension
```

`self.z_log_var` and `self.z_mean` are the parameters of the latent Gaussian distribution that we'll learn:

```
        self.z_log_var = None
        self.z_mean = None
```

4. Define some members that will store the inputs and outputs of the **VAE** network, as well as the three models; that is, `encoder`, `decoder`, and `vae`:

```
        self.inputs = None
        self.outputs = None

        self.encoder = None
        self.decoder = None
        self.vae = None
```

5. Define the `build_vae()` method, which builds the variational autoencoder architecture (notice that we are using dense layers instead of convolutions):

```
    def build_vae(self):
        self.inputs = Input(shape=(self.original_
    dimension,))
        x = Dense(self.encoding_dimension)(self.inputs)
```

```
x = ReLU()(x)
self.z_mean = Dense(self.latent_dimension)(x)
self.z_log_var = Dense(self.latent_dimension)(x)

z = Lambda(sampling)([self.z_mean,
                      self.z_log_var])
self.encoder = Model(self.inputs,
                     [self.z_mean,
                      self.z_log_var, z])
```

Notice that the encoder is just a fully connected network that produces three outputs: `self.z_mean`, which is the mean of the Gaussian distribution we are training to model, `self.z_log_var`, which is the logarithmic variance of this distribution, and `z`, a sample point in that probability space. In order to generate the `z` simple, we must wrap a custom function, `sampling()` (implemented in *Step 5*), in a `Lambda` layer.

6.  Next, define the decoder:

```
latent_inputs = Input(shape=(self.latent_
dimension,))
x = Dense(self.encoding_dimension)(latent_inputs)
x = ReLU()(x)
self.outputs = Dense(self.original_dimension)(x)
self.outputs = Activation('sigmoid')(self.
outputs)
self.decoder = Model(latent_inputs,
                     self.outputs)
```

7.  The decoder is just another fully connected network. The decoder will take samples from the latent dimension in order to reconstruct the inputs. Finally, connect the encoder and decoder to create the **VAE** model:

```
self.outputs = self.encoder(self.inputs)[2]
self.outputs = self.decoder(self.outputs)
self.vae = Model(self.inputs, self.outputs)
```

8.  Define the `train()` method, which trains the variational autoencoder. Therefore, it receives the train and test data, as well as the number of epochs and the batch size:

```
@tf.function
def train(self, X_train,
          X_test,
          epochs=50,
          batch_size=64):
```

9.  Define the reconstruction loss as the MSE between the inputs and outputs:

```
reconstruction_loss = mse(self.inputs,
                          self.outputs)
reconstruction_loss *= self.original_dimension
```

`kl_loss` is the **Kullback-Leibler** divergence between the learned latent distribution and the prior distribution. It is used as a regularization term for `reconstruction_loss`:

```
kl_loss = (1 + self.z_log_var -
          K.square(self.z_mean) -
          K.exp(self.z_log_var))
kl_loss = K.sum(kl_loss, axis=-1)
kl_loss *= -0.5


vae_loss = K.mean(reconstruction_loss + kl_loss)
```

10. Configure the `self.vae` model so that it uses `vae_loss` and `Adam()` as the optimizer (with a learning rate of 0.003). Then, fit the network over the specified number of epochs. Finally, return the three models:

```
self.vae.add_loss(vae_loss)
self.vae.compile(optimizer=Adam(lr=1e-3))
self.vae.fit(X_train,
             epochs=epochs,
             batch_size=batch_size,
             validation_data=(X_test, None))


return self.encoder, self.decoder, self.vae
```

11. Define a function that will generate a random sample or point from the latent space, given the two relevant parameters (passed in the `arguments` array); that is, `z_mean` and `z_log_var`:

```
def sampling(arguments):
    z_mean, z_log_var = arguments
    batch = K.shape(z_mean)[0]
    dimension = K.int_shape(z_mean)[1]

    epsilon = K.random_normal(shape=(batch, dimension))
    return z_mean + K.exp(0.5 * z_log_var) * epsilon
```

Notice that `epsilon` is a random Gaussian vector.

12. Define a function that will generate and plot images generated from the latent space. This will give us an idea of the **shapes** that are closer to the distribution, and the ones that are nearer to the tails of the curve:

```
def generate_and_plot(decoder, grid_size=5):
    cell_size = 28
    figure_shape = (grid_size * cell_size,
                    grid_size * cell_size)
    figure = np.zeros(figure_shape)
```

13. Create a range of values that span from -4 to 4 in both the X and Y axes. We'll use these to generate and visualize samples at each location:

```
    grid_x = np.linspace(-4, 4, grid_size)
    grid_y = np.linspace(-4, 4, grid_size)[::-1]
```

14. Use the decoder to generate a new sample for each combination of `z_mean` and `z_log_var`:

```
    for i, z_log_var in enumerate(grid_y):
        for j, z_mean in enumerate(grid_x):
            z_sample = np.array([[z_mean, z_log_var]])
            generated = decoder.predict(z_sample)[0]
```

15. Reshape the sample and place it in the corresponding cell in the grid:

```
fashion_item =
            generated.reshape(cell_size,
                              cell_size)

y_slice = slice(i * cell_size,
                (i + 1) * cell_size)
x_slice = slice(j * cell_size,
                (j + 1) * cell_size)
figure[y_slice, x_slice] = fashion_item
```

16. Add the ticks and axes labels, and then display the plot:

```
plt.figure(figsize=(10, 10))
start = cell_size // 2
end = (grid_size - 2) * cell_size + start + 1
pixel_range = np.arange(start, end, cell_size)

sample_range_x = np.round(grid_x, 1)
sample_range_y = np.round(grid_y, 1)

plt.xticks(pixel_range, sample_range_x)
plt.yticks(pixel_range, sample_range_y)
plt.xlabel('z_mean')
plt.ylabel('z_log_var')
plt.imshow(figure)
plt.show()
```

17. Load the `Fashion-MNIST` dataset. Normalize the images and add a color channel to them:

```
(X_train, _), (X_test, _) = fashion_mnist.load_data()

X_train = X_train.astype('float32') / 255.0
X_test = X_test.astype('float32') / 255.0
```

```
X_train = X_train.reshape((X_train.shape[0], -1))
X_test = X_test.reshape((X_test.shape[0], -1))
```

18. Instantiate and build the **variational autoencoder**:

```
vae = VAE(original_dimension=784,
          encoding_dimension=512,
          latent_dimension=2)
vae.build_vae()
```

19. Train the models for 100 epochs:

```
_, decoder_model, vae_model = vae.train(X_train, X_test,
                                        epochs=100)
```

20. Use the decoder to generate new images and plot the result:

```
generate_and_plot(decoder_model, grid_size=7)
```

Here's the result:

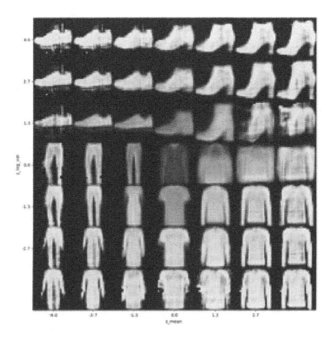

Figure 5.6 – Visualization of the latent space learned by the VAE

Here, we can see the collection of points that comprise the latent space and the corresponding clothing item for each of these points. This is a representation of the probability distribution the network learned, in which the item at the center of such a distribution resembles a T-shirt, while the ones at the edges look more like pants, sweaters, and shoes.

Let's move on to the next section.

## How it works...

In this recipe, we learned that a **variational autoencoder** is an advanced, more complex type of autoencoder that, instead of learning an arbitrary, vanilla function to map inputs to outputs, learns a probability distribution of the inputs. This gives it the ability to generate new, unseen images that make it a precursor of more modern generative models, such as **Generative Adversarial Networks** (**GANs**).

The architecture is not that different from the others autoencoder we studied in this chapter. The key to understanding the power of a **VAE** is that the link between the encoder and the decoder is a random sample, z, which we generate using the `sampling()` function, within a Lambda layer.

This means that in each iteration, the whole network is optimizing the z_mean and z_log_var parameters so that it closely resembles the probability distribution of the inputs. It does this because it's the only way the random samples (z) are going to be of such high quality that the decoder will be able to generate better, more realistic outputs.

## See also

A key component we can use to tune the **VAE** is the **Kullback-Leibler** divergence, which you can read more about here: `https://en.wikipedia.org/wiki/Kullback%E2%80%93Leibler_divergence`.

Note that **VAE**s are the perfect runway to generative models, which we'll cover in depth in the next chapter!

# 6
# Generative Models and Adversarial Attacks

Being able to differentiate between two or more classes is certainly impressive, and a healthy sign that deep neural networks do, in fact, learn.

But if traditional classification is impressive, then producing new content is staggering! That definitely requires a superior understanding of the domain. So, are there neural networks capable of such a feat? You bet there are!

In this chapter, we'll study one of the most captivating and promising types of neural networks: **Generative Adversarial Networks** (**GANs**). As the term implies, these networks are actually a system comprised of two sub-networks: the generator and the discriminator. The job of the generator is to produce images so good that they *could* come from the original distribution (but actually don't; they're generated from scratch), thereby fooling the discriminator, whose task is to discern between real and fake images.

**GANs** are the tip of the spear in areas such as semi-supervised learning and image-to-image translation, both topics that we will cover in this chapter. As a complement, the final recipe in this chapter teaches us how to perform an adversarial attack on a network using the **Fast Gradient Signed Method** (**FGSM**).

The recipes that we will cover in this chapter are as follows:

- Implementing a deep convolutional GAN

- Using a DCGAN for semi-supervised learning

- Translating images with Pix2Pix

- Translating unpaired images with CycleGAN

- Implementing an adversarial attack using the Fast Gradient Signed Method

# Technical requirements

GANs are great, but also extremely taxing in terms of computing power. Therefore, a GPU is a must-have in order to work on these recipes (and even then, most will run for several hours). In the *Getting ready* section, you'll find the preparations that are necessary, if any, for each recipe. The code for this chapter is available here: `https://github.com/PacktPublishing/Tensorflow-2.0-Computer-Vision-Cookbook/tree/master/ch6`.

Check out the following link to see the Code in Action video: `https://bit.ly/35Z8IYn`.

# Implementing a deep convolutional GAN

A **GAN** is comprised, in its simplest form, of two networks, a generator and a discriminator. The discriminator is just a regular **Convolutional Neural Network (CNN)** that must solve the binary classification problem of distinguishing real images from fakes. The generator, on the other hand, is similar to the decoder in an autoencoder because it has to produce an image from a `seed`, which is just a vector of Gaussian noise.

In this recipe, we'll implement a **Deep Convolutional Generative Adversarial Network (DCGAN)** to produce images akin to the ones present in `EMNIST`, a dataset that extends the well-known `MNIST` dataset with uppercase and lowercase handwritten letters on top of the digits from 0 to 9.

Let's begin!

# Getting ready

We'll need to install `tensorflow-datasets` to access `EMNIST` more easily. Also, in order to display a nice progress bar during the training of our GAN, we'll use `tqdm`.

Both dependencies can be installed as follows:

```
$> pip install tensorflow-datasets tqdm
```

We are good to go!

# How to do it…

Perform the following steps to implement a DCGAN on `EMNIST`:

1.  Import the necessary dependencies:

    ```
    import matplotlib.pyplot as plt
    import tensorflow as tf
    import tensorflow_datasets as tfds
    from tensorflow.keras.layers import *
    from tensorflow.keras.losses import BinaryCrossentropy
    from tensorflow.keras.models import Model
    from tensorflow.keras.optimizers import Adam
    from tqdm import tqdm
    ```

2.  Define an alias for the `AUTOTUNE` setting, which we'll use later to determine the number of parallel calls when processing the images in the dataset:

    ```
    AUTOTUNE = tf.data.experimental.AUTOTUNE
    ```

3.  Define a `DCGAN()` class to encapsulate our implementation. The constructor creates the discriminator, generator, loss function, and the respective optimizers for both sub-networks:

    ```
    class DCGAN(object):
        def __init__(self):
            self.loss = BinaryCrossentropy(from_logits=True)
            self.generator = self.create_generator()
            self.discriminator = self.create_discriminator()
            self.generator_opt = Adam(learning_rate=1e-4)
            self.discriminator_opt = Adam(learning_rate=1e-4)
    ```

4.  Define a static method to create the generator network. It reconstructs a 28x28x1 image from an input tensor of 100 elements. Notice the use of transposed convolutions (`Conv2DTranspose`) to expand the output volumes as we go deeper into the network. Also, notice the activation is `'tanh'`, which means the outputs will be in the range [-1, 1]:

```
@staticmethod
def create_generator(alpha=0.2):
    input = Input(shape=(100,))
    x = Dense(units=7 * 7 * 256,
              use_bias=False)(input)
    x = LeakyReLU(alpha=alpha)(x)
    x = BatchNormalization()(x)

    x = Reshape((7, 7, 256))(x)
```

5.  Add the first transposed convolution block, with 128 filters:

```
    x = Conv2DTranspose(filters=128,
                        strides=(1, 1),
                        kernel_size=(5, 5),
                        padding='same',
                        use_bias=False)(x)
    x = LeakyReLU(alpha=alpha)(x)
    x = BatchNormalization()(x)
```

6.  Create the second transposed convolution block, with 64 filters:

```
    x = Conv2DTranspose(filters=64,
                        strides=(2, 2),
                        kernel_size=(5, 5),
                        padding='same',
                        use_bias=False)(x)
    x = LeakyReLU(alpha=alpha)(x)
    x = BatchNormalization()(x)
```

7. Add the last transposed convolution block, with only one filter, corresponding to the output of the network:

```
x = Conv2DTranspose(filters=1,
                    strides=(2, 2),
                    kernel_size=(5, 5),
                    padding='same',
                    use_bias=False)(x)
output = Activation('tanh')(x)

return Model(input, output)
```

8. Define a static method to create the discriminator. This architecture is a regular CNN:

```
@staticmethod
def create_discriminator(alpha=0.2, dropout=0.3):
    input = Input(shape=(28, 28, 1))
    x = Conv2D(filters=64,
               kernel_size=(5, 5),
               strides=(2, 2),
               padding='same')(input)
    x = LeakyReLU(alpha=alpha)(x)
    x = Dropout(rate=dropout)(x)

    x = Conv2D(filters=128,
               kernel_size=(5, 5),
               strides=(2, 2),
               padding='same')(x)
    x = LeakyReLU(alpha=alpha)(x)
    x = Dropout(rate=dropout)(x)

    x = Flatten()(x)
    output = Dense(units=1)(x)

    return Model(input, output)
```

9. Define a method to calculate the discriminator's loss, which is the sum of the real and fake losses:

```
def discriminator_loss(self, real, fake):
    real_loss = self.loss(tf.ones_like(real), real)
    fake_loss = self.loss(tf.zeros_like(fake), fake)

    return real_loss + fake_loss
```

10. Define a method to calculate the generator's loss:

```
def generator_loss(self, fake):
    return self.loss(tf.ones_like(fake), fake)
```

11. Define a method to perform a single training step. We'll start by generating a vector of random Gaussian noise:

```
@tf.function
def train_step(self, images, batch_size):
    noise = tf.random.normal((batch_size,noise_
dimension))
```

12. Next, pass the random noise to the generator to produce fake images:

```
    with tf.GradientTape() as gen_tape, \
        tf.GradientTape() as dis_tape:
        generated_images = self.generator(noise,
                                training=True)
```

13. Pass the real and fake images to the discriminator and compute the losses of both sub-networks:

```
        real = self.discriminator(images,
                                training=True)
        fake = self.discriminator(generated_images,
                                training=True)

        gen_loss = self.generator_loss(fake)
        disc_loss = self.discriminator_loss(real,
                                fake)
```

14. Compute the gradients:

```
generator_grad = gen_tape \
    .gradient(gen_loss,
            self.generator.trainable_variables)
discriminator_grad = dis_tape \
    .gradient(disc_loss,
            self.discriminator.trainable_
variables)
```

15. Next, apply the gradients using the respective optimizers:

```
opt_args = zip(generator_grad,
            self.generator.trainable_variables)
self.generator_opt.apply_gradients(opt_args)


opt_args = zip(discriminator_grad,

        self.discriminator.trainable_variables)
self.discriminator_opt.apply_gradients(opt_args)
```

16. Finally, define a method to train the whole architecture. Every 10 epochs, we will plot the images the generator produces in order to visually assess their quality:

```
def train(self, dataset, test_seed, epochs,
        batch_size):
    for epoch in tqdm(range(epochs)):
        for image_batch in dataset:
            self.train_step(image_batch,
                        batch_size)


        if epoch == 0 or epoch % 10 == 0:


            generate_and_save_images(self.generator,
                                    epoch,
                                    test_seed)
```

17. Define a function to produce new images, and then save a 4x4 mosaic of them to disk:

```
def generate_and_save_images(model, epoch, test_input):
    predictions = model(test_input, training=False)

    plt.figure(figsize=(4, 4))

    for i in range(predictions.shape[0]):
        plt.subplot(4, 4, i + 1)
        image = predictions[i, :, :, 0] * 127.5 + 127.5
        image = tf.cast(image, tf.uint8)
        plt.imshow(image, cmap='gray')
        plt.axis('off')

    plt.savefig(f'{epoch}.png')
    plt.show()
```

18. Define a function to scale the images that come from the EMNIST dataset to the [-1, 1] interval:

```
def process_image(input):
    image = tf.cast(input['image'], tf.float32)
    image = (image - 127.5) / 127.5
    return image
```

19. Load the EMNIST dataset using tfds. We'll only use the 'train' split, which contains more than 600,000 images. We will also make sure to scale each image to the 'tanh' range:

```
BUFFER_SIZE = 1000
BATCH_SIZE = 512
train_dataset = (tfds
                 .load('emnist', split='train')
                 .map(process_image,
                      num_parallel_calls=AUTOTUNE)
                 .shuffle(BUFFER_SIZE)
                 .batch(BATCH_SIZE))
```

20. Create a test seed that will be used throughout the training of the DCGAN to generate images:

```
noise_dimension = 100
num_examples_to_generate = 16
seed_shape = (num_examples_to_generate,
                noise_dimension)
test_seed = tf.random.normal(seed_shape)
```

21. Finally, instantiate and train a DCGAN() instance for 200 epochs:

```
EPOCHS = 200
dcgan = DCGAN()
dcgan.train(train_dataset, test_seed, EPOCHS, BATCH_SIZE)
```

The first image generated by the GAN will look similar to this, just a collection of shapeless blobs:

Figure 6.1 – Images generated at epoch 0

At the end of the training process, the results are much better:

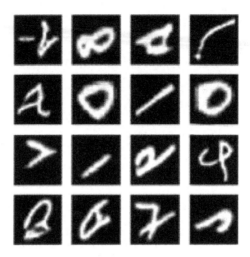

Figure 6.2 – Images generated at epoch 200

In *Figure 6.2*, we can distinguish familiar letters and numbers, including *A*, *d*, *9*, *X*, and *B*. However, in the first row, we notice a couple of ambiguous forms, which is a sign that the generator has room for improvement.

Let's see how it all works in the next section.

## How it works...

In this recipe, we learned that GANs work in tandem and, unlike autoencoders, they work against each other (hence the *adversarial* in the name) instead of cooperating. When our focus is on the generator, the discriminator is just a tool to train the latter, as is the case in this recipe. This means that after training, the discriminator is tossed out.

Our generator is actually a decoder that takes random Gaussian vectors of 100 elements and produces 28x28x1 images that are then passed to the discriminator, a regular CNN, which has to guess whether they are real or fake.

Because our goal is to create the best generator possible, the classification problem the discriminator tries to solve has nothing to do with the actual classes in EMNIST. For this reason, we don't explicitly label the images as real or fake beforehand, but in the `discriminator_loss()` method, where we know that all images in `real` come from EMNIST, and therefore we compute the loss against a tensor of ones (`tf.ones_like(real)`) and, analogously, all images in `fake` are synthetic, and we compute the loss against a tensor of zeros (`tf.zeros_like(fake)`).

The generator, on the other hand, takes into consideration the feedback received from the discriminator when computing its loss to improve its outputs.

It must be noted that the goal here is to achieve an equilibrium, instead of minimizing the loss. Therefore, visual inspection is crucial, and the reason why we save the images the generator produces every 10 epochs.

In the end, we went from random, shapeless blobs at epoch 0 to recognizable digits and letters at epoch 200, although the network can be improved further.

## See also

You can read more about EMNIST here: `https://arxiv.org/abs/1702.05373v1`.

# Using a DCGAN for semi-supervised learning

Data is the most important part of developing any deep learning model. However, good data is often scarce and expensive to acquire. The good news is that GANs can lend us a hand in these situations by artificially producing novel training examples, in a process known as **semi-supervised learning**.

In this recipe, we'll develop a special DCGAN architecture to train a classifier on a very small subset of `Fashion-MNIST` and still achieve a decent performance.

Let's begin, shall we?

## Getting ready

We won't require anything extra to access `Fashion-MNIST` because it comes bundled with TensorFlow. In order to display a nice-looking progress bar, let's install `tqdm`:

```
$> pip install tqdm
```

Let's now move on to the next section to start the recipe's implementation.

## How to do it...

Perform the following steps to complete the recipe:

1.  Let's start by importing the required packages:

    ```
    import numpy as np
    from numpy.random import *
    from tensorflow.keras import backend as K
    ```

```
from tensorflow.keras.datasets import fashion_mnist as
fmnist
from tensorflow.keras.layers import *
from tensorflow.keras.models import Model
from tensorflow.keras.optimizers import Adam
from tqdm import tqdm
```

2.  Define the pick_supervised_subset() function to pick a subset of the
    data. This will allow us to simulate a situation of scarce data, a perfect fit for semi-
    supervised learning:

```
def pick_supervised_subset(feats,
                           labels,
                           n_samples=1000,
                           n_classes=10):
    samples_per_class = int(n_samples / n_classes)

    X = []
    y = []
    for i in range(n_classes):
        class_feats = feats[labels == i]
        class_sample_idx = randint(low=0,

                                   high=len(class_feats),
                                   size=samples_per_class)

        X.extend([class_feats[j] for j in
                  class_sample_idx])
        y.extend([i] * samples_per_class)

    return np.array(X), np.array(y)
```

3.  Now, define a function to select a random sample of data for classification. This
    means that we'll use the labels from the original dataset:

```
def pick_samples_for_classification(feats, labels,
                                    n_samples):
    sample_idx = randint(low=0,
                         high=feats.shape[0],
                         size=n_samples)

    X = np.array([feats[i] for i in sample_idx])
    y = np.array([labels[i] for i in sample_idx])

    return X, y
```

4.  Define the `pick_samples_for_discrimination()` function in order
    to select a random sample for discrimination. The main difference with the last
    function is that the labels here are all 1, indicating that all images are real, which
    clearly indicates that this sample is intended for the discriminator:

```
def pick_samples_for_discrimination(feats, n_samples):
    sample_idx = randint(low=0,
                         high=feats.shape[0],
                         size=n_samples)

    X = np.array([feats[i] for i in sample_idx])
    y = np.ones((n_samples, 1))

    return X, y
```

5.  Implement the `generate_fake_samples()` function to produce a batch of latent points or, put another way, a sample of random noise vectors that the generator will use to generate fake images:

```
def generate_fake_samples(model, latent_size,
                          n_samples):
    z_input = generate_latent_points(latent_size,
                                     n_samples)
    images = model.predict(z_input)
    y = np.zeros((n_samples, 1))
    return images, y
```

6.  Create the `generate_fake_samples()` function to generate fake data using the generator:

```
def generate_fake_samples(model, latent_size,
                          n_samples):
    z_input = generate_latent_points(latent_size,
                                     n_samples)
    images = model.predict(z_input)
    y = np.zeros((n_samples, 1))
    return images, y
```

7.  We are ready to define our semi-supervised DCGAN, which we'll encapsulate in the `SSGAN()` class defined here. We'll start with the constructor:

```
class SSGAN(object):
    def __init__(self,
                 latent_size=100,
                 input_shape=(28, 28, 1),
                 alpha=0.2):
        self.latent_size = latent_size
        self.input_shape = input_shape
        self.alpha = alpha
```

8.  After storing the arguments as members, let's instantiate the discriminators:

```
        (self.classifier,
         self.discriminator) = self._create_
discriminators()
```

9.  Now, compile both the classifier and discriminator models:

```
clf_opt = Adam(learning_rate=2e-4, beta_1=0.5)
self.classifier.compile(
    loss='sparse_categorical_crossentropy',
    optimizer=clf_opt,
    metrics=['accuracy'])

dis_opt = Adam(learning_rate=2e-4, beta_1=0.5)
self.discriminator.compile(loss='binary_
crossentropy',
                            optimizer=dis_opt)
```

10. Create the generator:

```
self.generator = self._create_generator()
```

11. Create the GAN and compile it:

```
self.gan = self._create_gan()
gan_opt = Adam(learning_rate=2e-4, beta_1=0.5)
self.gan.compile(loss='binary_crossentropy',
                  optimizer=gan_opt)
```

12. Define the private `_create_discriminators()` method to create the discriminators. The inner `custom_activation()` function is used to activate the outputs of the classifier model and generate a value between 0 and 1 that will be used to discern whether the image is real or fake:

```
def _create_discriminators(self, num_classes=10):
    def custom_activation(x):
        log_exp_sum = K.sum(K.exp(x), axis=-1,
                            keepdims=True)
        return log_exp_sum / (log_exp_sum + 1.0)
```

13. Define the classifier architecture, which is just a regular softmax-activated CNN:

```
input = Input(shape=self.input_shape)
x = input

for _ in range(3):
```

```
       x = Conv2D(filters=128,
                  kernel_size=(3, 3),
                  strides=2,
                  padding='same')(x)
       x = LeakyReLU(alpha=self.alpha)(x)


   x = Flatten()(x)
   x = Dropout(rate=0.4)(x)
   x = Dense(units=num_classes)(x)
   clf_output = Softmax()(x)
   clf_model = Model(input, clf_output)
```

14. The discriminator shares weights with the classifier, but instead of softmax activating the outputs, it uses the `custom_activation()` function defined previously:

```
   dis_output = Lambda(custom_activation)(x)
   discriminator_model = Model(input, dis_output)
```

15. Return both the classifier and the discriminator:

```
   return clf_model, discriminator_model
```

16. Create the private `_create_generator()` method to implement the generator architecture, which is just a decoder, as explained in the first recipe in this chapter:

```
def _create_generator(self):
    input = Input(shape=(self.latent_size,))


    x = Dense(units=128 * 7 * 7)(input)
    x = LeakyReLU(alpha=self.alpha)(x)
    x = Reshape((7, 7, 128))(x)


    for _ in range(2):
        x = Conv2DTranspose(filters=128,
                            kernel_size=(4, 4),
                            strides=2,
                            padding='same')(x)
        x = LeakyReLU(alpha=self.alpha)(x)
```

```
        x = Conv2D(filters=1,
                   kernel_size=(7, 7),
                   padding='same')(x)
        output = Activation('tanh')(x)

        return Model(input, output)
```

17. Define the private `_create_gan()` method to create the GAN itself, which is just the connection between the generator and the discriminator:

```
    def _create_gan(self):
        self.discriminator.trainable = False
        output = \
            self.discriminator(self.generator.output)

        return Model(self.generator.input, output)
```

18. Finally, define `train()`, a function to train the whole system. We'll start by selecting the subset of `Fashion-MNIST` that we'll train on, and then we'll define the number of batches and training steps required to fit the architecture:

```
    def train(self, X, y, epochs=20, num_batches=100):
        X_sup, y_sup = pick_supervised_subset(X, y)

        batches_per_epoch = int(X.shape[0] / num_batches)
        num_steps = batches_per_epoch * epochs
        num_samples = int(num_batches / 2)
```

19. Pick samples for classification, and use these to fit the classifier:

```
        for _ in tqdm(range(num_steps)):
            X_sup_real, y_sup_real = \
                pick_samples_for_classification(X_sup,
                                                y_sup,
                                                num_samples)
            self.classifier.train_on_batch(X_sup_real,
                                           y_sup_real)
```

20. Pick real samples for discrimination, and use these to fit the discriminator:

```
X_real, y_real = \
        pick_samples_for_discrimination(X,
                                    num_samples)
self.discriminator.train_on_batch(X_real, y_real)
```

21. Use the generator to produce fake data, and use this to fit the discriminator:

```
X_fake, y_fake = \
        generate_fake_samples(self.generator,
                            self.latent_size,
                            num_samples)
self.discriminator.train_on_batch(X_fake,
                                y_fake)
```

22. Generate latent points, and use these to train the GAN:

```
X_gan = generate_latent_points(self.latent_
size,
                num_batches)
y_gan = np.ones((num_batches, 1))
self.gan.train_on_batch(X_gan, y_gan)
```

23. Load `Fashion-MNIST` and normalize both the training and test sets:

```
(X_train, y_train), (X_test, y_test) = fmnist.load_data()
X_train = np.expand_dims(X_train, axis=-1)
X_train = (X_train.astype(np.float32) - 127.5) / 127.5

X_test = np.expand_dims(X_test, axis=-1)
X_test = (X_test.astype(np.float32) - 127.5) / 127.5
```

24. Instantiate an `SSCGAN()` and train it for 30 epochs:

```
ssgan = SSGAN()
ssgan.train(X_train, y_train, epochs=30)
```

25. Report the accuracy of the classifier on both the training and test sets:

```
train_acc = ssgan.classifier.evaluate(X_train,
                                       y_train)[1]
train_acc *= 100
print(f'Train accuracy: {train_acc:.2f}%')

test_acc = ssgan.classifier.evaluate(X_test, y_test)[1]
test_acc *= 100
print(f'Test accuracy: {test_acc:.2f}%')
```

After the training finishes, both the training and test accuracy should be around 83%, which is pretty satisfying if we consider we only used 1,000 examples out of 50,000!

## How it works...

In this recipe, we implemented an architecture quite similar to the one implemented in the *Implementing a deep convolutional GAN* recipe that opened this chapter. The main difference resides in the fact that we have two discriminators: the first one is actually a classifier, which is trained on the small subset of labeled data at our disposal. The other is a regular discriminator, whose sole job is to not be fooled by the generator.

How does the classifier achieve such a respectable performance with so little data? The answer is shared weights. Both the classifier and the discriminator share the same feature extraction layers, differing only in the final output layer, which is activated with a plain old softmax function in the case of the classifier, and with a `Lambda()` layer that wraps our `custom_activation()` function in the case of the discriminator.

This means that these shared weights get updated each time the classifier trains on a batch of labeled data, and also when the discriminator trains on both real and fake images. In the end, we circumvent the data scarcity problem with the aid of the generator.

Pretty impressive, right?

## See also

You can consolidate your understanding of the semi-supervised training approach used in this recipe by reading the paper where it was first proposed: `https://arxiv.org/abs/1606.03498`.

# Translating images with Pix2Pix

One of the most interesting applications of GANs is image-to-image translation, which, as the name suggests, consists of translating the content from one image domain to another (for instance, sketches to photos, black and white images to RGB, and Google Maps to satellite views, among others).

In this recipe, we'll implement a fairly complex conditional adversarial network known as Pix2Pix. We'll focus solely on the practical aspects of the solution, but if you want to get familiar with the literature, check out the *See also* section at the end of the recipe.

## Getting ready

We'll use the `cityscapes` dataset, which is available here: `https://people.eecs.berkeley.edu/~tinghuiz/projects/pix2pix/datasets/cityscapes.tar.gz`. Download it and decompress it in a location of your choosing. For the purposes of this tutorial, we will assume that it's placed in the `~/.keras/datasets` directory, under the name `cityscapes`. To display a progress bar during training, install `tqdm`:

```
$> pip install tqdm
```

By the end of this recipe, we'll learn to generate the image on the left from the right one using Pix2Pix:

Figure 6.3 – We will use the segmented images on the right to produce real-world images like the one on the left

Let's get started!

# How to do it...

After completing these steps, you'll have implemented Pix2Pix from scratch!

1.  Import the dependencies:

```
import pathlib
import cv2
import numpy as np
import tensorflow as tf
import tqdm
from tensorflow.keras.layers import *
from tensorflow.keras.losses import BinaryCrossentropy
from tensorflow.keras.models import *
from tensorflow.keras.optimizers import Adam
```

2.  Define constants for TensorFlow's autotuning and resizing options, as well as the dimensions. We will resize all the images in the dataset:

```
AUTOTUNE = tf.data.experimental.AUTOTUNE
NEAREST_NEIGHBOR = tf.image.ResizeMethod.NEAREST_NEIGHBOR
IMAGE_WIDTH = 256
IMAGE_HEIGHT = 256
```

3.  Each image in the dataset is comprised of both the input and target, so after processing it, we need to split them into separate images. The load_image() function does this:

```
def load_image(image_path):
    image = tf.io.read_file(image_path)
    image = tf.image.decode_jpeg(image)

    width = tf.shape(image)[1]
    width = width // 2

    real_image = image[:, :width, :]
    input_image = image[:, width:, :]
```

```
input_image = tf.cast(input_image, tf.float32)
real_image = tf.cast(real_image, tf.float32)


return input_image, real_image
```

4.  Let's create the `resize()` function to resize both the input and target images:

```
def resize(input_image, real_image, height, width):
    input_image = tf.image.resize(input_image,
                                  size=(height,width),
                                  method=NEAREST_NEIGHBOR)
    real_image = tf.image.resize(real_image,
                                 size=(height, width),
                                 method=NEAREST_NEIGHBOR)


    return input_image, real_image
```

5.  Now, implement the `random_crop()` function to perform random cropping on the images:

```
def random_crop(input_image, real_image):
    stacked_image = tf.stack([input_image,
                              real_image],axis=0)
    size = (2, IMAGE_HEIGHT, IMAGE_WIDTH, 3)
    cropped_image = tf.image.random_crop(stacked_image,
                                         size=size)


    input_image = cropped_image[0]
    real_image = cropped_image[1]


    return input_image, real_image
```

6.  Next, code up the `normalize()` function to normalize the images to the range [-1, 1]:

```
def normalize(input_image, real_image):
    input_image = (input_image / 127.5) - 1
    real_image = (real_image / 127.5) - 1
```

```
return input_image, real_image
```

7. Define the `random_jitter()` function, which performs random jittering on the input images (notice that it uses the functions defined in *Step 4* and *Step 5*):

```
@tf.function
def random_jitter(input_image, real_image):
    input_image, real_image = resize(input_image,
                                     real_image,
                                     width=286,
                                     height=286)

    input_image, real_image = random_crop(input_image,
                                          real_image)

    if np.random.uniform() > 0.5:
        input_image = \
            tf.image.flip_left_right(input_image)
        real_image = \
            tf.image.flip_left_right(real_image)

    return input_image, real_image
```

8. Create the `load_training_image()` function to load and augment the training images:

```
def load_training_image(image_path):
    input_image, real_image = load_image(image_path)
    input_image, real_image = \
        random_jitter(input_image, real_image)

    input_image, real_image = \
        normalize(input_image, real_image)

    return input_image, real_image
```

9.  Let's now implement the `load_test_image()` function, which, as its name indicates, will be used to load test images:

```
def load_test_image(image_path):
    input_image, real_image = load_image(image_path)
    input_image, real_image = resize(input_image,
                                     real_image,
                                     width=IMAGE_WIDTH,
                                     height=IMAGE_HEIGHT)
    input_image, real_image = \
        normalize(input_image, real_image)

    return input_image, real_image
```

10. Now, let's proceed to create the `generate_and_save_images()` function to store synthetic images created by the generator model. The resulting images will be a concatenation of `input`, `target`, and `prediction`:

```
def generate_and_save_images(model, input, target, epoch):
    prediction = model(input, training=True)

    display_list = [input[0], target[0], prediction[0]]

    image = np.hstack(display_list)
    image *= 0.5
    image += 0.5
    image *= 255.0
    image = cv2.cvtColor(image, cv2.COLOR_RGB2BGR)

    cv2.imwrite(f'{epoch + 1}.jpg', image)
```

11. Next, define the `Pix2Pix()` class, which encapsulates this architecture implementation. Start with the constructor:

```
class Pix2Pix(object):
    def __init__(self, output_channels=3,
                 lambda_value=100):
        self.loss = BinaryCrossentropy(from_logits=True)
        self.output_channels = output_channels
```

```
        self._lambda = lambda_value

        self.generator = self.create_generator()
        self.discriminator = self.create_discriminator()

        self.gen_opt = Adam(learning_rate=2e-4,
                            beta_1=0.5)
        self.dis_opt = Adam(learning_rate=2e-4,
                            beta_1=0.5)
```

12. The constructor implemented in *Step 11* defines the loss function to be used (**binary cross-entropy**), the lambda value (used in *Step 18*), and instantiates the generator and the discriminator, as well as their respective optimizers. Our generator is a modified **U-Net**, which is a U-shaped network comprising downsampling and upsampling blocks. Let's create a static method to produce a downsample block:

```
    @staticmethod
    def downsample(filters, size, batch_norm=True):
        initializer = tf.random_normal_initializer(0.0,
    0.02)

        layers = Sequential()
        layers.add(Conv2D(filters=filters,
                          kernel_size=size,
                          strides=2,
                          padding='same',

                          kernel_initializer=initializer,
                          use_bias=False))

        if batch_norm:
            layers.add(BatchNormalization())

        layers.add(LeakyReLU())

        return layers
```

13. A downsample block is a convolution, optionally batch normalized, and activated with `LeakyReLU()`. Let's now implement a static method to create upsampling blocks:

```python
@staticmethod
def upsample(filters, size, dropout=False):
    init = tf.random_normal_initializer(0.0, 0.02)

    layers = Sequential()
    layers.add(Conv2DTranspose(filters=filters,
                               kernel_size=size,
                               strides=2,
                               padding='same',
                               kernel_initializer=init,
                               use_bias=False))

    layers.add(BatchNormalization())

    if dropout:
        layers.add(Dropout(rate=0.5))

    layers.add(ReLU())

    return layers
```

14. An upsampling block is a transposed convolution, optionally followed by dropout and with `ReLU()` activated. Let's now use these two convenience methods to implement the U-Net generator:

```python
def create_generator(self, input_shape=(256, 256,3)):
    down_stack = [self.downsample(64,4,batch_
norm=False)]
    for filters in (128, 256, 512, 512, 512, 512,
                    512):
        down_block = self.downsample(filters, 4)
        down_stack.append(down_block)
```

15. After defining the downsampling stack, let's do the same with the upsampling layers:

```
up_stack = []
for _ in range(3):
    up_block = self.upsample(512, 4,dropout=True)
    up_stack.append(up_block)

for filters in (512, 256, 128, 64):
    up_block = self.upsample(filters, 4)
    up_stack.append(up_block)
```

16. Thread the input through the down and up stacks, and also add skip connections to prevent the depth of the network from impeding its learning:

```
inputs = Input(shape=input_shape)
x = inputs

skip_layers = []
for down in down_stack:
    x = down(x)
    skip_layers.append(x)

skip_layers = reversed(skip_layers[:-1])

for up, skip_connection in zip(up_stack,
                               skip_layers):
    x = up(x)
    x = Concatenate()([x, skip_connection])
```

17. The output layers are a transposed convolution with 'tanh' activated:

```
init = tf.random_normal_initializer(0.0, 0.02)
output = Conv2DTranspose(
    filters=self.output_channels,
    kernel_size=4,
    strides=2,
    padding='same',
    kernel_initializer=init,
```

```
                    activation='tanh')(x)


        return Model(inputs, outputs=output)
```

18. Define a method to compute the generator loss, as the authors of Pix2Pix recommend. Notice the use of the self._lambda constant:

```
def generator_loss(self,
                        discriminator_generated output,
                        generator_output,
                        target):
    gan_loss = self.loss(
        tf.ones_like(discriminator_generated_output),
        discriminator_generated_output)

    # MAE
    error = target - generator_output
    l1_loss = tf.reduce_mean(tf.abs(error))
    total_gen_loss = gan_loss + (self._lambda *
                                    l1_loss)

    return total_gen_loss, gan_loss, l1_loss
```

19. The discriminator, defined in this step, receives two images; the input and the target:

```
def create_discriminator(self):
    input = Input(shape=(256, 256, 3))
    target = Input(shape=(256, 256, 3))


    x = Concatenate()([input, target])


    x = self.downsample(64, 4, False)(x)
    x = self.downsample(128, 4)(x)
    x = self.downsample(256, 4)(x)


    x = ZeroPadding2D()(x)
```

20. Notice that the last couple of layers are convolutions, instead of `Dense()` layers. This is because the discriminator works on patches of images at a time, and tells whether each patch is real or fake:

```python
init = tf.random_normal_initializer(0.0, 0.02)
x = Conv2D(filters=512,
           kernel_size=4,
           strides=1,
           kernel_initializer=init,
           use_bias=False)(x)
x = BatchNormalization()(x)
x = LeakyReLU()(x)
x = ZeroPadding2D()(x)
output = Conv2D(filters=1,
               kernel_size=4,
               strides=1,
               kernel_initializer=init)(x)


return Model(inputs=[input, target],
             outputs=output)
```

21. Define the discriminator loss:

```python
def discriminator_loss(self,
                       discriminator_real_output,
                       discriminator_generated_output):
    real_loss = self.loss(
        tf.ones_like(discriminator_real_output),
        discriminator_real_output)

    fake_loss = self.loss(
        tf.zeros_like(discriminator_generated_
output),
        discriminator_generated_output)

    return real_loss + fake_loss
```

22. Define a function to perform a single train step, named `train_step()`, consisting of taking the input image, passing through the generator, and then using the discriminator on the input image paired with the original target image, and then on the input imaged paired with the fake image output from the generator:

```
@tf.function
def train_step(self, input_image, target):
    with tf.GradientTape() as gen_tape, \
            tf.GradientTape() as dis_tape:
        gen_output = self.generator(input_image,
                                    training=True)

        dis_real_output = self.discriminator(
            [input_image, target], training=True)
        dis_gen_output = self.discriminator(
            [input_image, gen_output],
                training=True)
```

23. Next, the losses are computed, along with the gradients:

```
        (gen_total_loss, gen_gan_loss,
            gen_l1_loss) = \
            self.generator_loss(dis_gen_output,
                                gen_output,
                                target)
        dis_loss = \
            self.discriminator_loss(dis_real_output,

                dis_gen_output)

    gen_grads = gen_tape. \
        gradient(gen_total_loss,
                self.generator.trainable_variables)
    dis_grads = dis_tape. \
        gradient(dis_loss,
                self.discriminator.trainable_
    variables)
```

24. Use the gradients to update the models through the respective optimizers:

```
        opt_args = zip(gen_grads,
                       self.generator.trainable_
variables)
        self.gen_opt.apply_gradients(opt_args)

        opt_args = zip(dis_grads,
                       self.discriminator.trainable_
variables)
        self.dis_opt.apply_gradients(opt_args)
```

25. Implement `fit()`, a method to train the whole architecture. For each epoch, we'll save to disk the images generated to visually assess the performance of the model:

```
    def fit(self, train, epochs, test):
        for epoch in tqdm.tqdm(range(epochs)):
            for example_input, example_target in
                              test.take(1):
                generate_and_save_images(self.generator,
                                         example_input,
                                         example_target,
                                         epoch)

            for input_image, target in train:
                self.train_step(input_image, target)
```

26. Assemble the path to the training and test splits of the dataset:

```
    dataset_path = (pathlib.Path.home() / '.keras' /
                    'datasets' /'cityscapes')
    train_dataset_pattern = str(dataset_path / 'train' /
                                '*.jpg')
    test_dataset_pattern = str(dataset_path / 'val' /
                               '*.jpg')
```

27. Define the training and test datasets:

```
    BUFFER_SIZE = 400
    BATCH_SIZE = 1
```

```
train_ds = (tf.data.Dataset
            .list_files(train_dataset_pattern)
            .map(load_training_image,
                 num_parallel_calls=AUTOTUNE)
            .shuffle(BUFFER_SIZE)
            .batch(BATCH_SIZE))
test_ds = (tf.data.Dataset
           .list_files(test_dataset_pattern)
           .map(load_test_image)
           .batch(BATCH_SIZE))
```

28. Instantiate `Pix2Pix()` and fit it over 150 epochs:

```
pix2pix = Pix2Pix()
pix2pix.fit(train_ds, epochs=150, test=test_ds)
```

Here's a generated image at epoch 1:

Figure 6.4 – At first, the generator only produces noise

And here's one at epoch 150:

Figure 6.5 – At the end of its training run, the generator is capable of producing reasonable results

When the training ends, our Pix2Pix architecture can translate segmented images to real scenes, as demonstrated in *Figure 6.5*, where the first image is the input, the second is the target, and the rightmost is the generated one.

Let's connect the dots in the next section.

## How it works...

In this recipe, we implemented an architecture which was a bit hard, but was based, but based on the same ideas as all GANs. The main difference is that this time, the discriminator works on patches, instead of whole images. More specifically, the discriminator looks at patches of the original and fake images at a time and decides whether those patches belong to real or synthetized images.

Because image-to-image translation is a form of image segmentation, our generator is a modified U-Net, a groundbreaking type of CNN first used for biomedical image segmentation.

Because Pix2Pix is such a complex and deep network, the training process takes several hours to complete, but in the end, we obtained very good results translating the content of segmented city landscapes to real-looking predictions. Impressive!

If you want to take a look at other produced images, as well as a graphical representation of the generator and discriminator, consult the official repository at `https://github.com/PacktPublishing/Tensorflow-2.0-Computer-Vision-Cookbook/tree/master/ch6/recipe3`.

## See also

I recommend you read the original paper by Phillip Isola, Jun-Yan Zhu, Tinghui Zhou, and Alexei A. Efros, the authors of **Pix2Pix**, here: `https://arxiv.org/abs/1611.07004`. We used a U-Net as the generator, which you can read more about here: `https://arxiv.org/abs/1505.04597`.

# Translating unpaired images with CycleGAN

In the *Translating images with Pix2Pix* recipe, we discovered how to transfer images from one domain to another. However, in the end, it's supervised learning that requires a pairing of input and target images in order for Pix2Pix to learn the correct mapping. Wouldn't it be great if we could bypass this pairing condition, and let the network figure out on its own how to translate the characteristics from one domain to another, while preserving image consistency?

Well, that's what **CycleGAN** does, and in this recipe, we'll implement one from scratch to convert pictures of Yosemite National Park taken during the summer into their winter counterparts!

Let's get started.

## Getting ready

We'll use `OpenCV`, `tqdm`, and `tensorflow-datasets` in this recipe.

Install these simultaneously with `pip`:

```
$> pip install opencv-contrib-python tqdm tensorflow-datasets
```

Through the TensorFlow datasets, we'll access the `cyclegan/summer2winter_yosemite` dataset.

Here are some sample images of this dataset:

Figure 6.6 – Left: Yosemite during summer; right: Yosemite during winter

> **Tip**
> The implementation of CycleGAN is very similar to Pix2Pix. Therefore, we won't explain most of it in detail. Instead, I encourage you to complete the *Translating images with Pix2Pix* recipe before tackling this one.

# How to do it...

Perform the following steps to complete the recipe:

1. Import the necessary dependencies:

```
import cv2
import numpy as np
import tensorflow as tf
import tensorflow_datasets as tfds
from tensorflow.keras.layers import *
from tensorflow.keras.losses import BinaryCrossentropy
from tensorflow.keras.models import *
from tensorflow.keras.optimizers import Adam
from tqdm import tqdm
```

2. Define an alias for `tf.data.experimental.AUTOTUNE`:

```
AUTOTUNE = tf.data.experimental.AUTOTUNE
```

3. Define a function to perform the random cropping of an image:

```
def random_crop(image):
    return tf.image.random_crop(image, size=(256, 256,
                                               3))
```

4. Define a function to normalize images to the range [-1, 1]:

```
def normalize(image):
    image = tf.cast(image, tf.float32)
    image = (image / 127.5) - 1
    return image
```

5. Define a function to perform random jittering on an image:

```
def random_jitter(image):
    method = tf.image.ResizeMethod.NEAREST_NEIGHBOR
    image = tf.image.resize(image, (286, 286),
                            method=method)
    image = random_crop(image)
    image = tf.image.random_flip_left_right(image)
    return image
```

6. Define a function to preprocess and augment training images:

```
def preprocess_training_image(image, _):
    image = random_jitter(image)
    image = normalize(image)
    return image
```

7. Define a function to preprocess test images:

```
def preprocess_test_image(image, _):
    image = normalize(image)
    return image
```

8. Define a function to generate and save images using the generator model. The resulting images will be a concatenation of the input and the prediction:

```
def generate_images(model, test_input, epoch):
    prediction = model(test_input)

    image = np.hstack([test_input[0], prediction[0]])
    image *= 0.5
    image += 0.5
    image *= 255.0
    image = cv2.cvtColor(image, cv2.COLOR_RGB2BGR)

    cv2.imwrite(f'{epoch + 1}.jpg', image)
```

9. Define a custom instance normalization layer, starting with the constructor:

```
class InstanceNormalization(Layer):
    def __init__(self, epsilon=1e-5):
        super(InstanceNormalization, self).__init__()
        self.epsilon = epsilon
```

10. Now, define the `build()` method, which creates the inner components of the `InstanceNormalization()` class:

```
def build(self, input_shape):
    init = tf.random_normal_initializer(1.0, 0.02)
    self.scale = self.add_weight(name='scale',
                            shape=input_shape[-1:],
                                initializer=init,
                                trainable=True)

    self.offset = self.add_weight(name='offset',
                            shape=input_shape[-1:],
                                initializer='zeros',
                                trainable=True)
```

11. Create the `call()` method, which implements the logic to instance-normalize the input tensor, x:

```
def call(self, x):
    mean, variance = tf.nn.moments(x,
                                   axes=(1, 2),
                                   keepdims=True)
    inv = tf.math.rsqrt(variance + self.epsilon)
    normalized = (x - mean) * inv

    return self.scale * normalized + self.offset
```

12. Define a class to encapsulate the CycleGAN implementation. Start with the constructor:

```
class CycleGAN(object):
    def __init__(self, output_channels=3,
                 lambda_value=10):
        self.output_channels = output_channels
        self._lambda = lambda_value
        self.loss = BinaryCrossentropy(from_logits=True)

        self.gen_g = self.create_generator()
        self.gen_f = self.create_generator()

        self.dis_x = self.create_discriminator()
        self.dis_y = self.create_discriminator()

        self.gen_g_opt = Adam(learning_rate=2e-4,
                              beta_1=0.5)
        self.gen_f_opt = Adam(learning_rate=2e-4,
                              beta_1=0.5)

        self.dis_x_opt = Adam(learning_rate=2e-4,
                              beta_1=0.5)
        self.dis_y_opt = Adam(learning_rate=2e-4,
                              beta_1=0.5)
```

The main difference with Pix2Pix is that we have two generators (gen_g and gen_f) and two discriminators (dis_x and dis_y). gen_g learns how to transform image X to image Y, and gen_f learns how to transform image Y to image Y. Analogously, dis_x learns to differentiate between the real image X and the one generated by gen_f, while dis_y learns to differentiate between the real image Y and the one generated by gen_g.

13. Now, let's create a static method to produce downsampling blocks (this is the same as in the last recipe, only this time we use instance instead of batch normalization):

```python
@staticmethod
def downsample(filters, size, norm=True):
    initializer = tf.random_normal_initializer(0.0,
0.02)

    layers = Sequential()
    layers.add(Conv2D(filters=filters,
                      kernel_size=size,
                      strides=2,
                      padding='same',

                      kernel_initializer=initializer,
                      use_bias=False))

    if norm:
        layers.add(InstanceNormalization())

    layers.add(LeakyReLU())

    return layers
```

14. Now, define a static method to produce upsampling blocks (this is the same as in the last recipe, only this time we use instance instead of batch normalization):

```python
@staticmethod
def upsample(filters, size, dropout=False):
    init = tf.random_normal_initializer(0.0, 0.02)

    layers = Sequential()
```

```
        layers.add(Conv2DTranspose(filters=filters,
                                   kernel_size=size,
                                   strides=2,
                                   padding='same',

                                   kernel_initializer=init,
                                   use_bias=False))

        layers.add(InstanceNormalization())

        if dropout:
            layers.add(Dropout(rate=0.5))

        layers.add(ReLU())

        return layers
```

15. Define a method to build the generator. Start by creating the downsampling layers:

```
    def create_generator(self):
        down_stack = [
            self.downsample(64, 4, norm=False),
            self.downsample(128, 4),
            self.downsample(256, 4)]

        for _ in range(5):
            down_block = self.downsample(512, 4)
            down_stack.append(down_block)
```

16. Now, create the upsampling layers:

```
        for _ in range(3):
            up_block = self.upsample(512, 4,
                                     dropout=True)
            up_stack.append(up_block)

        for filters in (512, 256, 128, 64):
            up_block = self.upsample(filters, 4)
```

```
up_stack.append(up_block)
```

17. Thread the input through the downsampling and upsampling layers. Add skip connections to avoid the vanishing gradient problem:

```
inputs = Input(shape=(None, None, 3))
    x = inputs

    skips = []
    for down in down_stack:
        x = down(x)
        skips.append(x)

    skips = reversed(skips[:-1])

    for up, skip in zip(up_stack, skips):
        x = up(x)
        x = Concatenate()([x, skip])
```

18. The output layers are a `'tanh'` activated transposed convolution:

```
init = tf.random_normal_initializer(0.0, 0.02)
output = Conv2DTranspose(
    filters=self.output_channels,
    kernel_size=4,
    strides=2,
    padding='same',
    kernel_initializer=init,
    activation='tanh')(x)

return Model(inputs, outputs=output)
```

19. Define a method to calculate the generator loss:

```
def generator_loss(self, generated):
    return self.loss(tf.ones_like(generated),
                     generated)
```

20. Define a method to create the discriminator:

```python
def create_discriminator(self):
    input = Input(shape=(None, None, 3))
    x = input

    x = self.downsample(64, 4, False)(x)
    x = self.downsample(128, 4)(x)
    x = self.downsample(256, 4)(x)

    x = ZeroPadding2D()(x)
```

21. Add the last couple of layers, which are convolutional:

```python
init = tf.random_normal_initializer(0.0, 0.02)
x = Conv2D(filters=512,
           kernel_size=4,
           strides=1,
           kernel_initializer=init,
           use_bias=False)(x)
x = InstanceNormalization()(x)

x = LeakyReLU()(x)
x = ZeroPadding2D()(x)
output = Conv2D(filters=1,
               kernel_size=4,
               strides=1,
               kernel_initializer=init)(x)

return Model(inputs=input, outputs=output)
```

22. Define a method to compute the discriminator loss:

```python
def discriminator_loss(self, real, generated):
    real_loss = self.loss(tf.ones_like(real),
                          real)
    generated_loss =
        self.loss(tf.zeros_like(generated),
                  generated)
```

```
        total_discriminator_loss = real_loss + generated_
loss
        return total_discriminator_loss * 0.5
```

23. Define a method to compute the loss between the real and cycled images. This loss is in charge of quantifying the cycle consistency, which says that if you translate an image X to Y, and then Y to X, the result should be X, or close to X:

```
def calculate_cycle_loss(self, real_image,
                         cycled_image):
    error = real_image - cycled_image
    loss1 = tf.reduce_mean(tf.abs(error))
    return self._lambda * loss1
```

24. Define a method to compute the identity loss. This loss establishes that if you pass image Y through gen_g, we should obtain the real image Y or something close to it (the same applies to gen_f):

```
def identity_loss(self, real_image, same_image):
    error = real_image - same_image
    loss = tf.reduce_mean(tf.abs(error))
    return self._lambda * 0.5 * loss
```

25. Define a method to perform a single training step. It receives images X and Y from different domains. Then, it uses gen_g to translate X to Y, and gen_f to translate Y to X:

```
@tf.function
def train_step(self, real_x, real_y):
    with tf.GradientTape(persistent=True) as tape:
        fake_y = self.gen_g(real_x, training=True)
        cycled_x = self.gen_f(fake_y,
                              training=True)

        fake_x = self.gen_f(real_y, training=True)
        cycled_y = self.gen_g(fake_x,
                              training=True)
```

26. Now, pass X through `gen_f` and Y through `gen_y` to later compute the identity loss:

```
same_x = self.gen_f(real_x, training=True)
same_y = self.gen_g(real_y, training=True)
```

27. Pass real X and fake X to `dis_x`, and real Y, along with generated Y, to `dis_y`:

```
dis_real_x = self.dis_x(real_x,
                            training=True)
dis_real_y = self.dis_y(real_y,
                            training=True)
dis_fake_x = self.dis_x(fake_x,training=True)
dis_fake_y = self.dis_y(fake_y,
                            training=True)
```

28. Compute the generators' losses:

```
gen_g_loss = self.generator_loss(dis_fake_y)
gen_f_loss = self.generator_loss(dis_fake_x)
```

29. Compute the cycle loss:

```
cycle_x_loss = \
    self.calculate_cycle_loss(real_x,
                                cycled_x)
cycle_y_loss = \
    self.calculate_cycle_loss(real_y,
                                cycled_y)
total_cycle_loss = cycle_x_loss +
                        cycle_y_loss
```

30. Compute the identity loss and the total generator G loss:

```
identity_y_loss = \
    self.identity_loss(real_y, same_y)
total_generator_g_loss = (gen_g_loss +
                            total_cycle_loss +
                            identity_y_loss)
```

31. Repeat for generator F:

```
identity_x_loss = \
        self.identity_loss(real_x, same_x)
total_generator_f_loss = (gen_f_loss +
                            total_cycle_loss +
                            identity_x_loss)
```

32. Compute the discriminators' losses:

```
dis_x_loss = \
    self.discriminator_loss(dis_real_x,dis_fake_x)
dis_y_loss = \
    self.discriminator_loss(dis_real_y,dis_fake_y)
```

33. Compute the gradients for the generators:

```
gen_g_grads = tape.gradient(
    total_generator_g_loss,
    self.gen_g.trainable_variables)
gen_f_grads = tape.gradient(
    total_generator_f_loss,
    self.gen_f.trainable_variables)
```

34. Compute the gradients for the discriminators:

```
dis_x_grads = tape.gradient(
    dis_x_loss,
    self.dis_x.trainable_variables)
dis_y_grads = tape.gradient(
    dis_y_loss,
    self.dis_y.trainable_variables)
```

35. Apply the gradients to each generator using the respective optimizer:

```
gen_g_opt_params = zip(gen_g_grads,
                    self.gen_g.trainable_variables)
self.gen_g_opt.apply_gradients(gen_g_opt_params)


gen_f_opt_params = zip(gen_f_grads,
                    self.gen_f.trainable_
```

```
variables)
        self.gen_f_opt.apply_gradients(gen_f_opt_params)
```

36. Apply the gradients to each discriminator using the respective optimizer:

```
        dis_x_opt_params = zip(dis_x_grads,
                        self.dis_x.trainable_variables)
        self.dis_x_opt.apply_gradients(dis_x_opt_params)

        dis_y_opt_params = zip(dis_y_grads,
                        self.dis_y.trainable_variables)
        self.dis_y_opt.apply_gradients(dis_y_opt_params)
```

37. Define a method to fit the whole architecture. It will save to disk the images produced by generator G after each epoch:

```
    def fit(self, train, epochs, test):
        for epoch in tqdm(range(epochs)):
            for image_x, image_y in train:
                self.train_step(image_x, image_y)

            test_image = next(iter(test))
            generate_images(self.gen_g, test_image,
                            epoch)
```

38. Load the dataset:

```
    dataset, _ = tfds.load('cycle_gan/summer2winter_
    yosemite',
                        with_info=True,
                        as_supervised=True)
```

39. Unpack the training and test splits:

```
    train_summer = dataset['trainA']
    train_winter = dataset['trainB']

    test_summer = dataset['testA']
    test_winter = dataset['testB']
```

40. Define the data processing pipelines for the training spit:

```
BUFFER_SIZE = 400
BATCH_SIZE = 1

train_summer = (train_summer
                .map(preprocess_training_image,
                    num_parallel_calls=AUTOTUNE)
                .cache()
                .shuffle(BUFFER_SIZE)
                .batch(BATCH_SIZE))
train_winter = (train_winter
                .map(preprocess_training_image,
                    num_parallel_calls=AUTOTUNE)
                .cache()
                .shuffle(BUFFER_SIZE)
                .batch(BATCH_SIZE))
```

41. Define the data processing pipelines for the test split:

```
test_summer = (test_summer
                .map(preprocess_test_image,
                    num_parallel_calls=AUTOTUNE)
                .cache()
                .shuffle(BUFFER_SIZE)
                .batch(BATCH_SIZE))
test_winter = (test_winter
                .map(preprocess_test_image,
                    num_parallel_calls=AUTOTUNE)
                .cache()
                .shuffle(BUFFER_SIZE)
                .batch(BATCH_SIZE))
```

42. Create an instance of `CycleGAN()` and train it for 40 epochs:

```
cycle_gan = CycleGAN()
train_ds = tf.data.Dataset.zip((train_summer,
                                       train_winter))
cycle_gan.fit(train=train_ds,
              epochs=40,
              test=test_summer)
```

At epoch 1, we'll notice that the network hasn't learned much:

Figure 6.7 – Left: original image during summer; right: translated image (winter)

However, at epoch 40, the results are more promising:

Figure 6.8 – Left: original image during summer; right: translated image (winter)

As we can see in the preceding image, our `CycleGAN()` added a little more white to certain parts of the trail and the trees to make the translated image seem like it was taken during winter. Of course, training for more epochs can potentially lead to better results, which I encourage you to do to solidify your understanding of CycleGANs!

## How it works...

In this recipe, we learned that CycleGANs work in a very similar fashion to Pix2Pix. However, the biggest advantage is that a CycleGAN doesn't require a dataset of paired images to achieve its goal. Instead, it relies on two sets of generators and discriminators, which, in fact, create a learning cycle, hence the name.

In particular, CycleGANs work as follows:

- A generator G must learn a mapping from an image X to an image Y.

- A generator F must learn a mapping from an image Y to an image X.

- A discriminator D(X) must distinguish the real image X from the fake one generated by G.

- A discriminator D(Y) must distinguish the real image Y from the fake one generated by F.

There are two conditions that ensure that the translation preserves the meaning in both domains (very much like when we want to preserve the meaning of our words when we translate from English to Spanish, and vice versa):

- Cycle consistency: Going from X to Y and then from Y to X should produce the original X or something very similar to X. The same applies to Y.

- Identity consistency: Passing X to G should produce the same X or something very similar to X. The same applies to Y.

Using these four components, CycleGAN tries to preserve the cycle and identity consistency in the translation, which generates very satisfying results without the need for supervised, paired data.

## See also

You can read the original paper on CycleGANs here: `https://arxiv.org/abs/1703.10593`. Also, here is a very interesting thread to understand the difference between instance and batch normalization: `https://intellipaat.com/community/1869/instance-normalisation-vs-batch-normalisation`.

# Implementing an adversarial attack using the Fast Gradient Signed Method

We often think of highly accurate deep neural networks as robust models, but the **Fast Gradient Signed Method** (**FGSM**), proposed by no other than the father of GANs himself, Ian Goodfellow, showed otherwise. In this recipe, we'll perform an FGSM attack on a pre-trained model to see how, by introducing seemingly imperceptible changes, we can completely fool a network.

## Getting ready

Let's install OpenCV with pip.

We'll use it to save the perturbed images using the FGSM method:

```
$> pip install opencv-contrib-python
```

Let's begin.

## How to do it

After completing the following steps, you'll have successfully performed an adversarial attack:

1.  Import the dependencies:

    ```
    import cv2
    import tensorflow as tf
    from tensorflow.keras.applications.nasnet import *
    from tensorflow.keras.losses import
    CategoricalCrossentropy
    ```

2.  Define a function to preprocess an image, which entails resizing it and applying the same treatment as the pre-trained network we'll use (in this case, NASNetMobile):

    ```
    def preprocess(image, target_shape):
        image = tf.cast(image, tf.float32)
        image = tf.image.resize(image, target_shape)
        image = preprocess_input(image)
        image = image[None, :, :, :]
        return image
    ```

3. Define a function to get the human-readable image from a set of probabilities:

```
def get_imagenet_label(probabilities):
    return decode_predictions(probabilities, top=1)[0][0]
```

4. Define a function to save an image. This will use the pre-trained model to get the proper label and will utilize it as part of the filename of the image, which also contains the prediction confidence percentage. Prior to storing the image on disk, it ensures that it's in the expected [0, 255] range, as well as in BGR space, which is the one used by OpenCV:

```
def save_image(image, model, description):
    prediction = model.predict(image)
    _, label, conf = get_imagenet_label(prediction)
    image = image.numpy()[0] * 0.5 + 0.5
    image = (image * 255).astype('uint8')
    image = cv2.cvtColor(image, cv2.COLOR_RGB2BGR)

    conf *= 100
    img_name = f'{description}, {label} ({conf:.2f}%).
jpg'
    cv2.imwrite(img_name, image)
```

5. Define a function to create the adversarial pattern that will be used later on to perform the actual FGSM attack:

```
def generate_adv_pattern(model,
                         input_image,
                         input_label,
                         loss_function):
    with tf.GradientTape() as tape:
        tape.watch(input_image)
        prediction = model(input_image)
        loss = loss_function(input_label, prediction)

    gradient = tape.gradient(loss, input_image)
    signed_gradient = tf.sign(gradient)

    return signed_gradient
```

The pattern is pretty simple: It consists of a tensor with the sign of the gradient in each element. More specifically, `signed_gradient` will contain a `-1` for gradient values below `0`, `1` for values above `0`, and `0` if the gradient is, well, `0`.

6. Instantiate the pre-trained `NASNetMobile()` model and freeze its weights:

```
pretrained_model = NASNetMobile(include_top=True,
                                weights='imagenet')
pretrained_model.trainable = False
```

7. Load the test image and pass it through the network:

```
image = tf.io.read_file('dog.jpg')
image = tf.image.decode_jpeg(image)
image = preprocess(image, pretrained_model.input.
shape[1:-1])
image_probabilities = pretrained_model.predict(image)
```

8. One-hot encode the ground truth label of the original image, and use it to generate the adversarial pattern:

```
cce_loss = CategoricalCrossentropy()


pug_index = 254
label = tf.one_hot(pug_index, image_probabilities.shape[-
1])
label = tf.reshape(label, (1, image_probabilities.shape[-
1]))
disturbances = generate_adv_pattern(pretrained_model,
                                    image,
                                    label,
                                    cce_loss)
```

9. Perform a series of adversarial attacks using increasing, yet small, values of `epsilon`, which will be applied in the direction of the gradient, leveraging the pattern present in `disturbances`:

```
for epsilon in [0, 0.005, 0.01, 0.1, 0.15, 0.2]:
    corrupted_image = image + epsilon * disturbances
    corrupted_image = tf.clip_by_value(corrupted_image,
-1, 1)
```

```
save_image(corrupted_image,
           pretrained_model,
           f'Epsilon = {epsilon:.3f}')
```

For epsilon = 0 (no attack), the image looks like this, and the label is `pug` with an 80% confidence:

Figure 6.9 – Original image. Label: pug (80.23% confidence)

When epsilon = 0.005 (a very small perturbation), the label changes to `Brabancon_griffon`, with a 43.03% confidence:

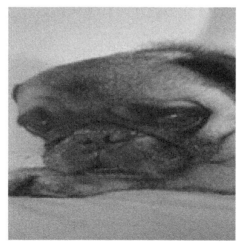

Figure 6.10 – Epsilon = 0.005 applied in the gradient direction. Label: Brabancon_gritton (43.03% confidence)

As can be seen from the preceding image, an imperceptible variation in the pixel values produced a drastically different response from the network. However, the situation worsens the more we increment the magnitude of epsilon. For a complete list of results, refer to `https://github.com/PacktPublishing/Tensorflow-2.0-Computer-Vision-Cookbook/tree/master/ch6/recipe5`.

## How it works...

In this recipe, we implemented a fairly simple attack based on the FGSM proposed by Ian Goodfellow, which simply consists of determining the direction (sign) of the gradient at each location and using that information to create an adversarial pattern. The underlying principle is that this technique maximizes the loss at each pixel value.

Next, we use this pattern to either add or subtract a small perturbation to each pixel in the image that gets passed to the network.

Although these changes are often imperceptible to the human eye, they have the power to completely confuse a network, resulting in nonsensical predictions, as demonstrated in the last step of this recipe.

## See also

Fortunately, many defenses against this type of attack (and more sophisticated ones) have emerged. You can read a pretty interesting survey of adversarial attacks and defenses here: `https://arxiv.org/abs/1810.00069`.

# 7
# Captioning Images with CNNs and RNNs

Equipping neural networks with the ability to describe visual scenes in a human-readable fashion has to be one of the most interesting yet challenging applications of deep learning. The main difficulty arises from the fact that this problem combines two major subfields of artificial intelligence: **Computer Vision** (**CV**) and **Natural Language Processing** (**NLP**).

The architectures of most image captioning networks use a **Convolutional Neural Network** (**CNN**) to encode images in a numeric format so that they're suitable for the consumption of the decoder, which is typically a **Recurrent Neural Network** (**RNN**). This is a kind of network specialized in learning from sequential data, such as time series, video, and text.

As we'll see in this chapter, the challenges of building a system with these capabilities start with preparing the data, which we'll cover in the first recipe. Then, we'll implement an image captioning solution from scratch. In the third recipe, we'll use this model to generate captions for our own pictures. Finally, in the fourth recipe, we'll learn how to include an attention mechanism in our architecture so that we can understand what parts of the image the network is looking at when generating each word in the output caption.

Pretty interesting, don't you agree?

Specifically, we'll cover the following recipes in this chapter:

- Implementing a reusable image caption feature extractor
- Implementing an image captioning network
- Generating captions for your own photos
- Implementing an image captioning network on COCO with attention
- Let's get started!

# Technical requirements

Image captioning is a problem that requires vast amounts of resources in terms of memory, storage, and computing power. My recommendation is that you use a cloud-based solution such as AWS or FloydHub to run the recipes in this chapter unless you have sufficiently capable hardware. As expected, a GPU is of paramount importance to complete the recipes in this chapter. In the *Getting ready* section of each recipe, you'll find what you'll need to prepare. The code of this chapter is available here: `https://github.com/PacktPublishing/Tensorflow-2.0-Computer-Vision-Cookbook/tree/master/ch7`.

Check out the following link to see the Code in Action video:

`https://bit.ly/3qmpVme`.

# Implementing a reusable image caption feature extractor

The first step of creating an image captioning, deep learning-based solution is to transform the data into a format that can be used by certain networks. This means we must encode images as vectors, or tensors, and the text as embeddings, which are vectorial representations of sentences.

In this recipe, we will implement a customizable and reusable component that will allow us to preprocess the data we'll need to implement an image captioner beforehand, thus saving us tons of time later on in the process.

Let's begin!

## Getting ready

The dependencies we need are tqdm (to display a nice progress bar) and Pillow (to load and manipulate images using TensorFlow's built-in functions):

```
$> pip install Pillow tqdm
```

We will use the Flickr8k dataset, which is available on **Kaggle**: https://www.kaggle.com/adityajn105/flickr8k. Log in or sign up, download it, and decompress it in a directory of your choosing. For the purposes of this tutorial, we assume the data is in the ~/.keras/datasets/flickr8k folder.

Here are some sample images:

Figure 7.1 – Sample images from Flickr8k

With that, we are good to go!

## How to do it...

Follow these steps to create a reusable feature extractor for image captioning problems:

1. Import all the necessary dependencies:

```
import glob
import os
import pathlib
import pickle
from string import punctuation
```

```
import numpy as np
import tqdm
from tensorflow.keras.applications.vgg16 import *
from tensorflow.keras.layers import *
from tensorflow.keras.preprocessing.image import *
from tensorflow.keras.preprocessing.sequence import \
    pad_sequences
from tensorflow.keras.preprocessing.text import Tokenizer
from tensorflow.keras.utils import to_categorical
from tqdm import tqdm
```

2.  Define the `ImageCaptionFeatureExtractor` class and its constructor:

```
class ImageCaptionFeatureExtractor(object):
    def __init__(self,
                 output_path,
                 start_token='beginsequence',
                 end_token='endsequence',
                 feature_extractor=None,
                 input_shape=(224, 224, 3)):
```

3.  Next, we must receive the path where the outputs will be stored, along with the tokens that we'll use to delimit the start and end of a text sequence. We must also take the input shape of the feature extractor as an argument. Next, let's store these values as members:

```
        self.input_shape = input_shape

        if feature_extractor is None:
            input = Input(shape=input_shape)
            self.feature_extractor = VGG16(input_
                                    tensor=input,
                                    weights='imagenet',
                                    include_top=False)
        else:
            self.feature_extractor = feature_extractor

        self.output_path = output_path
```

```
self.start_token = start_token
self.end_token = end_token
self.tokenizer = Tokenizer()
self.max_seq_length = None
```

4.  If we don't receive any `feature_extractor`, we'll use `VGG16` by default. Next, define a public method that will extract the features from an image, given its path:

```
def extract_image_features(self, image_path):
    image = load_img(image_path,
                     target_size=self.input_shape[:2])
    image = img_to_array(image)
    image = np.expand_dims(image, axis=0)
    image = preprocess_input(image)

    return self.feature_extractor.predict(image)[0]
```

5.  In order to clean the captions, we must get rid of all the punctuation characters and single-letter words (such as *a*). The `_clean_captions()` method performs this task, and also adds special tokens; that is, `self.start_token` and `self.end_token`:

```
def _clean_captions(self, captions):
    def remove_punctuation(word):
        translation = str.maketrans('', '',
                                    punctuation)
        return word.translate(translation)

    def is_valid_word(word):
        return len(word) > 1 and word.isalpha()

    cleaned_captions = []
    for caption in captions:
        caption = caption.lower().split(' ')
        caption = map(remove_punctuation, caption)
        caption = filter(is_valid_word, caption)

        cleaned_caption = f'{self.start_token} ' \
                          f'{" ".join(caption)} ' \
```

```
                                    f'{self.end_token}'
            cleaned_captions.append(cleaned_caption)


        return cleaned_captions
```

6.  We also need to compute the length of the longest caption, which we can do with the `_get_max_seq_length()` method. This is defined as follows:

```
        def _get_max_seq_length(self, captions):
            max_sequence_length = -1


            for caption in captions:
                caption_length = len(caption.split(' '))
                max_sequence_length =
                                max(max_sequence_length,
                                        caption_length)


        return max_sequence_length
```

7.  Define a public method, `extract_features()`, which receives a list of image paths and captions and uses them to extract features from both the images and text sequences:

```
        def extract_features(self, images_path, captions):
            assert len(images_path) == len(captions)
```

8.  Note that both lists must be of the same size. The next step is to clean the captions, compute the maximum sequence length, and fit a tokenizer to all the captions:

```
            captions = self._clean_captions(captions)
            self.max_seq_length=self._get_max_seq_
                                    length(captions)
            self.tokenizer.fit_on_texts(captions)
```

9. We'll iterate over each image path and caption pair, extracting the features from the image. Then, we'll save an entry in our `data_mapping` dict, associating the image ID (present in `image_path`) with the corresponding visual features and clean caption:

```
data_mapping = {}
print('\nExtracting features...')
for i in tqdm(range(len(images_path))):
    image_path = images_path[i]
    caption = captions[i]

    feats = self.extract_image_features(image_ path)

    image_id = image_path.split(os.path.sep)[-1]
    image_id = image_id.split('.')[0]

    data_mapping[image_id] = {
        'features': feats,
        'caption': caption
    }
```

10. We'll save this `data_mapping` to disk, in pickle format:

```
out_path = f'{self.output_path}/data_mapping.
  pickle'
with open(out_path, 'wb') as f:
    pickle.dump(data_mapping, f, protocol=4)
```

11. We'll complete this method by creating and storing the sequences that'll be inputted to an image captioning network in the future:

```
self._create_sequences(data_mapping)
```

12. The following method creates the input and output sequences that will be used to train an image captioning model (see the *How it works...* section for a deeper explanation). We will start by determining the number of output classes, which is the vocabulary size plus one (to account for out-of-vocabulary tokens). We must also define the lists where we'll store the sequences:

```
def _create_sequences(self, mapping):
    num_classes = len(self.tokenizer.word_index) + 1

    in_feats = []
    in_seqs = []
    out_seqs = []
```

13. Next, we'll iterate over each features-caption pair. We will transform the caption from a string into a sequence of numbers that represents the words in the sentence:

```
print('\nCreating sequences...')
for _, data in tqdm(mapping.items()):
    feature = data['features']
    caption = data['caption']

    seq = self.tokenizer.texts_to_
                sequences([caption])
    seq = seq[0]
```

14. Next, we'll generate as many input sequences as there are words in a caption. Each input sequence will be used to generate the next word in the sequence. Therefore, for a given index, `i`, the input sequence will be all the elements up to `i-1`, while the corresponding output sequence, or label, will be the one-hot encoded element at `i` (the next word). To ensure all the input sequences are the same length, we must pad them:

```
for i in range(1, len(seq)):
    input_seq = seq[:i]
    input_seq, =
        pad_sequences([input_seq],

            self.max_seq_length)
```

```
        out_seq = seq[i]
        out_seq = to_categorical([out_seq],

                                 num_classes)[0]
```

15. We then add the visual feature vector, the input sequence, and the output sequence to the corresponding lists:

```
in_feats.append(feature)
in_seqs.append(input_seq)
out_seqs.append(out_seq)
```

16. Finally, we must write the sequences to disk, in pickle format:

```
file_paths = [
    f'{self.output_path}/input_features.pickle',
    f'{self.output_path}/input_sequences.pickle',
    f'{self.output_path}/output_sequences.
                                    pickle']
sequences = [in_feats,
             in_seqs,
             out_seqs]

for path, seq in zip(file_paths, sequences):
    with open(path, 'wb') as f:
        pickle.dump(np.array(seq), f,
                    protocol=4)
```

17. Let's define the paths to the `Flickr8k` images and captions:

```
BASE_PATH = (pathlib.Path.home() / '.keras' / 'datasets'
                                    /'flickr8k')
IMAGES_PATH = str(BASE_PATH / 'Images')
CAPTIONS_PATH = str(BASE_PATH / 'captions.txt')
```

18. Create an instance of the feature extractor class we just implemented:

```
extractor = ImageCaptionFeatureExtractor(output_path='.')
```

19. List all the image files in the `Flickr8k` dataset:

```
image_paths = list(glob.glob(f'{IMAGES_PATH}/*.jpg'))
```

20. Read the contents of the captions file:

```
with open(CAPTIONS_PATH, 'r') as f:
    text = f.read()
    lines = text.split('\n')
```

21. Now, we must create a map that will associate each image with multiple captions. The key is the image ID, while the value is a list of all captions associated with such an image:

```
mapping = {}
for line in lines:
    if '.jpg' not in line:
        continue
    tokens = line.split(',', maxsplit=1)

    if len(line) < 2:
        continue

    image_id, image_caption = tokens
    image_id = image_id.split('.')[0]

    captions_per_image = mapping.get(image_id, [])
    captions_per_image.append(image_caption)

    mapping[image_id] = captions_per_image
```

22. We will only keep one caption per image:

```
captions = []
for image_path in image_paths:
    image_id = image_path.split('/')[-1].split('.')[0]

    captions.append(mapping[image_id][0])
```

23. Finally, we must use our extractor to produce the data mapping and corresponding input sequences:

```
extractor.extract_features(image_paths, captions)
```

This process may take a while. After several minutes, we should see the following files in the output path:

```
data_mapping.pickle        input_features.pickle      input_
sequences.pickle   output_sequences.pickle
```

We'll see how this all works in the next section.

## How it works...

In this recipe, we learned that one of the keys to creating a good image captioning system is to put the data in a suitable format. This allows the network to learn how to describe, with text, what's happening in a visual scenario.

There are many ways to frame an image captioning problem, but the most popular and effective way is to use each word to generate the next word in the caption. This way, we'll construct the sentence, word by word, passing each intermediate output as the input to the next cycle. (This is how **RNNs** work. To read more about them, refer to the *See also* section.)

You might be wondering how we pass the visual information to the network. This is where the feature extraction step is crucial, because we convert each image in our dataset into a numeric vector that summarizes the spatial information in each picture. Then, we pass the same feature vector along each input sequence when training the network. This way, the network will learn to associate all the words in a caption with the same image.

If we're not careful, we could get trapped in an endless loop of word generation. How can we prevent this? By using a special token to signal the end of a sequence (this means the network should stop producing words when it encounters such a token). In our case, this token is, by default, endsequence.

A similar problem is how to start a sequence. Which word should we use? In this case, we must also resort to a special token (our default is beginsequence). This acts as a seed that the network will use to start producing captions.

All of this might sound confusing now, and that's because we've only focused on the data preprocessing stage. In the remaining recipes of this chapter, we'll leverage the work we've done here to train many different image captioners, and all the pieces will fall into place!

## See also

Here's a great explanation of how **RNNs** work: `https://www.youtube.com/watch?v=UNmqTiOnRfg`.

# Implementing an image captioning network

An image captioning architecture is comprised of an encoder and a decoder. The encoder is a **CNN** (typically a pre-trained one), which converts input images into numeric vectors. These vectors are then passed, along with text sequences, to the decoder, which is an **RNN**, that will learn, based on these values, how to iteratively generate each word in the corresponding caption.

In this recipe, we'll implement an image captioner that's been trained on the `Flickr8k` dataset. We'll leverage the feature extractor we implemented in the *Implementing a reusable image caption feature extractor* recipe.

Let's begin, shall we?

## Getting ready

The external dependencies we'll be using in this recipe are `Pillow`, `nltk`, and `tqdm`. You can install them all at once with the following command:

```
$> pip install Pillow nltk tqdm
```

We will use the `Flickr8k` dataset, which you can get from **Kaggle**: `https://www.kaggle.com/adityajn105/flickr8k`. In order to fetch it, log in or sign up, download it, and decompress its contents in a location of your preference. For the purposes of this tutorial, we assume the data is in the `~/.keras/datasets/flickr8k` directory.

The following are some sample images from the `Flickr8k` dataset:

Figure 7.2 – Sample images from Flickr8k

Let's head over to the next section to start this recipe's implementation.

# How to do it...

Follow these steps to implement a deep learning-based image captioning system:

1. First, we must import all of the required packages:

```
import glob
import pathlib
import pickle

import numpy as np
from nltk.translate.bleu_score import corpus_bleu
from sklearn.model_selection import train_test_split
from tensorflow.keras.applications.vgg16 import *
from tensorflow.keras.callbacks import ModelCheckpoint
from tensorflow.keras.layers import *
from tensorflow.keras.models import *
from tensorflow.keras.preprocessing.sequence import \
    pad_sequences

from ch7.recipe1.extractor import
ImageCaptionFeatureExtractor
```

2. Define the paths to the images and captions, as well as the output path, which is where we'll store the artifacts that will be created in this recipe:

```
BASE_PATH = (pathlib.Path.home() / '.keras' / 'datasets'
                /'flickr8k')
IMAGES_PATH = str(BASE_PATH / 'Images')
CAPTIONS_PATH = str(BASE_PATH / 'captions.txt')
OUTPUT_PATH = '.'
```

3. Define a function that will load a list of image paths and their corresponding captions. This implementation is similar to *Steps 20* through *22* of the *Implementing a reusable image caption feature extractor* recipe:

```
def load_paths_and_captions():
    image_paths = list(glob.glob(f'{IMAGES_PATH}/*.jpg'))

    with open(f'{CAPTIONS_PATH}', 'r') as f:
```

```
        text = f.read()
        lines = text.split('\n')


    mapping = {}
    for line in lines:
        if '.jpg' not in line:
            continue
        tokens = line.split(',', maxsplit=1)


        if len(line) < 2:
            continue


        image_id, image_caption = tokens
        image_id = image_id.split('.')[0]


        captions_per_image = mapping.get(image_id, [])
        captions_per_image.append(image_caption)


        mapping[image_id] = captions_per_image
```

4. Compile all the captions:

```
    all_captions = []
    for image_path in image_paths:
        image_id = image_path.split('/')[-
                        1].split('.')[0]
        all_captions.append(mapping[image_id][0])


    return image_paths, all_captions
```

5. Define a function that will build the architecture of the network, which receives the vocabulary size, the maximum sequence length, and the encoder's input shape:

```
def build_network(vocabulary_size,
                    max_sequence_length,
                    input_shape=(4096,)):
```

6.  The first part of the network receives the feature vectors and passes them through a fully connected ReLU activated layer:

```
x = Dropout(rate=0.5)(feature_inputs)
x = Dense(units=256)(x)
feature_output = ReLU()(x)
```

7.  The second part of the layer receives the text sequences, transformed into numeric vectors, and trains an embedding of 256 elements. Then, it passes that embedding to an LSTM layer:

```
sequence_inputs =
        Input(shape=(max_sequence_length,))
y = Embedding(input_dim=vocabulary_size,
              output_dim=256,
              mask_zero=True)(sequence_inputs)
y = Dropout(rate=0.5)(y)
sequence_output = LSTM(units=256)(y)
```

8.  We concatenate the outputs of these two parts and pass the concatenation through a fully connected network, with an output layer with as many units as there are words in our vocabulary. By Softmax activating this output, we get a one-hot encoded vector that corresponds to a word in the vocabulary:

```
z = Add()([feature_output, sequence_output])
z = Dense(units=256)(z)
z = ReLU()(z)
z = Dense(units=vocabulary_size)(z)
outputs = Softmax()(z)
```

9.  Finally, we build the model, passing the image features and text sequences as inputs, and outputting the one-hot encoded vectors:

```
return Model(inputs=[feature_inputs,
             sequence_inputs],
             outputs=outputs)
```

10. Define a function that will convert an integer index into a word by using the tokenizer's internal mapping:

```python
def get_word_from_index(tokenizer, index):
    return tokenizer.index_word.get(index, None)
```

11. Define a function that will produce a caption. It will start by feeding the beginsequence token to the network, which will iteratively construct the sentence until the maximum sequence length is reached, or the endsequence token is encountered:

```python
def produce_caption(model,
                    tokenizer,
                    image,
                    max_sequence_length):
    text = 'beginsequence'

    for _ in range(max_sequence_length):
        sequence = tokenizer.texts_to_sequences([text])[0]
        sequence = pad_sequences([sequence],
                maxlen=max_sequence_length)

        prediction = model.predict([[image], sequence])
        index = np.argmax(prediction)

        word = get_word_from_index(tokenizer, index)

        if word is None:
            break

        text += f' {word}'

        if word == 'endsequence':
            break

    return text
```

12. Define a function that will evaluate the model's performance. First, we'll produce a caption for each feature corresponding to an image in the test dataset:

```
def evaluate_model(model, features, captions,
                     tokenizer,
                     max_seq_length):
    actual = []
    predicted = []

    for feature, caption in zip(features, captions):
        generated_caption = produce_caption(model,
                                             tokenizer,
                                             feature,
                                             max_seq_length)

        actual.append([caption.split(' ')])
        predicted.append(generated_caption.split(' '))
```

13. Next, we'll compute the **BLEU** score using different weights. Although the **BLEU** score is outside the scope of this recipe, you can find an excellent article that explains it in depth in the *See also* section. All you need to know is that it's used to measure how well a generated caption compares to a set of reference captions:

```
for index, weights in enumerate([(1, 0, 0, 0),
                                 (.5, .5, 0, 0),
                                 (.3, .3, .3, 0),
                                 (.25, .25, .25,
                                  .25)],
                                 start=1):
    b_score = corpus_bleu(actual, predicted, weights)
    print(f'BLEU-{index}: {b_score}')
```

14. Load the image paths and captions:

```
image_paths, all_captions = load_paths_and_captions()
```

15. Create the image extractor model:

```
extractor_model = VGG16(weights='imagenet')
inputs = extractor_model.inputs
outputs = extractor_model.layers[-2].output
extractor_model = Model(inputs=inputs, outputs=outputs)
```

16. Create the image caption feature extractor (passing the regular image extractor we created in *Step 15*) and use it to extract the sequences from the data:

```
extractor = ImageCaptionFeatureExtractor(
    feature_extractor=extractor_model,
    output_path=OUTPUT_PATH)
extractor.extract_features(image_paths, all_captions)
```

17. Load the pickled input and output sequences we created in *Step 16*:

```
pickled_data = []
for p in [f'{OUTPUT_PATH}/input_features.pickle',
          f'{OUTPUT_PATH}/input_sequences.pickle',
          f'{OUTPUT_PATH}/output_sequences.pickle']:
    with open(p, 'rb') as f:
        pickled_data.append(pickle.load(f))

input_feats, input_seqs, output_seqs = pickled_data
```

18. Use 80% of the data for training and 20% for testing:

```
(train_input_feats, test_input_feats,
 train_input_seqs, test_input_seqs,
 train_output_seqs,
 test_output_seqs) = train_test_split(input_feats,
                                      input_seqs,
                                      output_seqs,
                                      train_size=0.8,
                                      random_state=9)
```

19. Instantiate and compile the model. Because, in the end, this is a multi-class classification problem, we'll use `categorical_crossentropy` as our loss function:

```
vocabulary_size = len(extractor.tokenizer.word_index) + 1
model = build_network(vocabulary_size,
                      extractor.max_seq_length)
model.compile(loss='categorical_crossentropy',
              optimizer='adam')
```

20. Because the training process is so resource-intensive and the network tends to give the best results early on, let's create a `ModelCheckpoint` callback that will store the model with the lowest validation loss:

```
checkpoint_path = ('model-ep{epoch:03d}-
                        loss{loss:.3f}-'
                   'val_loss{val_loss:.3f}.h5')
checkpoint = ModelCheckpoint(checkpoint_path,
                             monitor='val_loss',
                             verbose=1,
                             save_best_only=True,
                             mode='min')
```

21. Fit the model over 30 epochs. Notice that we must pass two set of inputs or features, but only a set of labels:

```
EPOCHS = 30
model.fit(x=[train_input_feats, train_input_seqs],
          y=train_output_seqs,
          epochs=EPOCHS,
          callbacks=[checkpoint],
          validation_data=([test_input_feats,test_input_
                                                seqs],
                           test_output_seqs))
```

22. Load the best model. This may vary from run to run, but in this recipe, it's stored in the `model-ep003-loss3.847-val_loss4.328.h5` file:

```
model = load_model('model-ep003-loss3.847-
                    val_loss4.328.h5')
```

23. Load the data mapping, which contains all the features paired with the ground truth captions. Extract the features and mappings into separate collections:

```
with open(f'{OUTPUT_PATH}/data_mapping.pickle', 'rb') as
f:
    data_mapping = pickle.load(f)

feats = [v['features'] for v in data_mapping.values()]
captions = [v['caption'] for v in data_mapping.values()]
```

24. Evaluate the model:

```
evaluate_model(model,
               features=feats,
               captions=captions,
               tokenizer=extractor.tokenizer,
               max_seq_length=extractor.max_seq_length)
```

This step might take a while. In the end, you'll see an output similar to this:

```
BLEU-1: 0.35674398077995173
BLEU-2: 0.17030332240763874
BLEU-3: 0.12170338107914261
BLEU-4: 0.05493477725774873
```

Training an image captioner is not an easy task. However, by executing the proper steps, in the correct order, we were able to create a fairly capable one that performed well on the test set, based on the **BLEU** score shown in the preceding code block. Head over to the next section to see how it all works!

## How it works...

In this recipe, we implemented an image captioning network from scratch. Although this might seem complicated at first, we must remember it is a variation of an encoder-decoder architecture, similar to the ones we studied in *Chapter 5, Reducing Noise with Autoencoders*, and *Chapter 6, Generative Models and Adversarial Attacks*.

In this case, the encoder is just a fully connected and shallow network that maps the features we extracted from the pre-trained model on ImageNet, to a vector of 256 elements.

On the other hand, the decoder, instead of using transposed convolutions, uses an **RNN** that receives both text sequences (mapped to numeric vectors) and image features, concatenated into a long sequence of 512 elements.

The network is trained so that it learns to predict the next word in a sentence, given all the words it generated in previous time steps. Note that in each cycle, we pass the same feature vector that corresponds to the image, so the network learns to map certain words, in a particular order, to describe the visual data encoded in such a vector.

The output of the network is one-hot encoded, which means that only the position its corresponding to the words the network believes should come next in the sentence contains a 1, while the remaining positions contain a 0.

To generate captions, we follow a similar process. Of course, we somehow need to tell the model to start producing words. With this in mind, we pass the `beginsequence` token to the network and iterate until we reach the maximum sequence length, or the model outputs an `endsequence` token. Remember, we take the output of each iteration and use it as input for the next cycle.

This might seem confusing and cumbersome at first, but you now have the building blocks you need to tackle any image captioning problem!

## See also

Here's an excellent read if you wish to fully understand the **BLEU** score: `https://machinelearningmastery.com/calculate-bleu-score-for-text-python/`.

# Generating captions for your own photos

Training a good image captioning system is only one part of the equation. To actually use it, we must perform a series of steps, akin to the ones we executed during the training phase.

In this recipe, we'll use a trained image captioning network to produce textual descriptions of new images.

Let's get started!

# Getting ready

Although we don't need external dependencies for this particular recipe, we need access to a trained image captioning network, along with the cleaned captions that will be used to fit it. I highly recommend that you complete the *Implementing a reusable image caption feature extractor* and *Implementing an image captioning network* recipes before tackling this one.

Are you ready? Let's start captioning!

# How to do it...

Follow this series of steps to produce captions for your own images:

1.  As usual, let's begin by importing the necessary dependencies:

    ```
    import glob
    import pickle

    import matplotlib.pyplot as plt
    import numpy as np
    from tensorflow.keras.applications.vgg16 import *
    from tensorflow.keras.models import *
    from tensorflow.keras.preprocessing.sequence import \
        pad_sequences
    from tensorflow.keras.preprocessing.text import Tokenizer

    from ch7.recipe1.extractor import
    ImageCaptionFeatureExtractor
    ```

2.  Define a function that will translate an integer index into the corresponding word using the tokenizer's mapping:

    ```
    def get_word_from_index(tokenizer, index):
        return tokenizer.index_word.get(index, None)
    ```

3.  Define the `produce_caption()` function, which takes the captioning model, the tokenizer, an image to describe, and the maximum sequence length to generate a textual description of the input visual scene:

    ```
    def produce_caption(model,
                        tokenizer,
    ```

```
                        image,
                    max_sequence_length):
    text = 'beginsequence'

    for _ in range(max_sequence_length):
        sequence = tokenizer.texts_to_sequences([text])[0]
        sequence = pad_sequences([sequence],
                            maxlen=max_sequence_length)

        prediction = model.predict([[image], sequence])
        index = np.argmax(prediction)

        word = get_word_from_index(tokenizer, index)

        if word is None:
            break

        text += f' {word}'

        if word == 'endsequence':
            break

    return text
```

Note that we must keep generating words until we either encounter the endsequence token or we reach the maximum sequence length.

4. Define a pre-trained **VGG16** network, which we'll use as our image feature extractor:

```
extractor_model = VGG16(weights='imagenet')
inputs = extractor_model.inputs
outputs = extractor_model.layers[-2].output
extractor_model = Model(inputs=inputs, outputs=outputs)
```

5.  Pass the image extractor to an instance of
    `ImageCaptionFeatureExtractor()`:

```
extractor = ImageCaptionFeatureExtractor(
        feature_extractor=extractor_model)
```

6.  Load the cleaned captions we used to train the model. We need them to fit the
    tokenizer in *Step 7*:

```
with open('data_mapping.pickle', 'rb') as f:
        data_mapping = pickle.load(f)


captions = [v['caption'] for v in
                data_mapping.values()]
```

7.  Instantiate a `Tokenizer()` and fit it to all the captions. Also, compute the
    maximum sequence length:

```
tokenizer = Tokenizer()
tokenizer.fit_on_texts(captions)
max_seq_length = extractor._get_max_seq_length(captions)
```

8.  Load the trained network (in this case, the name of the network is `model-ep003-
    loss3.847-val_loss4.328.h5`):

```
model = load_model('model-ep003-loss3.847-
                        val_loss4.328.h5')
```

9.  Iterate over all the test images in the current location, extracting the corresponding
    numeric features:

```
for idx, image_path in enumerate(glob.glob('*.jpg'),
                                    start=1):
    img_feats = (extractor
                    .extract_image_features(image_path))
```

10. Produce the caption and remove the `beginsequence` and `endsequence` special
    tokens:

```
description = produce_caption(model,
                                tokenizer,
                                img_feats,
```

```
                                            max_seq_length)
description = (description
                .replace('beginsequence', '')
                .replace('endsequence', ''))
```

11. Open the image, add the generated caption as its title, and save it:

```
image = plt.imread(image_path)

plt.imshow(image)
plt.title(description)
plt.savefig(f'{idx}.jpg')
```

Here's an image where the network does a very good job of generating a proper caption:

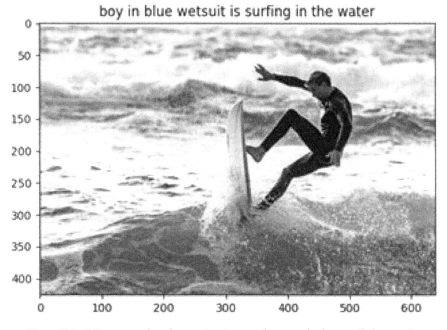

Figure 7.3 – We can see that the caption is very close to what's actually happening

Here's another example where the network is technically correct, although it could be more precise:

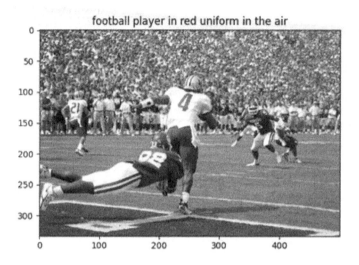

Figure 7.4 – A football player in a red uniform is, indeed, in the air, but there is more going on

Finally, here's an instance where the network is clueless:

Figure 7.5 – The network couldn't describe this scene

With that, we've seen that our model does well on some images, but still has room for improvement. We'll dive a bit deeper in the next section.

# How it works...

In this recipe, we learned that image captioning is a difficult problem that heavily depends on many factors. Some of these factors are as follows:

- A well-trained **CNN** to extract high-quality visual features

- A rich set of descriptive captions for each image

- Embeddings with enough capacity to encode the expressiveness of the vocabulary with minimal loss

- A powerful **RNN** to learn how to put all of this together

Despite these clear challenges, in this recipe, we used a trained network on the `Flickr8k` dataset to generate captions for new images. The process we followed is similar to the one we implemented to train the system in that, first, we must go from an image to a feature vector. Then, we must fit a tokenizer to our vocabulary to get a proper mechanism so that we can go from sequences to human-readable words. Finally, we assemble the captions one word at a time, passing the image features along with the sequence we've built so far. How do we know when to stop, though? We have two stopping criteria:

- The caption reached the maximum sequence length.

- The network encountered the `endsequence` token.

Lastly, we tested our solution on several images, with varied results. In some instances, the network is capable of producing very precise descriptions, while on other occasions, it generates somewhat vague captions. It also missed the mark completely in the last example, which is a clear indication of how much room for improvement there is.

If you want to take a look at other captioned images, consult the official repository: `https://github.com/PacktPublishing/Tensorflow-2.0-Computer-Vision-Cookbook/tree/master/ch7/recipe3`.

# Implementing an image captioning network on COCO with attention

A great way to understand how an image captioning network generates its descriptions is by adding an attention component to the architecture. This lets us appreciate what parts of the photo a network was looking at when it generated each word.

In this recipe, we'll train an end-to-end image captioning system on the more challenging **Common Objects in Context** (**COCO**) dataset. We'll also equip our network with an attention mechanism to improve its performance and to help us understand its inner reasoning.

This is a long and advanced recipe, but don't panic! We'll go step by step. If you want to dive deeper into the theory that supports this implementation, take a look at the *See also* section.

## Getting ready

Although we'll be using the COCO dataset, you don't need to do anything beforehand, because we'll download it as part of the recipe (however, you can read more about this seminal dataset here: `https://cocodataset.org/#home`).

The following is a sample from the COCO dataset:

Figure 7.6 – Sample images from COCO

Let's get to work!

## How to do it...

Follow these steps to complete this recipe:

1. Import all the necessary dependencies:

```
import json
import os
import time
import matplotlib.pyplot as plt
import numpy as np
import tensorflow as tf
from sklearn.model_selection import train_test_split
from sklearn.utils import shuffle
```

```
from tensorflow.keras.applications.inception_v3 import *
from tensorflow.keras.layers import *
from tensorflow.keras.losses import \
    SparseCategoricalCrossentropy
from tensorflow.keras.models import Model
from tensorflow.keras.optimizers import Adam
from tensorflow.keras.preprocessing.sequence import \
    pad_sequences
from tensorflow.keras.preprocessing.text import Tokenizer
from tensorflow.keras.utils import get_file
```

2. Define an alias for `tf.data.experimental.AUTOTUNE`:

```
AUTOTUNE = tf.data.experimental.AUTOTUNE
```

3. Define a function that will load an image. It must return both the image and its path:

```
def load_image(image_path):
    image = tf.io.read_file(image_path)
    image = tf.image.decode_jpeg(image, channels=3)
    image = tf.image.resize(image, (299, 299))
    image = preprocess_input(image)

    return image, image_path
```

4. Define a function that will get the maximum sequence length. This will be useful later on:

```
def get_max_length(tensor):
    return max(len(t) for t in tensor)
```

5. Define for the image captioning network a function that will load an image from disk (stored in NumPy format):

```
def load_image_and_caption(image_name, caption):
    image_name = image_name.decode('utf-8').split('/')
                                                    [-1]
    image_tensor = np.load(f'./{image_name}.npy')
    return image_tensor, caption
```

6.  Implement **Bahdanau's Attention** using model subclassing:

```python
class BahdanauAttention(Model):
    def __init__(self, units):
        super(BahdanauAttention, self).__init__()
        self.W1 = Dense(units)
        self.W2 = Dense(units)
        self.V = Dense(1)
```

7.  The previous block defined the network layers. Now, let's define the forward pass inside the `call()` method:

```python
def call(self, features, hidden):
    hidden_with_time_axis = tf.expand_dims(hidden,
                                           1)

    score = tf.nn.tanh(self.W1(features) +
                       self.W2(hidden_with_time_axis))

    attention_w = tf.nn.softmax(self.V(score),
                                axis=1)

    ctx_vector = attention_w * features
    ctx_vector = tf.reduce_sum(ctx_vector, axis=1)

    return ctx_vector, attention_w
```

8.  Define the image encoder. This is just a **CNN** that receives a feature vector and passes it through a dense layer, which is then activated with ReLU:

```python
class CNNEncoder(Model):
    def __init__(self, embedding_dim):
        super(CNNEncoder, self).__init__()
        self.fc = Dense(embedding_dim)

    def call(self, x):
        x = self.fc(x)
        x = tf.nn.relu(x)
```

```
          return x
```

9.  Define the decoder. This is an **RNN** that uses GRU and attention to learn how to produce captions from the visual feature vectors and the text input sequences:

```
class RNNDecoder(Model):
    def __init__(self, embedding_size, units,
                      vocab_size):
        super(RNNDecoder, self).__init__()
        self.units = units

        self.embedding = Embedding(vocab_size,
                                   embedding_size)
        self.gru = GRU(self.units,
                       return_sequences=True,
                       return_state=True,
                       recurrent_initializer='glorot_
                       uniform')
        self.fc1 = Dense(self.units)
        self.fc2 = Dense(vocab_size)

        self.attention = BahdanauAttention(self.units)
```

10.  Now that we've defined the layers in the **RNN** architecture, let's implement the forward pass. First, we must pass the inputs through the attention sub-network:

```
def call(self, x, features, hidden):
    context_vector, attention_weights = \
        self.attention(features, hidden)
```

11.  Then, we must pass the input sequence (x) through the embedding layer and concatenate it with the context vector we received from the attention mechanism:

```
x = self.embedding(x)
expanded_context = tf.expand_dims(context_vector,
                                  1)
x = Concatenate(axis=-1)([expanded_context, x])
```

12. Next, we must pass the merged tensor to the GRU layer, and then through the dense layers. This returns the output sequence, the state, and the attention weights:

```
output, state = self.gru(x)
x = self.fc1(output)
x = tf.reshape(x, (-1, x.shape[2]))
x = self.fc2(x)
```

13. Finally, we must define a method that will reset the hidden state:

```
def reset_state(self, batch_size):
    return tf.zeros((batch_size, self.units))
```

14. Define `ImageCaptionerClass`. The constructor instantiates the basic components, which are the encoder, the decoder, the tokenizer, and the optimizer and loss functions needed to train the whole system:

```
class ImageCaptioner(object):
    def __init__(self, embedding_size, units,
                 vocab_size,
                 tokenizer):
        self.tokenizer = tokenizer
        self.encoder = CNNEncoder(embedding_size)
        self.decoder = RNNDecoder(embedding_size,
                                  units,
                                  vocab_size)

        self.optimizer = Adam()
        self.loss = SparseCategoricalCrossentropy(
            from_logits=True,
            reduction='none')
```

15. Create a method that will compute the loss function:

```
def loss_function(self, real, predicted):
    mask = tf.math.logical_not(tf.math.equal(real,
                                             0))
    _loss = self.loss(real, predicted)

    mask = tf.cast(mask, dtype=_loss.dtype)
```

```
    _loss *= mask

    return tf.reduce_mean(_loss)
```

16. Next, define a function that will perform a single training step. We will start by creating the hidden state and the input, which is just a batch of singleton sequences containing the index of the <start> token, a special element used to signal the beginning of a sentence:

```
@tf.function
def train_step(self, image_tensor, target):
    loss = 0

    hidden =
    self.decoder.reset_state(target.shape[0])
    start_token_idx =
    self.tokenizer.word_index['<start>']
    init_batch = [start_token_idx] *
    target.shape[0]
    decoder_input = tf.expand_dims(init_batch, 1)
```

17. Now, we must encode the image tensor. Then, we'll iteratively pass the resulting features to the decoder, along with the outputted sequence so far, and the hidden state. For a deeper explanation on how **RNNs** work, head to the *See also* section:

```
with tf.GradientTape() as tape:
    features = self.encoder(image_tensor)

    for i in range(1, target.shape[1]):
        preds, hidden, _ =
        self.decoder(decoder_input,
                    features,
                    hidden)
        loss += self.loss_function(target[:, i],
                                    preds)
        decoder_input =
            tf.expand_dims(target[:, i],1)
```

18. Notice in the previous block that we computed the loss at each time step. To get the total loss, we must calculate the average. For the network to actually learn, we must backpropagate the total loss by computing the gradients and applying them via the optimizer:

```
total_loss = loss / int(target.shape[1])


trainable_vars = (self.encoder.trainable_
                                variables +
                        self.decoder.trainable_
                                variables)
gradients = tape.gradient(loss, trainable_vars)
self.optimizer.apply_gradients(zip(gradients,
                                trainable_vars))


return loss, total_loss
```

19. The last method in this class is in charge of training the system:

```
def train(self, dataset, epochs, num_steps):
    for epoch in range(epochs):
        start = time.time()
        total_loss = 0

        for batch, (image_tensor, target) \
                in enumerate(dataset):
            batch_loss, step_loss = \
                self.train_step(image_tensor, target)
            total_loss += step_loss
```

20. Every 100 epochs, we'll print the loss. At the end of each epoch, we will also print the epoch loss and elapsed time:

```
if batch % 100 == 0:
    loss = batch_loss.numpy()
    loss = loss / int(target.shape[1])
    print(f'Epoch {epoch + 1}, batch
                                {batch},'
          f' loss {loss:.4f}')
```

```
          print(f'Epoch {epoch + 1},'
                f' loss {total_loss /
                        num_steps:.6f}')
          epoch_time = time.time() - start
          print(f'Time taken: {epoch_time} seconds.
                \n')
```

21. Download and unzip the COCO dataset's annotation files. If they're already in the system, just store the file path:

```
INPUT_DIR = os.path.abspath('.')
annots_folder = '/annotations/'
if not os.path.exists(INPUT_DIR + annots_folder):
    origin_url = ('http://images.cocodataset.org/
            annotations''/annotations_trainval2014.zip')
    cache_subdir = os.path.abspath('.')
    annots_zip = get_file('all_captions.zip',
                          cache_subdir=cache_subdir,
                          origin=origin_url,
                          extract=True)
    annots_file = (os.path.dirname(annots_zip) +
                  '/annotations/captions_train2014.json')
    os.remove(annots_zip)
else:
    annots_file = (INPUT_DIR +
                  '/annotations/captions_train2014.json')
```

22. Download and unzip the COCO dataset's image files. If they're already in the system, just store the file path:

```
image_folder = '/train2014/'
if not os.path.exists(INPUT_DIR + image_folder):
    origin_url = ('http://images.cocodataset.org/zips/'
                  'train2014.zip')
    cache_subdir = os.path.abspath('.')
    image_zip = get_file('train2014.zip',
                         cache_subdir=cache_subdir,
```

```
                    origin=origin_url,
                    extract=True)
    PATH = os.path.dirname(image_zip) + image_folder
    os.remove(image_zip)
else:
    PATH = INPUT_DIR + image_folder
```

23. Load the image paths and the captions. We must add the special `<start>` and `<end>` tokens to each caption so that they're in our vocabulary. These special tokens let us specify where a sequence begins and ends, respectively:

```
with open(annots_file, 'r') as f:
    annotations = json.load(f)

captions = []
image_paths = []

for annotation in annotations['annotations']:
    caption = '<start>' + annotation['caption'] + '<end>'
    image_id = annotation['image_id']
    image_path = f'{PATH}COCO_train2014_{image_id:012d}.jpg'

    image_paths.append(image_path)
    captions.append(caption)
```

24. Because COCO is massive, and it would take ages to train a model on it, we'll select a random sample of 30,000 images, along with their captions:

```
train_captions, train_image_paths = shuffle(captions,
                                             image_paths,
                                             random_state=42)

SAMPLE_SIZE = 30000
train_captions = train_captions[:SAMPLE_SIZE]
train_image_paths = train_image_paths[:SAMPLE_SIZE]
train_images = sorted(set(train_image_paths))
```

25. Let's use a pre-trained instance of `InceptionV3` as our image feature extractor:

```
feature_extractor = InceptionV3(include_top=False,
                                weights='imagenet')
feature_extractor = Model(feature_extractor.input,
                          feature_extractor.layers[-
                                  1].output)
```

26. Create a `tf.data.Dataset` that maps image paths to tensors. Use it to go over all the images in our sample, convert them into feature vectors, and save them as NumPy arrays. This will allow us to save memory in the future:

```
BATCH_SIZE = 8
image_dataset = (tf.data.Dataset
                    .from_tensor_slices(train_images)
                    .map(load_image,
                        num_parallel_calls=AUTOTUNE)
                    .batch(BATCH_SIZE))

for image, path in image_dataset:
    batch_features = feature_extractor.predict(image)
    batch_features = tf.reshape(batch_features,
                            (batch_features.shape[0],
                                -1,
                                batch_features.shape[3]))

    for batch_feature, p in zip(batch_features, path):
        feature_path = p.numpy().decode('UTF-8')
        image_name = feature_path.split('/')[-1]
        np.save(f'./{image_name}', batch_feature.numpy())
```

27. Train a tokenizer on the top 5,000 words in our captions. Then, convert each text into a numeric sequence and pad them so that they are all the same size. Also, compute the maximum sequence length:

```
top_k = 5000
filters = '!"#$%&()*+.,-/:;=?@[\]^_`{|}~ '
tokenizer = Tokenizer(num_words=top_k,
                      oov_token='<unk>',
```

```
                              filters=filters)
tokenizer.fit_on_texts(train_captions)
tokenizer.word_index['<pad>'] = 0
tokenizer.index_word[0] = '<pad>'

train_seqs = tokenizer.texts_to_sequences(train_captions)
captions_seqs = pad_sequences(train_seqs,
                              padding='post')

max_length = get_max_length(train_seqs)
```

28. We'll use 20% of the data to test our model and the remaining 80% to train it:

```
(images_train, images_val, caption_train, caption_val) = \
    train_test_split(train_img_paths,
                     captions_seqs,
                     test_size=0.2,
                     random_state=42)
```

29. We'll load batches of 64 images (along with their captions) at a time. Notice that we're using the `load_image_and_caption()` function, defined in *Step 5*, which reads the feature vector corresponding to the images, stored in NumPy format. Moreover, because this function works at the NumPy level, we must wrap it with `tf.numpy_function` so that it can be used as a valid TensorFlow function within the `map()` method:

```
BATCH_SIZE = 64
BUFFER_SIZE = 1000
dataset = (tf.data.Dataset
           .from_tensor_slices((images_train,
                                caption_train))
           .map(lambda i1, i2:
                tf.numpy_function(
                    load_image_and_caption,
                    [i1, i2],
                    [tf.float32, tf.int32]),
                num_parallel_calls=AUTOTUNE)
           .shuffle(BUFFER_SIZE)
```

```
                    .batch(BATCH_SIZE)
                    .prefetch(buffer_size=AUTOTUNE))
```

30. Let's instantiate an `ImageCaptioner`. The embeddings will have 256 elements, and the number of units for the decoder and the attention model will be 512. The vocabulary size is 5,001. Finally, we must pass the fitted tokenizer from *Step 27*:

```
image_captioner = ImageCaptioner(embedding_size=256,
                                 units=512,
                                 vocab_size=top_k + 1,
                                 tokenizer=tokenizer)


EPOCHS = 30
num_steps = len(images_train) // BATCH_SIZE
image_captioner.train(dataset, EPOCHS, num_steps)
```

31. Define a function that will evaluate the image captioner on an image. It must receive the encoder, the decoder, the tokenizer, the image to caption, the maximum sequence length, and the shape of the attention vector. We will start by creating a placeholder array, which is where we'll store the subplots that comprise the attention plot:

```
def evaluate(encoder, decoder, tokenizer, image,
             max_length,
             attention_shape):
    attention_plot = np.zeros((max_length,
                               attention_shape))
```

32. Next, we must initialize the hidden state, extract the features from the input image, and pass them to the encoder. We must also initialize the decoder input by creating a singleton sequence with the `<start>` token index:

```
hidden = decoder.reset_state(batch_size=1)

temp_input = tf.expand_dims(load_image(image)[0],
                            0)
image_tensor_val = feature_extractor(temp_input)
image_tensor_val = tf.reshape(image_tensor_val,
                              (image_tensor_val.shape[0],
```

```
                                    -1,
                        image_tensor_val.shape[3]))

        feats = encoder(image_tensor_val)

        start_token_idx = tokenizer.word_index['<start>']
        dec_input = tf.expand_dims([start_token_idx], 0)
        result = []
```

33. Now, let's build the caption until we reach the maximum sequence length or encounter the <end> token:

```
        for i in range(max_length):
            (preds, hidden, attention_w) = \
                decoder(dec_input, feats, hidden)

            attention_plot[i] = tf.reshape(attention_w,
                                    (-1,)).numpy()

            pred_id = tf.random.categorical(preds,
                                1)[0][0].numpy()
            result.append(tokenizer.index_word[pred_id])

            if tokenizer.index_word[pred_id] == '<end>':
                return result, attention_plot

            dec_input = tf.expand_dims([pred_id], 0)

        attention_plot = attention_plot[:len(result), :]
        return result, attention_plot
```

34. Notice that for each word, we update attention_plot with the weights returned by the decoder.

35. Let's define a function that will plot the attention the network pays to each word in the caption. It receives the image, a list of the individual words that comprise the caption (`result`), `attention_plot` returned by `evaluate()`, and the output path where we'll store the graph:

```
def plot_attention(image, result,
                    attention_plot, output_path):
    tmp_image = np.array(load_image(image)[0])


    fig = plt.figure(figsize=(10, 10))
```

36. We'll iterate over each word to create a subplot of the corresponding attention graph, titled with the specific word it's linked to:

```
    for l in range(len(result)):
        temp_att = np.resize(attention_plot[l], (8, 8))
        ax = fig.add_subplot(len(result) // 2,
                                len(result) // 2,
                                l + 1)
        ax.set_title(result[l])
        image = ax.imshow(tmp_image)

        ax.imshow(temp_att,
                    cmap='gray',
                    alpha=0.6,
                    extent=image.get_extent())
```

37. Finally, we can save the full plot:

```
    plt.tight_layout()
    plt.show()
    plt.savefig(output_path)
```

38. Evaluate the network on a random image from the validation set:

```
attention_features_shape = 64
random_id = np.random.randint(0, len(images_val))
image = images_val[random_id]
```

39. Build and clean the actual (ground truth) caption:

```
actual_caption = ' '.join([tokenizer.index_word[i]
                          for i in caption_val[random_id]
                          if i != 0])
actual_caption = (actual_caption
                  .replace('<start>', '')
                  .replace('<end>', ''))
```

40. Generate the caption for the validation image:

```
result, attention_plot = evaluate(image_captioner
                                  encoder,
                        image_captioner.decoder,
                                  tokenizer,
                                  image,
                                  max_length,
                        attention_feats_shape)
```

41. Build and clean the predicted caption:

```
predicted_caption = (' '.join(result)
                     .replace('<start>', '')
                     .replace('<end>', ''))
```

42. Print the ground truth and generated captions, and then save the attention plot to disk:

```
print(f'Actual caption: {actual_caption}')
print(f'Predicted caption: {predicted_caption}')
output_path = './attention_plot.png'
plot_attention(image, result, attention_plot, output_
path)
```

43. In the following code block, we can appreciate the similarity between the real caption and the one outputted by our model:

> Actual caption: a lone giraffe stands in the midst of a grassy area

> Predicted caption: giraffe standing in a dry grass near trees

Now, let's take a look at the attention plot:

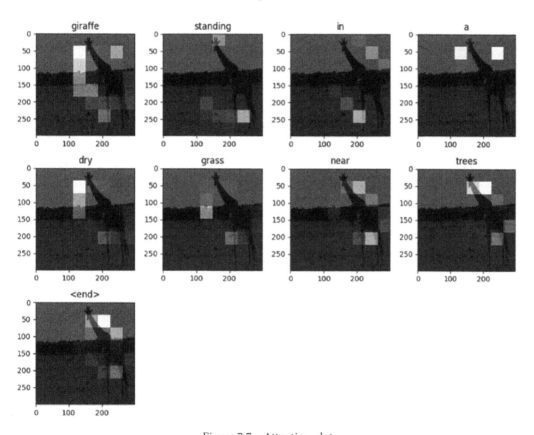

Figure 7.7 – Attention plot

Take note of the areas the network looked at when generating each word in the caption. Lighter squares mean that more attention was paid to those pixels. For instance, to produce the word *giraffe*, the network looked at the surroundings of the giraffe in the photo. Also, we can see that when the network generated the word *grass*, it looked at the giraffe legs, which have a grass portion behind them. Isn't that amazing?

We'll look at this in more detail in the *How it works...* section.

## How it works...

In this recipe, we implemented a more complete image captioning system, this time on the considerably more challenging COCO dataset, which is not only several orders of magnitude bigger than `Flickr8k`, but much more varied and, therefore, harder for the network to understand.

Nevertheless, we gave our network an advantage by providing it with an attention mechanism, inspired by the impressive breakthrough proposed by Dzmitry Bahdanau (take a look at the *See also* section for more details). This capability gives the model the power to perform a soft search for parts of the source caption that are relevant to predicting a target word or simply put, producing the best next word in the output sentence. Such an attention mechanism works as an advantage over the traditional approach, which consists of using a fixed-length vector (as we did in the *Implementing an image captioning network* recipe) from which the decoder generates the output sentence. The problem with such a representation is that it tends to act as a bottleneck when it comes to improving performance.

Also, the attention mechanism allows us to understand how the network thinks to produce captions in a more intuitive way.

Because neural networks are complex pieces of software (often akin to a black box), using visual techniques to inspect their inner workings is a great tool at our disposal that can aid us in the training, fine-tuning, and optimization process.

## See also

In this recipe, we implemented our architecture using the Model Subclassing pattern, which you can read more about here: `https://www.tensorflow.org/guide/keras/custom_layers_and_models`.

Take a look at the following link for a great refresher on **RNNs**: `https://www.youtube.com/watch?v=UNmqTiOnRfg`.

Finally, I highly encourage you to read Dzmitry Bahdanau's paper about the attention mechanism we just implemented and used: `https://arxiv.org/abs/1409.0473`.

# 8
# Fine-Grained Understanding of Images through Segmentation

Image segmentation is one of the biggest areas of study in computer vision. It consists of simplifying the visual contents of an image by grouping together pixels that share one or more defining characteristics, such as location, color, or texture. As is the case with many other subareas of computer vision, image segmentation has been greatly boosted by deep neural networks, mainly in industries such as medicine and autonomous driving.

While it's great to classify the contents of an image, more often than not, it's not enough. What if we want to know exactly where an object is? What if we're interested in its shape? What if we need its contour? These fine-grained needs cannot be met with traditional classification techniques. However, as we'll discover in this chapter, we can frame an image segmentation problem in a very similar way to a regular classification project. How? Instead of labeling the image as a whole, we'll label each pixel! This is known as image segmentation and is what constitutes the recipes in this chapter.

In this chapter, we will cover the following recipes:

- Creating a fully convolutional network for image segmentation
- Implementing a U-Net from scratch
- Implementing a U-Net with transfer learning
- Segmenting images using Mask-RCNN and TensorFlow Hub

Let's get started!

# Technical requirements

In order to implement and experiment with the recipes in this chapter, it's recommended that you have access to a GPU. If you have recourse to a cloud-based provider, such as AWS or FloydHub, that's great, but keep the fees attached to them in mind as they might skyrocket if you're not careful! In the *Getting ready* section of each recipe, you'll find everything you'll need to prepare for what lies ahead. The code for this chapter is available here: `https://github.com/PacktPublishing/Tensorflow-2.0-Computer-Vision-Cookbook/tree/master/ch8`.

Check out the following link to see the Code in Action video:

`https://bit.ly/2Na77IF`.

# Creating a fully convolutional network for image segmentation

If you were to create your first network for image segmentation while knowing that, at its core, segmenting is just pixel-wise classification, what would you do? You would probably take a battle-tested architecture and swap the final layers (usually fully connected ones) with convolutions in order to produce an output volume, instead of an output vector.

Well, that's exactly what we'll do in this recipe to build a **Fully Convolutional Network** (**FCN**) for image segmentation based on the famous **VGG16** network.

Let's get started!

# Getting ready

We need to install a couple of external libraries, starting with `tensorflow_docs`:

```
$> pip install git+https://github.com/tensorflow/docs
```

Next, we need to install TensorFlow Datasets, `Pillow`, and `OpenCV`:

```
$> pip install tensorflow-datasets Pillow opencv-contrib-python
```

Regarding the data, we will segment images from `the Oxford-IIIT Pet` dataset. The good news is that we'll access it using `tensorflow-datasets`, so we don't really need to do anything in that respect here. Each pixel in this dataset is classified as follows:

- 1: The pixel belongs to a pet (cat or dog).
- 2: The pixel belongs to the contour of a pet.
- 3: The pixel belongs to the surroundings.

Here are some sample images from the dataset:

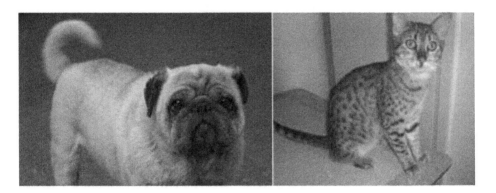

Figure 8.1 – Sample images from the Oxford-IIIT Pet dataset

Let's start implementing!

## How to do it...

Follow these steps to complete this recipe:

1. Import all the required packages:

```
import pathlib

import cv2
import matplotlib.pyplot as plt
import numpy as np
import tensorflow as tf
```

```
import tensorflow_datasets as tfds
import tensorflow_docs as tfdocs
import tensorflow_docs.plots
from tensorflow.keras.layers import *
from tensorflow.keras.losses import \
    SparseCategoricalCrossentropy
from tensorflow.keras.models import Model
from tensorflow.keras.optimizers import RMSprop
```

2.  Define an alias for `tf.data.experimental.AUTOTUNE`:

```
AUTOTUNE = tf.data.experimental.AUTOTUNE
```

3.  Define a function that will normalize the images in the dataset to the range [0, 1]. Just for consistency's sake, we'll subtract one from each pixel in the mask so that they go from 0 all the way to 2:

```
def normalize(input_image, input_mask):
    input_image = tf.cast(input_image, tf.float32) / 255.0
    input_mask -= 1

    return input_image, input_mask
```

4.  Define the `load_image()` function, which loads both the image and its mask, given a TensorFlow dataset element. We will seize the opportunity to resize the images to *256x256* here. Also, if the `train` flag is set to `True`, we can perform a bit of augmentation by randomly mirroring the image and its mask. Lastly, we must normalize the inputs:

```
@tf.function
def load_image(dataset_element, train=True):
    input_image = tf.image.resize(dataset_element['image'],
                                  (256, 256))
    input_mask = tf.image.resize(
        dataset_element['segmentation_mask'], (256, 256))

    if train and np.random.uniform() > 0.5:
        input_image =
            tf.image.flip_left_right(input_image)
```

```
        input_mask = tf.image.flip_left_right(input_mask)

    input_image, input_mask = normalize(input_image,
                                        input_mask)

    return input_image, input_mask
```

5. Implement the `FCN()` class, which encapsulates all the logic required to build, train, and evaluate our **FCN** image segmentation model. First, define the constructor:

```
class FCN(object):
    def __init__(self,
                 input_shape=(256, 256, 3),
                 output_channels=3):
        self.input_shape = input_shape
        self.output_channels = output_channels

        self.vgg_weights_path = str(pathlib.Path.home() /
                                    '.keras' /
                                    'models' /
                                    'vgg16_weights_tf_dim_'
                                    'ordering_tf_kernels.h5')

        self.model = self._create_model()

        loss = SparseCategoricalCrossentropy(from_
                                    logits=True)
        self.model.compile(optimizer=RMSprop(),
                           loss=loss,
                           metrics=['accuracy'])
```

In this step, we are creating the model, which we'll train using `RMSProp` as the optimizer and `SparseCategoricalCrossentropy` as the loss. Notice that `output_channels` is, by default, 3, because each pixel can be categorized into one of three classes. Also, notice that we are defining the path to the weights of the **VGG16** this model is based on. We'll use these weights to give our network a head start when training.

6.  Now, it's time to define the architecture itself:

```python
def _create_model(self):
    input = Input(shape=self.input_shape)

    x = Conv2D(filters=64,
               kernel_size=(3, 3),
               activation='relu',
               padding='same',
               name='block1_conv1')(input)
    x = Conv2D(filters=64,
               kernel_size=(3, 3),
               activation='relu',
               padding='same',
               name='block1_conv2')(x)
    x = MaxPooling2D(pool_size=(2, 2),
                     strides=2,
                     name='block1_pool')(x)
```

7.  We started by defining the input and the first block of convolutions and max pooling layers. Now, define the second block of convolutions, this time with 128 filters each:

```python
    x = Conv2D(filters=128,
               kernel_size=(3, 3),
               activation='relu',
               padding='same',
               name='block2_conv1')(x)
    x = Conv2D(filters=128,
               kernel_size=(3, 3),
               activation='relu',
               padding='same',
```

```
                    name='block2_conv2')(x)
        x = MaxPooling2D(pool_size=(2, 2),
                        strides=2,

                    name='block2_pool')(x)
```

8. The third block contains convolutions with 256 filters:

```
        x = Conv2D(filters=256,
                    kernel_size=(3, 3),
                    activation='relu',
                    padding='same',
                    name='block3_conv1')(x)
        x = Conv2D(filters=256,
                    kernel_size=(3, 3),
                    activation='relu',
                    padding='same',
                    name='block3_conv2')(x)
        x = Conv2D(filters=256,
                    kernel_size=(3, 3),
                    activation='relu',
                    padding='same',
                    name='block3_conv3')(x)
        x = MaxPooling2D(pool_size=(2, 2),
                        strides=2,
                        name='block3_pool')(x)
    block3_pool = x
```

9. The fourth block uses convolutions with 512 filters:

```
        x = Conv2D(filters=512,
                    kernel_size=(3, 3),
                    activation='relu',
                    padding='same',
                    name='block4_conv1')(x)
        x = Conv2D(filters=512,
                    kernel_size=(3, 3),
                    activation='relu',
```

```
                        padding='same',
                        name='block4_conv2')(x)
        x = Conv2D(filters=512,
                   kernel_size=(3, 3),
                   activation='relu',
                   padding='same',
                   name='block4_conv3')(x)
        block4_pool = MaxPooling2D(pool_size=(2, 2),
                                   strides=2,
                                   name='block4_pool')(x)
```

10. The fifth block is a repetition of block four, again with 512 filter-deep convolutions:

```
        x = Conv2D(filters=512,
                   kernel_size=(3, 3),
                   activation='relu',
                   padding='same',
                   name='block5_conv1')(block4_pool)
        x = Conv2D(filters=512,
                   kernel_size=(3, 3),
                   activation='relu',
                   padding='same',
                   name='block5_conv2')(x)
        x = Conv2D(filters=512,
                   kernel_size=(3, 3),
                   activation='relu',
                   padding='same',
                   name='block5_conv3')(x)
        block5_pool = MaxPooling2D(pool_size=(2, 2),
                                   strides=2,
                                   name='block5_pool')(x)
```

11. The reason we've been naming the layers so far is so that we can match them with the pre-trained weights we'll import next (notice `by_name=True`):

```
model = Model(input, block5_pool)
model.load_weights(self.vgg_weights_path,
                            by_name=True)
```

12. `output`, in a traditional **VGG16** architecture, is comprised of fully connected layers. However, we'll be replacing them with transposed convolutions. Notice we are connecting these layers to the output of the fifth block:

```
output = Conv2D(filters=self.output_channels,
                        kernel_size=(7, 7),
                        activation='relu',
                        padding='same',
                        name='conv6')(block5_pool)

conv6_4 = Conv2DTranspose(
        filters=self.output_channels,
        kernel_size=(4, 4),
        strides=4,
        use_bias=False)(output)
```

13. Create a 1x1 convolution, followed by a transposed convolution, and connect it to the output of the fourth block (this is, indeed, a skip connection):

```
pool4_n = Conv2D(filters=self.output_channels,
                        kernel_size=(1, 1),
                        activation='relu',
                        padding='same',
                        name='pool4_n')(block4_pool)
pool4_n_2 = Conv2DTranspose(
        filters=self.output_channels,
        kernel_size=(2, 2),
        strides=2,
        use_bias=False)(pool4_n)
```

14. Pass the output of the third block through a 1x1 convolution. Then, merge these three paths into one and pass them through a final transposed convolution. This will be activated with `Softmax`. This output constitutes the segmentation mask predicted by the model:

```
pool3_n = Conv2D(filters=self.output_channels,
                 kernel_size=(1, 1),
                 activation='relu',
                 padding='same',
                 name='pool3_n')(block3_pool)

output = Add(name='add')([pool4_n_2,
                          pool3_n,
                          conv6_4])
output = Conv2DTranspose
                (filters=self.output_channels,
                 kernel_size=(8, 8),
                 strides=8,
                 use_bias=False)(output)
output = Softmax()(output)
return Model(input, output)
```

15. Now, let's create a private helper method to plot the relevant training curves:

```
@staticmethod
def _plot_model_history(model_history, metric,
                        ylim=None):
    plt.style.use('seaborn-darkgrid')
    plotter = tfdocs.plots.HistoryPlotter()
    plotter.plot({'Model': model_history},
                 metric=metric)

    plt.title(f'{metric.upper()}')
    if ylim is None:
        plt.ylim([0, 1])
    else:
        plt.ylim(ylim)
```

```
        plt.savefig(f'{metric}.png')
        plt.close()
```

16. The `train()` method takes the training and validation datasets, as well as the number of epochs and training and validation steps to perform, in order to fit the model. It also saves the loss and accuracy plots to disk for later analysis:

```
def train(self, train_dataset, epochs,
                  steps_per_epoch,
              validation_dataset, validation_steps):
    hist = \
        self.model.fit(train_dataset,
                       epochs=epochs,
                       steps_per_epoch=steps_per_epoch,
                       validation_steps=validation_steps,
                       validation_data=validation_dataset)

    self._plot_model_history(hist, 'loss', [0., 2.0])
    self._plot_model_history(hist, 'accuracy')
```

17. Implement `_process_mask()`, which is used to make the segmentation masks compatible with OpenCV. What this function does is create a three-channeled version of a grayscale mask and upscale the class values to the [0, 255] range:

```
@staticmethod
def _process_mask(mask):
    mask = (mask.numpy() * 127.5).astype('uint8')
    mask = cv2.cvtColor(mask, cv2.COLOR_GRAY2RGB)

    return mask
```

18. The `_save_image_and_masks()` helper method creates a mosaic of the original image, the ground truth mask, and the predicted segmentation mask, and then saves it to disk for later revision:

```
def _save_image_and_masks(self, image,
                          ground_truth_mask,
                          prediction_mask,
                          image_id):
    image = (image.numpy() * 255.0).astype('uint8')
    gt_mask = self._process_mask(ground_truth_mask)
    pred_mask = self._process_mask(prediction_mask)

    mosaic = np.hstack([image, gt_mask, pred_mask])
    mosaic = cv2.cvtColor(mosaic, cv2.COLOR_RGB2BGR)

    cv2.imwrite(f'mosaic_{image_id}.jpg', mosaic)
```

19. In order to pass the output volume produced by the network to a valid segmentation mask, we must take the index with the highest value at each pixel location. This corresponds to the most likely category for that pixel. The `_create_mask()` method does this:

```
@staticmethod
def _create_mask(prediction_mask):
    prediction_mask = tf.argmax(prediction_mask,
                                axis=-1)
    prediction_mask = prediction_mask[...,
                                      tf.newaxis]

    return prediction_mask[0]
```

20. The _save_predictions() method uses the **FCN** to predict the mask of a sample of images in the input dataset. It then saves the result to disk using the _save_image_and_mask() helper method, which we defined in *Step 18*:

```
def _save_predictions(self, dataset,
                           sample_size=1):
    for id, (image, mask) in \
            enumerate(dataset.take(sample_size),
                                start=1):
        pred_mask = self.model.predict(image)
        pred_mask = self._create_mask(pred_mask)

        image = image[0]
        ground_truth_mask = mask[0]

        self._save_image_and_masks(image,
                                ground_truth_mask,
                                pred_mask,
                                image_id=id)
```

21. The evaluate() method computes the accuracy of the **FCN** on the test set and generates predictions for a sample of images, which are then stored on disk:

```
def evaluate(self, test_dataset, sample_size=5):
    result = self.model.evaluate(test_dataset)
    print(f'Accuracy: {result[1] * 100:.2f}%')

    self._save_predictions(test_dataset,
                                sample_size)
```

22. Download (or load, if cached) Oxford IIIT Pet Dataset, along with its metadata, using **TensorFlow Datasets**:

```
dataset, info = tfdata.load('oxford_iiit_pet',
                                with_info=True)
```

23. Use the metadata to define the corresponding number of steps the network will take over the training and validation datasets. Also, define the batch and buffer sizes:

```
TRAIN_SIZE = info.splits['train'].num_examples
VALIDATION_SIZE = info.splits['test'].num_examples
BATCH_SIZE = 32
STEPS_PER_EPOCH = TRAIN_SIZE // BATCH_SIZE

VALIDATION_SUBSPLITS = 5
VALIDATION_STEPS = VALIDATION_SIZE // BATCH_SIZE
VALIDATION_STEPS //= VALIDATION_SUBSPLITS

BUFFER_SIZE = 1000
```

24. Define the training and testing datasets' pipelines:

```
train_dataset = (dataset['train']
                    .map(load_image, num_parallel_
                 calls=AUTOTUNE)
                    .cache()
                    .shuffle(BUFFER_SIZE)
                    .batch(BATCH_SIZE)
                    .repeat()
                    .prefetch(buffer_size=AUTOTUNE))
test_dataset = (dataset['test']
                    .map(lambda d: load_image(d,train=False),
                       num_parallel_calls=AUTOTUNE)
                    .batch(BATCH_SIZE))
```

25. Instantiate the **FCN** and train it for 120 epochs:

```
fcn = FCN(output_channels=3)
fcn.train(train_dataset,
          epochs=120,
          steps_per_epoch=STEPS_PER_EPOCH,
          validation_steps=VALIDATION_STEPS,
          validation_dataset=test_dataset)
```

26. Lastly, evaluate the network on the test dataset:

```
unet.evaluate(test_dataset)
```

As shown in the following graph, the accuracy on the test set should be around 84% (specifically, I got 84.47%):

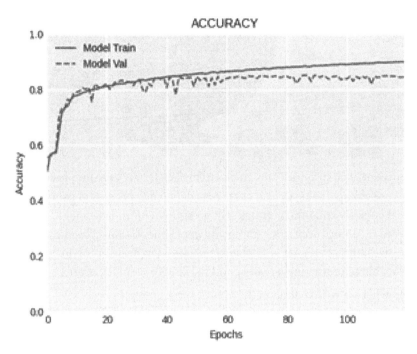

Figure 8.2 – Training and validation accuracy curves

The training curves display a healthy behavior, meaning that the network did, indeed, learn. However, the true test is to visually assess the results:

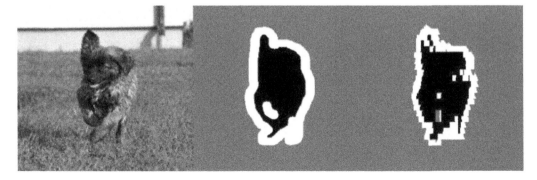

Figure 8.3 – The original image (left), the ground truth mask (center), and the predicted mask (right)

In the preceding image, we can see that the mask that was produced by the network follows the shape of the ground truth segmentation. However, there's an unsatisfying pixelated effect across the segments, as well as noise in the upper-right corner. Let's take a look at another example:

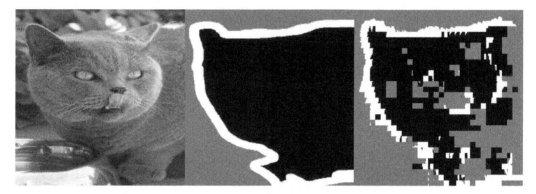

Figure 8.4 – The original image (left), the ground truth mask (center), and the predicted mask (right)

In the preceding image, we can see a very deficient, spotty, and overall low-quality mask that proves that the network still needs a lot of improvement. This could be achieved by doing more fine-tuning and experimentation. However, in the next recipe, we'll discover a network that's best suited to performing image segmentation and capable of producing a really good mask with way less effort.

We'll discuss what we've just done in the *How it works...* section.

## How it works...

In this recipe, we implemented an **FCN** for image segmentation. Even though we adapted a well-known architecture, **VGG16**, to our purposes, in reality, there are many different adaptations of **FCNs** that extend or modify other seminal architectures, such as **ResNet50**, **DenseNet**, and other variants of **VGG**.

What we need to remember is that **FCN** is more of a template than a concrete implementation. Such a template consists of swapping the fully connected layers at the end of these networks, which are often used for traditional image classification, with 1x1 convolutions and upsampling layers (either `UpSampling2D()` with bilinear interpolation or `ConvTranspose2D()`). The achieved result is that instead of classifying the whole image with an output vector of probabilities, we produce an output volume that has the same dimensions as the input image, where each pixel contains a probability distribution of the classes it can belong to. Such an output volume of pixel-wise likelihood is known as a predicted segmentation mask.

## See also

You can read more about **FCNs** here: `https://arxiv.org/abs/1411.4038`. If you want to find out more about `Oxford IIIT Pet Dataset`, visit the official site here: `https://www.robots.ox.ac.uk/~vgg/data/pets/`.

# Implementing a U-Net from scratch

It's difficult to talk about image segmentation without mentioning **U-Net**, one of the seminal architectures when it comes to pixel-wise classification.

A **U-Net** is a composite network comprised of an encoder and a decoder, whose layers, as the name suggests, are arranged in a U shape. It's intended for fast and precise segmentation, and in this recipe, we'll implement one from scratch.

Let's get started, shall we?

## Getting ready

In this example, we'll rely on several external libraries, such as TensorFlow Datasets, TensorFlow Docs, `Pillow`, and `OpenCV`. The good news is that we can easily install them all with `pip`. First, install `tensorflow_docs`, as follows:

```
$> pip install git+https://github.com/tensorflow/docs
```

Next, install the remaining libraries:

```
$> pip install tensorflow-datasets Pillow opencv-contrib-python
```

We will be using `Oxford-IIIT Pet Dataset` in this recipe. However, we don't need to do anything at this stage since we'll download it and manipulate it using `tensorflow-datasets`. In this dataset, the segmentation mask (an image where each location contains the class of the corresponding pixel in the original image) contains pixels categorized into three classes:

- 1: The pixel belongs to a pet (cat or dog).
- 2: The pixel belongs to the contour of a pet.
- 3: The pixel belongs to the surroundings.

Here are some sample images from the dataset:

Figure 8.5 – Sample images from the Oxford-IIIT Pet dataset

Great! Let's start implementing!

## How to do it...

Follow these steps to implement your own **U-Net** so that you can segment images of your own pets:

1.  Let's import all the necessary dependencies:

```
import cv2
import matplotlib.pyplot as plt
import numpy as np
import tensorflow as tf
import tensorflow_datasets as tfdata
import tensorflow_docs as tfdocs
import tensorflow_docs.plots
from tensorflow.keras.layers import *
from tensorflow.keras.losses import \
    SparseCategoricalCrossentropy
from tensorflow.keras.models import *
from tensorflow.keras.optimizers import RMSprop
```

2.  Define an alias for `tf.data.experimental.AUTOTUNE`:

```
AUTOTUNE = tf.data.experimental.AUTOTUNE
```

3.  Define a function that will normalize the images in the dataset. We must also normalize the masks so that the classes are numbered from 0 through 2, instead of from 1 through 3:

```
def normalize(input_image, input_mask):
```

```
      input_image = tf.cast(input_image, tf.float32) /
   255.0
      input_mask -= 1

      return input_image, input_mask
```

4.  Define a function that will load an image, given an element from a TensorFlow dataset data structure. Note that we resize both the image and the mask to *256x256*. Also, if the `train` flag is set to `True`, we perform augmentation by randomly mirroring the image and its mask. Finally, we normalize the inputs:

```
@tf.function
def load_image(dataset_element, train=True):
   input_image = tf.image.resize(dataset element['image'],
                                  (256, 256))
      input_mask = tf.image.resize(
         dataset_element['segmentation_mask'],(256, 256))

      if train and np.random.uniform() > 0.5:
         input_image = tf.image.flip_left_right(input_image)
         input_mask = tf.image.flip_left_right(input_mask)

      input_image, input_mask = normalize(input_image,
                                           input_mask)

      return input_image, input_mask
```

5.  Now, let's define a class, `UNet()`, that will contain all the logic necessary to build, train, and evaluate our **U-Net**. First, let's define the constructor:

```
class UNet(object):
   def __init__(self,
                  input_size=(256, 256, 3),
                  output_channels=3):
      self.input_size = input_size
      self.output_channels = output_channels

      self.model = self._create_model()
```

```
            loss = SparseCategoricalCrossentropy(from_
logits=True)
            self.model.compile(optimizer=RMSprop(),
                                loss=loss,
                                metrics=['accuracy'])
```

In this step, we are creating the model, which we'll train using `RMSProp` as the optimizer and `SparseCategoricalCrossentropy` as the loss. Note that `output_channels` is, by default, 3, because each pixel can be categorized into one of three classes.

6. Now, let's define the `_downsample()` helper method, which builds a downsampling block. This is a convolution that can be (optionally) batch normalized and that's activated with `LeakyReLU`:

```
@staticmethod
def _downsample(filters, size, batch_norm=True):
    initializer = tf.random_normal_initializer(0.0, 0.02)

    layers = Sequential()
    layers.add(Conv2D(filters=filters,
                      kernel_size=size,
                      strides=2,
                      padding='same',
                      kernel_initializer=initializer,
                      use_bias=False))

    if batch_norm:
        layers.add(BatchNormalization())

    layers.add(LeakyReLU())

    return layers
```

7. Conversely, the `_upsample()` helper method expands its input through a transposed convolution, which is also batch normalized and `ReLU` activated (optionally, we can add a dropout layer to prevent overfitting):

```python
def _upsample(filters, size, dropout=False):
    init = tf.random_normal_initializer(0.0, 0.02)

    layers = Sequential()
    layers.add(Conv2DTranspose(filters=filters,
                               kernel_size=size,
                               strides=2,
                               padding='same',
                               kernel_initializer=init,
                               use_bias=False))

    layers.add(BatchNormalization())

    if dropout:
        layers.add(Dropout(rate=0.5))

    layers.add(ReLU())

    return layers
```

8. Armed with `_downsample()` and `_upsample()`, we can iteratively build the full **U-Net** architecture. The encoding part of the network is just a stack of downsampling blocks, while the decoding portion is, as expected, comprised of a series of upsampling blocks:

```python
def _create_model(self):
    down_stack = [self._downsample(64, 4,
                                   batch_norm=False)]
    for filters in (128, 256, 512, 512, 512, 512,
                    512):
        down_block = self._downsample(filters, 4)
        down_stack.append(down_block)

    up_stack = []
```

```
for _ in range(3):
    up_block = self._upsample(512, 4,
                              dropout=True)
    up_stack.append(up_block)

for filters in (512, 256, 128, 64):
    up_block = self._upsample(filters, 4)
    up_stack.append(up_block)
```

9. In order to shield the network against the vanishing gradient problem (a phenomenon where very deep networks forget what they've learned), we must add skip connections at every level:

```
inputs = Input(shape=self.input_size)
x = inputs

skip_layers = []
for down in down_stack:
    x = down(x)
    skip_layers.append(x)

skip_layers = reversed(skip_layers[:-1])

for up, skip_connection in zip(up_stack,
                               skip_layers):
    x = up(x)
    x = Concatenate()([x, skip_connection])
```

The output layer of the **U-Net** is a transposed convolution whose dimensions are the same as the input image's, but it has as many channels as there are classes in the segmentation mask:

```
init = tf.random_normal_initializer(0.0, 0.02)
output = Conv2DTranspose(
    filters=self.output_channels,
    kernel_size=3,
    strides=2,
    padding='same',
    kernel_initializer=init)(x)
```

```
        return Model(inputs, outputs=output)
```

10. Let's define a `helper` method in order to plot the relevant training curves:

```
    @staticmethod
    def _plot_model_history(model_history, metric,
                            ylim=None):
        plt.style.use('seaborn-darkgrid')
        plotter = tfdocs.plots.HistoryPlotter()
        plotter.plot({'Model': model_history},
                     metric=metric)

        plt.title(f'{metric.upper()}')
        if ylim is None:
            plt.ylim([0, 1])
        else:
            plt.ylim(ylim)

        plt.savefig(f'{metric}.png')
        plt.close()
```

11. The `train()` method takes the training and validation datasets, as well as the number of epochs and training and validation steps to perform, in order to fit the model. It also saves the loss and accuracy plots to disk for later analysis:

```
    def train(self, train_dataset, epochs,
              steps_per_epoch,
              validation_dataset, validation_steps):
        hist = \
            self.model.fit(train_dataset,
                           epochs=epochs,
                           steps_per_epoch=steps_per_epoch,
                           validation_steps=validation_steps,
                           validation_data=validation_dataset)

        self._plot_model_history(hist, 'loss', [0., 2.0])
        self._plot_model_history(hist, 'accuracy')
```

12. Define a helper method named `_process_mask()`, which will be used to make the segmentation masks compatible with OpenCV. What this function does is create a three-channeled version of a grayscale mask and upscale the class values to the [0, 255] range:

```python
@staticmethod
def _process_mask(mask):
    mask = (mask.numpy() * 127.5).astype('uint8')
    mask = cv2.cvtColor(mask, cv2.COLOR_GRAY2RGB)

    return mask
```

13. The `_save_image_and_masks()` helper method creates a mosaic of the original image, the ground truth mask, and the predicted segmentation mask, and saves it to disk for later revision:

```python
def _save_image_and_masks(self, image,
                          ground_truth_mask,
                          prediction_mask,
                          image_id):
    image = (image.numpy() *
             255.0).astype('uint8')
    gt_mask = self._process_mask(ground_truth_mask)
    pred_mask = self._process_mask(prediction_mask)

    mosaic = np.hstack([image, gt_mask, pred_mask])
    mosaic = cv2.cvtColor(mosaic, cv2.COLOR_RGB2BGR)

    cv2.imwrite(f'mosaic_{image_id}.jpg', mosaic)
```

14. In order to pass the output volume produced by the network to a valid segmentation mask, we must take the index of the highest value at each pixel location, which corresponds to the most likely category for that pixel. The `_create_mask()` method does this:

```
@staticmethod
def _create_mask(prediction_mask):
    prediction_mask = tf.argmax(prediction_mask,
                                axis=-1)
    prediction_mask = prediction_mask[...,tf.newaxis]

    return prediction_mask[0]
```

The `_save_predictions()` method uses the **U-Net** to predict the mask of a sample of images in the input dataset and saves the result to disk. It does this using the `_save_image_and_mask()` helper method we defined in *Step 13*:

```
def _save_predictions(self, dataset,
                      sample_size=1):
    for id, (image, mask) in \
            enumerate(dataset.take(sample_size),
                      start=1):
        pred_mask = self.model.predict(image)
        pred_mask = self._create_mask(pred_mask)

        image = image[0]
        ground_truth_mask = mask[0]

        self._save_image_and_masks(image,
                                   ground_truth_mask,
                                   pred_mask,
                                   image_id=id)
```

15. The `evaluate()` method computes the accuracy of the **U-Net** on the test set, and also generates predictions for a sample of images, which are then stored on disk:

```python
def evaluate(self, test_dataset, sample_size=5):
    result = self.model.evaluate(test_dataset)
    print(f'Accuracy: {result[1] * 100:.2f}%')


    self._save_predictions(test_dataset,
                           sample_size)
```

16. Download (or load, if cached) `Oxford IIIT Pet Dataset`, along with its metadata, using TensorFlow Datasets:

```python
dataset, info = tfdata.load('oxford_iiit_pet',
                            with_info=True)
```

17. Use the metadata to define the corresponding number of steps the network will go over for the training and validation datasets. Also, define the batch and buffer sizes:

```python
TRAIN_SIZE = info.splits['train'].num_examples
VALIDATION_SIZE = info.splits['test'].num_examples
BATCH_SIZE = 64
STEPS_PER_EPOCH = TRAIN_SIZE // BATCH_SIZE


VALIDATION_SUBSPLITS = 5
VALIDATION_STEPS = VALIDATION_SIZE // BATCH_SIZE
VALIDATION_STEPS //= VALIDATION_SUBSPLITS


BUFFER_SIZE = 1000
```

18. Define the training and testing datasets' pipelines:

```python
train_dataset = (dataset['train']
                 .map(load_image, num_parallel_
                 calls=AUTOTUNE)
                 .cache()
                 .shuffle(BUFFER_SIZE)
                 .batch(BATCH_SIZE)
                 .repeat()
                 .prefetch(buffer_size=AUTOTUNE))
```

```
test_dataset = (dataset['test']
                .map(lambda d: load_image(d,
                    train=False),
                    num_parallel_calls=AUTOTUNE)
                .batch(BATCH_SIZE))
```

19. Instantiate the **U-Net** and train it for 50 epochs:

```
unet = UNet()
unet.train(train_dataset,
        epochs=50,
        steps_per_epoch=STEPS_PER_EPOCH,
        validation_steps=VALIDATION_STEPS,
        validation_dataset=test_dataset)
```

20. Lastly, evaluate the network on the test dataset:

```
unet.evaluate(test_dataset)
```

The accuracy on the test set should be around 83% (in my case, I got 83.49%):

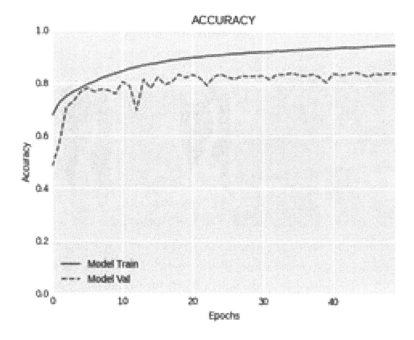

Figure 8.6 – Training and validation accuracy curves

Here, we can see that after about epoch 12, the gap between the training and validation accuracy curves slowly widens. This isn't a sign of overfitting, but an indication that we could do better. How does this accuracy translate to actual images?

Take a look at the following image, which shows the original image, the ground truth mask, and the produced mask:

Figure 8.7 – The original image (left), the ground truth mask (center), and the predicted mask (right)

Here, we can see that there's a good resemblance between the ground truth mask (center) and the predicted one (right), although there is some noise, such as the small white region and the pronounced bump on the lower half of the dog's silhouette, that could be cleaned up with more training:

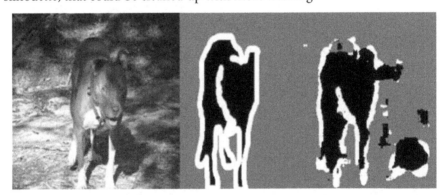

Figure 8.8 – The original image (left), the ground truth mask (center), and the predicted mask (right)

The preceding image clearly shows that the network could use more training or fine-tuning. This is because even though it gets the overall shape and location of the dog right, there's really too much noise for this mask to be usable in a real-world application.

Let's head over to the *How it works…* section to connect the dots.

# How it works...

In this recipe, we implemented and trained a **U-Net** from scratch to segment the body and contour of household pets. As we saw, the network did learn, but still offers room for improvement.

The ability to semantically segment the contents of an image is of paramount importance in several domains, such as in medicine, where what's more important than knowing if a condition, such as a malignant tumor, is present, is to determine the actual location, shape, and area of said ailment. The field of biomedicine is where **U-Net** made its debut. In 2015, it outperformed established methods for segmentation, such as sliding-windows convolutional networks, using far less data.

How does **U-Net** achieve such good results? As we learned in this recipe, the key is in its end-to-end nature, where both the encoder and decoder are comprised of convolutions that form a contracting path, whose job is to capture context and a symmetric expanding path, thereby enabling precise localization.

Both of the aforementioned paths can be as deep as needed, depending on the nature of the dataset. This depth customization is viable due to the presence of skip connections, which allow the gradients to flow farther down the network, thus preventing the vanishing gradient problem (this is similar to what **ResNet** does, as we learned in *Chapter 2*, *Performing Image Classification*).

In the next recipe, we'll combine a very powerful concept with this implementation of **U-Net** to increase the performance of Oxford IIIT Pet Dataset: transfer learning.

# See also

A great way to familiarize yourself with **U-Net** is to read the original paper: https://arxiv.org/abs/1505.04597. Also, if you want to find out more about Oxford IIIT Pet Dataset, visit the official site here: https://www.robots.ox.ac.uk/~vgg/data/pets/.

In this recipe, we mentioned the vanishing gradient problem a few times, so it's a good idea to understand the concept by reading this article: https://en.wikipedia.org/wiki/Vanishing_gradient_problem.

# Implementing a U-Net with transfer learning

Training a **U-Net** from scratch is a very good first step toward creating a performant image segmentation system. However, one of the biggest superpowers in deep learning that's applied to computer vision is being able to build solutions on top of the knowledge of other networks, which usually leads to faster and better results.

Image segmentation is no exception to this rule, and in this recipe, we'll implement a better segmentation network using transfer learning.

Let's begin.

## Getting ready

This recipe is very similar to the previous one (*Implementing a U-Net from scratch*), so we'll only go into depth on the parts that are different. For a deeper explanation, I recommend that you complete the *Implementing a U-Net from scratch* recipe before attempting this one. As expected, the libraries we'll need are the same as they were for that recipe, all of which can be installed using `pip`. Let's start with `tensorflow_docs`, as follows:

```
$> pip install git+https://github.com/tensorflow/docs
```

Now, let's set up the remaining dependencies:

```
$> pip install tensorflow-datasets Pillow opencv-contrib-python
```

Once again, we'll work with `Oxford-IIIT Pet Dataset`, which can be accessed through `tensorflow-datasets`. Each pixel in this dataset falls within one of these classes:

- 1: The pixel belongs to a pet (cat or dog).
- 2: The pixel belongs to the contour of a pet.
- 3: The pixel belongs to the surroundings.

The following image shows two sample images from the dataset:

Figure 8.9 – Sample images from the Oxford-IIIT Pet dataset

With that, we are good to go!

## How to do it...

Complete these steps to implement a transfer learning-powered **U-Net**:

1. Import all the needed packages:

```
import cv2
import matplotlib.pyplot as plt
import numpy as np
import tensorflow as tf
import tensorflow_datasets as tfdata
import tensorflow_docs as tfdocs
import tensorflow_docs.plots
from tensorflow.keras.applications import MobileNetV2
from tensorflow.keras.layers import *
from tensorflow.keras.losses import \
    SparseCategoricalCrossentropy
from tensorflow.keras.models import *
from tensorflow.keras.optimizers import RMSprop
```

2. Define an alias for `tf.data.experimental.AUTOTUNE`:

```
AUTOTUNE = tf.data.experimental.AUTOTUNE
```

3.  Define a function that will normalize the images and masks in the dataset:

```
def normalize(input_image, input_mask):
    input_image = tf.cast(input_image, tf.float32) /
                                        255.0
    input_mask -= 1

    return input_image, input_mask
```

4.  Define a function that will load an image and its corresponding mask, given an element from a TensorFlow Datasets data structure. Optionally, it should perform image mirroring on training images:

```
@tf.function
def load_image(dataset_element, train=True):
    input_image = tf.image.resize(dataset
                            element['image'], (256, 256))
    input_mask = tf.image.resize(
        dataset_element['segmentation_mask'], (256,256))

    if train and np.random.uniform() > 0.5:
        input_image = tf.image.flip_left_right(input_
                                            image)
        input_mask =
            tf.image.flip_left_right(input_mask)

    input_image, input_mask = normalize(input_image,
                                        input_mask)

    return input_image, input_mask
```

5.  Define `UNet()`, a container class for the logic necessary to build, train, and evaluate our transfer learning-aided **U-Net**. Start by defining the constructor:

```
class UNet(object):
    def __init__(self,
                    input_size=(256, 256, 3),
                    output_channels=3):
        self.pretrained_model = MobileNetV2(
```

```
                 input_shape=input_size,
                 include_top=False,
                 weights='imagenet')

        self.target_layers = [
            'block_1_expand_relu',
            'block_3_expand_relu',
            'block_6_expand_relu',
            'block_13_expand_relu',
            'block_16_project'
        ]

        self.input_size = input_size
        self.output_channels = output_channels

        self.model = self._create_model()
        loss = SparseCategoricalCrossentropy(from_
                                       logits=True)
        self.model.compile(optimizer=RMSprop(),
                           loss=loss,
                           metrics=['accuracy'])
```

In this step, we are creating the model, which we'll train using RMSProp as the optimizer and SparseCategoricalCrossentropy as the loss. Notice that output_channels is, by default, 3, because each pixel can be categorized into one of three classes. The encoder will be a pre-trained MobileNetV2. However, we'll only use a select group of layers, defined in self.target_layers.

6. Now, let's define the _upsample() helper method, which builds an upsampling block:

```
        @staticmethod
        def _upsample(filters, size, dropout=False):
            init = tf.random_normal_initializer(0.0, 0.02)

            layers = Sequential()
            layers.add(Conv2DTranspose(filters=filters,
                                       kernel_size=size,
```

```
                                     strides=2,
                                     padding='same',
                       kernel_initializer=init,
                                     use_bias=False))

        layers.add(BatchNormalization())

        if dropout:
            layers.add(Dropout(rate=0.5))

        layers.add(ReLU())

        return layers
```

7.  Armed with our pre-trained `MobileNetV2` and `_upsample()`, we can iteratively build the full **U-Net** architecture. The encoding part of the network is just a model of `self.target_layers`, which are frozen (`down_stack.trainable = False`), meaning we only train the decoder or upsampling blocks of the architecture:

```
def _create_model(self):
    layers = [self.pretrained_model.get_layer(l).output
              for l in self.target_layers]
    down_stack = Model(inputs=self.pretrained_model.
                            input, outputs=layers)
    down_stack.trainable = False

    up_stack = []

    for filters in (512, 256, 128, 64):
        up_block = self._upsample(filters, 4)
        up_stack.append(up_block)
```

8. Now, we can add the skip connections to facilitate the flow of the gradient throughout the network:

```python
inputs = Input(shape=self.input_size)
x = inputs

skip_layers = down_stack(x)
x = skip_layers[-1]
skip_layers = reversed(skip_layers[:-1])

for up, skip_connection in zip(up_stack,
                               skip_layers):
    x = up(x)
    x = Concatenate()([x, skip_connection])
```

9. The output layer of the **U-Net** is a transposed convolution that has the same dimensions as the input image, but has as many channels as there are classes in the segmentation mask:

```python
init = tf.random_normal_initializer(0.0, 0.02)
output = Conv2DTranspose(
    filters=self.output_channels,
    kernel_size=3,
    strides=2,
    padding='same',
    kernel_initializer=init)(x)

return Model(inputs, outputs=output)
```

10. Define `_plot_model_history()`, a helper method that plots the relevant training curves:

```python
@staticmethod
def _plot_model_history(model_history, metric,
                        ylim=None):
    plt.style.use('seaborn-darkgrid')
    plotter = tfdocs.plots.HistoryPlotter()
    plotter.plot({'Model': model_history},
                 metric=metric)
```

```
        plt.title(f'{metric.upper()}')
        if ylim is None:
            plt.ylim([0, 1])
        else:
            plt.ylim(ylim)

        plt.savefig(f'{metric}.png')
        plt.close()
```

11. Define the `train()` method, which is in charge of fitting the model:

```
    def train(self, train_dataset, epochs,
                  steps_per_epoch,
                validation_dataset, validation_steps):
        hist = \
            self.model.fit(train_dataset,
                           epochs=epochs,
                           steps_per_epoch=steps_per_epoch,
                           validation_steps=validation_steps,
                           validation_data=validation_dataset)

        self._plot_model_history(hist, 'loss', [0., 2.0])
        self._plot_model_history(hist, 'accuracy')
```

12. Define `_process_mask()`, a helper method that makes the segmentation masks compatible with OpenCV:

```
    @staticmethod
    def _process_mask(mask):
        mask = (mask.numpy() * 127.5).astype('uint8')
        mask = cv2.cvtColor(mask, cv2.COLOR_GRAY2RGB)

        return mask
```

13. Define the `_save_image_and_masks()` helper method to create a visualization of the original image, along with the real and predicted masks:

```
def _save_image_and_masks(self, image,
                          ground_truth_mask,
                          prediction_mask,
                          image_id):
    image = (image.numpy() * 255.0).astype('uint8')
    gt_mask = self._process_mask(ground_truth_mask)
    pred_mask = self._process_mask(prediction_mask)

    mosaic = np.hstack([image, gt_mask, pred_mask])
    mosaic = cv2.cvtColor(mosaic, cv2.COLOR_RGB2BGR)

    cv2.imwrite(f'mosaic_{image_id}.jpg', mosaic)
```

14. Define `_create_mask()`, which produces a valid segmentation mask from the network's predictions:

```
@staticmethod
def _create_mask(prediction_mask):
    prediction_mask = tf.argmax(prediction_mask,
                                axis=-1)
    prediction_mask = prediction_mask[...,
                                      tf.newaxis]

    return prediction_mask[0]
```

15. The `_save_predictions()` method uses the **U-Net** to predict the mask of a sample of images in the input dataset and saves the result to disk. It does this using the `_save_image_and_mask()` helper method, which we defined in *Step 13*:

```
def _save_predictions(self, dataset,
                      sample_size=1):
    for id, (image, mask) in \
            enumerate(dataset.take(sample_size),
                      start=1):
        pred_mask = self.model.predict(image)
        pred_mask = self._create_mask(pred_mask)
```

```
            image = image[0]
            ground_truth_mask = mask[0]


            self._save_image_and_masks(image,
                                       ground_truth_mask,
                                       pred_mask,
                                       image_id=id)
```

16. The `evaluate()` method computes the accuracy of the **U-Net** on the test set, while also generating predictions for a sample of images. These are then stored on disk:

```
def evaluate(self, test_dataset, sample_size=5):
    result = self.model.evaluate(test_dataset)
    print(f'Accuracy: {result[1] * 100:.2f}%')


    self._save_predictions(test_dataset, sample_size)
```

17. Download (or load, if cached) `Oxford IIIT Pet Dataset`, along with its metadata, using TensorFlow Datasets:

```
dataset, info = tfdata.load('oxford_iiit_pet',
                            with_info=True)
```

18. Use the metadata to define the corresponding number of steps the network will take over the training and validation datasets. Also, define the batch and buffer sizes:

```
TRAIN_SIZE = info.splits['train'].num_examples
VALIDATION_SIZE = info.splits['test'].num_examples
BATCH_SIZE = 64
STEPS_PER_EPOCH = TRAIN_SIZE // BATCH_SIZE

VALIDATION_SUBSPLITS = 5
VALIDATION_STEPS = VALIDATION_SIZE // BATCH_SIZE
VALIDATION_STEPS //= VALIDATION_SUBSPLITS

BUFFER_SIZE = 1000
```

19. Define the training and testing datasets' pipelines:

```
train_dataset = (dataset['train']
                     .map(load_image, num_parallel_
                     calls=AUTOTUNE)
                     .cache()
                     .shuffle(BUFFER_SIZE)
                     .batch(BATCH_SIZE)
                     .repeat()
                     .prefetch(buffer_size=AUTOTUNE))
test_dataset = (dataset['test']
                    .map(lambda d: load_image(d,
                        train=False),
                        num_parallel_calls=AUTOTUNE)
                    .batch(BATCH_SIZE))
```

20. Instantiate the **U-Net** and train it for 30 epochs:

```
unet = UNet()
unet.train(train_dataset,
           epochs=50,
           steps_per_epoch=STEPS_PER_EPOCH,
           validation_steps=VALIDATION_STEPS,
           validation_dataset=test_dataset)
```

21. Evaluate the network on the test dataset:

```
unet.evaluate(test_dataset)
```

The accuracy on the test set should be close to 90% (in my case, I obtained 90.78% accuracy):

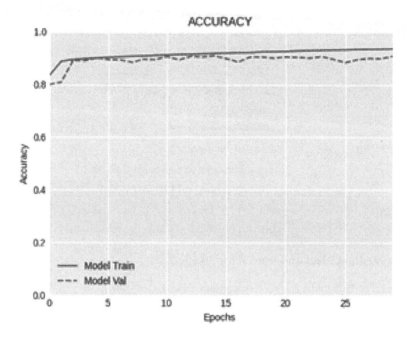

Figure 8.10 – Training and validation accuracy curves

The accuracy curves show that the network is not overfitting because both the training and validation plots follow the same trajectory, with a very thin gap. This also confirms that the knowledge the model is acquiring is transferrable and usable on unseen data.

Let's take a look at some of the outputs from the network, starting with the following image:

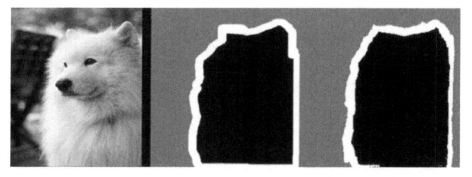

Figure 8.11 – The original image (left), the ground truth mask (center), and the predicted mask (right)

Compared to *Figure 8.7* in the *Implementing a U-Net from scratch* recipe, in the preceding image, we can see that the **U-Net** produces a much cleaner result, with the background (gray pixels), contour (white pixels), and pet (black pixels) clearly separated and almost identical to the ground truth mask (center):

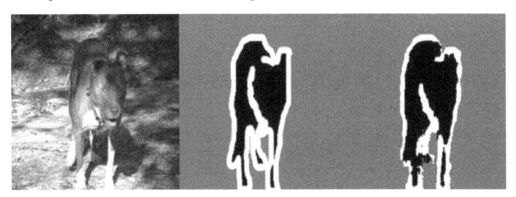

Figure 8.12 – The original image (left), the ground truth mask (center), and the predicted mask (right)

The preceding image is a great improvement in comparison to *Figure 8.8* in the *Implementing a U-Net from scratch* recipe. This time, the predicted mask (right), although not perfect, presents less noise and is much closer to the actual segmentation mask (center).

We'll dig deeper in the *How it works...* section.

## How it works...

In this recipe, we made a small yet substantial change to the **U-Net** architecture we implemented in *Implementing a U-Net from scratch*. Instead of training both the encoder and the decoder from scratch, we focused only on the upsampling layers (the decoder), leaving the encoding portion of the problem to a subset of target layers handpicked from a MobileNetV2 trained on the massive ImageNet dataset.

The reason transfer learning worked so well in this context is that there are hundreds of classes in ImageNet focused on different breeds of cats and dogs, meaning the overlap with Oxford IIIT Pet is very substantial. However, if this wasn't the case, this doesn't mean we should drop transfer learning entirely! What we should do in that situation is fine-tune the encoder by making some (or all) of its layers trainable.

By leveraging the knowledge encoded in MobileNetV2, we were able to bump the accuracy on the test set from 83% up to 90%, an impressive gain that translated into better, cleaner prediction masks, even on challenging examples.

## See also

You can read the original **U-Net** paper here: `https://arxiv.org/abs/1505.04597`. If you're interested in the details of `Oxford IIIT Pet Dataset`, please go to `https://www.robots.ox.ac.uk/~vgg/data/pets/`. To learn how to combat the vanishing gradient problem, read this article: `https://en.wikipedia.org/wiki/Vanishing_gradient_problem`.

# Segmenting images using Mask-RCNN and TensorFlow Hub

**Mask-RCNN** is a state-of-the-art architecture for object detection. However, as its name suggests, it's also excellent at performing image segmentation. In this recipe, we'll leverage an implementation of **Mask-RCNN** hosted in **TensorFlow Hub** (**TFHub**) that has been trained on the gargantuan `COCO` dataset. This will help us perform out-of-the-box object detection and image segmentation.

## Getting ready

First, we must install `Pillow` and **TFHub**, as follows:

```
$> pip install Pillow tensorflow-hub
```

We also need to install the **TensorFlow Object Detection API** since it contains a series of convenient visualization tools that'll come in handy for looking at the bounding boxes and segmentation masks. First, `cd` to a location of your preference and clone the `tensorflow/models` repository:

```
$> git clone --depth 1 https://github.com/tensorflow/models
```

Next, install the **TensorFlow Object Detection API**, like this:

```
$> sudo apt install -y protobuf-compiler
$> cd models/research
$> protoc object_detection/protos/*.proto --python_out=.
$> cp object_detection/packages/tf2/setup.py .
$> python -m pip install -q .
```

That's it! Let's get started.

# How to do it...

Follow these steps to learn how to segment your images using **Mask-RCNN**:

1. Import the necessary packages:

```
import glob
from io import BytesIO

import matplotlib.pyplot as plt
import numpy as np
import tensorflow as tf
import tensorflow_hub as hub
from PIL import Image
from object_detection.utils import ops
from object_detection.utils import visualization_utils as
viz
from object_detection.utils.label_map_util import \
    create_category_index_from_labelmap
```

2. Define a function that will load an image into a NumPy array:

```
def load_image(path):
    image_data = tf.io.gfile.GFile(path, 'rb').read()
    image = Image.open(BytesIO(image_data))

    width, height = image.size
    shape = (1, height, width, 3)

    image = np.array(image.getdata())
    image = image.reshape(shape).astype('uint8')

    return image
```

3. Define a function that will make predictions with **Mask-RCNN** and save the results to disk. Start by loading the image and passing it through the model:

```
def get_and_save_predictions(model, image_path):
    image = load_image(image_path)
    results = model(image)
```

4.  Convert the results into NumPy arrays:

```
model_output = {k: v.numpy() for k, v in
                results.items()}
```

5.  Extract both the detection masks and boxes from the model output and convert
    them into tensors:

```
detection_masks = model_output['detection_masks'][0]
detection_masks = tf.convert_to_tensor(detection_masks)

detection_boxes = model_output['detection_boxes'][0]
detection_boxes = tf.convert_to_tensor(detection_boxes)
```

6.  Reframe the box masks to image masks:

```
detection_masks_reframed = \
    ops.reframe_box_masks_to_image_masks(detection_
                                masks, detection_boxes,
                                image.shape[1],
                                image.shape[2])
detection_masks_reframed = \
    tf.cast(detection_masks_reframed > 0.5,
        tf.uint8)

model_output['detection_masks_reframed'] = \
    detection_masks_reframed.numpy()
```

7.  Create a visualization of the detections and their boxes, scores, classes, and masks:

```
boxes = model_output['detection_boxes'][0]
classes = \
    model_output['detection_classes'][0].astype('int')
scores = model_output['detection_scores'][0]
masks = model_output['detection_masks_reframed']

image_with_mask = image.copy()
viz.visualize_boxes_and_labels_on_image_array(
    image=image_with_mask[0],
    boxes=boxes,
```

```
            classes=classes,
            scores=scores,
            category_index=CATEGORY_IDX,
            use_normalized_coordinates=True,
            max_boxes_to_draw=200,
            min_score_thresh=0.30,
            agnostic_mode=False,
            instance_masks=masks,
            line_thickness=5
    )
```

8.  Save the result to disk:

```
        plt.figure(figsize=(24, 32))
        plt.imshow(image_with_mask[0])

        plt.savefig(f'output/{image_path.split("/")[-1]}')
```

9.  Load the COCO dataset's category index:

```
    labels_path = 'resources/mscoco_label_map.pbtxt'
    CATEGORY_IDX =create_category_index_from_labelmap(labels_
    path)
```

10. Load **Mask-RCNN** from **TFHub**:

```
    MODEL_PATH = ('https://tfhub.dev/tensorflow/mask_rcnn/'
                  'inception_resnet_v2_1024x1024/1')
    mask_rcnn = hub.load(MODEL_PATH)
```

11. Run **Mask-RCNN** over all the test images:

```
    test_images_paths = glob.glob('test_images/*')
    for image_path in test_images_paths:
        get_and_save_predictions(mask_rcnn, image_path)
```

After a while, the labeled images should be in the `output` folder. Let's review an easy one:

Figure 8.13– Single instance of segmentation

Here, we can see that the network correctly detected and segmented the dog with 100% accuracy! Let's try a more challenging one:

Figure 8.14 – Multiple instances of segmentation

This image is much more crowded than the previous one, and even then, the network correctly identified most of the objects in the scene (cars, people, trucks, and so on) – even occluded ones! However, the model fails in some circumstances, as shown in the following image:

Figure 8.15 – Segmentation with errors and redundancies

This time, the network correctly identified me and my dogs, as well as the coffee cup and the couch, but it threw duplicate and nonsensical detections, such as my leg being a person. This happened because I'm holding my dog, and parts of my body are disconnected in the photo, leading to incorrect or low confidence segmentations.

Let's head over to the next section.

## How it works...

In this recipe, we learned how to detect objects and perform image segmentation using one of the most powerful neural networks in existence: **Mask-RCNN**. Training such a model is not an easy task, let alone implementing it from scratch! Fortunately, thanks to **TensorFlow Hub**, we were able to use all its predicting power with just a few lines of code.

We must take into consideration that this pre-trained model will work best on images containing objects the network has been trained on. More precisely, the more the images that we pass to **Mask-RCNN** resemble those in COCO, the better the results will be. Nevertheless, a degree of tweaking and experimentation is always needed in order to achieve the best detections possible because, as we saw in the previous example, the network, although great, isn't perfect.

## See also

You can learn more about the model we used here: `https://tfhub.dev/ tensorflow/mask_rcnn/inception_resnet_v2_1024x1024/1`. Also, reading the **Mask-RCNN** paper is a sound decision: `https://arxiv.org/ abs/1703.06870`.

# 9
# Localizing Elements in Images with Object Detection

Object detection is one of the most common yet challenging tasks in computer vision. It's a natural evolution of image classification, where our goal is to work out what is in an image. On the other hand, object detection is not only concerned with the content of an image but also with the location of elements of interest in a digital image.

As with many other well-known tasks in computer vision, object detection has long been addressed with a wide array of techniques, ranging from naïve solutions (such as object matching) to machine learning-based ones (such as Haar Cascades). Nonetheless, the most effective detectors nowadays are powered by deep learning.

Implementing state-of-the-art object detectors (such as **You Only Look Once (YOLO)** and **Fast Region-based Convolutional Neural Network (Fast R-CNN)** from scratch is a very challenging task. However, there are many pre-trained solutions we can leverage, not only to make predictions but also to train our own models from zero, as we'll discover in this chapter.

Here is a list of the recipes we'll be working on in no time:

- Creating an object detector with image pyramids and sliding windows
- Detecting objects with YOLOv3
- Training your own object detector with TensorFlow's Object Detection **Application Programming Interface (API)**
- Detecting objects using **TensorFlow Hub (TFHub)**

# Technical requirements

Given the complexity of object detectors, having access to a **Graphics Processing Unit (GPU)** is a great idea. There are many cloud providers you can use to run the recipes in this chapter, my favorite being FloydHub, but you can use whichever you like the most! Of course, do keep in mind of the fees if you don't want any surprises! In the *Getting ready* sections, you'll find the preparatory steps for each recipe. The code for this chapter is available at `https://github.com/PacktPublishing/Tensorflow-2.0-Computer-Vision-Cookbook/tree/master/ch9`.

Check out the following link to see the Code in Action video:

`https://bit.ly/39wInla`.

# Creating an object detector with image pyramids and sliding windows

Traditionally, object detectors have worked following an iterative algorithm whereby a window is slid across the image, at different scales, in order to detect potential objects at every location and perspective. Although this approach is outdated due to its noticeable drawbacks (which we'll talk more about in the *How it works...* section), it has the great advantage of being agnostic about the type of image classifier we use, meaning we can use it as a framework to turn any classifier into an object detector. This is precisely what we'll do in this first recipe!

Let's begin.

## Getting ready

We need to install a couple of external libraries, such as `OpenCV`, `Pillow`, and `imutils`, which can easily be accomplished with this command:

```
$> pip install opencv-contrib-python Pillow imutils
```

We'll use a pre-trained model to power our object detector; therefore, we don't need any data for this recipe.

## How to do it...

Follow these steps to complete the recipe:

1. Import the necessary dependencies:

```
import cv2
import imutils
import numpy as np
from tensorflow.keras.applications import imagenet_utils
from tensorflow.keras.applications.inception_resnet_v2 \
    import *
from tensorflow.keras.preprocessing.image import img_to_
array
```

2. Next, let's define our `ObjectDetector()` class, starting with the constructor:

```
class ObjectDetector(object):
    def __init__(self,
                 classifier,
                 preprocess_fn=lambda x: x,
                 input_size=(299, 299),
                 confidence=0.98,
                 window_step_size=16,
                 pyramid_scale=1.5,
                 roi_size=(200, 150),
                 nms_threshold=0.3):
        self.classifier = classifier
        self.preprocess_fn = preprocess_fn
        self.input_size = input_size
        self.confidence = confidence
```

```
            self.window_step_size = window_step_size


            self.pyramid_scale = pyramid_scale
            self.roi_size = roi_size
            self.nms_threshold = nms_threshold
```

The `classifier` is just a trained network we'll use to classify each window, while `preprocess_fn` is the function used to process each window prior to passing it to the classifier. `confidence` is the minimum probability we'll allow detections to have in order to consider them valid. The remaining parameters will be explained in the next steps.

3.  Now, let's define a `sliding_window()` method, which extracts portions of the input image, with dimensions equal to `self.roi_size`. It's going to be slid across the image, both horizontally and vertically, at a rate of `self.window_step_size` pixels at a time (notice the use of `yield` instead of `return`—that's because this is a generator):

```
    def sliding_window(self, image):
        for y in range(0,
                        image.shape[0],
                        self.window_step_size):
            for x in range(0,
                           image.shape[1],
                           self.window_step_size):
                y_slice = slice(y, y + self.roi_size[1], 1)
                x_slice = slice(x, x + self.roi_size[0], 1)


                yield x, y, image[y_slice, x_slice]
```

4.  Next, define the `pyramid()` method, which generates smaller and smaller copies of the input image, until a minimum size is met (akin to the levels of a pyramid):

```
    def pyramid(self, image):
        yield image


        while True:
            width = int(image.shape[1] /
                        self.pyramid_scale)
```

```
        image = imutils.resize(image, width=width)

        if (image.shape[0] < self.roi_size[1] or
                image.shape[1] <
            self.roi_size[0]):
            break

        yield image
```

5. Because sliding a window across the same image at different scales is very prone to producing many detections related to the same object, we need a way to keep duplicates at a minimum. That's the purpose of our next method, non_max_suppression():

```
    def non_max_suppression(self, boxes, probabilities):
        if len(boxes) == 0:
            return []

        if boxes.dtype.kind == 'i':
            boxes = boxes.astype(np.float)

        pick = []

        x_1 = boxes[:, 0]
        y_1 = boxes[:, 1]
        x_2 = boxes[:, 2]
        y_2 = boxes[:, 3]

        area = (x_2 - x_1 + 1) * (y_2 - y_1 + 1)
        indexes = np.argsort(probabilities)
```

6.  We start by computing the area of all bounding boxes, and also sort them by their probability, in increasing order. Now, we'll pick the index of the bounding box with the highest probability, and add it to our final selection (`pick`) until we have `indexes` left to trim down:

```python
while len(indexes) > 0:
    last = len(indexes) - 1
    i = indexes[last]
    pick.append(i)
```

7.  We compute the overlap between the picked bounding box and the other ones, and then get rid of those boxes where the overlap is higher than `self.nms_ threshold`, which means that they probably refer to the same object:

```python
xx_1 = np.maximum(x_1[i],x_1[indexes[:last]])
yy_1 = np.maximum(y_1[i],y_1[indexes[:last]])
xx_2 = np.maximum(x_2[i],x_2[indexes[:last]])
yy_2 = np.maximum(y_2[i],y_2[indexes[:last]])

width = np.maximum(0, xx_2 - xx_1 + 1)
height = np.maximum(0, yy_2 - yy_1 + 1)

overlap = (width * height) /
          area[indexes[:last]]

redundant_boxes = \
    np.where(overlap >
             self.nms_threshold)[0]
to_delete = np.concatenate(
    ([last], redundant_boxes))
indexes = np.delete(indexes, to_delete)
```

8.  Return the picked bounding boxes:

```python
return boxes[pick].astype(np.int)
```

9.  The `detect()` method ties the object detection algorithm together. We start by defining a list of **regions of interest** (`rois`) and their corresponding `locations` (coordinates in the original image):

```
def detect(self, image):
    rois = []
    locations = []
```

10. Next, we'll generate different copies of the input image at several scales using the `pyramid()` generator, and at each level, we'll slide a window (with the `sliding_windows()` generator) to extract all possible ROIs:

```
for img in self.pyramid(image):
    scale = image.shape[1] /
            float(img.shape[1])

    for x, y, roi_original in \
            self.sliding_window(img):
        x = int(x * scale)
        y = int(y * scale)
        w = int(self.roi_size[0] * scale)
        h = int(self.roi_size[1] * scale)

        roi = cv2.resize(roi_original,
                         self.input_size)
        roi = img_to_array(roi)
        roi = self.preprocess_fn(roi)

        rois.append(roi)
        locations.append((x, y, x + w, y + h))

rois = np.array(rois, dtype=np.float32)
```

11. Pass all ROIs through the classifier at once:

```
predictions = self.classifier.predict(rois)
predictions = \
    imagenet_utils.decode_predictions(predictions,
                                      top=1)
```

12. Build a `dict` to map each label produced by the classifier to all the bounding boxes and their probabilities (notice we only keep those bounding boxes with a probability of at least `self.confidence`):

```
labels = {}
for i, pred in enumerate(predictions):
    _, label, proba = pred[0]

    if proba >= self.confidence:
        box = locations[i]

        label_detections = labels.get(label, [])
        label_detections.append({'box': box,
                                 'proba':
                                 proba})
        labels[label] = label_detections

return labels
```

13. Instantiate an `InceptionResnetV2` network trained on ImageNet to use as our classifier and pass it to a new `ObjectDetector`. Notice that we're also passing the `preprocess_function` as input:

```
model = InceptionResNetV2(weights='imagenet',
                          include_top=True)
object_detector = ObjectDetector(model, preprocess_input)
```

14. Load the input image, resize it to a width of 600 pixels maximum (the height will be computed accordingly to preserve the aspect ratio), and run it through the object detector:

```
image = cv2.imread('dog.jpg')
image = imutils.resize(image, width=600)
labels = object_detector.detect(image)
```

15. Go over all the detections corresponding to each label, and first draw all the bounding boxes:

```
GREEN = (0, 255, 0)
for i, label in enumerate(labels.keys()):
    clone = image.copy()

    for detection in labels[label]:
        box = detection['box']
        probability = detection['proba']

        x_start, y_start, x_end, y_end = box
        cv2.rectangle(clone, (x_start, y_start),
                      (x_end, y_end), (0, 255, 0), 2)

    cv2.imwrite(f'Before_{i}.jpg', clone)
```

Then, use **Non-Maximum Suppression** (**NMS**) to get rid of duplicates and draw the surviving bounding boxes:

```
    clone = image.copy()
    boxes = np.array([d['box'] for d in
                      labels[label]])
    probas = np.array([d['proba'] for d in
                       labels[label]])
    boxes = object_detector.non_max_suppression(boxes,
                                                 probas)

    for x_start, y_start, x_end, y_end in boxes:
        cv2.rectangle(clone, (x_start, y_start),
                      (x_end, y_end), GREEN, 2)

        if y_start - 10 > 10:
            y = y_start - 10
        else:
            y = y_start + 10

        cv2.putText(clone, label, (x_start, y),
```

```
                    cv2.FONT_HERSHEY_SIMPLEX, .45,
                    GREEN, 2)


cv2.imwrite(f'After_{i}.jpg', clone)
```

Here's the result without NMS:

Figure 9.1 – Overlapping detections of the same dog

And here's the result after applying NMS:

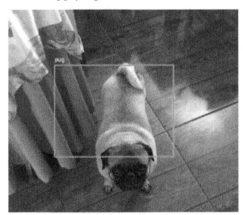

Figure 9.2 – With NMS, we got rid of the redundant detections

Although we successfully detected the dog in the previous photos, we notice that the bounding box doesn't tightly wrap the object as nicely as we might have expected. Let's talk about this and other issues regarding old-school object detection in the next section.

## How it works...

In this recipe, we implemented a reusable class that easily allows us to turn any image classifier into an object detector, by leveraging the iterative approach of extracting ROIs (sliding windows) at different levels of perspective (image pyramid) and passing them to such a classifier to determine where objects are in a photo, and what they are. Also, we used NMS to reduce the amount of non-informative, duplicate detections that are characteristic of this strategy.

Although this a great first attempt at creating an object detector, it has its flaws:

- It's incredibly slow, which makes it unusable in real-time situations.
- The accuracy of the bounding boxes depends heavily on the parameter selection for the image pyramid, the sliding window, and the ROI size.
- The architecture is not end-to-end trainable, which means that errors in bounding-box predictions are not backpropagated through the network in order to produce better, more accurate detections in the future, by updating its weights. Instead, we're stuck with pre-trained models that limit themselves to infer but not to learn because the framework does not allow them to.

However, don't rule out this approach yet! If you're working with images that present very little variation in size and perspective, and your application definitely doesn't operate in a real-time context, the strategy implemented in this recipe can work wonders for your project!

## See also

You can read more about NMS here:

```
https://towardsdatascience.com/non-maximum-suppression-nms-
93ce178e177c
```

# Detecting objects with YOLOv3

In the *Creating an object detector with image pyramids and sliding windows* recipe, we learned how to turn any image classifier into an object detector, by embedding it in a traditional framework that relies on image pyramids and sliding windows. However, we also learned that this approach isn't ideal because it doesn't allow the network to learn from its mistakes.

The reason why deep learning has conquered the field of object detection is due to its end-to-end approach. The network not only figures out how to classify an object, but also discovers how to produce the best bounding box possible to locate each element in the image.

On top of this, thanks to this end-to-end strategy, a network can detect a myriad objects in a single pass! Of course, this makes such object detectors incredibly efficient!

One of the seminal end-to-end object detectors is YOLO, and in this recipe, we'll learn how to detect objects with a pre-trained YOLOv3 model.

Let's begin!

## Getting ready

First, install `tqdm`, as follows:

```
$> pip install tqdm
```

Our implementation is heavily inspired by the amazing `keras-yolo3` repository implemented by *Huynh Ngoc Anh (on GitHub as experiencor)*, which you can consult here:

`https://github.com/experiencor/keras-yolo3`

Because we'll use a pre-trained YOLO model, we need to download the weights. They're available here: `https://pjreddie.com/media/files/yolov3.weights`. For the purposes of this tutorial, we assume they're inside the `ch9/recipe2/resources` folder, in the companion repository, as `yolov3.weights`. These weights are the same ones used by the original authors of YOLO. Refer to the *See also* section to learn more about YOLO.

We are good to go!

## How to do it...

Follow these steps to complete the recipe:

1.  Start by importing the relevant dependencies:

```
import glob
import json
import struct
import matplotlib.pyplot as plt
import numpy as np
```

```
import tqdm
from matplotlib.patches import Rectangle
from tensorflow.keras.layers import *
from tensorflow.keras.models import *
from tensorflow.keras.preprocessing.image import *
```

2.  Define a `WeightReader()` class that automatically loads the YOLO weights in whichever format the original authors used. Notice that this is a very low-level solution, but we don't need to understand it fully in order to leverage it. Let's begin with the constructor:

```
class WeightReader:
    def __init__(self, weight_file):
        with open(weight_file, 'rb') as w_f:
            major, = struct.unpack('i', w_f.read(4))
            minor, = struct.unpack('i', w_f.read(4))
            revision, = struct.unpack('i', w_f.read(4))

            if (major * 10 + minor) >= 2 and \
                    major < 1000 and \
                    minor < 1000:
                w_f.read(8)
            else:
                w_f.read(4)

            binary = w_f.read()

        self.offset = 0
        self.all_weights = np.frombuffer(binary,
                                        dtype='float32')
```

3.  Next, define a method to read a given number of bytes from the `weights` file:

```
def read_bytes(self, size):
    self.offset = self.offset + size
    return self.all_weights[self.offset-
                            size:self.offset]
```

4.  The `load_weights()` method loads the weights for each of the 106 layers that comprise the YOLO architecture:

```
def load_weights(self, model):
    for i in tqdm.tqdm(range(106)):
        try:
            conv_layer = model.get_layer(f'conv_{i}')

            if i not in [81, 93, 105]:
                norm_layer =
model.get_layer(f'bnorm_{i}')
                size = np.prod(norm_layer.

                    get_weights()[0].shape)
                bias = self.read_bytes(size)
                scale = self.read_bytes(size)
                mean = self.read_bytes(size)
                var = self.read_bytes(size)

                norm_layer.set_weights([scale,
                                        bias, mean,
                                        var])
```

5.  Load the weights of the convolutional layers:

```
            if len(conv_layer.get_weights()) > 1:
                bias = self.read_bytes(np.prod(
conv_layer.get_weights()[1].shape))

                kernel = self.read_bytes(np.prod(
conv_layer.get_weights()[0].shape))

                kernel =
kernel.reshape(list(reversed(
conv_layer.get_weights()[0].shape)))

                kernel = kernel.transpose([2, 3,
                                           1, 0])
```

```
                    conv_layer.set_weights([kernel,
                                            bias])
            else:
                kernel = self.read_bytes(np.prod(
                conv_layer.get_weights()[0].shape))

                kernel =
                kernel.reshape(list(reversed(

                conv_layer.get_weights()[0].shape)))
                kernel = kernel.transpose([2, 3, 1, 0])

                conv_layer.set_weights([kernel])
        except ValueError:
            pass
```

6. Define a method to reset the offset:

```
    def reset(self):
        self.offset = 0
```

7. Define a `BoundBox()` class that encapsulates the vertices of a bounding box, along with the confidence that the enclosed elements are an object (`objness`):

```
class BoundBox(object):
    def __init__(self, x_min, y_min, x_max, y_max,
                 objness=None,
                 classes=None):
        self.xmin = x_min
        self.ymin = y_min
        self.xmax = x_max
        self.ymax = y_max
        self.objness = objness
        self.classes = classes
        self.label = -1
        self.score = -1
```

```
def get_label(self):
    if self.label == -1:
        self.label = np.argmax(self.classes)

    return self.label

def get_score(self):
    if self.score == -1:
        self.score = self.classes[self.get_label()]

    return self.score
```

8.  Define a YOLO() class that encapsulates both the construction of the network and the detection logic. Let's begin with the constructor:

```
class YOLO(object):
    def __init__(self, weights_path,
                 anchors_path='resources/anchors.json',
                 labels_path='resources/coco_labels.txt',
                 class_threshold=0.65):
        self.weights_path = weights_path
        self.model = self._load_yolo()

        self.labels = []
        with open(labels_path, 'r') as f:
            for l in f:
                self.labels.append(l.strip())

        with open(anchors_path, 'r') as f:
            self.anchors = json.load(f)

        self.class_threshold = class_threshold
```

The output of YOLO is a set of encoded bounding boxes defined in the context of anchor boxes that were carefully chosen by the authors of YOLO. This is based on an analysis of the size of objects in the COCO dataset. That's why we store the anchors in self.anchors, and COCO's labels in self.labels. Also, we rely on the self._load_yolo() method (defined later) to build the model.

9.  YOLO is comprised of a series of convolutional blocks and optional skip connections. The `_conv_block()` helper method allows us to instantiate such blocks easily:

```python
def _conv_block(self, input, convolutions,
                skip=True):
    x = input
    count = 0
    for conv in convolutions:
        if count == (len(convolutions) - 2) and
            skip:
            skip_connection = x

        count += 1

        if conv['stride'] > 1:
            x = ZeroPadding2D(((1, 0), (1, 0)))(x)

        x = Conv2D(conv['filter'],
                   conv['kernel'],
                   strides=conv['stride'],
                   padding=('valid' if
                   conv['stride'] > 1
                        else 'same'),

                   name=f'conv_{conv["layer_idx"]}',
                   use_bias=(False if
                        conv['bnorm']
                        else True))(x)
```

10. Check if we need to add batch normalization, leaky ReLU activations, and skip connections:

```python
if conv['bnorm']:
    name = f'bnorm_{conv["layer_idx"]}'
    x = BatchNormalization(epsilon=1e-3,
                           name=name)(x)
if conv['leaky']:
    name = f'leaky_{conv["layer_idx"]}'
    x = LeakyReLU(alpha=0.1, name=name)(x)

return Add()([skip_connection, x]) if skip else x
```

11. The _make_yolov3_architecture() method, defined as follows, builds the YOLO network by stacking a series of convolutional blocks, using the _conv_block() method defined previously:

```python
def _make_yolov3_architecture(self):
    input_image = Input(shape=(None, None, 3))

    # Layer  0 => 4
    x = self._conv_block(input_image, [
        {'filter': 32, 'kernel': 3, 'stride': 1,
         'bnorm': True,
         'leaky': True, 'layer_idx': 0},
        {'filter': 64, 'kernel': 3, 'stride': 2,
         'bnorm': True,
         'leaky': True, 'layer_idx': 1},
        {'filter': 32, 'kernel': 1, 'stride': 1,
         'bnorm': True,
         'leaky': True, 'layer_idx': 2},
        {'filter': 64, 'kernel': 3, 'stride': 1,
         'bnorm': True,
         'leaky': True, 'layer_idx': 3}])
    ...
```

Because this method is quite large, please refer to the companion repository for the full implementation.

12. The `_load_yolo()` method creates the architecture, loads the weights, and instantiates a trained YOLO model in a format TensorFlow understands:

```
def _load_yolo(self):
    model = self._make_yolov3_architecture()
    weight_reader = WeightReader(self.weights_path)
    weight_reader.load_weights(model)
    model.save('model.h5')

    model = load_model('model.h5')

    return model
```

13. Define a static method to compute the Sigmoid value of a tensor:

```
@staticmethod
def _sigmoid(x):
    return 1.0 / (1.0 + np.exp(-x))
```

14. The `_decode_net_output()` method decodes the candidate bounding boxes and class predictions produced by YOLO:

```
def _decode_net_output(self,
                       network_output,
                       anchors,
                       obj_thresh,
                       network_height,
                       network_width):
    grid_height, grid_width = network_output.shape[:2]
    nb_box = 3
    network_output = network_output.reshape(
        (grid_height, grid_width, nb_box, -1))

    boxes = []
    network_output[..., :2] = \
        self._sigmoid(network_output[..., :2])
    network_output[..., 4:] = \
```

```
        self._sigmoid(network_output[..., 4:])
network_output[..., 5:] = \
    (network_output[..., 4][..., np.newaxis] *
    network_output[..., 5:])
network_output[..., 5:] *= \
    network_output[..., 5:] > obj_thresh


for i in range(grid_height * grid_width):
    r = i / grid_width
    c = i % grid_width
```

15. We skip those bounding boxes that don't confidently describe an object:

```
for b in range(nb_box):
    objectness = \
        network_output[int(r)][int(c)][b][4]


    if objectness.all() <= obj_thresh:
        continue
```

16. We extract the coordinates and classes from the network output, and use them to create BoundBox() instances:

```
x, y, w, h = \
    network_output[int(r)][int(c)][b][:4]
x = (c + x) / grid_width
y = (r + y) / grid_height
w = (anchors[2 * b] * np.exp(w) /
    network_width)
h = (anchors[2 * b + 1] * np.exp(h) /
    network_height)


classes = network_output[int(r)][c][b][5:]
box = BoundBox(x_min=x - w / 2,
               y_min=y - h / 2,
               x_max=x + w / 2,
               y_max=y + h / 2,
               objness=objectness,
```

```
                                     classes=classes)
                boxes.append(box)


        return boxes
```

17. The `_correct_yolo_boxes()` method rescales the bounding boxes to the dimensions of the original image:

```
    @staticmethod
    def _correct_yolo_boxes(boxes,
                                image_height,
                                image_width,
                                network_height,
                                network_width):
        new_w, new_h = network_width, network_height

        for i in range(len(boxes)):
            x_offset = (network_width - new_w) / 2.0
            x_offset /= network_width
            x_scale = float(new_w) / network_width

            y_offset = (network_height - new_h) / 2.0
            y_offset /= network_height
            y_scale = float(new_h) / network_height

            boxes[i].xmin = int((boxes[i].xmin - x_
                                 offset) /
                                 x_scale * image_width)
            boxes[i].xmax = int((boxes[i].xmax - x_
                                 offset) /x_scale * image_
                                 width)
            boxes[i].ymin = int((boxes[i].ymin - y_
                                 offset) /
                                 y_scale * image_height)
            boxes[i].ymax = int((boxes[i].ymax - y_
                                 offset) /
                                 y_scale * image_height)
```

18. We'll perform NMS in a bit, in order to reduce the number of redundant detections. For that matter, we need a way to compute the amount of overlap between two intervals:

```python
@staticmethod
def _interval_overlap(interval_a, interval_b):
    x1, x2 = interval_a
    x3, x4 = interval_b

    if x3 < x1:
        if x4 < x1:
            return 0
        else:
            return min(x2, x4) - x1
    else:
        if x2 < x3:
            return 0
        else:
            return min(x2, x4) - x3
```

19. Next, we can calculate the **Intersection Over Union (IoU)** between two bounding boxes, relying on the _interval_overlap() method defined before:

```python
def _bbox_iou(self, box1, box2):
    intersect_w = self._interval_overlap(
        [box1.xmin, box1.xmax],
        [box2.xmin, box2.xmax])
    intersect_h = self._interval_overlap(
        [box1.ymin, box1.ymax],
        [box2.ymin, box2.ymax])

    intersect = intersect_w * intersect_h

    w1, h1 = box1.xmax - box1.xmin, box1.ymax - box1.ymin
    w2, h2 = box2.xmax - box2.xmin, box2.ymax - box2.ymin
```

```
    union = w1 * h1 + w2 * h2 - intersect
    return float(intersect) / union
```

20. Armed with these methods, we can apply NMS to the bounding boxes in order to keep the number of duplicate detections to a minimum:

```
def _non_max_suppression(self, boxes, nms_thresh):
    if len(boxes) > 0:
        nb_class = len(boxes[0].classes)
    else:
        return

    for c in range(nb_class):
        sorted_indices = np.argsort(
            [-box.classes[c] for box in boxes])

        for i in range(len(sorted_indices)):
            index_i = sorted_indices[i]

            if boxes[index_i].classes[c] == 0:
                continue

            for j in range(i + 1,
            len(sorted_indices)):
                index_j = sorted_indices[j]
                iou = self._bbox_iou(boxes[index_i],

                boxes[index_j])
                if iou >= nms_thresh:
                    boxes[index_j].classes[c] = 0
```

21. The `_get_boxes()` method keeps only those boxes with a confidence score higher than the `self.class_threshold` method defined in the constructor (0.6 or 60% by default):

```
def _get_boxes(self, boxes):
    v_boxes, v_labels, v_scores = [], [], []

    for box in boxes:
        for i in range(len(self.labels)):
            if box.classes[i] >
            self.class_threshold:
                v_boxes.append(box)
                v_labels.append(self.labels[i])
                v_scores.append(box.classes[i] *
                100)

    return v_boxes, v_labels, v_scores
```

22. `_draw_boxes()` plots the most confident detections in an input image, which means that each bounding box is accompanied by its class label and its probability:

```
@staticmethod
def _draw_boxes(filename, v_boxes, v_labels,
                v_scores):
    data = plt.imread(filename)
    plt.imshow(data)

    ax = plt.gca()

    for i in range(len(v_boxes)):
        box = v_boxes[i]

        y1, x1, y2, x2 = \
            box.ymin, box.xmin, box.ymax, box.xmax

        width = x2 - x1
        height = y2 - y1
```

```
                rectangle = Rectangle((x1, y1), width,
                                      height,
                                      fill=False,
                                      color='white')

                ax.add_patch(rectangle)
                label = f'{v_labels[i]} ({v_scores[i]:.3f})'
                plt.text(x1, y1, label, color='green')
         plt.show()
```

23. The only public method in the `YOLO()` class is `detect()`, which implements the end-to-end logic to detect objects in an input image. First, it passes the image through the model:

```
def detect(self, image, width, height):
    image = np.expand_dims(image, axis=0)
    preds = self.model.predict(image)

    boxes = []
```

24. Then, it decodes the outputs of the network:

```
for i in range(len(preds)):
    boxes.extend(
        self._decode_net_output(preds[i][0],
                                self.anchors[i],
                                self.class_threshold,
                                416,
                                416))
```

25. Next, it corrects the boxes so that they have proper proportions in relation to the input image. It also applies NMS to get rid of redundant detections:

```
self._correct_yolo_boxes(boxes, height, width,
                         416,
                         416)
self._non_max_suppression(boxes, .5)
```

26. Lastly, it gets the valid bounding boxes and draws them in the input image:

```
valid_boxes, valid_labels, valid_scores = \
    self._get_boxes(boxes)

for i in range(len(valid_boxes)):
    print(valid_labels[i], valid_scores[i])

self._draw_boxes(image_path,
                 valid_boxes,
                 valid_labels,
                 valid_scores)
```

27. With the YOLO() class defined, we can instantiate it as follows:

```
model = YOLO(weights_path='resources/yolov3.weights')
```

28. The final step is to iterate over all test images and run the model on them:

```
for image_path in glob.glob('test_images/*.jpg'):
    image = load_img(image_path, target_size=(416,
                                              416))
    image = img_to_array(image)
    image = image.astype('float32') / 255.0

    original_image = load_img(image_path)
    width, height = original_image.size

    model.detect(image, width, height)
```

Here's the first example:

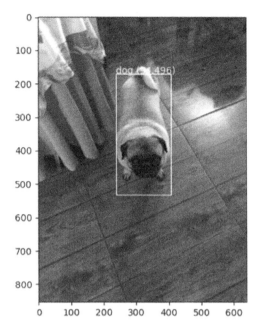

Figure 9.3 – YOLO detected the dog, with a very high confidence score

We can observe that YOLO confidently detected my dog as such, with a confidence score of 94.5%! Awesome! Let's look at the second test image:

Figure 9.4 – YOLO detected multiple objects at varying scales in a single pass

Even though the result is crowded, a quick glance reveals the network was able to identify both cars in the foreground, as well as the people in the background. This is an interesting example because it demonstrates the incredible power of YOLO as an end-to-end object detector, which in a single pass was capable of classifying and localizing many different objects, at varying scales. Impressive, isn't it?

Let's head to the *How it works…* section to connect the dots.

## How it works...

In this recipe, we discovered the immense power of end-to-end object detectors—particularly, one of the most famous and impressive of all: YOLO.

Although YOLO was originally implemented in C++, we leveraged the fantastic Python adaptation by *Huynh Ngoc Anh* to perform object detection in our own images using a pre-trained version (specifically, version 3) of this architecture on the seminal COCO dataset.

As you might have noticed, YOLO and many other end-to-end object detectors are very complex networks, but their advantage over traditional approaches such as image pyramids and sliding windows is evident. Not only are the results way better, but they also come through faster thanks to the ability of YOLO to look once at the input image in order to produce all the relevant detections.

But what if you want to train an end-to-end object detector on your own data? Are you doomed to rely on out-of-the-box solutions? Do you need to spend hours deciphering cryptic papers in order to implement such networks?

Well, that's one option, but there's another one, which we'll explore in the next recipe, and it entails the TensorFlow Object Detection API, an experimental repository of state-of-the-art architectures that will ease and boost your object detection endeavors!

## See also

YOLO is a milestone when it comes to deep learning and object detection, so reading the paper is a pretty smart time investment. You can find it here:

```
https://arxiv.org/abs/1506.02640
```

You can learn more about YOLO directly from the author's website, here:

```
https://pjreddie.com/darknet/yolo/
```

If you are interested in exploring `keras-yolo3`, the tool we based our implementation on, refer to this link:

```
https://github.com/experiencor/keras-yolo3
```

# Training your own object detector with TensorFlow's Object Detection API

It's no secret that modern object detectors rank among the most complex and challenging architectures to implement and get it right! However, that doesn't mean we can't take advantage of the most recent advancements in this domain in order to train object detectors on our own datasets. *How?*, you ask. Enter TensorFlow's Object Detection API!

In this recipe, we'll install this API, prepare a custom dataset for training, tweak a couple of configuration files, and use the resulting model to localize objects on test images. This recipe is a bit different from the ones you've worked on so far, because we'll be switching back and forth between Python and the command line.

Are you ready? Then let's get started.

## Getting ready

There are several dependencies we need to install for this recipe to work. Let's begin with the most important one: the TensorFlow Object Detection API. First, `cd` to a location of your preference and clone the `tensorflow/models` repository:

```
$> git clone --depth 1 https://github.com/tensorflow/models
```

Next, install the TensorFlow Object Detection API, like this:

```
$> sudo apt install -y protobuf-compiler
$> cd models/research
$> protoc object_detection/protos/*.proto --python_out=.
$> cp object_detection/packages/tf2/setup.py .
$> python -m pip install -q .
```

For the purposes of this recipe, we'll assume it's installed at the same level as the ch9 folder (`https://github.com/PacktPublishing/Tensorflow-2.0-Computer-Vision-Cookbook/tree/master/ch9`). Now, we must install `pandas` and `Pillow`:

```
$> pip install pandas Pillow
```

The dataset we will use is `Fruit Images for Object Detection`, hosted on Kaggle, which you can access here: `https://www.kaggle.com/mbkinaci/fruit-images-for-object-detection`. Log in or sign up and download the data to a location of your preference as `fruits.zip` (the data is available in the `ch9/recipe3` folder in the companion repository for this book). Finally, decompress it:

Figure 9.5 – Sample images of the three classes in the dataset: apple, orange, and banana

The labels in this dataset are in **Pascal VOC** format, where **VOC** stands for **Visual Object Classes**. Refer to the *See also…* section to learn more about it.

Now, we're all set! Let's begin implementing.

## How to do it...

By the end of these steps, you'll have trained your own state-of-the-art object detector using the TensorFlow Object Detection API:

1.  We'll work with two files in this recipe: the first one is used to prepare the data (you can find it as `prepare.py` in the repository), and the second one is used to make inferences with the object detector (`inference.py` in the repository). Open `prepare.py` and import all the needed packages:

```
import glob
import io
import os
from collections import namedtuple
from xml.etree import ElementTree as tree
import pandas as pd
import tensorflow.compat.v1 as tf
from PIL import Image
from object_detection.utils import dataset_util
```

2. Define the `encode_class()` function, which maps the text labels to their integer counterparts:

```
def encode_class(row_label):
    class_mapping = {'apple': 1, 'orange': 2,
                     'banana': 3}

    return class_mapping.get(row_label, None)
```

3. Define a function to split a dataframe of labels (which we'll create later) into groups:

```
def split(df, group):
    Data = namedtuple('data', ['filename', 'object'])
    groups = df.groupby(group)
    return [Data(filename, groups.get_group(x))
            for filename, x
            in zip(groups.groups.keys(),
        groups.groups)]
```

4. The TensorFlow Object Detection API works with a data structure known as `tf.train.Example`. The next function takes the path to an image and its label (which is the set of bounding boxes and the ground-truth classes of all objects contained in it) and creates the corresponding `tf.train.Example`. First, load the image and its properties:

```
def create_tf_example(group, path):
    groups_path = os.path.join(path, f'{group.filename}')
    with tf.gfile.GFile(groups_path, 'rb') as f:
        encoded_jpg = f.read()

    image = Image.open(io.BytesIO(encoded_jpg))
    width, height = image.size

    filename = group.filename.encode('utf8')
    image_format = b'jpg'
```

5.  Now, store the dimensions of the bounding boxes, along with the classes of each object contained in the image:

```
xmins = []
xmaxs = []
ymins = []
ymaxs = []
classes_text = []
classes = []

for index, row in group.object.iterrows():
    xmins.append(row['xmin'] / width)
    xmaxs.append(row['xmax'] / width)
    ymins.append(row['ymin'] / height)
    ymaxs.append(row['ymax'] / height)
    classes_text.append(row['class'].encode('utf8'))
    classes.append(encode_class(row['class']))
```

6.  Create a `tf.train.Features` object that will contain relevant information about the image and its objects:

```
features = tf.train.Features(feature={
    'image/height':
        dataset_util.int64_feature(height),
    'image/width':
        dataset_util.int64_feature(width),
    'image/filename':
        dataset_util.bytes_feature(filename),
    'image/source_id':
        dataset_util.bytes_feature(filename),
    'image/encoded':
        dataset_util.bytes_feature(encoded_jpg),
    'image/format':
        dataset_util.bytes_feature(image_format),
    'image/object/bbox/xmin':
        dataset_util.float_list_feature(xmins),
    'image/object/bbox/xmax':
        dataset_util.float_list_feature(xmaxs),
```

```
        'image/object/bbox/ymin':
            dataset_util.float_list_feature(ymins),
        'image/object/bbox/ymax':
            dataset_util.float_list_feature(ymaxs),
        'image/object/class/text':
            dataset_util.bytes_list_feature(classes_text),
        'image/object/class/label':
            dataset_util.int64_list_feature(classes)
    })
```

7.  Return a `tf.train.Example` structure initialized with the features created previously:

```
        return tf.train.Example(features=features)
```

8.  Define a function to transform an **Extensible Markup Language** (**XML**) file— with information about the bounding boxes in an image—to an equivalent one in **Comma-Separated Values** (**CSV**) format:

```
def bboxes_to_csv(path):
    xml_list = []

    bboxes_pattern = os.path.sep.join([path, '*.xml'])
    for xml_file in glob.glob(bboxes_pattern):
        t = tree.parse(xml_file)
        root = t.getroot()

        for member in root.findall('object'):
            value = (root.find('filename').text,
                        int(root.find('size')[0].text),
                        int(root.find('size')[1].text),
                        member[0].text,
                        int(member[4][0].text),
                        int(member[4][1].text),
                        int(member[4][2].text),
                        int(member[4][3].text))
            xml_list.append(value)
```

```
column_names = ['filename', 'width', 'height',
            'class','xmin', 'ymin', 'xmax', 'ymax']
df = pd.DataFrame(xml_list, columns=column_names)
return df
```

9. Iterate over the `test` and `train` subsets in the `fruits` folder, converting the labels from CSV to XML:

```
base = 'fruits'
for subset in ['test', 'train']:
    folder = os.path.sep.join([base, f'{subset}_zip',
                            subset])

    labels_path = os.path.sep.join([base,f'{subset}_
                                    labels.
                                    csv'])
    bboxes_df = bboxes_to_csv(folder)
    bboxes_df.to_csv(labels_path, index=None)
```

10. Then, use the same labels to produce the `tf.train.Examples` corresponding to the current subset of data being processed:

```
writer = (tf.python_io.
        TFRecordWriter(f'resources/{subset}.record'))
examples = pd.read_csv(f'fruits/{subset}_labels.csv')
grouped = split(examples, 'filename')

path = os.path.join(f'fruits/{subset}_zip/{subset}')
for group in grouped:
    tf_example = create_tf_example(group, path)
    writer.write(tf_example.SerializeToString())

writer.close()
```

11. After running the `prepare.py` script implemented in *Step 1* through *Step 10*, you'll have the data in the necessary shape for the TensorFlow Object Detection API to train on it. The next step is to download the weights of `EfficientDet`, a state-of-the-art architecture we'll fine-tune shortly. Download the weights from this **Uniform Resource Locator (URL)**, and then decompress them into a location of your preference: `http://download.tensorflow.org/models/object_detection/tf2/20200711/efficientdet_d0_coco17_tpu-32.tar.gz`. I placed them in my `Desktop` folder.

12. Create a file to map the classes to integers. Name it `label_map.txt` and place it inside `ch9/recipe3/resources`:

```
item {
    id: 1
    name: 'apple'
}
item {
    id: 2
    name: 'orange'
}
item {
    id: 3
    name: 'banana'
}
```

13. Next, we must change the configuration file for this network to adapt it to our dataset. You can either locate it in `models/research/object_detection/configs/tf2/ssd_efficientdet_d0_512x512_coco17_tpu-8.config` (assuming you installed the TensorFlow Object Detection API at the same level of the `ch9` folder in the companion repository), or download it directly from this URL: `https://github.com/tensorflow/models/blob/master/research/object_detection/configs/tf2/ssd_efficientdet_d0_512x512_coco17_tpu-8.config`. Whichever option you choose, place a copy inside `ch9/recipe3/resources` and modify *line 13* to reflect the number of classes in our dataset:

```
num_classes: 3
```

Then, modify *line 140* to point to the `EfficientDet` weights we downloaded in *Step 7*:

```
fine_tune_checkpoint: "/home/jesus/Desktop/efficientdet_
d0_coco17_tpu-32/checkpoint/ckpt-0"
```

Change `fine_tune_checkpoint_type` from `classification` to `detection` on *line 143*:

```
fine_tune_checkpoint_type: "detection"
```

Modify *line 180* to point to the `label_map.txt` file created in *Step 8*:

```
label_map_path: "/home/jesus/Desktop/tensorflow-computer-
vision/ch9/recipe3/resources/label_map.txt"
```

Modify *line 182* to point to the `train.record` file created in *Step 11*, corresponding to the prepared training data:

```
input_path: "/home/jesus/Desktop/tensorflow-computer-
vision/ch9/recipe3/resources/train.record"
```

Modify *line 193* to point to the `label_map.txt` file created in *Step 12*:

```
label_map_path: "/home/jesus/Desktop/tensorflow-computer-
vision/ch9/recipe3/resources/label_map.txt"
```

Modify *line 197* to point to the `test.record` file created in *Step 11*, corresponding to the prepared test data:

```
input_path: "/home/jesus/Desktop/tensorflow-computer-
vision/ch9/recipe3/resources/test.record"
```

14. Time to train the model! First, assuming you're at the root level of the companion repository, `cd` into the `object_detection` folder in the TensorFlow Object Detection API:

```
$> cd models/research/object_detection
```

Then, train the model with this command:

```
$> python model_main_tf2.py --pipeline_config_
path=../../../ch9/recipe3/resources/ssd_efficientdet_
d0_512x512_coco17_tpu-8.config --model_dir=../../../ch9/
recipe3/training --num_train_steps=10000
```

Here, we are training the model for 10000 steps. Also, we'll save the results in the training folder inside ch9/recipe3. Finally, we're specifying the location of the configuration file with the --pipeline_config_path option. This step will take several hours.

15. Once the network has been fine-tuned, we must export it as a frozen graph in order to use it for inference. For that matter, cd once again to the object_detection folder in the TensorFlow Object Detection API:

```
$> cd models/research/object_detection
```

Now, execute the following command:

```
$> python exporter_main_v2.py --trained_checkpoint_
dir=../../../ch9/recipe3/training/ --pipeline_
config_path=../../../ch9/recipe3/resources/
ssd_efficientdet_d0_512x512_coco17_tpu-8.config --output_
directory=../../../ch9/recipe3/resources/inference_graph
```

The trained_checkpoint_dir parameter is used to point to the location where the trained model is, while pipeline_config_path points to the model's configuration file. Finally, the frozen inference graph will be saved inside the ch9/recipe3/resources/inference_graph folder, as stated by the output_directory flag.

16. Open a file named inference.py, and import all the relevant dependencies:

```
import glob
import random
from io import BytesIO


import matplotlib.pyplot as plt
import numpy as np
import tensorflow as tf
from PIL import Image
from object_detection.utils import ops
from object_detection.utils import visualization_utils as
viz
from object_detection.utils.label_map_util import \
    create_category_index_from_labelmap
```

17. Define a function to load an image from disk as a NumPy array:

```python
def load_image(path):
    image_data = tf.io.gfile.GFile(path, 'rb').read()
    image = Image.open(BytesIO(image_data))

    width, height = image.size
    shape = (height, width, 3)

    image = np.array(image.getdata())
    image = image.reshape(shape).astype('uint8')

    return image
```

18. Define a function to run the model on a single image. First, convert the image into a tensor:

```python
def infer_image(net, image):
    image = np.asarray(image)
    input_tensor = tf.convert_to_tensor(image)
    input_tensor = input_tensor[tf.newaxis, ...]
```

19. Pass the tensor to the network, extract the number of detections, and keep as many values in the resulting dictionary as there are detections:

```python
num_detections = int(result.pop('num_detections'))
result = {key: value[0, :num_detections].numpy()
          for key, value in result.items()}
result['num_detections'] = num_detections

result['detection_classes'] = \
    result['detection_classes'].astype('int64')
```

20. If there are detection masks present, reframe them to image masks and return the results:

```python
if 'detection_masks' in result:
    detection_masks_reframed = \
        ops.reframe_box_masks_to_image_masks(
            result['detection_masks'],
```

```
                    result['detection_boxes'],
                    image.shape[0],
                    image.shape[1])

        detection_masks_reframed = \
            tf.cast(detection_masks_reframed > 0.5,
                    tf.uint8)

        result['detection_masks_reframed'] = \
            detection_masks_reframed.numpy()

    return result
```

21. Create a category index from the `label_map.txt` file we created in *Step 12*, and also load the model from the frozen inference graph produced in *Step 15*:

```
labels_path = 'resources/label_map.txt'
CATEGORY_IDX = \
    create_category_index_from_labelmap(labels_path,
                                    use_display_name=True)
model_path = 'resources/inference_graph/saved_model'
model = tf.saved_model.load(model_path)
```

22. Pick three random test images:

```
test_images = list(glob.glob('fruits/test_zip/test/*.
jpg'))
random.shuffle(test_images)
test_images = test_images[:3]
```

23. Run the model over the sample images, and save the resulting detections:

```
for image_path in test_images:
    image = load_image(image_path)
    result = infer_image(model, image)

    masks = result.get('detection_masks_reframed',
                        None)
    viz.visualize_boxes_and_labels_on_image_array(
```

```
        image,
        result['detection_boxes'],
        result['detection_classes'],
        result['detection_scores'],
        CATEGORY_IDX,
        instance_masks=masks,
        use_normalized_coordinates=True,
        line_thickness=5)

    plt.figure(figsize=(24, 32))
    plt.imshow(image)
    plt.savefig(f'detections_{image_path.split("/")
[-1]}')
```

We see the results in *Figure 9.6*:

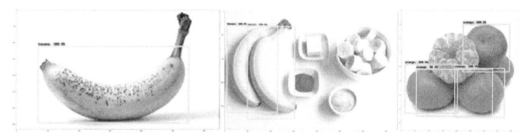

Figure 9.6 – EfficientDet detection results on a random sample of test images

We can see in *Figure 9.6* that our fine-tuned network produced fairly accurate and confident detections. Considering we only concerned ourselves with data preparation and inference, and that regarding the architecture itself we just adapted a configuration file to our needs, the results are pretty impressive!

Let's move on to the *How it works…* section.

## How it works...

In this recipe, we discovered that training an object detector is a hard and challenging feat. The good news, however, is that we have the TensorFlow Object Detection API at our disposal to train a wide range of vanguardist networks.

Because the TensorFlow Object Detection API is an experimental tool, it uses different conventions than regular TensorFlow, and therefore in order to use it, we need to perform a little bit of processing work on the input data to put it into a shape that the API understands. This is done by converting the labels in the `Fruits for Object Detection` dataset (originally in XML format) to CSV and then into serialized `tf.train.Example` objects.

Then, to use the trained model, we exported it as an inference graph using the `exporter_main_v2.py` script and leveraged some of the visualization tools in the API to display the detections on the sample test images.

What about the training? This is arguably the easiest part, entailing three major steps:

- Creating a mapping from text labels to integers (*Step 12*)
- Modifying the configuration file corresponding to the model to fine-tune it in all the relevant places (*Step 13*)
- Running the `model_main_tf2.py` file to train the network, passing it the proper parameters (*Step 14*)

This recipe provides you with a template you can tweak and adapt to train virtually any modern object detector (supported by the API) on any dataset of your choosing. Pretty cool, right?

## See also

You can learn more about the TensorFlow Object Detection API here:

```
https://github.com/tensorflow/models/tree/master/research/
object_detection
```

Also, I encourage you to read this great article to learn more about `EfficientDet`:

```
https://towardsdatascience.com/a-thorough-breakdown-of-
efficientdet-for-object-detection-dc6a15788b73
```

If you want to learn a great deal about the **Pascal VOC** format, then you must watch this video:

```
https://www.youtube.com/watch?v=-f6TJpHcAeM
```

# Detecting objects using TFHub

TFHub is a cornucopia of state-of-the-art models when it comes to object detection. As we'll discover in this recipe, using them to spot elements of interest in our images is a fairly straightforward task, especially considering they've been trained on the gigantic COCO dataset, which make them an excellent choice for out-of-the-box object detection.

## Getting ready

First, we must install `Pillow` and TFHub, as follows:

```
$> pip install Pillow tensorflow-hub
```

Also, because some visualization tools we'll use live in the TensorFlow Object Detection API, we must install it. First, `cd` to a location of your preference and clone the `tensorflow/models` repository:

```
$> git clone --depth 1 https://github.com/tensorflow/models
```

Next, install the TensorFlow Object Detection API, like this:

```
$> sudo apt install -y protobuf-compiler
$> cd models/research
$> protoc object_detection/protos/*.proto --python_out=.
$> cp object_detection/packages/tf2/setup.py .
$> python -m pip install -q .
```

That's it! Let's get started.

## How to do it...

Follow these steps to learn how to use TFHub to detect objects in your own photos:

1.  Import the packages we'll need:

    ```
    import glob
    from io import BytesIO

    import matplotlib.pyplot as plt
    import numpy as np
    import tensorflow as tf
    import tensorflow_hub as hub
    ```

```
from PIL import Image
from object_detection.utils import visualization_utils as
viz
from object_detection.utils.label_map_util import \
    create_category_index_from_labelmap
```

2.  Define a function to load an image into a NumPy array:

```
def load_image(path):
    image_data = tf.io.gfile.GFile(path, 'rb').read()
    image = Image.open(BytesIO(image_data))

    width, height = image.size
    shape = (1, height, width, 3)

    image = np.array(image.getdata())
    image = image.reshape(shape).astype('uint8')

    return image
```

3.  Define a function to make predictions with a model, and save the results to disk. Start by loading the image and passing it through the model:

```
def get_and_save_predictions(model, image_path):
    image = load_image(image_path)
    results = model(image)
```

4.  Convert the results to NumPy arrays:

```
model_output = {k: v.numpy() for k, v in results.items()}
```

5.  Create a visualization of the detections with their boxes, scores, and classes:

```
    boxes = model_output['detection_boxes'][0]
    classes = \
        model_output['detection_classes'][0].astype('int')
    scores = model_output['detection_scores'][0]

    clone = image.copy()
    viz.visualize_boxes_and_labels_on_image_array(
```

```
        image=clone[0],
        boxes=boxes,
        classes=classes,
        scores=scores,
        category_index=CATEGORY_IDX,
        use_normalized_coordinates=True,
        max_boxes_to_draw=200,
        min_score_thresh=0.30,
        agnostic_mode=False,
        line_thickness=5
    )
```

6. Save the result to disk:

```
        plt.figure(figsize=(24, 32))
        plt.imshow(image_with_mask[0])

        plt.savefig(f'output/{image_path.split("/")[-1]}')
```

7. Load COCO's category index:

```
labels_path = 'resources/mscoco_label_map.pbtxt'
CATEGORY_IDX =create_category_index_from_labelmap(labels_
path)
```

8. Load Faster R-CNN from TFHub:

```
MODEL_PATH = ('https://tfhub.dev/tensorflow/faster_rcnn/'
              'inception_resnet_v2_1024x1024/1')
model = hub.load(MODEL_PATH)
```

9. Run Faster R-CNN over all test images:

```
test_images_paths = glob.glob('test_images/*')
for image_path in test_images_paths:
    get_and_save_predictions(model, image_path)
```

After a while, the labeled images should be in the output folder. The first example showcases the power of the network, which detected with 100% confidence the two elephants in the photo:

Figure 9.7 – Both elephants were detected, with a perfect score

However, there are instances where the model makes some mistakes, like this:

Figure 9.8 – The network mistakenly detected a person in the tablecloth

In this example, the network detected a person in the tablecloth, with 42% certainty, although it correctly identified my dog as a Pug, with 100% accuracy. This, and other false positives, can be prevented by increasing the `min_score_thresh` value passed to the `visualize_boxes_and_labels_on_image_array()` method in *Step 5*.

Let's head to the next section.

## How it works...

In this recipe, we leveraged the ease of use of the powerful models that live in TFHub to perform out-of-the-box object detection with fairly good results.

Why should we consider TFHub a viable option to satisfy our object detection needs? Well, the vast majority of the models there are really challenging to implement when starting from scratch, let alone training them to achieve decent results. On top of this, these complex architectures have been trained on COCO, a massive corpus of images tailored for object detection and image segmentation tasks. Nevertheless, we must keep in mind that we cannot retrain these networks and, therefore, they will work best on images containing objects that exist in COCO. If we need to create our own custom object detectors, the other strategies covered in this chapter should suffice.

## See also

You can access the list of all available object detectors in TFHub here:

`https://tfhub.dev/tensorflow/collections/object_detection/1`

# 10
# Applying the Power of Deep Learning to Videos

Computer vision is focused on the understanding of visual data. Of course, that includes videos, which, at their core, are a sequence of images, which means we can leverage most of our knowledge regarding deep learning for image processing to videos and reap great results.

In this chapter, we'll start training a convolutional neuronal network to detect emotions in human faces, and then we'll learn how to apply it in a real-time context using our webcam.

Then, in the remaining recipes, we'll use very advanced implementations of architectures, hosted in **TensorFlow Hub** (**TFHub**), specially tailored to tackle interesting video-related problems such as action recognition, frames generation, and text-to-video retrieval.

Here are the recipes that we will be covering shortly:

- Detecting emotions in real time
- Recognizing actions with TensorFlow Hub

- Generating the middle frames of a video with TensorFlow Hub
- Performing text-to-video retrieval with TensorFlow Hub

# Technical requirements

As usual, having access to a GPU is a great plus, particularly for the first recipe, where we'll implement a network from scratch. Because the rest of the chapter leverages models in TFHub, your CPU should be enough, although a GPU will give you a pretty nice speed boost! In the *Getting ready* section, you'll find the preparatory steps for each recipe. You can find the code for this chapter here: `https://github.com/PacktPublishing/Tensorflow-2.0-Computer-Vision-Cookbook/tree/master/ch10`.

Check out the following link to see the Code in Action video:

`https://bit.ly/3qkTJ2l`.

# Detecting emotions in real time

At its most basic form, a video is just a series of images. By leveraging this seemingly simple or trivial fact, we can adapt what we know about image classification to create very interesting video processing pipelines powered by deep learning.

In this recipe, we'll build an algorithm to detect emotions in real time (webcam streaming) or from video files. Pretty interesting, right?

Let's begin.

## Getting ready

First, we must install several external libraries, such as `OpenCV` and `imutils`. Execute the following command to install them:

```
$> pip install opencv-contrib-python imutils
```

To train an emotion classifier network, we'll use the dataset from the Kaggle competition **Challenges in Representation Learning: Facial Expression Recognition Challenge**, which is available here: `https://www.kaggle.com/c/challenges-in-representation-learning-facial-expression-recognition-challenge/data`. You must sign in or sign up in order to download the dataset. Place the file in a location of your preference (we'll assume it's located in the `~/.keras/datasets` folder), extract it as `emotion_recognition`, and then unzip the `fer2013.tar.gz` file.

Here are some sample images:

Figure 10.1 – Sample images. Emotions from left to right: sad, angry, scared, surprised, happy, and neutral

Let's get started!

# How to do it...

By the end of this recipe, you'll have your own emotion detector!

1. Import all the dependencies:

```
import csv
import glob
import pathlib
import cv2
import imutils
import numpy as np
from tensorflow.keras.callbacks import ModelCheckpoint
from tensorflow.keras.layers import *
from tensorflow.keras.models import *
from tensorflow.keras.optimizers import Adam
from tensorflow.keras.preprocessing.image import *
from tensorflow.keras.utils import to_categorical
```

2. Define a list of all possible emotions in our dataset, along with a color associated with each one:

```
EMOTIONS = ['angry', 'scared', 'happy', 'sad',
            'surprised','neutral']

COLORS = {'angry': (0, 0, 255),
    'scared': (0, 128, 255),
    'happy': (0, 255, 255),
```

```
      'sad': (255, 0, 0),
      'surprised': (178, 255, 102),
      'neutral': (160, 160, 160)
  }
```

3. Define a method to build the emotion classifier architecture. It receives the input shape and the number of classes in the dataset:

```
def build_network(input_shape, classes):
    input = Input(shape=input_shape)
    x = Conv2D(filters=32,
               kernel_size=(3, 3),
               padding='same',
               kernel_initializer='he_normal')(input)
    x = ELU()(x)
    x = BatchNormalization(axis=-1)(x)
    x = Conv2D(filters=32,
               kernel_size=(3, 3),
               kernel_initializer='he_normal',
               padding='same')(x)
    x = ELU()(x)
    x = BatchNormalization(axis=-1)(x)
    x = MaxPooling2D(pool_size=(2, 2))(x)
    x = Dropout(rate=0.25)(x)
```

4. Each block in the network is comprised of two ELU activated, batch-normalized convolutions, followed by a max pooling layer, and ending with a dropout layer. The block defined previously had 32 filters per convolution, while the following one has 64 filters per convolution:

```
    x = Conv2D(filters=64,
               kernel_size=(3, 3),
               kernel_initializer='he_normal',
               padding='same')(x)
    x = ELU()(x)
    x = BatchNormalization(axis=-1)(x)
    x = Conv2D(filters=64,
               kernel_size=(3, 3),
```

```
                       kernel_initializer='he_normal',
                       padding='same')(x)
x = ELU()(x)
x = BatchNormalization(axis=-1)(x)
x = MaxPooling2D(pool_size=(2, 2))(x)
x = Dropout(rate=0.25)(x)
```

5.  The third block has 128 filters per convolution:

```
x = Conv2D(filters=128,
           kernel_size=(3, 3),
           kernel_initializer='he_normal',
           padding='same')(x)
x = ELU()(x)
x = BatchNormalization(axis=-1)(x)
x = Conv2D(filters=128,
           kernel_size=(3, 3),
           kernel_initializer='he_normal',
           padding='same')(x)
x = ELU()(x)
x = BatchNormalization(axis=-1)(x)
x = MaxPooling2D(pool_size=(2, 2))(x)
x = Dropout(rate=0.25)(x)
```

6.  Next, we have two dense, ELU activated, batch-normalized layers, also followed by a dropout, each with 64 units:

```
x = Flatten()(x)
x = Dense(units=64,
          kernel_initializer='he_normal')(x)
x = ELU()(x)
x = BatchNormalization(axis=-1)(x)
x = Dropout(rate=0.5)(x)


x = Dense(units=64,
          kernel_initializer='he_normal')(x)
x = ELU()(x)
x = BatchNormalization(axis=-1)(x)
```

```
x = Dropout(rate=0.5)(x)
```

7. Finally, we encounter the output layer, with as many neurons as classes in the dataset. Of course, it's softmax-activated:

```
x = Dense(units=classes,
          kernel_initializer='he_normal')(x)
output = Softmax()(x)


return Model(input, output)
```

8. `load_dataset()` loads both the images and labels for the training, validation, and test datasets:

```
def load_dataset(dataset_path, classes):
    train_images = []
    train_labels = []
    val_images = []
    val_labels = []
    test_images = []
    test_labels = []
```

9. The data in this dataset is in a CSV file, separated into `emotion`, `pixels`, and `Usage` columns. Let's parse the `emotion` column first. Although the dataset contains faces for seven classes, we'll combine *disgust* and *angry* (encoded as 0 and 1, respectively) because both share most of the facial features, and merging them leads to better results:

```
with open(dataset_path, 'r') as f:
    reader = csv.DictReader(f)
    for line in reader:
        label = int(line['emotion'])

        if label <= 1:
            label = 0  # This merges classes 1 and 0.

        if label > 0:
            label -= 1  # All classes start from 0.
```

10. Next, we parse the `pixels` column, which is 2,034 whitespace-separated integers, corresponding to the grayscale pixels for the image (48x48=2034):

```
image = np.array(line['pixels'].split
                              (' '),
                    dtype='uint8')
image = image.reshape((48, 48))
image = img_to_array(image)
```

11. Now, to figure out to which subset this image and label belong, we must look at the `Usage` column:

```
if line['Usage'] == 'Training':
    train_images.append(image)
    train_labels.append(label)
elif line['Usage'] == 'PrivateTest':
    val_images.append(image)
    val_labels.append(label)
else:
    test_images.append(image)
    test_labels.append(label)
```

12. Convert all the images to NumPy arrays:

```
train_images = np.array(train_images)
val_images = np.array(val_images)
test_images = np.array(test_images)
```

13. Then, one-hot encode all the labels:

```
train_labels =
to_categorical(np.array(train_labels),
                        classes)
val_labels = to_categorical(np.array(val_labels),
                        classes)
test_labels = to_categorical(np.array(test_labels),
                        classes)
```

14. Return all the images and labels:

```
return (train_images, train_labels), \
```

```
        (val_images, val_labels), \
        (test_images, test_labels)
```

15. Define a function to compute the area of a rectangle. We'll use this later to get the largest face detection:

```
def rectangle_area(r):
    return (r[2] - r[0]) * (r[3] - r[1])
```

16. We'll now create a bar plot to display the probability distribution of the emotions detected in each frame. The following function is used to plot each bar, corresponding to a particular emotion, in said plot:

```
def plot_emotion(emotions_plot, emotion, probability,
                 index):
    w = int(probability * emotions_plot.shape[1])
    cv2.rectangle(emotions_plot,
                  (5, (index * 35) + 5),
                  (w, (index * 35) + 35),
                  color=COLORS[emotion],
                  thickness=-1)

    white = (255, 255, 255)
    text = f'{emotion}: {probability * 100:.2f}%'
    cv2.putText(emotions_plot,
                text,
                (10, (index * 35) + 23),
                fontFace=cv2.FONT_HERSHEY_COMPLEX,
                fontScale=0.45,
                color=white,
                thickness=2)

    return emotions_plot
```

17. We'll also draw a bounding box around the detected face, captioned with the recognized emotion:

```
def plot_face(image, emotion, detection):
    frame_x, frame_y, frame_width, frame_height =
detection
    cv2.rectangle(image,
                  (frame_x, frame_y),
                  (frame_x + frame_width,
                   frame_y + frame_height),
                  color=COLORS[emotion],
                  thickness=2)
    cv2.putText(image,
                emotion,
                (frame_x, frame_y - 10),
                fontFace=cv2.FONT_HERSHEY_COMPLEX,
                fontScale=0.45,
                color=COLORS[emotion],
                thickness=2)

    return image
```

18. Define the `predict_emotion()` function, which takes the emotion classifier and an input image and returns the predictions output by the model:

```
def predict_emotion(model, roi):
    roi = cv2.resize(roi, (48, 48))
    roi = roi.astype('float') / 255.0
    roi = img_to_array(roi)
    roi = np.expand_dims(roi, axis=0)

    predictions = model.predict(roi)[0]
    return predictions
```

19. Load a saved model if there is one:

```
checkpoints = sorted(list(glob.glob('./*.h5')),
reverse=True)
if len(checkpoints) > 0:
    model = load_model(checkpoints[0])
```

20. Otherwise, train the model from scratch. First, build the path to the CSV with the data and then compute the number of classes in the dataset:

```
else:
    base_path = (pathlib.Path.home() / '.keras' /
                 'datasets' /
                 'emotion_recognition' / 'fer2013')
    input_path = str(base_path / 'fer2013.csv')
    classes = len(EMOTIONS)
```

21. Then, load each subset of data:

```
(train_images, train_labels), \
(val_images, val_labels), \
(test_images, test_labels) = load_dataset(input_path,
                                          classes)
```

22. Build the network and compile it. Also, define a `ModelCheckpoint` callback to save the best performing model, based on the validation loss:

```
model = build_network((48, 48, 1), classes)
model.compile(loss='categorical_crossentropy',
              optimizer=Adam(lr=0.003),
              metrics=['accuracy'])

checkpoint_pattern = ('model-ep{epoch:03d}-
                       loss{loss:.3f}'
                      '-val_loss{val_loss:.3f}.h5')
checkpoint = ModelCheckpoint(checkpoint_pattern,
                             monitor='val_loss',
                             verbose=1,
                             save_best_only=True,
                             mode='min')
```

23. Define the augmenters and generator for the training and validation sets. Notice that we're only augmenting the training set, while we just rescale the images in the validation set:

```
BATCH_SIZE = 128
train_augmenter = ImageDataGenerator(rotation_
                        range=10,zoom_range=0.1,
                            horizontal_flip=True,
                                rescale=1. / 255.,
                            fill_mode='nearest')
train_gen = train_augmenter.flow(train_images,
                            train_labels,
                        batch_size=BATCH_SIZE)
train_steps = len(train_images) // BATCH_SIZE


val_augmenter = ImageDataGenerator(rescale=1. / 255.)
val_gen = val_augmenter.flow(val_images,val_labels,
                    batch_size=BATCH_SIZE)
```

24. Fit the model for 300 epochs and then evaluate it on the test set (we only rescale the images in this subset):

```
EPOCHS = 300
model.fit(train_gen,
            steps_per_epoch=train_steps,
            validation_data=val_gen,
            epochs=EPOCHS,
            verbose=1,
            callbacks=[checkpoint])

test_augmenter = ImageDataGenerator(rescale=1. / 255.)
test_gen = test_augmenter.flow(test_images,
                            test_labels,
                        batch_size=BATCH_SIZE)
test_steps = len(test_images) // BATCH_SIZE
_, accuracy = model.evaluate(test_gen,
                        steps=test_steps)
```

```
print(f'Accuracy: {accuracy * 100}%')
```

25. Instantiate a `cv2.VideoCapture()` object to fetch the frames in a test video. If you want to use your webcam, replace `video_path` with 0:

```
video_path = 'emotions.mp4'
camera = cv2.VideoCapture(video_path)   # Pass 0 to use
webcam
```

26. Create a **Haar Cascades** face detector (this is a topic outside the scope of this book. If you want to learn more about Haar Cascades, refer to the *See also* section in this recipe):

```
cascade_file = 'resources/haarcascade_frontalface_
default.xml'
det = cv2.CascadeClassifier(cascade_file)
```

27. Iterate over each frame in the video (or webcam stream), exiting only if there are no more frames to read, or if the user presses the Q key:

```
while True:
    frame_exists, frame = camera.read()

    if not frame_exists:
        break
```

28. Resize the frame to have a width of 380 pixels (the height will be computed automatically to preserve the aspect ratio). Also, create a canvas of where to draw the emotions bar plot, and a copy of the input frame in terms of where to plot the detected faces:

```
frame = imutils.resize(frame, width=380)
emotions_plot = np.zeros_like(frame,
                                dtype='uint8')
copy = frame.copy()
```

29. Because Haar Cascades work on grayscale images, we must convert the input frame to black and white. Then, we run the face detector on it:

```
gray = cv2.cvtColor(frame, cv2.COLOR_BGR2GRAY)

detections = \
    det.detectMultiScale(gray,scaleFactor=1.1,
                         minNeighbors=5,
                         minSize=(35, 35),

                         flags=cv2.CASCADE_SCALE_IMAGE)
```

30. Verify whether there are any detections and fetch the one with the largest area:

```
if len(detections) > 0:
    detections = sorted(detections,
                        key=rectangle_area)
    best_detection = detections[-1]
```

31. Extract the region of interest (roi) corresponding to the detected face and extract the emotions from it:

```
(frame_x, frame_y,
 frame_width, frame_height) = best_detection

roi = gray[frame_y:frame_y + frame_height,
           frame_x:frame_x + frame_width]
predictions = predict_emotion(model, roi)
label = EMOTIONS[predictions.argmax()]
```

32. Create the emotion distribution plot:

```
for i, (emotion, probability) in \
        enumerate(zip(EMOTIONS, predictions)):
    emotions_plot = plot_emotion(emotions_plot,
                                 emotion,
                                 probability,
                                 i)
```

33. Plot the detected face along with the emotion it displays:

```
clone = plot_face(copy, label, best_detection)
```

34. Show the result:

```
cv2.imshow('Face & emotions',
           np.hstack([copy, emotions_plot]))
```

35. Check whether the user pressed Q, and if they did, break out of the loop:

```
if cv2.waitKey(1) & 0xFF == ord('q'):
    break
```

36. Finally, release the resources:

```
camera.release()
cv2.destroyAllWindows()
```

After 300 epochs, I obtained a test accuracy of 65.74%. Here you can see some snapshots of the emotions detected in the test video:

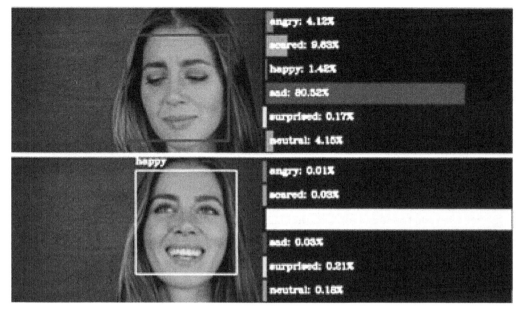

Figure 10.2 – Emotions detected in two different snapshots

We can see that the network correctly identifies sadness in the top frame, and happiness in the bottom one. Let's take a look at another example:

Figure 10.3 – Emotions detected in three different snapshots

In the first frame, the girl clearly has a neutral expression, which was correctly picked up by the network. In the second frame, her face shows anger, which the classifier also detects. The third frame is more interesting, because her expression displays surprise, but it could also be interpreted as fear. Our detector seems to be split between these two emotions as well.

Let's head over to the next section, shall we?

## How it works...

In this recipe, we implemented a fairly capable emotion detector for video streams, either from a built-in webcam, or a stored video file. We started by parsing the FER 2013 data, which, unlike most other image datasets, is in CSV format. Then, we trained an emotion classifier on its images, achieving a respectable 65.74% accuracy on the test set.

We must take into consideration the fact that facial expressions are tricky to interpret, even for humans. At a given time, we might display mixed emotions. Also, there are many expressions that share traits, such as *anger* and *disgust*, and *fear* and *surprise*, among others.

The last step in this first recipe consisted of passing each frame in the input video stream to a Haar Cascade face detector, and then getting the emotions, using the trained classifier, from the regions of interest corresponding to the detected faces.

Although this approach works well for this particular problem, we must take into account that we overlooked a crucial assumption: each frame is independent. Simply put, we treated each frame in the video as an isolated image, but in reality, that's not the case when we're dealing with videos, because there's a time dimension that, when accounted for, yields more stable and better results.

## See also

Here's a great resource for understanding the Haar Cascade classifier: https://docs.opencv.org/3.4/db/d28/tutorial_cascade_classifier.html.

# Recognizing actions with TensorFlow Hub

A very interesting application of deep learning to video processing involves action recognition. This is a challenging problem, because it not only presents the typical difficulties associated with classifying the contents of an image, but also includes a temporal component. An action in a video can vary depending on the order in which the frames are presented to us.

The good news is that there is an architecture that is perfectly suited to this kind of problem, known as **Inflated 3D Convnet (I3D)**, and in this recipe we'll use a trained version hosted in TFHub to recognize actions in a varied selection of videos!

Let's get started.

# Getting ready

We need to install several supplementary libraries, such as OpenCV, TFHub, and imageio. Execute the following command:

```
$> pip install opencv-contrib-python tensorflow-hub imageio
```

That's it! Let's begin implementing.

# How to do it...

Perform the following steps to complete the recipe:

1. Import all the required dependencies:

```
import os
import random
import re
import ssl
import tempfile
from urllib import request
import cv2
import imageio
import numpy as np
import tensorflow as tf
import tensorflow_hub as tfhub
from tensorflow_docs.vis import embed
```

2. Define the path to the UCF101 - Action Recognition dataset, from where we'll fetch the test videos that we will pass to the model later on:

```
UCF_ROOT = 'https://www.crcv.ucf.edu/THUMOS14/UCF101/
UCF101/'
```

3. Define the path to the labels file of the Kinetics dataset, the one used to train the 3D convolutional network we'll use shortly:

```
KINETICS_URL = ('https://raw.githubusercontent.com/
deepmind/'
                'kinetics-i3d/master/data/label_map.txt')
```

4.  Create a temporary directory to cache the downloaded resources:

```
CACHE_DIR = tempfile.mkdtemp()
```

5.  Create an unverified SSL context. We need this to be able to download data from UCF's site (at the time of writing this book, it appears that their certificate has expired):

```
UNVERIFIED_CONTEXT = ssl._create_unverified_context()
```

6.  Define the `fetch_ucf_videos()` function, which downloads the list of the possible videos we'll choose from to test our action recognizer:

```
def fetch_ucf_videos():
    index = \
        (request
        .urlopen(UCF_ROOT,
                 context=UNVERIFIED_CONTEXT)
        .read()
        .decode('utf-8'))
    videos = re.findall('(v_[\w]+\.avi)', index)
    return sorted(set(videos))
```

7.  Define the `fetch_kinetics_labels()` function, used to download and parse the labels of the `Kinetics` dataset:

```
def fetch_kinetics_labels():
    with request.urlopen(KINETICS_URL) as f:
        labels = [line.decode('utf-8').strip()
                  for line in f.readlines()]

    return labels
```

8.  Define the `fetch_random_video()` function, which selects a random video from our list of UCF101 videos and downloads it to the temporary directory created in *Step 4*:

```
def fetch_random_video(videos_list):
    video_name = random.choice(videos_list)
    cache_path = os.path.join(CACHE_DIR, video_name)
```

```
    if not os.path.exists(cache_path):
        url = request.urljoin(UCF_ROOT, video_name)

        response = (request
                    .urlopen(url,

                        context=UNVERIFIED_CONTEXT)
                    .read())
        with open(cache_path, 'wb') as f:
            f.write(response)

    return cache_path
```

9.  Define the `crop_center()` function, which takes an image and crops a squared selection corresponding to the center of the received frame:

```
def crop_center(frame):
    height, width = frame.shape[:2]
    smallest_dimension = min(width, height)

    x_start = (width // 2) - (smallest_dimension // 2)
    x_end = x_start + smallest_dimension

    y_start = (height // 2) - (smallest_dimension // 2)
    y_end = y_start + smallest_dimension

    roi = frame[y_start:y_end, x_start:x_end]
    return roi
```

10. Define the `read_video()` function, which reads up to `max_frames` from a video stored in our cache and returns a list of all the read frames. It also crops the center of each frame, resizes it to 224x224x3 (the input shape expected by the network), and normalizes it:

```
def read_video(path, max_frames=32, resize=(224, 224)):
    capture = cv2.VideoCapture(path)

    frames = []
```

```
while len(frames) <= max_frames:
    frame_read, frame = capture.read()

    if not frame_read:
        break

    frame = crop_center(frame)
    frame = cv2.resize(frame, resize)
    frame = cv2.cvtColor(frame, cv2.COLOR_BGR2RGB)
    frames.append(frame)

capture.release()

frames = np.array(frames)

return frames / 255.
```

11. Define the `predict()` function, used to get the top five most likely actions recognized by the model in the input video:

```
def predict(model, labels, sample_video):
    model_input = tf.constant(sample_video,
                              dtype=tf.float32)
    model_input = model_input[tf.newaxis, ...]

    logits = model(model_input)['default'][0]
    probabilities = tf.nn.softmax(logits)

    print('Top 5 actions:')
    for i in np.argsort(probabilities)[::-1][:5]:
        print(f'{labels[i]}: {probabilities[i] *
100:5.2f}%')
```

12. Define the `save_as_gif()` function, which takes a list of frames corresponding to a video, and uses them to create a GIF representation:

```python
def save_as_gif(images, video_name):
    converted_images = np.clip(images * 255, 0, 255)
    converted_images = converted_images.astype(np.uint8)

    imageio.mimsave(f'./{video_name}.gif',
                    converted_images,
                    fps=25)
```

13. Fetch the videos and labels:

```python
VIDEO_LIST = fetch_ucf_videos()
LABELS = fetch_kinetics_labels()
```

14. Fetch a random video and read its frames:

```python
video_path = fetch_random_video(VIDEO_LIST)
sample_video = read_video(video_path)
```

15. Load the I3D from TFHub:

```python
model_path = 'https://tfhub.dev/deepmind/i3d-kinetics-400/1'
model = tfhub.load(model_path)
model = model.signatures['default']
```

16. Finally, pass the video through the network to obtain the predictions, and then save the video as a GIF:

```python
predict(model, LABELS, sample_video)
video_name = video_path.rsplit('/', maxsplit=1)[1][:-4]
save_as_gif(sample_video, video_name)
```

Here's the first frame of the random video I obtained:

Figure 10.4 – Frame of the random UCF101 video

And here are the top five predictions produced by the model:

```
Top 5 actions:
mopping floor:  75.29%
cleaning floor:  21.11%
sanding floor:  0.85%
spraying:  0.69%
sweeping floor:  0.64%
```

It appears that the network understands that the action portrayed in the video has to do with the floor, because four out of five predictions have to do with it. However, `mopping floor` is the correct one.

Let's now move to the *How it works…* section.

## How it works...

In this recipe, we leveraged the power of a 3D convolutional network to recognize actions in videos. A 3D convolution, as the name suggests, is a natural extension of a bi-dimensional convolution, which moves in two directions. Naturally, 3D convolutions consider width and height, but also depth, making them the perfect fit for special kinds of images, such as Magnetic Resonance Imaging (MRI) or, in this case, videos, which are just a series of images stacked together.

We started by fetching a series of videos from the `UCF101` dataset and a set of action labels from the `Kinetics` dataset. It's important to remember that the I3D we downloaded from TFHub was trained on Kinetics. Therefore, the videos we passed to it are unseen.

Next, we implemented a series of helper functions to obtain, preprocess, and shape each input video in the way the I3D expects. Then, we loaded the aforementioned network from TFHub and used it to display the top five actions it recognized in the video.

One interesting extension you can make to this solution is to read custom videos from your filesystem, or better yet, pass a stream of images from your webcam to the network in order to see how well it performs!

## See also

I3D is a groundbreaking architecture for video processing, so I highly recommend you read the original paper here: `https://arxiv.org/abs/1705.07750`. Here's a pretty interesting article that explains the difference between 1D, 2D, and 3D convolutions: `https://towardsdatascience.com/understanding-1d-and-3d-convolution-neural-network-keras-9d8f76e29610`. You can learn more about the `UCF101` dataset here: `https://www.crcv.ucf.edu/data/UCF101.php`. If you're interested in the `Kinetics` dataset, access this link: `https://deepmind.com/research/open-source/kinetics`. Lastly, you can find more details about the I3D implementation we used here: `https://tfhub.dev/deepmind/i3d-kinetics-400/1`.

# Generating the middle frames of a video with TensorFlow Hub

Another interesting application of deep learning to videos involves frame generation. A fun and practical example of this technique is slow motion, where a network decides, based on the context, how to create intervening frames, thus expanding the length of a video and creating the illusion it was recorded with a high-speed camera (if you want to read more about it, refer to the *See also...* section).

In this recipe, we'll use a 3D convolutional network to produce the middle frames of a video, given only its first and last frames.

For this purpose, we'll rely on TFHub.

Let's start this recipe.

## Getting ready

We must install TFHub and `TensorFlow Datasets`:

```
$> pip install tensorflow-hub tensorflow-datasets
```

The model we'll use was trained on the `BAIR Robot Pushing Videos` dataset, which is available in `TensorFlow Datasets`. However, if we access it through the library, we'll download way more data than we need for the purposes of this recipe. Instead, we'll use a smaller subset of the test set. Execute the following command to download it and place it inside the `~/.keras/datasets/bair_robot_pushing` folder:

```
$> wget -nv https://storage.googleapis.com/download.tensorflow.
org/data/bair_test_traj_0_to_255.tfrecords -O ~/.keras/
datasets/bair_robot_pushing/traj_0_to_255.tfrecords
```

Now we're all set! Let's begin implementing.

## How to do it...

Perform the following steps to learn how to generate middle frames using **Direct 3D Convolutions**, through a model hosted in TFHub:

1.  Import the dependencies:

    ```
    import pathlib
    import matplotlib.pyplot as plt
    import numpy as np
    import tensorflow as tf
    import tensorflow_hub as tfhub
    from tensorflow_datasets.core import SplitGenerator
    from tensorflow_datasets.video.bair_robot_pushing import \
        BairRobotPushingSmall
    ```

2.  Define the `plot_first_and_last_for_sample()` function, which creates a plot of the first and last frames of a sample of four videos:

    ```
    def plot_first_and_last_for_sample(frames, batch_size):
        for i in range(4):
            plt.subplot(batch_size, 2, 1 + 2 * i)
            plt.imshow(frames[i, 0] / 255.)
    ```

```
        plt.title(f'Video {i}: first frame')
        plt.axis('off')

        plt.subplot(batch_size, 2, 2 + 2 * i)
        plt.imshow(frames[i, 1] / 255.)
        plt.title(f'Video {i}: last frame')
        plt.axis('off')
```

3. Define the `plot_generated_frames_for_sample()` function, which graphs the middle frames generated for a sample of four videos:

```
def plot_generated_frames_for_sample(gen_videos):
    for video_id in range(4):
        fig = plt.figure(figsize=(10 * 2, 2))
        for frame_id in range(1, 16):
            ax = fig.add_axes(
                [frame_id / 16., 0, (frame_id + 1) /
                    16., 1],
                xmargin=0, ymargin=0)
            ax.imshow(gen_videos[video_id, frame_id])
            ax.axis('off')
```

4. We need to patch the `BarRobotPushingSmall()` (see *Step 6*) dataset builder to only expect the test split to be available, instead of both the training and test ones. Therefore, we must create a custom `SplitGenerator()`:

```
def split_gen_func(data_path):
    return [SplitGenerator(name='test',
                           gen_kwargs={'filedir':
                               data_path})]
```

5. Define the path to the data:

```
DATA_PATH = str(pathlib.Path.home() / '.keras' /
                'datasets' /
                'bair_robot_pushing')
```

6.  Create a `BarRobotPushingSmall()` builder, pass it the custom split generator created in *Step 4*, and then prepare the dataset:

```
builder = BairRobotPushingSmall()
builder._split_generators = lambda _:split_gen_func(DATA_
PATH)
builder.download_and_prepare()
```

7.  Get the first batch of videos:

```
BATCH_SIZE = 16


dataset = builder.as_dataset(split='test')
test_videos = dataset.batch(BATCH_SIZE)


for video in test_videos:
    first_batch = video
    break
```

8.  Keep only the first and last frame of each video in the batch:

```
input_frames = first_batch['image_aux1'][:, ::15]
input_frames = tf.cast(input_frames, tf.float32)
```

9.  Load the generator model from TFHub:

```
model_path = 'https://tfhub.dev/google/tweening_conv3d_
bair/1'
model = tfhub.load(model_path)
model = model.signatures['default']
```

10. Pass the batch of videos through the model to generate the middle frames:

```
middle_frames = model(input_frames)['default']
middle_frames = middle_frames / 255.0
```

11. Concatenate the first and last frames of each video in the batch with the corresponding middle frames produced by the network in *Step 10*:

```
generated_videos = np.concatenate(
    [input_frames[:, :1] / 255.0,  # All first frames
    middle_frames,  # All inbetween frames
```

```
    input_frames[:, 1:] / 255.0],  # All last frames
  axis=1)
```

12. Finally, plot the first and last frames, and also the middle frames:

```
plt.figure(figsize=(4, 2 * BATCH_SIZE))
plot_first_and_last_for_sample(input_frames,
                               BATCH_SIZE)
plot_generated_frames_for_sample(generated_videos)
plt.show()
```

In *Figure 10.5*, we can observe the first and last frame of each video in our sample of four:

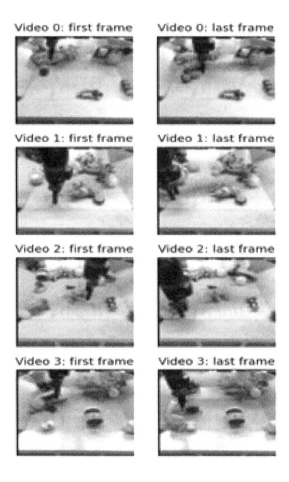

Figure 10.5 – First and last frame of each video in the sample

In *Figure 10.6*, we observe the 14 middle frames generated by the model for each video. Close inspection reveals they are coherent with the first and last real frames passed to the network:

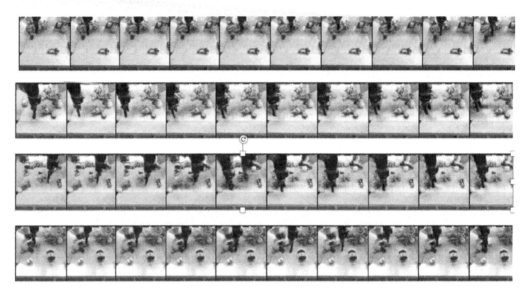

Figure 10.6 – Middle frames produced by the model for each sample video

Let's go to the *How it works...* section to review what we did.

## How it works...

In this recipe, we learned about another useful and interesting application of deep learning to videos, particularly 3D convolutional networks, in the context of generative models.

We took a state-of-the-art architecture trained on the BAIR Robot Pushing Videos dataset, hosted in TFHub, and used it to produce an entirely new video sequence, taking only as seeds the first and last frames of a video.

Because downloading the entire 30 GBs of the BAIR dataset would have been an overkill, given we only needed a way smaller subset to test our solution, we couldn't rely directly on the TensorFlow dataset's load() method. Instead, we downloaded a subset of the test videos and made the necessary adjustments to the BairRobotPushingSmall() builder to load and prepare the sample videos.

It must be mentioned that this model was trained on a very specific dataset, but it certainly showcases the powerful generation capabilities of this architecture. I encourage you to check out the *See also* section for a list of useful resources that could be of help if you want to implement a video generation network on your own data.

## See also

You can learn more about the `BAIR Robot Pushing Videos` dataset here: `https://arxiv.org/abs/1710.05268`. I encourage you to read the paper entitled **Video Inbetweening Using Direct 3D Convolutions**, where the network we used in this recipe was proposed: `https://arxiv.org/abs/1905.10240`. You can find the TFHub model we relied on at the following link: `https://tfhub.dev/google/tweening_conv3d_bair/1`. Lastly, here's an interesting read about an AI that transforms regular footage into slow motion: `https://petapixel.com/2020/09/08/this-ai-can-transform-regular-footage-into-slow-motion-with-no-artifacts/`.

# Performing text-to-video retrieval with TensorFlow Hub

The applications of deep learning to videos are not limited to classification, categorization, or even generation. One of the biggest resources of neural networks is their internal representation of data features. The better a network is at a given task, the better their internal mathematical model is. We can take advantage of the inner workings of state-of-the-art models to build interesting applications on top of them.

In this recipe, we'll create a small search engine based on the embeddings produced by an **S3D** model, trained and ready to be used, which lives in TFHub.

Are you ready? Let's begin!

## Getting ready

First, we must install `OpenCV` and TFHub, as follows:

```
$> pip install opencv-contrib-python tensorflow-hub
```

That's all we need, so let's start this recipe!

## How to do it...

Perform the following steps to learn how to perform text-to-video retrieval using TFHub:

1. The first step is to import all the dependencies that we'll use:

```
import math
import os
import uuid

import cv2
import numpy as np
import tensorflow as tf
import tensorflow_hub as tfhub
from tensorflow.keras.utils import get_file
```

2. Define a function to produce the text and video embeddings using an instance of S3D:

```
def produce_embeddings(model, input_frames, input_words):
    frames = tf.cast(input_frames, dtype=tf.float32)
    frames = tf.constant(frames)
    video_model = model.signatures['video']
    video_embedding = video_model(frames)
    video_embedding = video_embedding['video_embedding']

    words = tf.constant(input_words)
    text_model = model.signatures['text']
    text_embedding = text_model(words)
    text_embedding = text_embedding['text_embedding']

    return video_embedding, text_embedding
```

3. Define the `crop_center()` function, which takes an image and crops a squared selection corresponding to the center of the received frame:

```
def crop_center(frame):
    height, width = frame.shape[:2]
    smallest_dimension = min(width, height)
```

```
    x_start = (width // 2) - (smallest_dimension // 2)
    x_end = x_start + smallest_dimension


    y_start = (height // 2) - (smallest_dimension //
                                        2)
    y_end = y_start + smallest_dimension


    roi = frame[y_start:y_end, x_start:x_end]
    return roi
```

4. Define the `fetch_and_read_video()` function, which, as its name indicates, downloads a video and then reads it. For this last part, we use OpenCV. Let's start by getting the video from a given URL:

```
def fetch_and_read_video(video_url,
                         max_frames=32,
                         resize=(224, 224)):
    extension = video_url.rsplit(os.path.sep,
                                 maxsplit=1)[-1]
    path = get_file(f'{str(uuid.uuid4())}.{extension}',
                    video_url,
                    cache_dir='.',
                    cache_subdir='.')
```

We extract the video format from the URL. Then, we save the video in the current folder, with a random UUID as its name.

5. Next, we'll load `max_frames` of this fetched video:

```
    capture = cv2.VideoCapture(path)
    frames = []
    while len(frames) <= max_frames:
        frame_read, frame = capture.read()

        if not frame_read:
            break

        frame = crop_center(frame)
        frame = cv2.resize(frame, resize)
```

```
        frame = cv2.cvtColor(frame, cv2.COLOR_BGR2RGB)
        frames.append(frame)


    capture.release()
    frames = np.array(frames)
```

6. If the video doesn't have enough frames, we'll repeat the process until we reach the desired capacity:

```
    if len(frames) < max_frames:
        repetitions = math.ceil(float(max_frames) /
                                len(frames))
        repetitions = int(repetitions)
        frames = frames.repeat(repetitions, axis=0)
```

7. Return the normalized frames:

```
    frames = frames[:max_frames]


    return frames / 255.0
```

8. Define the URLs of the videos:

```
URLS = [
    ('https://media.giphy.com/media/'
     'WWYSFIZo4fsLC/source.gif'),
    ('https://media.giphy.com/media/'
     'fwhIy2QQtu5vObfjrs/source.gif'),
    ('https://media.giphy.com/media/'
     'W307DdkjIsRHVWvoFE/source.gif'),
    ('https://media.giphy.com/media/'
     'FOcbaDiNEaqqY/source.gif'),
    ('https://media.giphy.com/media/'
     'VJwck53yG6y8s2H3Og/source.gif')]
```

9. Fetch and read each video:

```
VIDEOS = [fetch_and_read_video(url) for url in URLS]
```

10. Define the queries (captions) associated with each video. Notice that they must be in the correct order:

```
QUERIES = ['beach', 'playing drums', 'airplane taking
           off',
           'biking', 'dog catching frisbee']
```

11. Load S3D from TFHub:

```
model = tfhub.load
('https://tfhub.dev/deepmind/mil-nce/s3d/1')
```

12. Obtain the text and video embeddings:

```
video_emb, text_emb = produce_embeddings(model,
                              np.stack(VIDEOS, axis=0),
np.array(QUERIES))
```

13. Compute the similarity scores between the text and video embeddings:

```
scores = np.dot(text_emb, tf.transpose(video_emb))
```

14. Take the first frame of each video, rescale it back to [0, 255], and then convert it to BGR space so that we can display it with OpenCV. We do this to display the results of our experiment:

```
first_frames = [v[0] for v in VIDEOS]
first_frames = [cv2.cvtColor((f * 255.0).astype('uint8'),
                             cv2.COLOR_RGB2BGR) for f
                      in  first_frames]
```

15. Iterate over each (query, video, score) triplet and display the most sim\*ilar videos for each query:

```
for query, video, query_scores in
zip(QUERIES,VIDEOS,scores):
    sorted_results = sorted(list(zip(QUERIES,
                                     first_frames,
                                     query_scores)),
                            key=lambda p: p[-1],
                            reverse=True)
```

```
    annotated_frames = []
    for i, (q, f, s) in enumerate(sorted_results,
                                  start=1):
        frame = f.copy()
        cv2.putText(frame,
                    f'#{i} - Score: {s:.2f}',
                    (8, 15),
                    fontFace=cv2.FONT_HERSHEY_SIMPLEX,
                    fontScale=0.6,
                    color=(0, 0, 255),
                    thickness=2)
        annotated_frames.append(frame)
    cv2.imshow(f'Results for query "{query}"',
               np.hstack(annotated_frames))
    cv2.waitKey(0)
```

First, we'll see the result of the *beach* query:

Figure 10.7 – Ranked results for the BEACH query

As expected, the first result, which is the highest score, is an image of a beach. Let's now try with *playing drums*:

Figure 10.8 – Ranked results for the PLAYING DRUMS query

Awesome! It seems that the similarity between the query text and the images is stronger in this instance. Up next, a more difficult one:

Figure 10.9 – Ranked results for the AIRPLANE TAKING OFF query

Although *airplane taking off* is a somewhat more complex query, our solution had no problem producing the correct results. Let's now try with *biking*:

Figure 10.10 – Ranked results for the BIKING query

Another match! How about *dog catching frisbee*?

Figure 10.11 – Ranked results for the DOG CATCHING FRISBEE query

No problem at all! The satisfying results we've seen are due to the great job S3D does at mapping images with the words that best describe them. If you have read the paper where S3D was introduced, you won't be surprised by this fact, given the humongous amount of data it was trained on.

Let's now proceed to the next section.

## How it works...

In this recipe, we exploited the ability of the S3D model to generate embeddings, both for text and video, to create a small database we used as the basis of a toy search engine. This way, we demonstrated the usefulness of having a network capable of producing richly informative vectorial two-way mappings between images and text.

## See also

I highly recommend that you read the paper where the model we used in this recipe was published as it's very interesting! Here's the link: `https://arxiv.org/pdf/1912.06430.pdf`. Speaking of the model, you'll find it here: `https://tfhub.dev/deepmind/mil-nce/s3d/1`.

# 11
# Streamlining Network Implementation with AutoML

Computer vision, particularly when combined with deep learning, is a field that's not suitable for the faint of heart! While in traditional computer programming, we have a limited set of options for debugging and experimentation, this is not the case in machine learning.

Of course, the stochastic nature of machine learning itself plays a role in making the process of creating a good enough solution difficult, but so do the myriad of parameters, variables, knobs, and settings we need to get right to unlock the true power of a neural network for a particular problem.

Selecting a proper architecture is just the beginning because we also need to consider preprocessing techniques, learning rates, optimizers, loss functions, and data splits, among a multiplicity of other factors.

My point is that deep learning is hard! Where do you start? Wouldn't it be great if we had a way to ease the burden of searching through such an ample spectrum of combinations?

Well, it exists! It's called **Automatic Machine Learning** (**AutoML**), and in this chapter, we'll learn how to leverage one of the most promising tools in this field, built on top of TensorFlow, known as **AutoKeras**.

In this chapter, we are going to cover the following recipes:

- Creating a simple image classifier with AutoKeras
- Creating a simple image regressor with AutoKeras
- Exporting and importing a model in AutoKeras
- Controlling architecture generation with AutoKeras' AutoModel
- Predicting age and gender with AutoKeras

Let's get started!

# Technical requirements

One of the first things you'll notice is that **AutoML** is very resource-intensive, so accessing a **GPU** is a must if you want to replicate and extend the recipes we'll discuss in this chapter. Also, because we'll be using **AutoKeras** in all the examples provided, install it as follows:

```
$> pip install git+https://github.com/keras-team/keras-tuner.
git@1.0.2rc2 autokeras pydot graphviz
```

The **AutoKeras** version we'll be using in this chapter only works with TensorFlow 2.3, so ensure you have it installed as well (if you prefer, you can create a different environment altogether). In the *Getting ready* section of each recipe, you'll find any preparatory information needed. As usual, the code shown in this chapter is available at https://github.com/PacktPublishing/Tensorflow-2.0-Computer-Vision-Cookbook/tree/master/ch11.

Check out the following link to see the Code in Action video:

https://bit.ly/2Na6XRz.

# Creating a simple image classifier with AutoKeras

Image classification must be the de facto application of neural networks for computer vision. However, as we know, depending on the complexity of the dataset, the availability of information, and countless other factors, the process of creating a proper image classifier can be quite cumbersome at times.

In this recipe, we'll implement an image classifier effortlessly thanks to the magic of **AutoML**. Don't believe me? Let's begin and see for ourselves!

## How to do it...

By the end of this recipe, you'll have implemented an image classifier in a dozen lines of code or less! Let's get started:

1. Import all the required modules:

```
from autokeras import ImageClassifier
from tensorflow.keras.datasets import fashion_mnist as fm
```

For the sake of simplicity, we'll use the well-known `Fashion-MNIST` dataset, a more challenging version of the famous `MNIST`.

2. Load the train and test data:

```
(X_train, y_train), (X_test, y_test) = fm.load_data()
```

3. Normalize the images to the range [0, 1]:

```
X_train = X_train.astype('float32') / 255.0
X_test = X_test.astype('float32') / 255.0
```

4. Define the number of epochs we'll allow each possible network (known as a trial) to train:

```
EPOCHS = 10
```

5. Here's where the magic happens. Define an instance of `ImageClassifier()`:

```
classifier = ImageClassifier(seed=9, max_trials=10)
```

Notice that we are seeding the classifier with 9 and allowing it to find a suitable network 10 times. We're doing this so that the **Neural Architecture Search** (**NAS**) process terminates in a reasonable amount of time (to learn more about **NAS**, please refer to the *See also* section).

6.  Fit the classifier on the test data over 10 epochs (per trial):

```
classifier.fit(X_train, y_train, epochs=EPOCHS)
```

7.  Lastly, evaluate the best classifier on the test set and print out the accuracy:

```
print(classifier.evaluate(X_test, y_test))
```

After a while (let's not forget the library is training 10 models with varying complexity), we should obtain an accuracy of 93%, give or take. That's not bad, considering we didn't even write 10 lines of code!

We'll discuss what we've done a bit more in the *How it works...* section.

## How it works...

In this recipe, we created the most effortless image classifier ever! We delegated all major decisions to the **AutoML** tool, **AutoKeras**. From selecting an architecture, to which optimizer to use, all such decisions were made by the framework.

You might have noticed that we limited the search space by specifying a maximum of 10 trials and 10 epochs per trial. We did this so that the program terminates in a reasonable amount of time, but as you might suspect, these parameters can also be trusted to **AutoKeras**.

Despite all the autonomy **AutoML** has, we can guide the framework if we wish. What **AutoML** offers is, as its name suggests, a way to automate the search for a good enough combination for a particular problem. However, this doesn't mean that human expertise and prior knowledge is not necessary. In fact, it is often the case that a well-crafted network, typically the product of thoroughly studying the data, often performs better than one found by **AutoML** with no prior information whatsoever.

In the end, **AutoML** is a tool, and as such, it should be used to enhance our mastery of deep learning, not to replace it – because it can't.

## See also

You can learn more about **NAS** here: https://en.wikipedia.org/wiki/Neural_architecture_search.

# Creating a simple image regressor with AutoKeras

The power and usefulness of **AutoKeras** is not limited to image classification. Although not as popular, image regression is a similar problem where we want to predict a continuous quantity based on the spatial information in an image.

In this recipe, we'll train an image regressor to predict people's ages while using **AutoML**.

Let's begin.

## Getting ready

We'll be using `APPA-REAL` dataset in this recipe, which contains 7,591 images labeled with the real and apparent ages for a wide range of subjects. You can read more about the dataset and download it from `http://chalearnlap.cvc.uab.es/dataset/26/description/#`. Decompress the data in a directory of your preference. For the purposes of this recipe, we'll assume the dataset is located within the `~/.keras/datasets/appa-real-release` folder.

Here are some sample images:

Figure 11.1 – Sample images from the APPA-REAL dataset

Let's implement this recipe!

## How to do it...

Follow these steps to complete this recipe:

1. Import the modules we will be using:

```
import csv
import pathlib
import numpy as np
from autokeras import ImageRegressor
from tensorflow.keras.preprocessing.image import *
```

2.  Each subset (train, test, and validation) of the dataset is defined in a CSV file. There, among many other columns, we have the path to the image and the real age of the person depicted in a photo. In this step, we will define the `load_mapping()` function, which will create a map from the image paths to the labels that we'll use to load the actual data in memory:

```python
def load_mapping(csv_path, faces_path):
    mapping = {}
    with open(csv_path, 'r') as f:
        reader = csv.DictReader(f)
        for line in reader:
            file_name = line["file_name"].rsplit(".")[0]
            key = f'{faces_path}/{file_name}.jpg_face.jpg'
            mapping[key] = int(line['real_age'])

    return mapping
```

3.  Define the `get_image_and_labels()` function, which takes the mapping produced by the `load_mapping()` function and returns an array of images (normalized to the range [-1, 1]) and an array of the corresponding ages:

```python
def get_images_and_labels(mapping):
    images = []
    labels = []
    for image_path, label in mapping.items():
        try:
            image = load_img(image_path, target_size=(64,
                                                      64))
            image = img_to_array(image)

            images.append(image)
            labels.append(label)
        except FileNotFoundError:
            continue

    return (np.array(images) - 127.5) / 127.5, \
        np.array(labels).astype('float32')
```

Notice that each image has been resized so that its dimensions are 64x64x3. This is necessary because the images in the dataset don't have homogeneous dimensions.

4. Define the paths to the CSV files to create the data mappings for each subset:

```
base_path = (pathlib.Path.home() / '.keras' / 'datasets'
             /'appa-real-release')
train_csv_path = str(base_path / 'gt_train.csv')
test_csv_path = str(base_path / 'gt_test.csv')
val_csv_path = str(base_path / 'gt_valid.csv')
```

5. Define the paths to the directories where the images for each subset live:

```
train_faces_path = str(base_path / 'train')
test_faces_path = str(base_path / 'test')
val_faces_path = str(base_path / 'valid')
```

6. Create the mappings for each subset:

```
train_mapping = load_mapping(train_csv_path,
                             train_faces_path)
test_mapping = load_mapping(test_csv_path,
                            test_faces_path)
val_mapping = load_mapping(val_csv_path,
                           val_faces_path)
```

7. Get the images and labels for each subset:

```
X_train, y_train = get_images_and_labels(train_mapping)
X_test, y_test = get_images_and_labels(test_mapping)
X_val, y_val = get_images_and_labels(val_mapping)
```

8. We'll train each network in a trial for a maximum of 15 epochs:

```
EPOCHS = 15
```

9.  We instantiate an `ImageRegressor()` object, which encapsulates the **AutoML** logic that searches for the best regressor. It will perform 10 trials, and for the sake of reproducibility, we'll seed it with 9. Notice that we are explicitly telling **AutoKeras** to use `adam` as the optimizer:

```
regressor = ImageRegressor(seed=9,
                           max_trials=10,
                           optimizer='adam')
```

10. Fit the regressor. Notice that we are passing our own validation set. If we don't do this, **AutoKeras** takes 20% of the training data to validate its experiments by default:

```
regressor.fit(X_train, y_train,
              epochs=EPOCHS,
              validation_data=(X_val, y_val))
```

11. Finally, we must evaluate the best regressor on the test data and print its performance metric:

```
print(regressor.evaluate(X_test, y_test))
```

After a while, we should obtain a test loss of 241.248, which is not bad if we take into account that the bulk of our work consisted of loading the dataset.

Let's move on to the *How it works…* section.

## How it works...

In this recipe, we delegated the creation of a model to an **AutoML** framework, similar to what we did in the *Creating a simple image classifier with AutoKeras* recipe. However, this time, our goal was to solve a regression problem, namely predicting the age of a person based on a photo of their face, instead of a classification one.

This time, because we used a real-world dataset, we had to implement several helper functions to load the data and make it the proper shape for **AutoKeras** to use it. However, after doing this, we let the framework take the wheel, leveraging its built-in **NAS** algorithm to find the best possible model in a span of 15 iterations.

We obtained a respectable 241.248 loss on the test set. Predicting the age of a person is not an easy task, even though it might appear that it is at first. I invite you to take a closer look at the *APPA-REAL* CSV files so that you can see the deviation in the human estimates of people's ages!

## See also

You can learn more about **NAS** here: `https://en.wikipedia.org/wiki/Neural_architecture_search`.

# Exporting and importing a model in AutoKeras

One worry we might have when working with **AutoML** is the black-box nature of the tools available. Do we have control over the produced models? Can we extend them? Understand them? Reuse them?

Of course we can! The good thing about **AutoKeras** is that it is built on top of TensorFlow, so despite its sophistication, under the hood, the models being trained are just TensorFlow graphs that we can export and tweak and tune later if we need to.

In this recipe, we'll learn how to export a model trained on **AutoKeras**, and then import it as a plain old TensorFlow network.

Are you ready? Let's begin.

## How to do it...

Follow these steps to complete this recipe:

1. Import the necessary dependencies:

```
from autokeras import *
from tensorflow.keras.datasets import fashion_mnist as fm
from tensorflow.keras.models import load_model
from tensorflow.keras.utils import plot_model
```

2. Load the train and test splits of the `Fashion-MNIST` dataset:

```
(X_train, y_train), (X_test, y_test) = fm.load_data()
```

3.  Normalize the data to the [0, 1] interval:

```
X_train = X_train.astype('float32') / 255.0
X_test = X_test.astype('float32') / 255.0
```

4.  Define the number of epochs we'll train each network for:

```
EPOCHS = 10
```

5.  Create an `ImageClassifier()` that'll try to find to best possible classifier, over 20 trials, with each one trained for 10 epochs. We will instruct **AutoKeras** to use adam as the optimizer and seed `ImageClassifier()` for the sake of reproducibility:

```
classifier = ImageClassifier(seed=9,
                             max_trials=20,
                             optimizer='adam')
```

6.  Fit the classifier. We'll allow **AutoKeras** to automatically pick 20% of the training data for validation:

```
classifier.fit(X_train, y_train, epochs=EPOCHS)
```

7.  Export the best model and save it to disk:

```
model = classifier.export_model()
model.save('model.h5')
```

8.  Load the model back into memory:

```
model = load_model('model.h5',
                   custom_objects=CUSTOM_OBJECTS)
```

9.  Evaluate the training model on the test set:

```
print(classifier.evaluate(X_test, y_test))
```

10. Print a text summary of the best model:

```
print(model.summary())
```

11. Lastly, generate a graph of the architecture of the best model found by **AutoKeras**:

```
plot_model(model,
           show_shapes=True,
           show_layer_names=True,
           to_file='model.png')
```

After 20 trials, the best model that was created by **AutoKeras** achieves 91.5% accuracy on the test set. The following screenshot shows the model's summary:

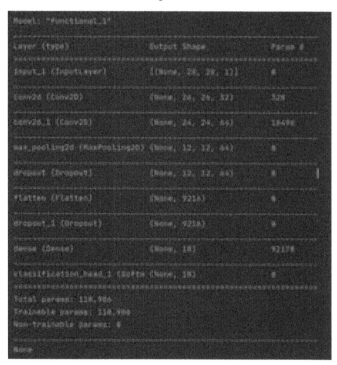

Figure 11.2 – AutoKeras' best model summary

The following diagram shows the model's architecture:

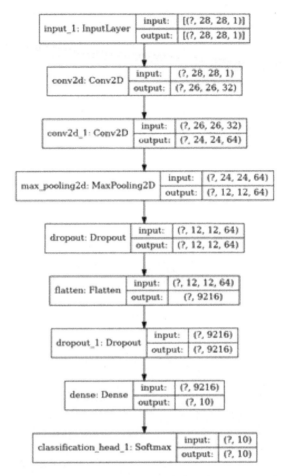

Figure 11.3 – AutoKeras' best model architecture

In *Figure 11.2*, we can see the network **AutoKeras** deemed the most suitable for **Fashion-MNIST**, at least within the bounds we established. You can take a closer look at the full architecture in the companion GitHub repository.

Let's move on to the next section.

## How it works...

In this recipe, we demonstrated that **AutoML** can work as a great starting point when we're tackling a new computer vision problem. How? We can use it to produce well-performing models out of the gate, which we can then extend based on our domain knowledge of the dataset at hand.

The formula to do this is straightforward: let **AutoML** do the grunt work for a while; then, export the best network and import it into the confines of TensorFlow so that you can build your solution on top of it.

This not only showcases the usability of tools such as **AutoKeras**, but allows us to peak behind the curtain, understanding the building blocks of the models engendered by **NAS**.

## See also

The basis of **AutoKeras** is **NAS**. You can read more about it here (it's pretty interesting!): `https://en.wikipedia.org/wiki/Neural_architecture_search`.

# Controlling architecture generation with AutoKeras' AutoModel

Letting **AutoKeras** automagically figure out what architecture works best is great, but it can be time-consuming – unacceptably so at times.

Can we exert more control? Can we hint at which options work best for our particular problem? Can we meet **AutoML** halfway by providing a set of guidelines it must follow according to our prior knowledge or preference, but still give it enough leeway to experiment?

Yes, we can, and in this recipe, you'll learn how by utilizing a special feature in **AutoKeras** known as AutoModel!

## How to do it...

Follow these steps to learn how to customize the search space of the **NAS** algorithm with `AutoModel`:

1. The first thing we need to do is import all the necessary dependencies:

```
from autokeras import *
from tensorflow.keras.datasets import fashion_mnist as fm
from tensorflow.keras.models import load_model
from tensorflow.keras.utils import *
```

2. Because we'll be training our customized model on `Fashion-MNIST`, we must load the train and test splits, respectively:

```
(X_train, y_train), (X_test, y_test) = fm.load_data()
```

3. To avoid numerical instability issues, let's normalize the images of both splits so that they're in the range [0, 1]:

```
X_train = X_train.astype('float32')
X_test = X_test.astype('float32')
```

4. Define the `create_automodel()` function, which defines the custom search space of the underlying **NAS** algorithm as a series of blocks arranged in a graph structure. Each `Block` is in charge of a defined task, such as image augmentation, normalization, image processing, or classification. First, we must define the input block, which will be normalized and augmented through the `Normalization()` and `ImageAugmentation()` blocks, respectively:

```
def create_automodel(max_trials=10):
    input = ImageInput()
    x = Normalization()(input)
    x = ImageAugmentation(horizontal_flip=False,
                         vertical_flip=False)(x)
```

Notice that we disabled horizontal and vertical flipping in the `ImageAugmentation()` block. This is because these operations alter the class of images in `Fashion-MNIST`.

5. Now, we'll bifurcate the graph. The left branch searches for vanilla convolutional layers, thanks to `ConvBlock()`. On the right branch, we'll explore more sophisticated Xception-like architectures (for more information about the **Xception** architecture, refer to the *See also* section):

```
left = ConvBlock()(x)
right = XceptionBlock(pretrained=True)(x)
```

In the previous snippet, we instructed **AutoKeras** to only explore **Xception** architectures pre-trained on ImageNet.

6. We'll merge the left and right branches, flatten them, and pass the result through a `DenseBlock()`, which, as its name suggests, searches for fully connected combinations of layers:

```
x = Merge()([left, right])
x = SpatialReduction(reduction_type='flatten')(x)
x = DenseBlock()(x)
```

7. The output of this graph will be a `ClassificationHead()`. This is because we're dealing with a classification problem. Notice that we don't specify the number of classes. This is because **AutoKeras** infers this information from the data:

```
output = ClassificationHead()(x)
```

8. We can close `create_automodel()` by building and returning an `AutoModel()` instance. We must specify the inputs and outputs, as well as the maximum number of trials to perform:

```
return AutoModel(inputs=input,
                 outputs=output,
                 overwrite=True,
                 max_trials=max_trials)
```

9. Let's train each trial model for 10 epochs:

```
EPOCHS = 10
```

10. Create the `AutoModel` and fit it:

```
model = create_automodel()
model.fit(X_train, y_train, epochs=EPOCHS)
```

11. Let's export the best model:

```
model = model.export_model()
```

12. Evaluate the model on the test set:

```
print(model.evaluate(X_test, to_categorical(y_test)))
```

13. Plot the architecture of the best model:

```
plot_model(model,
           show_shapes=True,
           show_layer_names=True,
           to_file='automodel.png')
```

The final architecture I obtained achieved 90% accuracy on the test set, although your results may vary. What's even more interesting is the structure of the generated model:

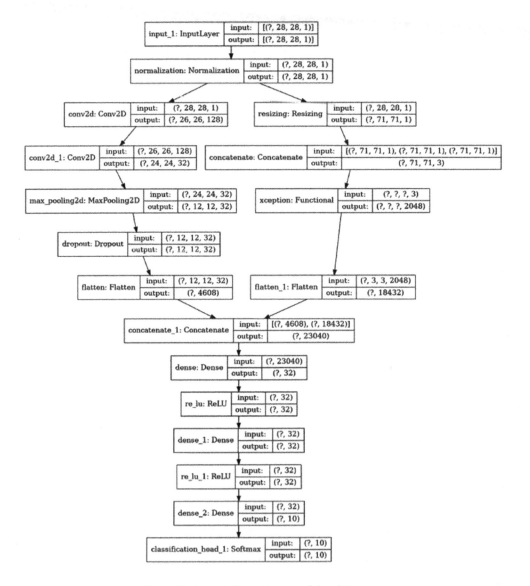

Figure 11.4 – AutoKeras' best model architecture

The preceding diagram reveals that `AutoModel` produced a network according to the blueprint we laid out in `create_automodel()`.

Now, let's move on to the *How it works...* section.

# How it works...

In this recipe, we took advantage of **AutoKeras'** `AutoModel` module to trim down the search space. This is a very useful feature when we have an idea of what our final model should look like. This leads to huge time gains because we don't allow **AutoKeras** to waste time trying out unfruitful, useless combinations. One example of such bad combinations can be seen in *Step 4*, where we told **AutoKeras** not to try to flip images as part of its image augmentation scheme. This is because, due to the characteristics of our problem, this operation changes the classes of the numbers in **Fashion-MNIST**.

Proof that we steered **AutoKeras** down the path we wanted is in the architecture of the final model, where we had layers that correspond to each of the blocks specified in the search graph defined in the `create_automodel()` function.

Impressive, right?

# See also

One thing we didn't do here is implement our own `Block`, which is possible in **AutoKeras**. Why don't you give it a try? You can start by reading the docs here: `https://autokeras.com/tutorial/customized/`. For a list of all available blocks, go to `https://autokeras.com/block/`. In this recipe, we used Xception-like layers. To find out more about Xception, you can read the original paper: `https://arxiv.org/abs/1610.02357`.

# Predicting age and gender with AutoKeras

In this recipe, we'll study a practical application of AutoML that can be used as a template to create prototypes, MVPs, or just to tackle real-world applications with the help of AutoML.

More concretely, we'll create an age and gender classification program with a twist: the architecture of both the gender and age classifiers will be the responsibility of **AutoKeras**. We'll be in charge of getting and shaping the data, as well as creating the framework to test the solution on our own images.

I hope you're ready because we are about to begin!

## Getting ready

We need a couple of external libraries, such as OpenCV, `scikit-learn`, and `imutils`. All these dependencies can be installed at once, as follows:

```
$> pip install opencv-contrib-python scikit-learn imutils
```

On the data side, we'll use the **Adience** dataset, which contains 26,580 images of 2,284 subjects, along with their gender and age. To download the data, go to https://talhassner.github.io/home/projects/Adience/Adience-data.html.

Next, you'll need to navigate to the **Download** section and enter your name and email, as shown in the following screenshot:

Figure 11.5 – Enter your information to receive the credentials of the FTP server where the data is

Once you hit the **Submit** button, you'll get the credentials required for the FTP server where the data is located. You can access this here: http://www.cslab.openu.ac.il/download/.

Make sure that you click on the first link, labeled **Adience OUI Unfiltered faces for gender and age classification**:

## CSlab FTP SERVER

### Tal Hassner's datasets are availble from (same username and password as FTP server )

Adience OUI Unfiltered faces for gender and age classification

Action Similarity Labeling benchmark (ASLAN)

Face frontalization MATLAB code and LFW3D

Violent Flows benchmark and data set

YouTube Faces (YTF) data set

Figure 11.6 – Going to the highlighted link

Enter the credentials you received previously and access the second link, named **AdienceBenchmarkOfUnfilteredFacesForGenderAndAgeClassification**:

# Index of /adiencedb

| [ICO] | Name | Last modified | Size |
|---|---|---|---|
| [PARENTDIR] | Parent Directory | | - |
| [DIR] | AdienceBenchmarkOfUn..> | 2014-12-15 09:59 | - |

Figure 11.7 – Clicking the highlighted link

Finally, download `aligned.tar.gz`, `fold_frontal_0_data.txt`, `fold_frontal_1_data.txt`, `fold_frontal_2_data.txt`, `fold_frontal_3_data.txt`, and `fold_frontal_4_data.txt`:

# Index of /adiencedb/AdienceBenchmark

| [ICO] | Name | Last modified | Size | Description |
|---|---|---|---|---|
| [PARENTDIR] | Parent Directory | | | |
| [TXT] | (old a) fold_0_data.txt | 2014-11-20 16:36 | 355K | |
| [TXT] | (old a) fold_1_data.txt | 2014-11-20 16:36 | 297K | |
| [TXT] | (old a) fold_2_data.txt | 2014-11-20 16:36 | 310K | |
| [TXT] | (old a) fold_3_data.txt | 2014-11-20 16:36 | 279K | |
| [TXT] | (old a) fold_4_data.txt | 2014-11-20 16:36 | 307K | |
| [TXT] | (old a) fold_frontal_> | 2014-11-20 16:36 | 253K | |
| [TXT] | (old a) fold_frontal_> | 2014-11-20 16:36 | 242K | |
| [TXT] | (old a) fold_frontal_> | 2014-11-20 16:36 | 190K | |
| [TXT] | (old a) fold_frontal_> | 2014-11-20 16:36 | 202K | |
| [TXT] | (old a) fold_frontal_> | 2014-11-20 16:36 | 192K | |
| [TXT] | LICENSE.txt | 2016-11-22 20:35 | 1.8K | |
| [ ] | aligned.tar.gz | 2014-06-18 16:51 | 2.6G | |
| [ ] | faces.tar.gz | 2014-06-18 15:04 | 1.2G | |
| [TXT] | fold_0_data.txt | 2014-12-15 09:57 | 355K | |
| [TXT] | fold_1_data.txt | 2014-12-15 09:57 | 297K | |
| [TXT] | fold_2_data.txt | 2014-12-15 09:57 | 310K | |
| [TXT] | fold_3_data.txt | 2014-12-15 09:57 | 279K | |
| [TXT] | fold_4_data.txt | 2014-12-15 09:57 | 307K | |
| [TXT] | fold_frontal_0_data.txt | 2014-12-15 09:57 | 253K | |
| [TXT] | fold_frontal_1_data.txt | 2014-12-15 09:57 | 242K | |
| [TXT] | fold_frontal_2_data.txt | 2014-12-15 09:57 | 190K | |
| [TXT] | fold_frontal_3_data.txt | 2014-12-15 09:57 | 202K | |
| [TXT] | fold_frontal_4_data.txt | 2014-12-15 09:57 | 192K | |

Figure 11.8 – Downloading aligned.tar.gz and all the fold_frontal_*_data.txt files

Unzip `aligned.tar.gz` into a directory of your preference as `adience`. Inside that directory, create a subdirectory named `folds`, and move all the `fold_frontal_*_data.txt` files inside it. For the purposes of this recipe, we'll assume the dataset is located within `~/.keras/datasets/adience`.

Here are some sample images:

Figure 11.9 – Sample images from the Adience dataset

Let's implement this recipe!

## How to do it...

Complete these steps to implement an age and gender classifier using **AutoML**:

1. The first thing we need to do is import all the necessary dependencies:

```
import csv
import os
import pathlib
from glob import glob
import cv2
import imutils
import numpy as np
from autokeras import *
from sklearn.preprocessing import LabelEncoder
from tensorflow.keras.models import load_model
from tensorflow.keras.preprocessing.image import *
```

2. Define the base path to the Adience dataset, as well as the folds (which contain the relationships between the images and the ages and genders of their subjects, in CSV format):

```
base_path = (pathlib.Path.home() / '.keras' / 'datasets'
             / 'adience')
folds_path = str(base_path / 'folds')
```

3.  The ages in `Adience` are expressed as intervals, groups, or brackets. Here, we will define an array that we will use to map the reported age in the folds to the correct bracket:

```
AGE_BINS = [(0, 2), (4, 6), (8, 13), (15, 20), (25, 32),
            (38, 43), (48, 53), (60, 99)]
```

4.  Define the `age_to_bin()` function, which takes an input as it appears in a fold CSV row and maps it to the corresponding bin. For instance, if the input is `(27, 29)`, the output will be `25_32`:

```
def age_to_bin(age):
    age = age.replace('(', '').replace(')', '').
                                        split(',')
    lower, upper = [int(x.strip()) for x in age]

    for bin_low, bin_up in AGE_BINS:
        if lower >= bin_low and upper <= bin_up:
            label = f'{bin_low}_{bin_up}'
            return label
```

5.  Define a function that will compute the area of a rectangle. We'll use this later to get the largest face detection possible:

```
def rectangle_area(r):
    return (r[2] - r[0]) * (r[3] - r[1])
```

6.  We'll also draw a bounding box around the detected face, captioned with the recognized age and gender:

```
def plot_face(image, age_gender, detection):
    frame_x, frame_y, frame_width, frame_height =
detection
    cv2.rectangle(image,
                    (frame_x, frame_y),
                    (frame_x + frame_width,
                    frame_y + frame_height),
                  color=(0, 255, 0),
                  thickness=2)
    cv2.putText(image,
```

```
        age_gender,
        (frame_x, frame_y - 10),
        fontFace=cv2.FONT_HERSHEY_SIMPLEX,
        fontScale=0.45,
        color=(0, 255, 0),
        thickness=2)

    return image
```

7. Define the `predict()` function, which we'll use to predict both the age and gender (depending on `model`) of a person whose face was passed into the `roi` parameter:

```
def predict(model, roi):
    roi = cv2.resize(roi, (64, 64))
    roi = roi.astype('float32') / 255.0
    roi = img_to_array(roi)
    roi = np.expand_dims(roi, axis=0)

    predictions = model.predict(roi)[0]
    return predictions
```

8. Define the lists where we'll store all the images, ages, and genders of the dataset:

```
images = []
ages = []
genders = []
```

9. Iterate over each fold file. These will be in CSV format:

```
folds_pattern = os.path.sep.join([folds_path, '*.txt'])
for fold_path in glob(folds_pattern):
    with open(fold_path, 'r') as f:
        reader = csv.DictReader(f, delimiter='\t')
```

10. If the age or gender fields are not well-defined, skip the current line:

```
for line in reader:
    if ((line['age'][0] != '(') or
            (line['gender'] not in {'m', 'f'})):
        Continue
```

11. Map the age to a valid bin. If we get None from age_to_bin(), this means the age doesn't correspond to any of our defined categories, so we must skip this record:

```
age_label = age_to_bin(line['age'])
if age_label is None:
    continue
```

12. Load the image:

```
aligned_face_file = \
                (f'landmark_aligned_face.'
                    f'{line["face_id"]}.'
                f'{line["original_image"]}')
image_path = os.path.sep.join(
                [str(base_path),
                line["user_id"],
                aligned_face_file])

image = load_img(image_path,
                target_size=(64, 64))
image = img_to_array(image)
```

13. Append the image, age, and gender to the corresponding collections:

```
images.append(image)

ages.append(age_label)

genders.append(line['gender'])
```

14. Create two copies of the images, one for each problem (age classification and gender prediction):

```
age_images = np.array(images).astype('float32') / 255.0
gender_images = np.copy(images)
```

15. Encode the age and genders:

```
gender_enc = LabelEncoder()
age_enc = LabelEncoder()
gender_labels = gender_enc.fit_transform(genders)
age_labels = age_enc.fit_transform(ages)
```

16. Define the number of trials and epochs per trial. These parameters affect both models:

```
EPOCHS = 100
MAX_TRIALS = 10
```

17. If there's a trained version of the age classifier, load it; otherwise, train an `ImageClassifier()` from scratch and save it to disk:

```
if os.path.exists('age_model.h5'):
    age_model = load_model('age_model.h5')
else:
    age_clf = ImageClassifier(seed=9,
                              max_trials=MAX_TRIALS,
                              project_name='age_clf',
                              overwrite=True)
    age_clf.fit(age_images, age_labels, epochs=EPOCHS)
    age_model = age_clf.export_model()
    age_model.save('age_model.h5')
```

18. If there's a trained version of the gender classifier, load it; otherwise, train an `ImageClassifier()` from scratch and save it to disk:

```
if os.path.exists('gender_model.h5'):
    gender_model = load_model('gender_model.h5')
else:
    gender_clf = ImageClassifier(seed=9,
```

```
                          max_trials=MAX_TRIALS,
                        project_name='gender_clf',
                             overwrite=True)
    gender_clf.fit(gender_images, gender_labels,
                   epochs=EPOCHS)
    gender_model = gender_clf.export_model()
    gender_model.save('gender_model.h5')
```

19. Read a test image from disk:

```
    image = cv2.imread('woman.jpg')
```

20. Create a **Haar Cascades** face detector. (This is a topic outside the scope of this book. If you want to learn more about Haar Cascades, go to the *See also* section of this recipe.) Use the following code to do so:

```
    cascade_file = 'resources/haarcascade_frontalface_
    default.xml'
    det = cv2.CascadeClassifier(cascade_file)
```

21. Resize the image so that it is 380 pixels wide. Thanks to the `imutils.resize()` function, we can rest assured that the result will preserve the aspect ratio. This is because the function computes the height automatically to guarantee this condition:

```
    image = imutils.resize(image, width=380)
```

22. Create a copy of the original image so that we can draw the detections on it:

```
    copy = image.copy()
```

23. Convert the image into grayscale and pass it through the face detector:

```
    gray = cv2.cvtColor(image, cv2.COLOR_BGR2GRAY)
    detections = \
        det.detectMultiScale(gray,
                            scaleFactor=1.1,
                            minNeighbors=5,
                            minSize=(35, 35),
                            flags=cv2.CASCADE_SCALE_IMAGE)
```

24. Verify whether there are detections and fetch the one with the largest area:

```
if len(detections) > 0:
    detections = sorted(detections, key=rectangle_area)
    best_detection = detections[-1]
```

25. Extract the region of interest (`roi`) corresponding to the detected face and extract its age and gender:

```
(frame_x, frame_y,
  frame_width, frame_height) = best_detection

roi = image[frame_y:frame_y + frame_height,
            frame_x:frame_x + frame_width]

age_pred = predict(age_model, roi).argmax()
age = age_enc.inverse_transform([age_pred])[0]

gender_pred = predict(gender_model, roi).argmax()
gender = gender_enc.inverse_transform([gender_pred])
[0]
```

Notice that we use each encoder to revert back to a human-readable label for both the predicted age and gender.

26. Plot the predicted age and gender on the original image and show the result:

```
clone = plot_face(copy,
                  f'Gender: {gender} - Age:
                  {age}',
                  best_detection)

cv2.imshow('Result', copy)
cv2.waitKey(0)
```

> **Important note**
> The first time you execute this script, you'll have to wait a very long time –
> probably more than 24 hours (depending on your hardware). This is because
> each model is trained for a high number of trials and epochs. However,
> subsequent runs should be way faster because the program will load the trained
> classifiers.

We can see an example of a successful prediction of both age and gender in the
following screenshot:

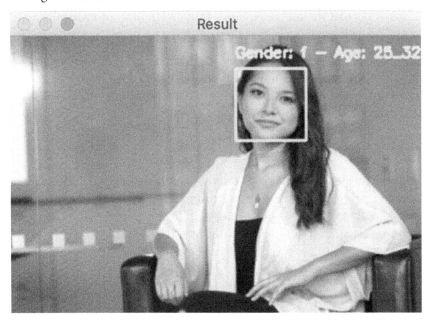

Figure 11.10 – Our models state the person in the photo is female and is between 25 and 32 years of age.
Seems about right, doesn't it?

Isn't it truly amazing how the heavy lifting was done by **AutoKeras**? We're living in the
future!

## How it works...

In this recipe, we implemented a practical solution to a surprisingly challenging problem:
age and gender prediction.

Why is this challenging? The apparent age of a person can vary, depending on multiple
factors, such as ethnicity, gender, health, and other life conditions. We humans are not as
great as we think we are at estimating the age of a man or a woman based solely on their
physical features.

For instance, a mostly healthy 25-year-old person will look vastly different than another 25-year-old that's a heavy drinker and smoker.

Either way, we trusted the power of **AutoML** to find two models: one for gender classification and another for age prediction. We must highlight that, in this case, we framed age prediction as a classification problem instead of a regression one. This is because it makes it a bit easier to select an age range instead of producing a precise quantity.

After a long wait (we trained both models over 100 epochs per trial), we obtained two competent networks that we integrated into a framework that automatically detects a face in a photo, and using these models, tags them with the predicted age and gender.

As you may have noticed, we relied on `ImageClassifier()`, which means we gave 100% control of the network creation process to **AutoKeras**. An interesting extension is to use `AutoModel` to narrow down the search space, therefore arriving at potentially better solutions at a fraction of the time. Why don't you give it a try?

## See also

Read the following paper to learn how the authors of the **Adience** dataset solve this problem: `https://talhassner.github.io/home/projects/cnn_agegender/CVPR2015_CNN_AgeGenderEstimation.pdf`. To learn more about the Haar Cascade classifier we used previously, read this tutorial: `https://docs.opencv.org/3.4/db/d28/tutorial_cascade_classifier.html`.

# 12

# Boosting Performance

More often than not, the leap between good and great doesn't involve drastic changes, but instead subtle tweaks and fine-tuning.

It is often said that 20% of the effort can get you 80% of the results (this is known as the **Pareto principle**). But what about that gap between 80% and 100%? What do we need to do to exceed expectations, to improve our solutions, to squeeze as much performance out of our computer vision algorithms as possible?

Well, as with all things deep learning, the answer is a mixture of art and science. The good news is that in this chapter, we'll focus on simple tools you can use to boost the performance of your neural networks!

In this chapter, we will cover the following recipes:

- Using convolutional neural network ensembles to improve accuracy
- Using test time augmentation to improve accuracy
- Using rank-N accuracy to evaluate performance
- Using label smoothing to increase performance
- Checkpointing models

- Customizing the training process using `tf.GradientTape`
- Visualizing class activation maps to better understand your network

Let's get started!

# Technical requirements

As usual, you'll get the most out of these recipes if you can access a GPU, given that some of the examples in this chapter are quite resource-intensive. Also, if there are any preparatory steps you'll need to perform in order to complete a recipe, you'll find them in the *Getting ready* sections provided. As a last remark, the code for this chapter is available in the companion repository on GitHub: `https://github.com/PacktPublishing/Tensorflow-2.0-Computer-Vision-Cookbook/tree/master/ch12`.

Check out the following link to see the Code in Action video:

`https://bit.ly/2Ko3H3K`.

# Using convolutional neural network ensembles to improve accuracy

In machine learning, one of the most robust classifiers is, in fact, a meta-classifier, known as an ensemble. An ensemble is comprised of what's known as weak classifiers, predictive models just a tad better than random guessing. However, when combined, they result in a rather robust algorithm, especially against high variance (overfitting). Some of the most famous examples of ensembles we may encounter include Random Forest and Gradient Boosting Machines.

The good news is that we can leverage the same principle when it comes to neural networks, thus creating a whole that's more than the sum of its parts. Do you want to learn how? Keep reading!

## Getting ready

This recipe depends on `Pillow` and `tensorflow_docs`, which can be easily installed like this:

```
$> pip install Pillow git+https://github.com/tensorflow/docs
```

We'll also be using the famous `Caltech 101` dataset, available here: `http://www.vision.caltech.edu/Image_Datasets/Caltech101/`. Download and decompress `101_ObjectCategories.tar.gz` to your preferred location. For the purposes of this recipe, we'll place it in `~/.keras/datasets/101_ObjectCategories`.

The following are some sample images:

Figure 12.1 – Caltech 101 sample images

Let's start this recipe, shall we?

# How to do it...

Follow these steps to create an ensemble of **Convolutional Neural Networks (CNNs)**:

1.  Import all the required modules:

```python
import os
import pathlib
from glob import glob
import numpy as np
from sklearn.metrics import accuracy_score
from sklearn.model_selection import train_test_split
from sklearn.preprocessing import LabelBinarizer
from tensorflow.keras import Model
from tensorflow.keras.layers import *
from tensorflow.keras.preprocessing.image import *
```

2. Define the `load_images_and_labels()` function, which reads the images and categories of the `Caltech 101` dataset and returns them as NumPy arrays:

```
def load_images_and_labels(image_paths,
                           target_size=(64, 64)):
    images = []
    labels = []

    for image_path in image_paths:
        image = load_img(image_path,
                         target_size=target_size)
        image = img_to_array(image)

        label = image_path.split(os.path.sep)[-2]

        images.append(image)
        labels.append(label)

    return np.array(images), np.array(labels)
```

3. Define the `build_model()` function, which is in charge of building a VGG-like convolutional neural network:

```
def build_network(width, height, depth, classes):
    input_layer = Input(shape=(width, height, depth))

    x = Conv2D(filters=32,
               kernel_size=(3, 3),
               padding='same')(input_layer)
    x = ReLU()(x)
    x = BatchNormalization(axis=-1)(x)
    x = Conv2D(filters=32,
               kernel_size=(3, 3),
               padding='same')(x)
    x = ReLU()(x)
    x = BatchNormalization(axis=-1)(x)
    x = MaxPooling2D(pool_size=(2, 2))(x)
    x = Dropout(rate=0.25)(x)
```

```
    x = Conv2D(filters=64,
               kernel_size=(3, 3),
               padding='same')(x)
    x = ReLU()(x)
    x = BatchNormalization(axis=-1)(x)
    x = Conv2D(filters=64,
               kernel_size=(3, 3),
               padding='same')(x)
    x = ReLU()(x)
    x = BatchNormalization(axis=-1)(x)
    x = MaxPooling2D(pool_size=(2, 2))(x)
    x = Dropout(rate=0.25)(x)
```

Now, build the fully connected part of the network:

```
    x = Flatten()(x)
    x = Dense(units=512)(x)
    x = ReLU()(x)
    x = BatchNormalization(axis=-1)(x)
    x = Dropout(rate=0.25)(x)


    x = Dense(units=classes)(x)
    output = Softmax()(x)


    return Model(input_layer, output)
```

4.  Define the `plot_model_history()` function, which we'll use to plot the training and validation curves of the networks in the ensemble:

```
def plot_model_history(model_history, metric,
                       plot_name):
    plt.style.use('seaborn-darkgrid')
    plotter = tfdocs.plots.HistoryPlotter()
    plotter.plot({'Model': model_history},
                 metric=metric)


    plt.title(f'{metric.upper()}')
    plt.ylim([0, 1])
```

```
        plt.savefig(f'{plot_name}.png')
        plt.close()
```

5. To enhance reproducibility, set a random seed:

```
SEED = 999
np.random.seed(SEED)
```

6. Compile the paths to the images of Caltech 101, as well as the classes:

```
base_path = (pathlib.Path.home() / '.keras' /
                'datasets' /
                '101_ObjectCategories')
images_pattern = str(base_path / '*' / '*.jpg')
image_paths = [*glob(images_pattern)]
image_paths = [p for p in image_paths if
                p.split(os.path.sep)[-2] !='BACKGROUND_
Google']
CLASSES = {p.split(os.path.sep)[-2] for p in image_paths}
```

7. Load the images and labels while normalizing the images and one-hot encoding the labels:

```
X, y = load_images_and_labels(image_paths)
X = X.astype('float') / 255.0
y = LabelBinarizer().fit_transform(y)
```

8. Reserve 20% of the data for test purposes and use the rest to train the models:

```
(X_train, X_test,
 y_train, y_test) = train_test_split(X, y,
                                    test_size=0.2,
                                    random_state=SEED)
```

9. Define the batch size, the number of epochs, and the number of batches per epoch:

```
BATCH_SIZE = 64
STEPS_PER_EPOCH = len(X_train) // BATCH_SIZE
EPOCHS = 40
```

10. We'll use data augmentation here to perform a series of random transformations, such as horizontal flipping, rotations, and zooming:

```
augmenter = ImageDataGenerator(horizontal_flip=True,
                               rotation_range=30,
                               width_shift_range=0.1,
                               height_shift_range=0.1,
                               shear_range=0.2,
                               zoom_range=0.2,
                               fill_mode='nearest')
```

11. Our ensemble will be comprised of 5 models. We'll save the predictions of each network in the ensemble in the `ensemble_preds` list:

```
NUM_MODELS = 5
ensemble_preds = []
```

12. We'll train each model in a similar fashion. We'll start by creating and compiling the network itself:

```
for n in range(NUM_MODELS):
    print(f'Training model {n + 1}/{NUM_MODELS}')

    model = build_network(64, 64, 3, len(CLASSES))
    model.compile(loss='categorical_crossentropy',
                  optimizer='rmsprop',
                  metrics=['accuracy'])
```

13. Then, we'll fit the model using data augmentation:

```
    train_generator = augmenter.flow(X_train, y_train,
                                     BATCH_SIZE)
    hist = model.fit(train_generator,
                     steps_per_epoch=STEPS_PER_EPOCH,
                     validation_data=(X_test, y_test),
                     epochs=EPOCHS,
                     verbose=2)
```

14. Compute the accuracy of the model on the test set, plot its training and validation accuracy curves, and store its predictions in `ensemble_preds`:

```
predictions = model.predict(X_test,
                            batch_size=BATCH_SIZE)
accuracy = accuracy_score(y_test.argmax(axis=1),
                         predictions.argmax(axis=1))
print(f'Test accuracy (Model #{n + 1}): {accuracy}')
plot_model_history(hist, 'accuracy', f'model_{n +1}')


ensemble_preds.append(predictions)
```

15. The last step consists of averaging the predictions of each member of the ensemble, effectively producing a joint prediction for the whole meta-classifier, and then computing the accuracy on the test set:

```
ensemble_preds = np.average(ensemble_preds, axis=0)
ensemble_acc = accuracy_score(y_test.argmax(axis=1),
                             ensemble_preds.argmax(axis=1))
print(f'Test accuracy (ensemble): {ensemble_acc}')
```

Because we are training five networks, this program can take a while to complete. When it does, you should see accuracies similar to the following for each member of the ensemble:

```
Test accuracy (Model #1): 0.6658986175115207
Test accuracy (Model #2): 0.6751152073732719
Test accuracy (Model #3): 0.673963133640553
Test accuracy (Model #4): 0.6491935483870968
Test accuracy (Model #5): 0.6756912442396313
```

Here, we can observe the accuracy ranges between 65% and 67.5%. The following figure shows the training and validation curves for models 1 to 5 (from left to right, models 1, 2, and 3 on the top row; models 4 and 5 on the bottom row):

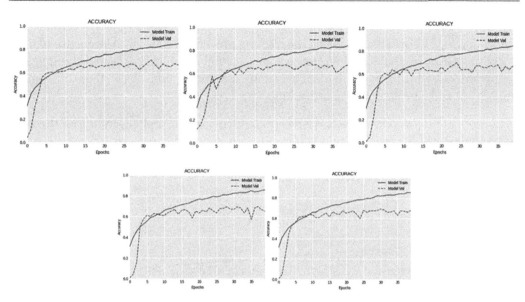

Figure 12.2 – Curves for the training and validation accuracy for the five models in the ensemble

However, the most interesting result is the accuracy of the ensemble, which is the result of averaging the predictions of each model:

```
Test accuracy (ensemble): 0.7223502304147466
```

Truly impressive! Just by combining the predictions of the five networks, we bumped our accuracy all the way to 72.2%, on a very challenging dataset – `Caltech 101`! Let's discuss this a bit further in the next section.

## How it works...

In this recipe, we leveraged the power of ensembles by training five neural networks on the challenging `Caltech 101` dataset. It must be noted that our process was pretty straightforward and unremarkable. We started by loading and shaping the data in a format suitable for training and then using the same template to train several copies of a VGG-inspired architecture.

To create more robust classifiers, we used data augmentation and trained each network for 40 epochs. Besides these details, we didn't change the architecture of the networks, nor did we tweak each particular member. The result is that each model was between 65% and 67% accurate on the test set. However, when combined, they reached a decent 72%!

Why did this happen, though? The rationale behind ensemble learning is that each model develops its own biases during the training process, which is a consequence of the stochastic nature of deep learning. However, when combining their decisions through a voting process (which is basically what averaging their predictions does), these differences smooth out and give far more robust results.

Of course, training several models is a resource-intensive task, and depending on the size and complexity of the problem, it might be outright impossible to do so. Nevertheless, it's a very useful tool that can boost your predicting power just by creating and combining multiple copies of the same network.

Not bad, huh?

## See also

If you want to understand the mathematical basis behind ensembles, read this article about **Jensen's Inequality**: `https://en.wikipedia.org/wiki/Jensen%27s_inequality`.

# Using test time augmentation to improve accuracy

Most of the time, when we're testing the predictive power of a network, we use a test set to do so. This test set is comprised of images the model has never seen. Then, we present them to the model and ask it what class each belongs to. The thing is… we do it *once*.

What if we were more forgiving and gave the model multiple chances to do this? Would its accuracy improve? Well, more often than not, it does!

This technique is known as **Test Time Augmentation (TTA)**, and it's the focus of this recipe.

## Getting ready

In order to load the images in the dataset, we need `Pillow`. Install it using the following command:

```
$> pip install Pillow
```

Then, download the `Caltech 101` dataset, which is available here: `http://www.vision.caltech.edu/Image_Datasets/Caltech101/`. Download and decompress `101_ObjectCategories.tar.gz` to a location of your choosing. For the rest of this recipe, we'll work under the assumption that the dataset is in `~/.keras/datasets/101_ObjectCategories`.

Here's a sample of what you can find inside `Caltech 101`:

Figure 12.3 – Caltech 101 sample images

We are ready to begin!

## How to do it...

Follow these steps to learn the benefits of TTA:

1. Import the dependencies we need:

```
import os
import pathlib
from glob import glob
import numpy as np
from sklearn.metrics import accuracy_score
from sklearn.model_selection import train_test_split
from sklearn.preprocessing import LabelBinarizer
from tensorflow.keras import Model
from tensorflow.keras.layers import *
from tensorflow.keras.preprocessing.image import *
```

2. Define the `load_images_and_labels()` function in order to read the data from `Caltech 101` (in NumPy format):

```
def load_images_and_labels(image_paths,
                           target_size=(64, 64)):
```

```
        images = []
        labels = []


    for image_path in image_paths:
        image = load_img(image_path,
                              target_size=target_size)
        image = img_to_array(image)


        label = image_path.split(os.path.sep)[-2]


        images.append(image)
        labels.append(label)


    return np.array(images), np.array(labels)
```

3. Define the `build_model()` function, which returns a network based on the famous **VGG** architecture:

```
def build_network(width, height, depth, classes):
    input_layer = Input(shape=(width, height, depth))


    x = Conv2D(filters=32,
               kernel_size=(3, 3),
               padding='same')(input_layer)
    x = ReLU()(x)
    x = BatchNormalization(axis=-1)(x)
    x = Conv2D(filters=32,
               kernel_size=(3, 3),
               padding='same')(x)
    x = ReLU()(x)
    x = BatchNormalization(axis=-1)(x)
    x = MaxPooling2D(pool_size=(2, 2))(x)
    x = Dropout(rate=0.25)(x)


    x = Conv2D(filters=64,
               kernel_size=(3, 3),
               padding='same')(x)
```

```
    x = ReLU()(x)
    x = BatchNormalization(axis=-1)(x)
    x = Conv2D(filters=64,
               kernel_size=(3, 3),
               padding='same')(x)
    x = ReLU()(x)
    x = BatchNormalization(axis=-1)(x)
    x = MaxPooling2D(pool_size=(2, 2))(x)
    x = Dropout(rate=0.25)(x)
```

Now, build the fully connected part of the network:

```
    x = Flatten()(x)
    x = Dense(units=512)(x)
    x = ReLU()(x)
    x = BatchNormalization(axis=-1)(x)
    x = Dropout(rate=0.25)(x)


    x = Dense(units=classes)(x)
    output = Softmax()(x)


    return Model(input_layer, output)
```

4.  The `flip_augment()` function is the basis of our **TTA** scheme. It takes an image and produces copies of it that can be randomly flipped (horizontally) with a 50% probability:

```
def flip_augment(image, num_test=10):
    augmented = []
    for i in range(num_test):
        should_flip = np.random.randint(0, 2)
        if should_flip:
            flipped = np.fliplr(image.copy())
            augmented.append(flipped)
        else:
            augmented.append(image.copy())

    return np.array(augmented)
```

5.  To ensure reproducibility, set a random seed:

```
SEED = 84
np.random.seed(SEED)
```

6.  Compile the paths to the images of `Caltech 101`, as well as its classes:

```
base_path = (pathlib.Path.home() / '.keras' /
                 'datasets' /'101_ObjectCategories')
images_pattern = str(base_path / '*' / '*.jpg')
image_paths = [*glob(images_pattern)]
image_paths = [p for p in image_paths if
                  p.split(os.path.sep)[-2]
                 !='BACKGROUND_Google']
CLASSES = {p.split(os.path.sep)[-2] for p in
             image_paths}
```

7.  Load the images and labels while normalizing the images and one-hot encoding the labels:

```
X, y = load_images_and_labels(image_paths)
X = X.astype('float') / 255.0
y = LabelBinarizer().fit_transform(y)
```

8.  Use 20% of the data for test purposes and leave the rest to train the models:

```
(X_train, X_test,
 y_train, y_test) = train_test_split(X, y, test_size=0.2,
                                     random_state=SEED)
```

9.  Define the batch size and the number of epochs:

```
BATCH_SIZE = 64
EPOCHS = 40
```

10. We'll randomly horizontally flip the images in the train set:

```
augmenter = ImageDataGenerator(horizontal_flip=True)
```

11. Build and compile the network:

```
model = build_network(64, 64, 3, len(CLASSES))
model.compile(loss='categorical_crossentropy',
              optimizer='adam',
              metrics=['accuracy'])
```

12. Fit the model:

```
train_generator = augmenter.flow(X_train, y_train,
                                 BATCH_SIZE)
model.fit(train_generator,
          steps_per_epoch=len(X_train) // BATCH_SIZE,
          validation_data=(X_test, y_test),
          epochs=EPOCHS,
          verbose=2)
```

13. Make predictions on the test set and use them to compute the accuracy of the model:

```
predictions = model.predict(X_test,
                            batch_size=BATCH_SIZE)
accuracy = accuracy_score(y_test.argmax(axis=1),
                          predictions.argmax(axis=1))
print(f'Accuracy, without TTA: {accuracy}')
```

14. Now, we'll use **TTA** on the test set. We'll store the predictions for each copy of an image in the test set in the predictions list. We'll create 10 copies of each image:

```
predictions = []
NUM_TEST = 10
```

15. Next, we will iterate over each image of the test set, creating a batch of copies of it and passing it through the model:

```
for index in range(len(X_test)):
    batch = flip_augment(X_test[index], NUM_TEST)
    sample_predictions = model.predict(batch)
```

16. The final prediction of each image will be the most predicted class in the batch of copies:

```
sample_predictions = np.argmax(
        np.sum(sample_predictions, axis=0))
predictions.append(sample_predictions)
```

17. Finally, we will compute the accuracy on the predictions made by the model using TTA:

```
accuracy = accuracy_score(y_test.argmax(axis=1),
                            predictions)
print(f'Accuracy with TTA: {accuracy}')
```

After a while, we'll see results similar to these:

```
Accuracy, without TTA: 0.6440092165898618
Accuracy with TTA: 0.6532258064516129
```

The network achieves an accuracy of 64.4% without TTA, while it increases to 65.3% if we give the model more chances to generate correct predictions. Cool, right?

Let's move on to the *How it works...* section.

## How it works...

In this recipe, we learned that **test time augmentation** is a simple technique that entails only a few changes once the network has been trained. The reasoning behind this is that if we present the network with copies of images in the test set that have been altered in a similar way to the ones it saw during training, the network should do better.

However, the key is that these transformations, which are done during the evaluation phase, should match the ones that were done during the training period; otherwise, we would be feeding the model incongruent data!

There's a caveat, though: TTA is really, really slow! After all, we are multiplying the size of the test set by the augmentation factor, which in our case was 10. This means that instead of evaluating one image at a time, the network must process 10 instead.

Of course, TTA is not suitable for real-time or speed-constrained applications, but it can be useful when time or speed are not an issue.

# Using rank-N accuracy to evaluate performance

Most of the time, when we're training deep learning-based image classifiers, we care about the accuracy, which is a binary measure of a model's performance, based on a one-on-one comparison between its predictions and the ground-truth labels. When the model says there's a *leopard* in a photo, is there actually a *leopard* there? In other words, we measure how *precise* the model is.

However, for more complex datasets, this way of assessing a network's learning might be counterproductive and even unfair, because it's too restrictive. What if the model didn't classify the feline in the picture as a *leopard* but as a *tiger*? Moreover, what if the second most probable class was, indeed, a *leopard*? This means the model has some more learning to do, but it's getting there! That's valuable!

This is the reasoning behind **rank-N accuracy**, a more lenient and fairer way of measuring a predictive model's performance, which counts a prediction as correct if the ground-truth label is in the top-N most probable classes output by the model. In this recipe, we'll learn how to implement it and use it.

Let's get started.

## Getting ready

Install `Pillow`:

```
$> pip install Pillow
```

Next, download and unzip the `Caltech 101` dataset, which is available here: `http://www.vision.caltech.edu/Image_Datasets/Caltech101/`. Make sure to click on the `101_ObjectCategories.tar.gz` file. Once downloaded, place it in a location of your choosing. For the rest of this recipe, we'll work under the assumption that the dataset is in `~/.keras/datasets/101_ObjectCategories`.

Here's a sample of `Caltech 101`:

Figure 12.4 – Caltech 101 sample images

Let's implement this recipe!

## How to do it...

Follow these steps to implement and use **rank-N accuracy**:

1.  Import the necessary modules:

```
import os
import pathlib
from glob import glob
import numpy as np
from sklearn.metrics import accuracy_score
from sklearn.model_selection import train_test_split
from sklearn.preprocessing import LabelBinarizer
from tensorflow.keras import Model
from tensorflow.keras.layers import *
from tensorflow.keras.preprocessing.image import *
```

2.  Define the `load_images_and_labels()` function in order to read the data from `Caltech 101`:

```
def load_images_and_labels(image_paths,
                           target_size=(64, 64)):
    images = []
    labels = []

    for image_path in image_paths:
        image = load_img(image_path,
```

```
                    target_size=target_size)
        image = img_to_array(image)


        label = image_path.split(os.path.sep)[-2]


        images.append(image)
        labels.append(label)


    return np.array(images), np.array(labels)
```

3. Define the `build_model()` function to create a **VGG**-inspired network:

```
def build_network(width, height, depth, classes):
    input_layer = Input(shape=(width, height, depth))


    x = Conv2D(filters=32,
               kernel_size=(3, 3),
               padding='same')(input_layer)
    x = ReLU()(x)
    x = BatchNormalization(axis=-1)(x)
    x = Conv2D(filters=32,
               kernel_size=(3, 3),
               padding='same')(x)
    x = ReLU()(x)
    x = BatchNormalization(axis=-1)(x)
    x = MaxPooling2D(pool_size=(2, 2))(x)
    x = Dropout(rate=0.25)(x)


    x = Conv2D(filters=64,
               kernel_size=(3, 3),
               padding='same')(x)
    x = ReLU()(x)
    x = BatchNormalization(axis=-1)(x)
    x = Conv2D(filters=64,
               kernel_size=(3, 3),
               padding='same')(x)
    x = ReLU()(x)
```

```
    x = BatchNormalization(axis=-1)(x)
    x = MaxPooling2D(pool_size=(2, 2))(x)
    x = Dropout(rate=0.25)(x)
```

Now, build the fully connected part of the network:

```
    x = Flatten()(x)
    x = Dense(units=512)(x)
    x = ReLU()(x)
    x = BatchNormalization(axis=-1)(x)
    x = Dropout(rate=0.25)(x)


    x = Dense(units=classes)(x)
    output = Softmax()(x)


    return Model(input_layer, output)
```

4.  Define the `rank_n()` function, which computes the **rank-N accuracy** based on the
    predictions and ground-truth labels. Notice that it produces a value between 0 and
    1, where a "hit" or correct prediction is accounted for when the ground-truth label
    is in the N most probable categories:

```
def rank_n(predictions, labels, n):
    score = 0.0

    for prediction, actual in zip(predictions, labels):
        prediction = np.argsort(prediction)[::-1]

        if actual in prediction[:n]:
            score += 1

    return score / float(len(predictions))
```

5.  For the sake of reproducibility, set a random seed:

```
SEED = 42
np.random.seed(SEED)
```

6. Compile the paths to the images of `Caltech 101`, as well as its classes:

```
base_path = (pathlib.Path.home() / '.keras' / 'datasets'
/
                '101_ObjectCategories')
images_pattern = str(base_path / '*' / '*.jpg')
image_paths = [*glob(images_pattern)]
image_paths = [p for p in image_paths if
        p.split(os.path.sep)[-2] !='BACKGROUND_Google']
CLASSES = {p.split(os.path.sep)[-2] for p in image_paths}
```

7. Load the images and labels while normalizing the images and one-hot encoding the labels:

```
X, y = load_images_and_labels(image_paths)
X = X.astype('float') / 255.0
y = LabelBinarizer().fit_transform(y)
```

8. Use 20% of the data for test purposes and leave the rest to train the models:

```
(X_train, X_test,
 y_train, y_test) = train_test_split(X, y,
                            test_size=0.2,
                            random_state=SEED)
```

9. Define the batch size and the number of epochs:

```
BATCH_SIZE = 64
EPOCHS = 40
```

10. Define an `ImageDataGenerator()` to augment the images in the training set with random flips, rotations, and other transformations:

```
augmenter = ImageDataGenerator(horizontal_flip=True,
                            rotation_range=30,
                            width_shift_range=0.1,
                            height_shift_range=0.1,
                            shear_range=0.2,
```

```
                                    zoom_range=0.2,
                                    fill_mode='nearest')
```

11. Build and compile the network:

```
model = build_network(64, 64, 3, len(CLASSES))
model.compile(loss='categorical_crossentropy',
              optimizer='adam',
              metrics=['accuracy'])
```

12. Fit the model:

```
train_generator = augmenter.flow(X_train, y_train,
                                 BATCH_SIZE)
model.fit(train_generator,
          steps_per_epoch=len(X_train) // BATCH_SIZE,
          validation_data=(X_test, y_test),
          epochs=EPOCHS,
          verbose=2)
```

13. Make predictions on the test set:

```
predictions = model.predict(X_test,
                            batch_size=BATCH_SIZE)
```

14. Compute rank-1 (regular accuracy), rank-3, rank-5, and rank-10 accuracies:

```
y_test = y_test.argmax(axis=1)
for n in [1, 3, 5, 10]:
    rank_n_accuracy = rank_n(predictions, y_test, n=n) *
100
    print(f'Rank-{n}: {rank_n_accuracy:.2f}%')
```

Here are the results:

```
Rank-1: 64.29%
Rank-3: 78.05%
Rank-5: 83.01%
Rank-10: 89.69%
```

Here, we can observe that 64.29% of the time, the network produces an exact match. However, 78.05% of the time, the correct prediction is in the top 3, 83.01% of the time it's in the top 5, and almost 90% of the time it's in the top 10. These are pretty interesting and encouraging results, considering our dataset is comprised of 101 classes that are very different from each other.

We'll dig deeper in the *How it works...* section.

## How it works...

In this recipe, we learned about the existence and utility of rank-N accuracy. We also implemented it with a simple function, `rank_n()`, which we then tested on a network that had been trained on the challenging `Caltech-101` dataset.

Rank-N, particularly the rank-1 and rank-5 accuracies, are common in the literature of networks that have been trained on massive, challenging datasets, such as COCO or ImageNet, where even humans have a hard time discerning between categories. It is particularly useful when we have fine-grained classes that share a common parent or ancestor, such as *Pug* and *Golden Retriever*, both being *Dog* breeds.

The reason why rank-N is meaningful is a well-trained model that has truly learned to generalize will produce contextually similar classes in its top-N predictions (typically, the top 5).

Of course, we can take rank-N accuracy too far, to the point where it loses its meaning and utility. For instance, a rank-5 accuracy on `MNIST`, a dataset comprised of 10 categories, would be almost useless.

## See also

Want to see rank-N being used in the wild? Take a look at the results section of this paper: `https://arxiv.org/pdf/1610.02357.pdf`.

# Using label smoothing to increase performance

One of the constant battles we have to fight against in machine learning is overfitting. There are many techniques we can use to prevent a model from losing generalization power, such as dropout, L1 and L2 regularization, and even data augmentation. A recent addition to this group is **label smoothing**, a more forgiving alternative to one-hot encoding.

Whereas in one-hot encoding we represent each category as a binary vector where the only non-zero element corresponds to the class that's been encoded, with **label smoothing**, we represent each label as a probability distribution where all the elements have a non-zero probability. The one with the highest probability, of course, is the one that corresponds to the encoded class.

For instance, a smoothed version of the *[0, 1, 0]* vector would be *[0.01, 0.98, 0.01]*.

In this recipe, we'll learn how to use **label smoothing**. Keep reading!

## Getting ready

Install `Pillow`, which we'll need to manipulate the images in the dataset:

```
$> pip install Pillow
```

Head to the `Caltech 101` website: `http://www.vision.caltech.edu/Image_Datasets/Caltech101/`. Download and unzip the file named `101_ObjectCategories.tar.gz` in a location of your preference. From now on, we'll assume the data is in `~/.keras/datasets/101_ObjectCategories`.

Here's a sample from `Caltech 101`:

Figure 12.5 – Caltech 101 sample images

Let's begin!

## How to do it...

Follow these steps to complete this recipe:

1.  Import the necessary dependencies:

    ```
    import os
    import pathlib
    ```

```
from glob import glob
import numpy as np
from sklearn.metrics import accuracy_score
from sklearn.model_selection import train_test_split
from sklearn.preprocessing import LabelBinarizer
from tensorflow.keras import Model
from tensorflow.keras.layers import *
from tensorflow.keras.losses import
CategoricalCrossentropy
from tensorflow.keras.preprocessing.image import *
```

2. Create the `load_images_and_labels()` function in order to read the data from `Caltech 101`:

```
def load_images_and_labels(image_paths,
                           target_size=(64, 64)):
    images = []
    labels = []

    for image_path in image_paths:
        image = load_img(image_path,
                         target_size=target_size)
        image = img_to_array(image)

        label = image_path.split(os.path.sep)[-2]

        images.append(image)
        labels.append(label)

    return np.array(images), np.array(labels)
```

3. Implement the `build_model()` function to create a **VGG**-based network:

```
def build_network(width, height, depth, classes):
    input_layer = Input(shape=(width, height, depth))

    x = Conv2D(filters=32,
               kernel_size=(3, 3),
```

```
                      padding='same')(input_layer)
x = ReLU()(x)
x = BatchNormalization(axis=-1)(x)
x = Conv2D(filters=32,
            kernel_size=(3, 3),
            padding='same')(x)
x = ReLU()(x)
x = BatchNormalization(axis=-1)(x)
x = MaxPooling2D(pool_size=(2, 2))(x)
x = Dropout(rate=0.25)(x)


x = Conv2D(filters=64,
            kernel_size=(3, 3),
            padding='same')(x)
x = ReLU()(x)
x = BatchNormalization(axis=-1)(x)
x = Conv2D(filters=64,
            kernel_size=(3, 3),
            padding='same')(x)
x = ReLU()(x)
x = BatchNormalization(axis=-1)(x)
x = MaxPooling2D(pool_size=(2, 2))(x)
x = Dropout(rate=0.25)(x)
```

Now, build the fully connected part of the network:

```
x = Flatten()(x)
x = Dense(units=512)(x)
x = ReLU()(x)
x = BatchNormalization(axis=-1)(x)
x = Dropout(rate=0.25)(x)


x = Dense(units=classes)(x)
output = Softmax()(x)


return Model(input_layer, output)
```

4. Set a random seed to enhance reproducibility:

```
SEED = 9
np.random.seed(SEED)
```

5. Compile the paths to the images of `Caltech 101`, as well as its classes:

```
base_path = (pathlib.Path.home() / '.keras' / 'datasets'
                /'101_ObjectCategories')
images_pattern = str(base_path / '*' / '*.jpg')
image_paths = [*glob(images_pattern)]
image_paths = [p for p in image_paths if
        p.split(os.path.sep)[-2] !='BACKGROUND_Google']
CLASSES = {p.split(os.path.sep)[-2] for p in image_paths}
```

6. Load the images and labels while normalizing the images and one-hot encoding the labels:

```
X, y = load_images_and_labels(image_paths)
X = X.astype('float') / 255.0
y = LabelBinarizer().fit_transform(y)
```

7. Use 20% of the data for test purposes and leave the rest to train the models:

```
(X_train, X_test,
 y_train, y_test) = train_test_split(X, y,
                                     test_size=0.2,
                                     random_state=SEED)
```

8. Define the batch size and the number of epochs:

```
BATCH_SIZE = 128
EPOCHS = 40
```

9. Define an `ImageDataGenerator()` to augment the images in the training set with random flips, rotations, and other transformations:

```
augmenter = ImageDataGenerator(horizontal_flip=True,
                               rotation_range=30,
                               width_shift_range=0.1,
                               height_shift_range=0.1,
                               shear_range=0.2,
```

```
                              zoom_range=0.2,
                          fill_mode='nearest')
```

10. We'll train two models: one with and an other without **label smoothing**. This will allow us to compare their performance and assess whether **label smoothing** has an impact on performance. The logic is pretty much the same in both cases, starting with the model creation process:

```
for with_label_smoothing in [False, True]:
    model = build_network(64, 64, 3, len(CLASSES))
```

11. If with_label_smoothing is True, then we'll set the smoothing factor to 0.1. Otherwise, the factor will be 0, which implies we'll use regular one-hot encoding:

```
if with_label_smoothing:
    factor = 0.1
else:
    factor = 0
```

12. We apply **label smoothing** through the loss function – in this case, CategoricalCrossentropy():

```
    loss = CategoricalCrossentropy(label_
smoothing=factor)
```

13. Compile and fit the model:

```
    model.compile(loss=loss,
                    optimizer='rmsprop',
                    metrics=['accuracy'])

    train_generator = augmenter.flow(X_train, y_train,
                                        BATCH_SIZE)
    model.fit(train_generator,
                steps_per_epoch=len(X_train) //
                BATCH_SIZE,
                validation_data=(X_test, y_test),
```

```
                    epochs=EPOCHS,
                    verbose=2)
```

14. Make predictions on the test set and compute the accuracy:

```
predictions = model.predict(X_test,
                            batch_size=BATCH_SIZE)
accuracy = accuracy_score(y_test.argmax(axis=1),
                          predictions.argmax(axis=1))

print(f'Test accuracy '
      f'{"with" if with_label_smoothing else
        "without"} '
      f'label smoothing: {accuracy * 100:.2f}%')
```

The script will train two models: one without **label smoothing**, using traditional one-hot encoded labels, and a second one with **label smoothing** applied through the `loss` function. Here are the results:

```
Test accuracy without label smoothing: 65.09%
Test accuracy with label smoothing: 65.78%
```

Just by using **label smoothing**, we improved our test score by almost 0.7%, a non-negligible boost considering the size of our dataset and its complexity. We'll dive deeper in the next section.

## How it works...

In this recipe, we learned how to apply **label smoothing** to a multi-class classification problem and witnessed how it improved the performance of our network on the test set. We didn't do anything particularly special, besides passing a smoothing factor to the `CategoricalCrossentropy()` loss function, which is used to measure the network's learning.

Why does label smoothing work, though? Despite its widespread use in many areas of deep learning, including **Natural Language Processing** (**NLP**) and, of course, **computer vision**, **label smoothing** is still poorly understood. However, what many have observed (including ourselves, in this example) is that by softening the targets, the generalization and learning speed of a network often improves significantly, preventing it from becoming overconfident, thus shielding us against the harmful effects of overfitting.

For a very interesting insight into **label smoothing**, read the paper mentioned in the *See also* section.

## See also

This paper explores the reasons why **label smoothing** helps, as well as when it does not. It's a worthy read! You can download it here: `https://arxiv.org/abs/1906.02629`.

# Checkpointing model

Training a deep neural network is an expensive process in terms of time, storage, and resources. Retraining a network each time we want to use it is preposterous and impractical. The good news is that we can use a mechanism to automatically save the best versions of a network during the training process.

In this recipe, we'll talk about such a mechanism, known as checkpointing.

## How to do it...

Follow these steps to learn about the different modalities of checkpointing you have at your disposal in TensorFlow:

1. Import the modules we will be using:

```
import numpy as np
import tensorflow as tf
from sklearn.model_selection import train_test_split
from sklearn.preprocessing import LabelBinarizer
from tensorflow.keras.callbacks import ModelCheckpoint
from tensorflow.keras.datasets import fashion_mnist as fm
from tensorflow.keras.layers import *
from tensorflow.keras.models import *
```

2. Define a function that will load `Fashion-MNIST` into `tf.data.Datasets`:

```
def load_dataset():
    (X_train, y_train), (X_test, y_test) = fm.load_data()

    X_train = X_train.astype('float32') / 255.0
    X_test = X_test.astype('float32') / 255.0
```

```
X_train = np.expand_dims(X_train, axis=3)
X_test = np.expand_dims(X_test, axis=3)

label_binarizer = LabelBinarizer()
y_train = label_binarizer.fit_transform(y_train)
y_test = label_binarizer.fit_transform(y_test)
```

3. Use 20% of the training data to validate the dataset:

```
(X_train, X_val,
 y_train, y_val) = train_test_split(X_train, y_train,
                                    train_size=0.8)
```

4. Convert the train, test, and validation subsets into `tf.data.Dataset`s:

```
train_ds = (tf.data.Dataset
                .from_tensor_slices((X_train,
                                     y_train)))
val_ds = (tf.data.Dataset
            .from_tensor_slices((X_val, y_val)))
test_ds = (tf.data.Dataset
                .from_tensor_slices((X_test, y_test)))

train_ds = (train_ds.shuffle(buffer_size=BUFFER_SIZE)
               .batch(BATCH_SIZE)
               .prefetch(buffer_size=BUFFER_SIZE))
val_ds = (val_ds
             .batch(BATCH_SIZE)
             .prefetch(buffer_size=BUFFER_SIZE))
test_ds = test_ds.batch(BATCH_SIZE)

return train_ds, val_ds, test_ds
```

5. Define the `build_network()` method, which, as its name suggests, creates the model we'll train on `Fashion-MNIST`:

```
def build_network():
    input_layer = Input(shape=(28, 28, 1))
    x = Conv2D(filters=20,
               kernel_size=(5, 5),
               padding='same',
               strides=(1, 1))(input_layer)
    x = ELU()(x)
    x = BatchNormalization()(x)
    x = MaxPooling2D(pool_size=(2, 2),
                     strides=(2, 2))(x)
    x = Dropout(0.5)(x)


    x = Conv2D(filters=50,
               kernel_size=(5, 5),
               padding='same',
               strides=(1, 1))(x)
    x = ELU()(x)
    x = BatchNormalization()(x)
    x = MaxPooling2D(pool_size=(2, 2),
                     strides=(2, 2))(x)
    x = Dropout(0.5)(x)
```

Now, build the fully connected part of the network:

```
    x = Flatten()(x)
    x = Dense(units=500)(x)
    x = ELU()(x)
    x = Dropout(0.5)(x)


    x = Dense(10)(x)
    output = Softmax()(x)


    return Model(inputs=input_layer, outputs=output)
```

6.  Define the `train_and_checkpoint()` function, which loads the dataset and then builds, compiles, and fits the network, saving the checkpoints according to the logic established by the `checkpointer` parameter:

```
def train_and_checkpoint(checkpointer):
    train_dataset, val_dataset, test_dataset = load_
dataset()

    model = build_network()
    model.compile(loss='categorical_crossentropy',
                  optimizer='adam',
                  metrics=['accuracy'])
    model.fit(train_dataset,
              validation_data=val_dataset,
              epochs=EPOCHS,
              callbacks=[checkpointer])
```

7.  Define the batch size, the number of epochs to train the model for, and the buffer size of each subset of data:

```
BATCH_SIZE = 256
BUFFER_SIZE = 1024
EPOCHS = 100
```

8.  The first way to generate checkpoints is by just saving a different model after each iteration. To do this, we must pass `save_best_only=False` to `ModelCheckpoint()`:

```
checkpoint_pattern = (
    'save_all/model-ep{epoch:03d}-loss{loss:.3f}'
    '-val_loss{val_loss:.3f}.h5')
checkpoint = ModelCheckpoint(checkpoint_pattern,
                             monitor='val_loss',
                             verbose=1,
                             save_best_only=False,
                             mode='min')
train_and_checkpoint(checkpoint)
```

Notice that we save all the checkpoints in the `save_all` folder, with the epoch, the loss, and the validation loss in the checkpointed model name.

9.  A more efficient way of checkpointing is to just save the best model so far. We can achieve this by setting `save_best_only` to `True` in `ModelCheckpoint()`:

```
checkpoint_pattern = (
    'best_only/model-ep{epoch:03d}-loss{loss:.3f}'
    '-val_loss{val_loss:.3f}.h5')
checkpoint = ModelCheckpoint(checkpoint_pattern,
                             monitor='val_loss',
                             verbose=1,
                             save_best_only=True,
                             mode='min')
train_and_checkpoint(checkpoint)
```

We'll save the results in the `best_only` directory.

10. A leaner way to generate checkpoints is to just save one, corresponding to the best model so far, instead of storing each incrementally improved model. To achieve this, we can remove any parameters from the checkpoint name:

```
checkpoint_pattern = 'overwrite/model.h5'
checkpoint = ModelCheckpoint(checkpoint_pattern,
                             monitor='val_loss',
                             verbose=1,
                             save_best_only=True,
                             mode='min')
train_and_checkpoint(checkpoint)
```

After running these three experiments, we can examine each output folder to see how many checkpoints were generated. In the first experiment, we saved a model after each epoch, as shown in the following screenshot:

Figure 12.6 – Experiment 1 results

The downside of this approach is that we end up with a lot of useless snapshots. The upside is that, if we want, we can resume training from any epoch by loading the corresponding epoch. A better approach is to save only the best model so far, which, as the following screenshot shows, produces fewer models. By inspecting the checkpoint names, we can see that each one has a validation loss that's lower than the one before it:

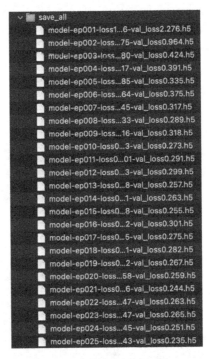

Figure 12.7 – Experiment 2 results

Lastly, we can just save the best model, as shown in the following screenshot:

Figure 12.8 – Experiment 3 results

Let's move on to the next section.

## How it works...

In this recipe, we learned how to checkpoint models, which saves us a huge amount of time as we don't need to retrain a model from scratch. Checkpointing is great because we can save the best model according to our own criteria, such as the validation loss, training accuracy, or any other measurement.

By leveraging the `ModelCheckpoint()` callback, we can save a snapshot of the network after each completed epoch, thus keeping only the best model or a history of the best models produced during training.

Each strategy has its pros and cons. For instance, generating models after each epoch has the upside of allowing us to resume training from any epoch, but at the cost of occupying lots of space on disk, while saving the best model only preserves space but reduces our flexibility to experiment.

What strategy will you use in your next project?

# Customizing the training process using tf.GradientTape

One of the biggest competitors of TensorFlow is another well-known framework: PyTorch. What made PyTorch so attractive until the arrival of TensorFlow 2.x was the level of control it gives to its users, particularly when it comes to training neural networks.

If we are working with somewhat traditional neural networks to solve common problems, such as image classification, we don't need that much control over how to train a model, and therefore can rely on TensorFlow's (or the Keras API's) built-in capabilities, loss functions, and optimizers without a problem.

But what if we are researchers that are exploring new ways to do things, as well as new architectures and novel strategies to solve challenging problems? That's when, in the past, we had to resort to PyTorch, due to it being considerably easier to customize the training models than using TensorFlow 1.x, but not anymore! TensorFlow 2.x's `tf.GradientTape` allows us to create custom training loops for models implemented in Keras and low-level TensorFlow more easily, and in this recipe, we'll learn how to use it.

## How to do it...

Follow these steps to complete this recipe:

1.  Import the modules we will be using:

```
import time
import numpy as np
import tensorflow as tf
from tensorflow.keras.datasets import fashion_mnist as fm
from tensorflow.keras.layers import *
from tensorflow.keras.losses import categorical_
```

```
crossentropy
from tensorflow.keras.models import Model
from tensorflow.keras.optimizers import RMSprop
from tensorflow.keras.utils import to_categorical
```

2. Define a function that will load and prepare Fashion-MNIST:

```
def load_dataset():
    (X_train, y_train), (X_test, y_test) = fm.load_data()

    X_train = X_train.astype('float32') / 255.0
    X_test = X_test.astype('float32') / 255.0

    # Reshape grayscale to include channel dimension.
    X_train = np.expand_dims(X_train, axis=-1)
    X_test = np.expand_dims(X_test, axis=-1)

    y_train = to_categorical(y_train)
    y_test = to_categorical(y_test)

    return (X_train, y_train), (X_test, y_test)
```

3. Define the build_network() method, which, as its name suggests, creates the
   model we'll train on Fashion-MNIST:

```
def build_network():
    input_layer = Input(shape=(28, 28, 1))
    x = Conv2D(filters=20,
               kernel_size=(5, 5),
               padding='same',
               strides=(1, 1))(input_layer)
    x = ELU()(x)
    x = BatchNormalization()(x)
    x = MaxPooling2D(pool_size=(2, 2),
                     strides=(2, 2))(x)
    x = Dropout(0.5)(x)

    x = Conv2D(filters=50,
```

```
                    kernel_size=(5, 5),
                    padding='same',
                    strides=(1, 1))(x)
    x = ELU()(x)
    x = BatchNormalization()(x)
    x = MaxPooling2D(pool_size=(2, 2),
                    strides=(2, 2))(x)
    x = Dropout(0.5)(x)
```

Now, build the fully connected part of the network:

```
    x = Flatten()(x)
    x = Dense(units=500)(x)
    x = ELU()(x)
    x = Dropout(0.5)(x)


    x = Dense(10)(x)
    output = Softmax()(x)


    return Model(inputs=input_layer, outputs=output)
```

4. To demonstrate how to use `tf.GradientTape`, we'll implement the `training_step()` function, which obtains the gradients for a batch of data and then backpropagates them using an optimizer:

```
def training_step(X, y, model, optimizer):
    with tf.GradientTape() as tape:
        predictions = model(X)
        loss = categorical_crossentropy(y, predictions)

    gradients = tape.gradient(loss,
                            model.trainable_variables)
    optimizer.apply_gradients(zip(gradients,
                            model.trainable_variables))
```

5.  Define the batch size and the number of epochs to train the model for:

```
BATCH_SIZE = 256
EPOCHS = 100
```

6.  Load the dataset:

```
(X_train, y_train), (X_test, y_test) = load_dataset()
```

7.  Create the optimizer and the network:

```
optimizer = RMSprop()
model = build_network()
```

8.  Now, we'll create our custom training loop. First, we'll go over each epoch, measuring the time it takes to complete:

```
for epoch in range(EPOCHS):
    print(f'Epoch {epoch + 1}/{EPOCHS}')
    start = time.time()
```

9.  Now, we'll iterate over each batch of data and pass them, along with the network and the optimizer, to our `training_step()` function:

```
for i in range(int(len(X_train) / BATCH_SIZE)):
    X_batch = X_train[i * BATCH_SIZE:
                      i * BATCH_SIZE + BATCH_SIZE]
    y_batch = y_train[i * BATCH_SIZE:
                      i * BATCH_SIZE + BATCH_SIZE]

    training_step(X_batch, y_batch, model,
                  optimizer)
```

10. Then, we'll print the epoch's elapsed time:

```
    elapsed = time.time() - start
    print(f'\tElapsed time: {elapsed:.2f} seconds.')
```

11. Lastly, evaluate the network on the test set to make sure it learned without any problems:

```
model.compile(loss=categorical_crossentropy,
              optimizer=optimizer,
```

```
                        metrics=['accuracy'])
    results = model.evaluate(X_test, y_test)


    print(f'Loss: {results[0]}, Accuracy: {results[1]}')
```

Here are the results:

```
Loss: 1.7750033140182495, Accuracy: 0.9083999991416931
```

Let's move on to the next section.

## How it works...

In this recipe, we learned how to create our own custom training loop. Although we didn't do anything particularly interesting in this instance, we highlighted the components (or ingredients, if you will) to cook up a custom deep learning training loop with tf.GradientTape:

- The network architecture itself
- The loss function used to compute the model loss
- The optimizer used to update the model weights based on the gradients
- The step function, which implements a forward pass (compute the gradients) and a backward pass (apply the gradients through the optimizers)

If you want to study more realistic and appealing uses of tf.GradientTape, you can refer to *Chapter 6, Generative Models and Adversarial Attacks*; *Chapter 7, Captioning Images with CNNs and RNNs*; and *Chapter 8, Fine-Grained Understanding of Images through Segmentation*. However, you can just read the next recipe, where we'll learn how to visualize class activation maps in order to debug deep neural networks!

# Visualizing class activation maps to better understand your network

Despite their incontestable power and usefulness, one of the biggest gripes about deep neural networks is their mysterious nature. Most of the time, we use them as black boxes, where we know they work but not why they do.

In particular, it's truly challenging to say why a network arrived at a particular result, which neurons were activated and why, or where the network is looking at to figure out the class or nature of an object in an image.

In other words, how can we trust something we don't understand? How can we improve it or fix it if it breaks?

Fortunately, in this recipe, we'll study a novel method to shine some light on these topics, known as **Gradient Weighted Class Activation Mapping**, or **Grad-CAM** for short.

Are you ready? Let's get going!

## Getting ready

For this recipe, we need `OpenCV`, `Pillow`, and `imutils`. You can install them in one go like this:

```
$> pip install Pillow opencv-python imutils
```

Now, we are ready to implement this recipe.

## How to do it...

Follow these steps to complete this recipe:

1.  Import the modules we will be using:

    ```python
    import cv2
    import imutils
    import numpy as np
    import tensorflow as tf
    from tensorflow.keras.applications import *
    from tensorflow.keras.models import Model
    from tensorflow.keras.preprocessing.image import *
    ```

2.  Define the `GradCAM` class, which will encapsulate the **Grad-CAM** algorithm, allowing us to produce a heatmap of the activation maps of a given layer. Let's start by defining the constructor:

    ```python
    class GradGAM(object):
        def __init__(self, model, class_index,
                     layer_name=None):
            self.class_index = class_index

            if layer_name is None:
                for layer in reversed(model.layers):
    ```

```
            if len(layer.output_shape) == 4:
                layer_name = layer.name
                break


        self.grad_model = \
                self._create_grad_model(model,


                                        layer_name)
```

3.  Here, we are receiving the `class_index` of a class we want to inspect, and the `layer_name` of a layer whose activations we want to visualize. If we don't receive a `layer_name`, we'll take the outermost output layer of our `model` by default. Finally, we create `grad_model` by relying on the `_create_grad_model()` method, as defined here:

```
    def _create_grad_model(self, model, layer_name):
        return Model(inputs=[model.inputs],
                     outputs=[
                         model.get_layer(layer_name).
                         output,model.output])
```

This model takes the same inputs as `model`, but outputs both the activations of the layer of interest, and the predictions of `model` itself.

4.  Next, we must define the `compute_heatmap()` method. First, we must pass the input image to `grad_model`, obtaining both the activation map of the layer of interest and the predictions:

```
    def compute_heatmap(self, image, epsilon=1e-8):
        with tf.GradientTape() as tape:
            inputs = tf.cast(image, tf.float32)
            conv_outputs, preds = self.grad_model(inputs)
            loss = preds[:, self.class_index]
```

5.  We can calculate the gradients based on the loss corresponding to the `class_index`:

```
    grads = tape.gradient(loss, conv_outputs)
```

6.  We can compute guided gradients by, basically, finding positive values in both `float_conv_outputs` and `float_grads`, and multiplying those by the gradients, which will enable us to visualize what neurons are activating:

```
guided_grads = (tf.cast(conv_outputs > 0,
                  'float32') *
                    tf.cast(grads > 0, 'float32') *
              grads)
```

7.  Now, we can compute the gradient weights by averaging the guided gradients, and then use those weights to add the pondered maps to our **Grad-CAM** visualization:

```
conv_outputs = conv_outputs[0]
guided_grads = guided_grads[0]

weights = tf.reduce_mean(guided_grads,
                          axis=(0, 1))
cam = tf.reduce_sum(
      tf.multiply(weights, conv_outputs),
      axis=-1)
```

8.  Then, we take the **Grad-CAM** visualization, resize it to the dimensions of the input image, and min-max normalize it before returning it:

```
height, width = image.shape[1:3]
heatmap = cv2.resize(cam.numpy(), (width,
                      height))

min = heatmap.min()
max = heatmap.max()
heatmap = (heatmap - min) / ((max - min) +
                              epsilon)
heatmap = (heatmap * 255.0).astype('uint8')

return heatmap
```

9.  The last method of the `GradCAM` class overlays a heatmap onto the original image. This lets us get a better sense of the visual cues the network is looking at when making predictions:

```python
def overlay_heatmap(self,
                    heatmap,
                    image, alpha=0.5,
                    colormap=cv2.COLORMAP_VIRIDIS):
    heatmap = cv2.applyColorMap(heatmap, colormap)
    output = cv2.addWeighted(image,
                             alpha,
                             heatmap,
                             1 - alpha,
                             0)

    return heatmap, output
```

10. Let's instantiate a **ResNet50** trained on ImageNet:

```python
model = ResNet50(weights='imagenet')
```

11. Load the input image, resize it to the dimensions expected by ResNet50, turn it into a NumPy array, and preprocess it:

```python
image = load_img('dog.jpg', target_size=(224, 224))
image = img_to_array(image)
image = np.expand_dims(image, axis=0)
image = imagenet_utils.preprocess_input(image)
```

12. Pass the image through the model and extract the index of the most probable class:

```python
predictions = model.predict(image)
i = np.argmax(predictions[0])
```

13. Instantiate a **GradCAM** object and calculate the heatmap:

```
cam = GradGAM(model, i)
heatmap = cam.compute_heatmap(image)
```

14. Overlay the heatmap on top of the original image:

```
original_image = cv2.imread('dog.jpg')
heatmap = cv2.resize(heatmap, (original_image.shape[1],
                               original_image.shape[0]))
heatmap, output = cam.overlay_heatmap(heatmap,
                                      original_image,
                                      alpha=0.5)
```

15. Decode the predictions to make it human-readable:

```
decoded = imagenet_utils.decode_predictions(predictions)
_, label, probability = decoded[0][0]
```

16. Label the overlaid heatmap with the class and its associated probability:

```
cv2.rectangle(output, (0, 0), (340, 40), (0, 0, 0), -1)
cv2.putText(output, f'{label}: {probability * 100:.2f}%',
            (10, 25), cv2.FONT_HERSHEY_SIMPLEX, 0.8,
            (255, 255, 255), 2)
```

17. Lastly, merge the original image, the heatmap, and the labeled overlay into a single image and save it to disk:

```
output = np.hstack([original_image, heatmap, output])
output = imutils.resize(output, height=700)
cv2.imwrite('output.jpg', output)
```

Here is the result:

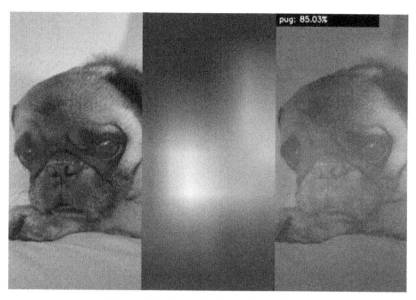

Figure 12.9 – Visualization of Grad-CAM

As we can see, the network classified my dog as a Pug, which is correct, with a confidence of 85.03%. Moreover, the heatmap reveals the network activates around the nose and eyes of my dog's face, which means these are important features and the model is behaving as expected.

## How it works...

In this recipe, we learned and implemented **Grad-CAM**, a very useful algorithm for visually inspecting the activations of a neural network. This can be an effective way of debugging its behavior as it ensures it's looking at the right parts of an image.

This is a very important tool because the high accuracy or performance of our model may have less to do with the actual learning, and more to do with factors that have been unaccounted for. For instance, if we are working on a pet classifier to distinguish between dogs and cats, we should use **Grad-CAM** to verify that the network looks at features inherent to these animals in order to properly classify them, and not at the surroundings, background noise, or less important elements in the images.

## See also

You can expand your knowledge of **Grad-CAM** by reading the following paper: https://arxiv.org/abs/1610.02391.

# Other Books You May Enjoy

If you enjoyed this book, you may be interested in these other books by Packt:

**Mastering Computer Vision with TensorFlow 2.x**

Krishnendu Kar

ISBN: 978-1-83882-706-9

- Explore methods of feature extraction and image retrieval and visualize different layers of the neural network model
- Use TensorFlow for various visual search methods for real-world scenarios
- Build neural networks or adjust parameters to optimize the performance of models
- Understand TensorFlow DeepLab to perform semantic segmentation on images and DCGAN for image inpainting
- Evaluate your model and optimize and integrate it into your application to operate at scale
- Get up to speed with techniques for performing manual and automated image annotation

**Applied Deep Learning and Computer Vision for Self-Driving Cars**

Sumit Ranjan , Dr. S. Senthamilarasu

ISBN: 978-1-83864-630-1

- Implement deep neural network from scratch using the Keras library
- Understand the importance of deep learning in self-driving cars
- Get to grips with feature extraction techniques in image processing using the OpenCV library
- Design a software pipeline that detects lane lines in videos
- Implement a convolutional neural network (CNN) image classifier for traffic signal signs
- Train and test neural networks for behavioral-cloning by driving a car in a virtual simulator
- Discover various state-of-the-art semantic segmentation and object detection architectures

# Leave a review - let other readers know what you think

Please share your thoughts on this book with others by leaving a review on the site that you bought it from. If you purchased the book from Amazon, please leave us an honest review on this book's Amazon page. This is vital so that other potential readers can see and use your unbiased opinion to make purchasing decisions, we can understand what our customers think about our products, and our authors can see your feedback on the title that they have worked with Packt to create. It will only take a few minutes of your time, but is valuable to other potential customers, our authors, and Packt. Thank you!

# Index

## A

accuracy
  improving, with convolutional neural network ensembles 462-470
  improving, with Test Time Augmentation (TTA) 470-476
actions
  recognizing, with TensorFlow Hub (TFHub) 412-419
adversarial attack
  implementing, with FGSM 252-256
application programming interface (API) 352
attention
  image captioning network, implementing on COCO with 283-300
autoencoder
  about 162
  used, for denoising image 175-182
  used, for spotting outliers 182-187
AutoKeras
  about 434
  age and gender, predicting with 449-460
  image classifier, creating with 435, 436
  image regressor, creating with 437-440

model, exporting in 441-445
model, importing in 441-445
Automatic Machine Learning (AutoML) 434
AutoModel
  architecture generation, controlling with 445-449

## B

Bahdanau's Attention 286
binary classifier
  creating, to detect smiles 34-39
BLEU score
  reference link 277
building blocks, of Keras API
  working with 3-7

## C

captions
  generating, for 278-283
  generating, for photos 277
class activation maps
  visualizing, to understand network 501-506

classifier
    spot-checking 97-104
    training, on extracted features 94-97
    training, with incremental
        learning 104-109
Comma-Separated Values (CSV) 383
Common Objects in Context (COCO)
    about 284
    image captioning network,
        implementing with
        attention on 283-300
Computer Vision (CV) 257, 489
convolutional autoencoder
    creating 168-174
    working 174
Convolutional Neural Network (CNN)
    about 40, 151, 204, 257, 463
    ensembles, using to improve
        accuracy 462-470
custom images
    style transfer, applying to 141-146
CycleGAN
    reference link 251
    unpaired images, translating
        with 236-251
    working 251

## D

data augmentation
    using, to improve performance
        with Keras API 68-75
    using, to improve performance with
        tf.data and tf.image APIs 75-83
Decision Trees 94
Deep Convolutional Generative
    Adversarial Network (DCGAN)
    about 204

implementing 204-212
used, for semi-supervised
    learning 213-221
working 213
DeepDream
    implementing 122-128
    reference link 123
deep learning
    used, for creating inverse image
        search index 188-193
    used, for improving image
        resolution 151-159
DenseNet 318
Direct 3D Convolutions 420
directed acyclic graph (DAG) 6
dreamy images
    generating 128-133

## E

emotions
    detecting, in real time 398-412
ensemble 462
Extensible Markup Language (XML) 383
extracted features
    classifier, training on 94-97

## F

Fashion-MNIST
    reference link 32, 168
Fast Gradient Signed Method (FGSM)
    about 252
    adversarial attack, implementing
        with 252-256
Fast Region-based Convolutional Neural
    Network (Fast R-CNN) 351
feature extractor

implementing, with pre-trained
    network 87-93
spot-checking 97-104
fully connected autoencoder
    creating 162-167
    working 167
Fully Convolutional Network (FCN)
    about 159
    creating, for image
        segmentation 304-318
    reference link 319

## G

Gaussian noise 179
Generative Adversarial Networks
    (GANs) 201
Gradient Weighted Class Activation
    Mapping (Grad-CAM)
    about 502
    implementing 507
    reference link 507
Gram Matrix 136
    reference link 141

## H

Haar Cascade classifier
    reference link 412, 460
Haar Cascades 408
Haar Cascades face detector
    creating 457

## I

image captioning network
    implementing 268-277
    implementing, on COCO with

attention 283-300
image classifier
    creating 25-32
    creating, with AutoKeras 435, 436
image pyramids
    object detector, creating with 352-361
image regressor
    creating, with AutoKeras 437-440
image resolution
    improving, with deep learning 151-159
images
    classifying, with pre-trained network
        using Keras API 60-63
    classifying, with pre-trained network
        using TensorFlow Hub 64-67
    denoising, with autoencoder 175-182
    loading, with Keras API 7-12
    loading, with tf.data.Dataset API 12-16
    segmenting, with Mask-RCNN 344-350
    segmenting, with TensorFlow
        Hub (TFHub) 344-350
    translating, with Pix2Pix 222-235
image segmentation
    fully convolutional network
        (FCN), creating 304-318
images, with Keras
    reference link 12
incremental learning
    about 104
    using, to train classifier 104-109
Inflated 3D Convnet (I3D) 412
instance normalization, versus
    batch normalization
    reference link 251
Intersection Over Union (IoU) 372
inverse image search index
    creating, with deep learning 188-193

# K

Kaggle
  reference link 268
Keras API
  data augmentation, using to improve
    performance with 68-75
  images, classifying with pre-trained
    network using 60-63
  used, for fine-tuning network 109-115
  used, for loading images 7-12
Keras pre-trained models
  reference link 64
Kullback-Leibler divergence
  about 197
  reference link 201

# L

label smoothing
  about 483
  reference link 490
  using, to increase performance 483-489
LeNet 27, 36
Logistic Regression 94

# M

Mask-RCNN
  about 344
  reference link 350
  used, for segmenting images 344-350
middle frames
  generating, of video with TensorFlow
    Hub (TFHub) 419-425
MNIST dataset
  reference link 213

# model

  checkpointing 490-496
  exporting, in AutoKeras 441-445
  importing, in AutoKeras 441-445
  loading 16-19
  saving 16-19
model's architecture
  visualizing 20-25
model sub-classing API 7
multi-class classifier
  creating, to play rock paper
    scissors 39-44
multi-label classifier
  creating, to label watches 45-52

# N

Natural Language Processing
    (NLP) 64, 257, 489
network
  fine-tuning, with Keras API 109-115
  fine-tuning, with TensorFlow
    Hub (TFHub) 115-119
Neural Architecture Search (NAS)
  about 436
  reference link 436
neural style transfer
  about 25, 143
  implementing 134-140
Non-Maximum Suppression (NMS) 359

# O

object detector
  creating, with image pyramids 352-361
  creating, with sliding windows 352-361
  training, with TensorFlow's Object
    Detection API 379-391

object detectors, in TFHub
    reference link  396
objects
    detecting, with TensorFlow
        Hub (TFHub)  392-396
    detecting, with YOLOv3  361-378
octaves  126
outliers
    spotting, with autoencoder  182-187

# P

Pareto principle  461
Pascal VOC  391
Passive Aggressive Classifier  104
Pix2Pix
    about  222
    images, translating with  222-235
pre-trained network
    Keras API, used for classifying
        images with  60-63
    TensorFlow Hub (TFHub), used for
        classifying images with  64-67
    used, for implementing feature
        extractor  87-93

# R

rank-N accuracy
    about  477
    using, to improve performance  477-482
    working  483
rank-N accuracy, using in wild
    reference link  483
Recurrent Neural Network (RNN)
    about  257
    reference link  268

regions of interest (rois)  357
Residual Network (ResNet)
    implementing  52-59
    working  59, 60
ResNet  93
ResNet50  318
ResNetV1152  115
reusable image caption feature extractor
    implementing  258-267
RMSProp  113
rock paper scissors
    multi-class classifier, creating
        to play  39-44

# S

scikit-learn  97, 104
semi-supervised learning
    about  213
    DCGAN, using for  213-221
SGD  114
sliding windows
    object detector, creating with  352-361
SMILEs dataset
    reference link  39
style transfer
    applying, to custom images  141-146
    applying, with TensorFlow
        Hub (TFHub)  147-151
Support Vector Machines  94

# T

TensorFlow Datasets  315
TensorFlow Hub (TFHub)
    about  344, 352
    actions, recognizing with  412-419

518

images, classifying with pre-trained
    network using  64-67
middle frames, generating of
    video with  419-425
objects, detecting with  392-396
text-to-video retrieval,
    performing with  425-432
used, for applying style transfer  147-151
used, for fine-tuning network  115-119
used, for segmenting images  344-350
TensorFlow Object Detection API
    object detector, training with  379-391
    references  391
Test Time Augmentation (TTA)
    about  470
    using, to improve accuracy  470-476
    working  476
text-to-video retrieval
    performing, with TensorFlow
        Hub (TFHub)  425-432
tf.data and tf.image APIs
    data augmentation, using to
        improve performance  75-83
tf.data.Dataset API
    reference link  16
    used, for loading images  12-16
tf.GradientTape
    using, to customize training
        process  497-501
TFHub module
    reference link  151
training process
    customizing, with
        tf.GradientTape  497-501
transfer learning
    U-Net, implementing with  332-343
transposed convolutions
    reference link  175

Tree-LSTMs
    reference link  7

## U

U-Net  227
    implementing  319-330
    implementing, with transfer
        learning  332-343
    reference link  344
    working  331
Uniform Resource Locator (URL)  385
unpaired images
    translating, with CycleGAN  236-251

## V

variational autoencoder (VAE)
    about  194
    implementing  194-201
    working  201
VGG16  93
VGG network  51

## Y

YOLOv3
    objects, detecting with  361-378
You Only Look Once (YOLO)  351

Made in United States
North Haven, CT
02 December 2021